This work is intended as a contribution to the d the reasons for London's freedom from seriou: century when the city's rulers faced mountin, , population growth, spiralling prices, impoverishment, and crime.

Throughout the study Dr Archer acknowledges the reality of the tensions in metropolitan society, and stresses the key importance of the solidarity of the elite, unscathed by serious religious conflict or clashes of economic interest, in restraining popular unrest. Nevertheless, in the absence of a highly developed apparatus of control, the authorities had to show some responsiveness, however limited, to popular grievances. It was crucial to the city's stability that Londoners were locked into a matrix of overlapping communities, the livery companies, wards, and parishes, all of which created claims on their loyalties and gave them a framework within which redress of grievances could be pursued. The highly developed structures of government in the capital also enjoyed considerable success in mobilising resources for poor relief: in the most comprehensive reconstruction of the sources of charity yet attempted for an English urban centre, Dr Archer demonstrates that although relief was limited in scale, the ways in which it was distributed served to emphasise the dependence of the poor. In considering those groups which were not so successfully integrated, it is suggested that the criminal underworld was neither so coherent, nor the authorities so impotent against it, as the traditional accounts would suggest.

This is the first effort at a holistic approach to interpreting early modern London society, based on the full range of London sources.

Cambridge Studies in Early Modern British History

THE PURSUIT OF STABILITY

Cambridge Studies in Early Modern British History

Series editors

ANTHONY FLETCHER
Professor of Modern History, University of Durham

JOHN GUY
*Richard L. Turner Professor in the Humanities and
Professor of History, University of Rochester, NY*

and JOHN MORRILL
*Lecturer in History, University of Cambridge, and
Fellow and Tutor of Selwyn College*

This is a series of monographs and studies covering many aspects of the history of the British Isles between the late fifteenth century and the early eighteenth century. It includes the work of established scholars and pioneering work by a new generation of scholars. It includes both reviews and revisions of major topics and books which open up new historical terrain or which reveal startling new perspectives on familiar subjects. All the volumes set detailed research into broader perspectives and the books are intended for the use of students as well as of their teachers.

For a list of titles in the series, see end of book.

THE PURSUIT OF STABILITY

Social Relations in Elizabethan London

IAN W. ARCHER

Fellow and Director of Studies in History,
Downing College, Cambridge

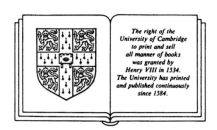

The right of the
University of Cambridge
to print and sell
all manner of books
was granted by
Henry VIII in 1534.
The University has printed
and published continuously
since 1584.

CAMBRIDGE UNIVERSITY PRESS

Cambridge
New York   Port Chester
Melbourne   Sydney

PUBLISHED BY THE PRESS SYNDICATE OF THE UNIVERSITY OF CAMBRIDGE
The Pitt Building, Trumpington Street, Cambridge, United Kingdom

CAMBRIDGE UNIVERSITY PRESS
The Edinburgh Building, Cambridge CB2 2RU, UK
40 West 20th Street, New York NY 10011–4211, USA
477 Williamstown Road, Port Melbourne, VIC 3207, Australia
Ruiz de Alarcón 13, 28014 Madrid, Spain
Dock House, The Waterfront, Cape Town 8001, South Africa

http://www.cambridge.org

First published 1991
First paperback edition 2002

A catalogue record for this book is available from the British Library

Library of Congress Cataloguing in Publication data
Archer, Ian.
The pursuit of stability: social relations in Elizabethan London
Ian W. Archer.
p.   cm. – (Cambridge studies in early modern British history)
Revision of the author's thesis.
Includes bibliographical references.
ISBN 0 521 37315 8
1. London (England – History – 16th century.   2. London (England) –
Social conditions.   I. Title.   II. Series.
DA680.A74   1991
942.1′2055–dc20   90-33136   CIP

ISBN 0 521 37315 8   hardback
ISBN 0 521 52216 1   paperback

For my father and in memory of my mother

CONTENTS

FIGURES

TABLES

ACKNOWLEDGEMENTS

The years of this book's gestation have left me with many debts. Much of the work at the archival coal-face was financed by a Department of Education and Science Major State Studentship. The revision of the thesis from which this book emerged took place during my tenure of a British Academy Post-Doctoral Fellowship in 1988–9. To both bodies I am deeply grateful. I have been fortunate in my associations with four Oxbridge colleges, Trinity College and Lady Margaret Hall in Oxford, both of which elected me to Temporary Lectureships, Girton College, Cambridge, which elected me to a Research Fellowship, and Downing College, Cambridge, at which I have just commenced a Teaching Fellowship. All have provided congenial environments for research and writing. Three individuals in those colleges stand out for the support they have given: Peter Carey at Trinity for providing the encouragement which launched me on a career of research, Susan Reynolds at L.M.H. for characteristically invigorating discussions and her constant goading to action, and Miri Rubin at Girton, for providing a constant intellectual stimulus over the past three years.

My debts to the wider scholarly community are legion. Penry Williams supervised my doctoral thesis, restraining its excesses and patiently insisting on clarity. For his friendship and support over more years than I care to admit I am extremely thankful. My examiners, Robert Ashton and Paul Slack, made suggestions which have assisted the metamorphosis of the thesis into book. John Morrill's generous enthusiasm proved a powerful spur to publication. Without the critical insight provided by Caroline Barron, Joanna Innes, and John Walter, this book would have been very much impoverished. I am also grateful for the comments of those who at various stages read parts of it, including Mark Benbow, George Bernard, Susan Brigden, Richard Cairns, Cliff Davies, David Dean, Alan Fellows, Paul Griffiths, Steve Hindle, Robin Hughes, Derek Keene, Valerie Pearl, Andrew Pettegree, Steve Rappaport, and Tim Wales. Others have provided the stimulus of discussion, enriching my understanding of early modern London, from their often different perspectives. Among these I would like to thank

James Alexander, Lee Beier, Jeremy Boulton, Mike Braddick, Mike Berlin, Martha Carlin, Patrick Collinson, Trevor Griffiths, Steve Gunn, Peter Gwyn, Vanessa Harding, Mark Jenner, Julia Merritt, David Palliser, Michael Power, James Robertson, Gervase Rosser, Judith Richards, Conrad Russell, Helen Weinstein, and Keith Wrightson. Earlier versions of most of the chapters have been hawked about the Oxford–London–Cambridge seminar circuit, and I am grateful for the opportunities to refine my ideas that they provided.

Particular thanks are due to Dr J. H. Baker for his loan of a xerox of the fragment of the Newgate gaol delivery calendar in the National Library of Wales, to Mark Benbow for a preliminary print-out of his 'Index of London Citizens Active in Government, 1558–1603', to Christopher Coleman for the loan of his microfilm of Richard Stonley's diary, to Caroline Barron and Alan Fellows for providing copies of other manuscripts in American libraries, and to Steve Rappaport who, in spite of our differences of interpretation, has always generously shared data and given me the benefit of numerous lively discussions.

I should like to register my appreciation of the staff of the various record offices, libraries, and archives I have used. To Betty Masters, formerly Deputy Keeper at the Corporation of London Records Office, Chris Cooper, formerly archivist at the Guildhall Library, and David Wickham, archivist of the Clothworkers' Company, I owe particularly heavy debts. To the staff of those repositories listed in the bibliography I must add the librarians of the Bodleian and History Faculty Libraries in Oxford, and the Cambridge University Library.

Finally I should like to thank my students, who have borne with my enthusiasms, whose irreverent wit has often sustained me, and whose questioning has sharpened this work's arguments at many points.

ABBREVIATIONS

A.P.C.	*Acts of the Privy Council of England*, ed. J. R. Dasent, vols. I–XXXII (1890–1907)
B.I.H.R.	*Bulletin of the Institute of Historical Research*
B.C.B.	Bridewell Court Book
B.L.	British Library
Bodl.	Bodleian Library, Oxford
Br. Sr. Co.	Barber Surgeons' Company
C.J.	*Journals of the House of Commons*, vol. I (1852)
C.L.R.O.	Corporation of London Record Office
C.M.	Court Minutes
C.P.R.	*Calendar of the Patent Rolls, Edward VI, Philip and Mary, and Elizabeth* (1924–)
C.W.A.	Churchwardens' Accounts
Cw. Co.	Clothworkers' Company
Dp. Co.	Drapers' Company
E.E.T.S.	Early English Text Society
Ec.H.R.	*Economic History Review*
E.H.R.	*English Historical Review*
G.L.	Guildhall Library
G.L.R.O.	Greater London Record Office
Gs. Co.	Goldsmiths' Company
H.L.R.O.	House of Lords Records Office
H.M.C.	*Historical Manuscripts Commission Reports*
Jour.	Journal of the Court of Common Council
L.J.	*Journals of the House of Lords*, vols. I–II (1846)
L.P.L.	Lambeth Palace Library
Mc. Co.	Mercers' Company
MT. Co.	Merchant Tailors' Company
P.R.O.	Public Record Office
Rep.	Repertory of the Court of Aldermen
S.B.H.	Saint Bartholomew's Hospital

Sk. Co.	Skinners' Company
S.T.C.	*Short-Title Catalogue of Books Printed in England, Scotland and Ireland, and of English Books Printed Abroad, 1475–1640*, ed. A. W. Pollard and G. R. Redgrave (2nd revised edition, 1976–86)
T.E.D.	*Tudor Economic Documents*, ed. R. H. Rawney and E. Power (3 vols., 1924)
T.R.H.S.	*Transactions of the Royal Historical Society*
T.R.P.	*Tudor Royal Proclamations*, ed. P. L. Hughes and J. F. Larkin, 3 vols. (1964–9)
V.M.	Vestry Minutes
W.A.M.	Westminster Abbey Muniments
W.P.L.	Westminster Public Library
Wright	T. Wright, *Queen Elizabeth and her Times* (2 vols., 1838)

1

Introduction: the problem of order

On the evening of Sunday 29 June 1595 a crowd of London apprentices reported to have been one thousand strong marched on Tower Hill, intending to ransack gunmakers' shops, and then stoned the City's officers who had been sent to pacify them. Their ultimate intentions are unclear, but in the legal proceedings which followed it was alleged that they planned 'to robbe, steale, pill and spoile the welthy and well disposed inhabitaunts of the saide cytye, and to take the sworde of aucthorytye from the magistrats and governours lawfully aucthorised'. Particularly ominous were the tearing down of pillories in Cheapside and the report that a gallows had been set up outside the house of the unpopular mayor, Sir John Spencer.[1] This disturbance was the culmination of a series of riots in the preceding months. A riot on Shrove Tuesday had not indicated that anything was seriously amiss, since this was traditionally a time of apprentice misrule.[2] But more alarming, because so unusual in the city, had been the food riots over the price of fish and butter on 12 and 13 June. And there was mounting evidence of coordination between apprentices and a discontented soldiery. Rumours were circulating that they were conspiring to 'play an Irish trick with the lord mayor, who should not have his head upon his shoulders within one hour after'.[3] The speed with which the aldermen moved to suppress a pamphlet promoted by members of the Weavers' Company expressing hostility to strangers shows that they feared that the tense situation in the city might lead to further riots against the aliens, tapping a rich vein of popular xenophobia.[4]

---

[1] R. B. Manning, 'The Prosecution of Sir Michael Blount, Lieutenant of the Tower of London, 1595', *B.I.H.R.*, 57 (1984), 222; *A Student's Lamentation that hath Sometime been in London an Apprentice, for the Rebellious Tumults lately in the Citie Hapning* (1595); J. Stow, *The Annales or Generall Chronicle of England* (1615), pp. 768–9; B.L., Lansdowne MSS 78/64; 114/1; P.R.O., SP 12/252/94.
[2] C.L.R.O., Rep. 23, fos. 365ᵛ, 369.   [3] *H.M.C., Hatfield House*, V. 249–50.
[4] C.L.R.O., Remembrancia II, no. 98; Rep. 23, fo. 406ᵛ; F. Consitt, *The London Weavers' Company* (Oxford, 1933), pp. 312–18.

Although their initial response to the food riots had been mild, involving the public whipping of rioters, the failure of the traditional sanctions and the persistence of trouble panicked the authorities into harsh repressive measures. For the rest of the summer the capital was subject to martial law as the Crown appointed Sir Thomas Wilford as provost marshal to round up vagrants and suppress any further disturbances.[5] A special commission was set up to coordinate action against vagrants in the city and suburbs.[6] Meanwhile, five apprentices, accused of levying war against the Crown on a very dubious interpretation of the 1571 treason legislation, were sentenced to be hanged, drawn, and quartered, an extremely rare use of the ultimate sanction against rioters.[7]

The verdicts of historians on these disturbances are varied. Penry Williams sees the riots of 1595 as the culmination of a series of disorders which marked a more violent aspect to the city from the late 1580s onwards. He emphasises the dangers posed by the threatened conjunction between apprentices and discontented soldiers and by the disillusionment with the government of the City apparent in the repeated attacks on Spencer. Peter Clark concludes that 'at certain times, as in London in 1595, it seemed as if the whole fabric of the urban community might be about to disintegrate'. Steve Rappaport, on the other hand, stresses the essential orderliness of the capital. He emphasises the short duration of the disturbances in 1595, the lack of casualties, the absence of damage to property, and the relative calm of the city in subsequent years. Although reluctantly conceding that disturbances were more serious in 1595 than at other times, he argues that they were untypical, since disorders usually reflected youthful high spirits, 'chiefly the antics and brawling of apprentices and journeymen' rather than action aiming at the attainment of specific and realistic goals. He is tempted by the view that rioting was essentially mindless: he suggests that anti-alien feeling provided excuses for violence which would have occurred anyway, and his preferred explanation for apprentice disorder is that 'boys will be boys'.[8] In

---

[5] L. O. J. Boynton, 'The Tudor Provost Marshal', *E.H.R.*, 77 (1962), 451–4; T. Rymer, *Foedera, Conventiones, Litterae* (1704–15), XVI. 279–80; *T.R.P.*, III. 82–3, 143; *Orders Prescribed for the Observation of Her Maiesties Present Proclamation* (1595). These documents must be dated to 1595, not 1591, as Hughes and Larkin assert. Wilford's commission was withdrawn in early September: C.L.R.O., Remembrancia II, no. 103.

[6] B.L., Lansdowne MSS 66/93–5; 78/53.

[7] B.L., Harleian MS 6997, fo. 64; J. Bellamy, *The Tudor Law of Treason: an Introduction* (1979), pp. 78–9; *Student's Lamentation*. Cf. J. Walter, '"A Rising of the People"? The Oxfordshire Rising of 1596', *Past and Present*, 107 (1985), 127–30.

[8] P. H. Williams, *The Tudor Regime* (Oxford, 1979), pp. 328–30; P. Clark, 'A Crisis Contained? The Condition of English Towns in the 1590s', in *The European Crisis of the 1590s*, ed. P. Clark (1985), pp. 53–4, 56; S. Rappaport, *Worlds Within Worlds: Structures of Life in Sixteenth-Century London* (Cambridge, 1989), pp. 6–17; R. B. Manning, *Village Revolts: Social Protest and Popular Disturbances in England, 1509–1640* (Oxford, 1988), ch. VIII.

what follows I shall put these contrasting judgements to test by looking at the types of disorder which characterised London in the years before 1595, and the degree to which the 1590s marked new developments.

The apparent absence of riots may in part be a function of the absence of sources. For the Elizabethan period we lack any sessions material for the City proper; that surviving for the Middlesex suburbs is extremely fragmentary; and the records of the Elizabethan Star Chamber remain intractable. The discovery of many more riots during the early seventeenth century reflects not increasing disorder but increasing documentation.[9] It would be wrong, for example, to interpret the lack of references to Shrove Tuesday riots in the Middlesex sessions before 1598 as indicating a lack of such disturbances, although their appearance thereafter may reflect an increased willingness to prosecute such rioters in the more socially polarised conditions of the later 1590s.[10] Mayoral precepts requiring that apprentices be kept indoors and the watch doubled suggest that Shrove Tuesday, like May Day, had long been associated with disorder. The character of these disturbances remains obscure, but they do not appear to have posed a serious threat to authority. The strictures of the aldermen in a precept of 1576 against 'showtinges, hooping noyses, soundinge of drumes or instrumentes, shootinge of gunnes or usinge of squybbes' are more suggestive of rowdy sporting competitions than any threat to authority.[11] By the early seventeenth century Shrove Tuesday was associated with attacks on brothels. Although there are no Elizabethan references to such practices, it seems unlikely that the tradition was so recently developed because the most convincing explanation for the selection of the brothels as targets lies in the onset of the stricter moral regime associated with Lent, and the quest among apprentices for an outlet for their struggles with their sexuality.[12] But however common such disturbances may have been, it is difficult to see them as posing a real threat to the hierarchy because brothel keepers were frequently punished by the authorities. The apprentices were hardly reflecting an alternative value system.

Perhaps more threatening, because of the social tensions underlying them, were the clashes which pitted apprentices against gentlemen, particularly of the Inns of Court, and against their servingmen. In June 1581 there was a broil between apprentices and the servingmen of Sir Thomas Stanhope in Smithfield in which one Thomas Butcher, brewer, was accused of inciting one thousand apprentices 'to make a rebellion against the gentlemen &

[9] K. Lindley, 'Riot Prevention and Control in Early Stuart London', *T.RH.S.*, fifth series, 33 (1983), 109–26.

[10] G.L.R.O., MJ/SR 353/43; 377/38; 399/16–18, 22, 28, 49; 400/118, 130.

[11] Lindley, 'Riot Prevention', pp. 109–10; P. Burke, 'Popular Culture in Seventeenth-Century London', *London Journal*, 3 (1977), 144–5; C.L.R.O., Jour. 20, fo. 390.

[12] A. Yarborough, 'Bristol's Apprentices in the Sixteenth Century: the Cultural and Regional Mobility of an Age Group' (Catholic University of America Ph.D., 1977), pp. 73–6.

servingmen'. When Butcher was whipped for his offence, apprentices rescued him from the cart on which he was being punished.[13] Recorder Fleetwood (incidentally, he is our only source) records a series of similar disturbances in June 1584. Three brawls on two successive days outside the Curtain Theatre escalated into riots, two of them apparently involving 500 and 1,000 people respectively; apprentices conspired to rescue their imprisoned fellows; and the disturbances ended with attacks on the Inns of Court. In all cases the trouble began with a brawl between an apprentice and a gentleman. One gentleman, for example, is recorded as having exclaimed that 'the apprentice was but a rascal, and some there were littel better than roogs that tooke upon them the name of gentlemen, and saide the prentizes were but the skumme of the worlde'.[14] The well-known riots against Lincoln's Inn in 1590 probably had their origins in similar tensions.[15] Such disturbances were not mindless violence because they reflected the status uncertainties of apprentices, which derived from gentry snobbery about the demeaning effects of trade. Such attitudes had a sharper cutting edge in London because many apprentices were recruited from the younger sons of the gentry or from the ranks of the yeomanry, the same groups as provided so many servingmen in gentry households.[16] The disturbances demonstrated an apprentice solidarity that must have been alarming to the authorities.

But the anxieties of the aldermen centred on relations between the citizens and the alien population. Evil May Day haunted the consciousness of the late-sixteenth-century metropolitan magistrate. Tensions were particularly acute in the later 1560s and early 1570s when alien immigration was at its height, and again in the later 1580s and early 1590s when the alien presence provided a convenient scapegoat for economic difficulties. In 1567 there appeared libels showing 'galowys and as it were hangyng of strangers', and in 1572 mayoral precepts warned against the dangers of allowing strangers out of doors.[17] In April 1586 the aldermen noted 'some dislyke ... amongst divers her highnes subiectes of the meaner sorte in respects of the dearthe and scarcytie increased in some places of this Realm aswell by the number of

[13] *Holinshed's Chronicles of England, Scotland and Ireland* (6 vols., 1807–9), IV. 445–6; Stow, *Annales*, p. 694; C.L.R.O., Remembrancia I, nos. 222, 232, 233; Rep. 20, fo. 224; Jour. 21, fo. 127ᵛ; Folger Library, MS V.a.459, fos. 6, 10; *A Transcript of the Registers of the Stationers' Company, 1554–1640*, ed. E. Arber (5 vols., London and Birmingham, 1875–94), II. 397.
[14] Wright, II. 227–9; C.L.R.O., Jour. 21, fos. 347ᵛ, 356.
[15] *T.R.P.*, III. 60–1; *A.P.C.*, XX. 63–5; W. Darrell, *A Short Discourse of the Life of Servingmen* (1578), sig. A iii; C.L.R.O., Jour. 20, fos. 276ᵛ, 277; Jour. 22, fos. 417ᵛ, 418, 421ᵛ.
[16] V. B. Elliott, 'Mobility and Marriage in Pre-Industrial England' (Cambridge Ph.D., 1978), p. 62; L. Stevenson O'Connell, 'The Elizabethan Bourgeois Hero-Tale: Aspects of an Adolescent Social Consciousness', in *After the Reformation: Essays in Honour of J. H. Hexter*, ed. B. Malament (Manchester, 1980), 267–90.
[17] *Three Fifteenth-Century Chronicles with Historical Memoranda*, ed. J. Gairdner (Camden Society, new series, XXVIII, 1880), pp. 140–1; C.L.R.O., Rep. 17, fo. 372.

strangers'.[18] Recorder Fleetwood uncovered a plot to destroy the strangers in September of that year, while libels continued to circulate the following spring.[19] In 1592 the lord mayor warned that harsh proceedings against rioting feltmakers might produce further disturbances against the strangers. His anxieties appear well founded because vicious libels against the aliens appeared in the tense weeks before May 1593.[20] This was not mindless violence: rather the threat of popular action should be seen as a negotiating strategy, designed to remind the magistrates of their obligations to redress apprentice grievances. Moreover, as later sections of this book will demonstrate, it was a negotiating strategy which met with a fair degree of success.[21]

The significant thing about the three targets of apprentice violence discussed thus far – brothels, servingmen, and stranger artisans – is that they all represented groups or activities marginal to city life. In normal circumstances the elite escaped direct criticism. Anti-alien feeling in particular was significant in earthing discontent since strangers provided a suitable scapegoat for all the ills that afflicted Londoners: they were responsible for inflation and increases in house prices; they took away jobs which might be performed by the English; they were poor and disease flourished among them.[22] The aldermen usually took up a mediatorial position in disturbances, recognising the legitimacy of apprentice grievances. For example, they often supported restrictive measures against aliens. A typical response to disorder was that of Lord Mayor Webb in June 1592. Writing to the privy council in the wake of a riot of feltmakers against the knight marshal's men, he argued for leniency because the residents claimed that the blame lay with the marshalmen, and any action which might be construed as partiality would merely 'give soom occasion to such seditious persons to kindle the coals of a further disorder, which wear better prevented by equal severitie or favour to both parts'.[23] Such mediation ensured that the neutrality of the magisterial office was appreciated, and helps explain why it was that the presence of the lord mayor alone was often enough to persuade rioters to return home.[24]

But the mediatorial position of the elite was under severe strain in 1595 because the lord mayor himself had become an object of apprentice grievances. This is shown by the case of the silkweaver who declared that Spencer was mad and was committed to Bedlam, only to be rescued by other

[18] C.L.R.O., Jour. 22, fo. 18.   [19] Wright, II. 308; C.L.R.O., Jour. 22, fos. 54, 97.

[20] B.L., Lansdowne MS 71/17; C.L.R.O., Rep. 23, fos. 57ᵛ; Jour. 23, fo. 225ᵛ; A.P.C., XXIV. 187, 200, 222, 488; J. Strype, *Annals of the Reformation and Establishment of Religion ... During Queen Elizabeth's Happy Reign* (4 vols., Oxford, 1824), IV. 234–6.

[21] Below, pp. 131–40.

[22] A. Pettegree, *Foreign Protestant Communities in Sixteenth-Century London* (Oxford, 1986), pp. 282–6.

[23] B.L., Lansdowne MS 71/17.

[24] Ibid.; *The Great Chronicle of London*, ed. A. H. Thomas and I. D. Thornley (1938), pp. 248–9.

apprentices, by the libels against the mayor, and, most graphically, by the reports of the gallows outside his house.[25] In other respects too the riots of 1595 represented alarming new developments in the capital. They appear to have been the first food riots in London since the 1520s.[26] And the threat of a conjunction between apprentice grievances and a discontented soldiery was taken very seriously indeed.[27]

Peter Clark's verdict, however, seems unwarranted. Disillusionment with the elite does not appear to have been generalised. One of the libels of 1595 praised Sir Richard Martin at Spencer's expense.[28] The disorders of that year owed a lot to Spencer's peculiarly unpleasant personality.[29] Moreover, the disorders, when examined individually, do not seem particularly threatening. It is true that in the food riots the apprentices appropriated some of the magisterial functions in the markets. The 300 apprentices who assembled in Southwark on 13 June took upon themselves the office of clerk of the market, selling butter at 3d. per pound whereas the owners demanded 5d. They also issued a proclamation demanding that butter be brought to the markets and not sold in inns or private houses.[30] The other food riot occurred when apprentices sent to purchase mackerel at Billingsgate found that the stocks had been bought up by fishwives. A crowd of between sixty and eighty apprentices pursued the fishwives and took their fish, paying for it at the rates appointed by the lord mayor.[31] But this account makes it clear how disciplined these crowds were. It is a pattern familiar to students of riot: disciplined crowds operating according to values which were shared to some extent by the elite in actions designed to remind the magistrates of their duties.[32] In attacking hucksters and those who sold in inns the apprentices were singling out groups and practices which were periodically the objects of magisterial correction.[33] The magistrates took seriously the warnings from the crowd that they were failing to discharge their duties properly, for the repression of rioters was accompanied by measures to tighten the machinery of market regulation.[34] Although the failure of the traditional sanctions to defuse tensions immediately demonstrates that the situation was unusually

[25] H.M.C., *Hatfield House*, V. 249; B.L., Lansdowne MS 78/64–65; P.R.O., SP 12/252/94.
[26] C.L.R.O., Rep. 7, fos. 202ᵛ, 218.
[27] For military disorders, see Clark, 'Crisis Contained?', p. 55.
[28] B.L., Lansdowne MS 78/64.   [29] Below, p. 56.
[30] Stow, *Annales*, p. 769; B.L., Harleian MS 2143, fo. 57ᵛ; C.L.R.O., Remembrancia II, no. 98.
[31] C.L.R.O., Remembrancia II, no. 97.
[32] E. P. Thompson, 'The Moral Economy of the English Crowd in the Eighteenth Century', *Past and Present*, 50 (1971), 76–136; J. Walter and K. Wrightson, 'Dearth and the Social Order in Early Modern England', *Past and Present*, 71 (1976), 22–42; P. Clark, 'Popular Protest and Disturbance in Kent, 1558–1640', *Ec.H.R.*, second series, 29 (1976), 365–82.
[33] C.L.R.O., Jour. 23, fo. 334, Jour. 24, fos. 3, 98ᵛ.
[34] *Hugh Alley's 'Caveat': the London Markets in 1598*, ed. I. W. Archer, C. M. Barron and V. Harding (London Topographical Society, 1988).

tense, this does not look like a general social crisis. Two further pieces of evidence support this contention. *The Student's Lamentation*, a tract issued within a few weeks of the Tower riot, emphasises that discontent was not universal because the better sort of apprentices reported on the conspiracy to their masters, suggesting that there were limits to apprentice solidarity.[35] Finally, the readiness with which the lieutenant of the Tower resisted the efforts of the City's officers to quell the disturbances in the Tower liberty in order to score another point in his interminable jurisdictional conflict with the City shows that there was no generalised social crisis in which all men of property feared for their lives.[36]

However, it will also be clear that Rappaport's characterisation of apprentice violence as aimless is misleading. His account is at its weakest in his description of the context of the disturbances because he fails to relate crowd action to the social tensions underlying riots, he does not examine the other means by which those tensions might be expressed, and he fails to look at the responses of the elite to popular pressure, whether in the form of ameliorative action or repression. In other words he does not look at riot as part of the process of interaction between rulers and ruled.

Once we appreciate that riot was a negotiating strategy, we may become sensitive to other means by which pressure was brought to bear upon the elite, and other ways in which the tensions in the civic polity were expressed. Libels, those 'proclamations and trumpets of sedition' as one government minister put it in 1593, with the threat of action that they conveyed, were one such means.[37] There never was an actual anti-alien riot in Elizabethan London, but there were, as we have seen, plenty of libels threatening action. The absence of riots may reflect the particular diligence of magistrates and the difficulties of conspiracy among apprentices in a world ruled by householders, but it may also be an indication that the libels fulfilled their functions in encouraging the rulers of the companies supported by the aldermanic elite to take action against strangers. Libels, frequently left under the lord mayor's door, were used in other contexts too.[38] Although there were no riots in 1596, the City authorities reported the discovery of several libels.[39] Unfortunately, none of them survives and we do not know what grievances they expressed. But it is likely that they provided some commentary on the worsening dearth conditions in the capital: in 1596 a ballad on the scarcity of corn was causing the authorities some concern, while in 1597

---

[35] *Student's Lamentation.*   [36] Manning, 'Prosecution of Blount'.
[37] B.L., Harleian MS 6849, fo. 330.
[38] C.L.R.O., Rep. 20, fo. 133ᵛ; Rep. 21, fo. 334; B.L., Lansdowne MSS 26/68; 78/64; Folger Library, MS V.a. 459, fo. 21ᵛ.
[39] B.L., Lansdowne MSS 81/28, 30, 32.

libels reporting that the lord mayor was engaged in a *pacte de famine* were circulating in London.[40] If this was typical of the later 1590s, then libels might be seen as a mechanism, short of riot, by which the aldermen were reminded of their functions in the markets.

Rappaport is also misleading about the quality of social relations in the Elizabethan metropolis because he underestimates the extent to which the escalation of disturbances alarmed the elite, and contributed to a sense of perceived crisis. There are some signs of this even before 1595: when riots against aliens threatened in 1593, the privy council authorised the use of torture in the discovery of libellers, and a vestry minute of St Alban Wood Street on 22 April records the exceptional appointment of nine householders to be ready at one hour's notice to aid the lord mayor 'in the suppression of tumults'.[41] Correspondence between the City and the privy council conveys a sense of the fragile crust on which the aldermen moved in the 1590s. Writing to the council against Darcy's controversial patent for sealing leather in March 1592, the aldermen warned:

What great mischiefs have risen of lesse beginnings your Lordships can consider & experience hath taught us in this Citie beefore, whear popular multitudes beeing once incited and assembled togither can hardly bee suppressed and kept within obedience by any authoritie of Magistrate whatsoever.[42]

The sense of perceived crisis is clearest in the reaction to the disturbances of 1595: the declaration of martial law, the hanging of rioters, and the City's appointment early in the following year of two marshals of its own with twelve attendants to exercise general police functions and suppress 'any further distemperature that may arise by youth'.[43] That this represented a higher profile for policing in London is clear from the large number of fines taken from constables for their failure to convey vagrants to ward on the instructions of the marshals.[44] The continuing nervousness of the elite is evident in the speeches of Recorder Croke at the presentation of the mayor at Westminster with their remarks on the contempt of the people for their magistrates.[45] Elite concerns found an answering echo among the middling sort in the rhetoric of wardmote petitions: in 1597 the wardmote of Tower ward expressed its anxieties about the negligence of constables in terms of the general collapse in obedience that threatened:

it will come to pass yt the people will shortly growe careless of lawes & maiestrates,

[40] *T.R.P.*, III. 182–3; B.L., Lansdowne MS 81/30.
[41] *A.P.C.*, XXIV. 222; G.L., MS 1264/1, fo. 10.
[42] C.L.R.O., Remembrancia I, no. 651.
[43] B.L., Lansdowne MS 114/1; C.L.R.O., Jour. 24, fos. 95, 150ᵛ; Stow, *Annales*, pp. 768–9.
[44] C.L.R.O., Rep. 23, fos. 526ᵛ, 529ᵛ; Rep. 24, fos. 23, 36ᵛ, 40, 68, 101ᵛ, 453; Jour. 24, fos. 113ᵛ, 150ᵛ.
[45] Buckinghamshire Record Office, D138/22/1.

and in thend fall to flat disobedience & open contempt whereof we do perceive & fynd to our greatt greafes a marvelous inclynacion & beginning already.[46]

A sense of perceived crisis might therefore have been important in effecting a tightening of the machinery of social regulation, and the absence of riots after 1595 may reflect tightened control rather than the restoration of social calm.

The fundamental stability of the City is not in question. But because Rappaport defines his position in terms of reaction against an extremist position never seriously held (that London was characterised by a pattern of 'pervasive instability'), he is prone to underestimate the tensions in civic society.[47] It might be objected that his primary concern is with explaining metropolitan stability, and that the tensions in society are irrelevant to this concern. However, a preoccupation with the fact of stability makes his account of the reasons for it deficient. It will be one of the main contentions of this book that metropolitan stability can only be properly understood in terms of the dynamics of interaction between rulers and ruled, in particular through the ways in which the system dealt with grievances.

THE 'CRISIS' OF THE 1590S

Disagreements among historians about the severity of disorder in the 1590s reflect broader disagreements both about the scale of the problems of the 1590s, and about the underlying sources of resilience in metropolitan society. Historians since E. P. Cheyney (1926) have seen the last decade of the sixteenth century as a period of crisis, characterised by plague, repeated harvest failure, massive price inflation, heavy taxation, depression both in overseas trade and in the volume of domestic demand, large-scale unemployment, and escalating crime and vagrancy.[48] Plague stalked the city in 1592–3. In the second year, 10,675 plague deaths were recorded in the metropolitan area, constituting 14.3 per cent of the population. Because the level of morbidity was twice as high as that of mortality, and because the authorities demanded that afflicted houses be quarantined, the effect on the economy was devastating, and the agencies of poor relief inadequately equipped to deal with the huge extra demand placed on their services.[49] The

---

[46] C.L.R.O., Samuel Barton's Book, fo. 46.

[47] S. Rappaport, 'Social Structure and Mobility in Sixteenth-Century London: Part I', *London Journal*, 9 (1983), 107–8.

[48] E. P. Cheyney, *A History of England from the Defeat of the Armada to the Death of Elizabeth* (2 vols., 1914–26), II, chs. XXV–XXVI; J. B. Black, *The Reign of Elizabeth, 1558–1603* (Oxford, 1936), pp. 355–6.

[49] P. Slack, *The Impact of Plague in Tudor and Stuart England* (1985), pp. 151, 154, 158, 162, 175–6 and 'Metropolitan Government in Crisis: the Response to Plague', in *London, 1500–1700: the Making of the Metropolis*, ed. A. L. Beier and R. Finlay (1986), pp. 60–81.

plague years were followed by the failure of four successive harvests between 1594 and 1597. Prices sky-rocketed. The Phelps Brown and Hopkins price index of a composite basket of consumables, with the average prices of the period 1451–75 as a base of 100, stood at 356 in 1593, and rose to a peak of 685 in 1597, before falling back to 459 in 1600. Real wages inevitably spiralled downwards. The index figure for a building craftsman fell from 56 in 1593 to 29 in 1597, and real wages were on average 22 per cent lower in the 1590s than in the preceding decade.[50] Acute distress in the countryside encouraged the swarm of subsistence migrants who descended on London in this decade in the hope of employment or relief, thereby compounding the capital's own problems.[51] The chances of their hopes being fulfilled were slender because of diminishing employment opportunities in the capital. Cloth exports stagnated, and the yield of the dues on sales of cloth at Blackwell Hall dropped precipitously reflecting a sluggish domestic demand.[52] The misery was deepened by the continuing war, and the demands for money the Crown placed on the City. There were payments in parliamentary subsidy every year during the 1590s apart from 1598, and in parliamentary fifteenths every year apart from 1597. To these were added the special levies to finance the Crown's demands for troops and ships. The total volume of direct taxation in London arising from the Crown's demands (and including loans which were not repaid) averaged £12,246 p.a. between 1585 and 1603 (£15,778 p.a. during the worst years of the 'crisis', 1594–8), compared to just £3,595 p.a. during the twenty years preceding the outbreak of war. Even in 1593, before the harvest failures, members of parliament alleged that the poor were selling pots and pans to pay their taxes.[53] The sense of cumulative hardship is well captured in the complaints of the aldermen and common council of the City to the privy council in December 1596 when confronted by another request for shipping:

The great dearth of victual which hath been continued now these three years, besides three years' plague before, which so hath impoverished the general estate of this whole city, that many persons, before known to be of good wealth, are greatly

[50] E. H. Phelps Brown and S. V. Hopkins, *A Perspective of Wages and Prices* (1981).
[51] A. L. Beier, *Masterless Men: the Vagrancy Problem in England, 1560–1640* (1985), pp. 30–2, 37.
[52] F. J. Fisher, 'Commercial Trends and Policy in Sixteenth-Century England', *Ec.H.R.*, 10 (1940), 95–117 and 'London's Export Trade in the Early Seventeenth Century', *Ec.H.R.*, second series, 3 (1950), 151–61; R. Davis, *English Overseas Trade, 1500–1700* (1973), p. 53; D. W. Jones, 'The "Hallage" Receipts of the London Cloth Markets, 1562–1720', *Ec.H.R.*, second series, 25 (1972), 568.
[53] *T.E.D*, II. 240–1. The calculations of the burden of taxation are based on P.R.O., E359/51–7 (the enrolled accounts of the collectors of the subsidy in the Exchequer), livery company accounts (for expenditure on soldiers raised through the companies, the predominant method of recruitment before 1585), and on estimates of the yield of City fifteenths (theoretically a fixed-yield tax) and of taxes based on subsidy assessments (for the calculation of which the Exchequer accounts have been used as a base). I hope to publish a full-scale study of taxation in which these calculations will be justified, in due course. Cf. G. Gronquist,

decayed and utterly disabled for all public service, being hardly able by their uttermost endeavours to maintain the charges of their private families in very mean sort: divers of them being enforced to relinquish their trades, and to dissolve their households, which public calamity is greatly increased by the decay of traffic in foreign countries.[54]

This was clearly the worst decade sixteenth-century Londoners experienced.

But historians have recently become much more reluctant to apply the term 'crisis' to the 1590s. They have tended both to emphasise the underlying sources of resilience in the metropolitan economy and to downplay the severity of the pressures to which it was subjected at the turn of the century.[55] Lee Beier has shown how diversified craft production in London was, suggesting that it may therefore have been less vulnerable to depression because it was not dependent on key staples like cloth.[56] Brian Dietz has emphasised that although cloth exports may have been stagnating, imports, particularly of raw materials, were increasing in the later sixteenth century, and many of the spin-off industries associated with these imports were located in the London area.[57] London's rising role as a social centre for the gentry has been underscored by Christopher Brooks' recent demonstration of the huge increase of litigation in the Elizabethan period. The city's requirements for grain were 11.5 per cent higher during the law terms, and as the gentry thronged to the capital to wage law, demand for London's goods and services increased. This was a demand which was more resilient than that in other sections of society because the gentry were among the beneficiaries of the social changes of the sixteenth century.[58] The resilience of the economy was reflected in the high wage differential between London and the rest of the country: wages in London were 50 per cent higher than in provincial England.[59]

Moreover, the decline in living standards was not as catastrophic as previously thought. A new real wage index for London constructed by Steve

'The Relationship Between the City of London and the Crown, 1509–47' (Cambridge Ph.D., 1986), p. 206.

[54] *H.M.C., Hatfield House*, VI. 534–5.

[55] Apart from the specific items listed below, see the following general surveys: Clark, 'A Crisis Contained'; M. J. Power, 'London and the Control of the "Crisis" of the 1590s', *History*, 70 (1985), 371–85 and 'A "Crisis" Reconsidered: Social and Demographic Dislocation in London in the 1590s', *London Journal*, 12 (1986), 134–45.

[56] A. L. Beier, 'Engine of Manufacture: the Trades of London', in *London, 1500–1700*, ed. Beier and Finlay, pp. 141–67.

[57] B. Dietz, 'Overseas Trade and Metropolitan Growth', in *London, 1500–1700*, ed. Beier and Finlay, pp. 121–9.

[58] C. W. Brooks, *Pettyfoggers and Vipers of the Commonwealth: the "Lower Branch" of the Legal Profession in Early Modern England* (Cambridge, 1986), ch. IV; F. J. Fisher, 'The Development of London as a Centre of Conspicuous Consumption in the Sixteenth and Seventeenth Centuries', *T.R.H.S.*, fourth series, 30 (1948), 37–50; *T.E.D.*, II, 159.

[59] J. A. Chartres, 'Food Consumption and Internal Trade', in *London, 1500–1700*, ed. Beier and Finlay, pp. 170–2.

Rappaport, and much improved on that of Phelps Brown and Hopkins, because it is based on retail prices which rose less rapidly than wholesale prices reflecting the high labour component in food processing, stands on 69 for the decade 1590–9, compared to 44 on the Phelps Brown and Hopkins index. Thus the fall in real wages over the sixteenth century was in fact only half that previously thought. Rappaport acknowledges that the 1590s saw severe cuts in living standards as real wages plunged by 20 per cent from an average index of 76 in 1590–3 to 61 in 1596–8, but he suggests that there was some improvement thereafter, and that people may have achieved some relief from spiralling prices by shifting their patterns of consumption towards less expensive types of food such as fish and poultry.[60] Such a conclusion is supported by the very limited evidence that the dearth caused mortality crises in the capital. There was higher than usual mortality in 1597, but it came only in the fourth year of the food crisis, was only evident in the suburban parishes, and was much less serious than in provincial towns.[61]

The severity of the fiscal pressures has received rather less attention from recent historians. This is an area currently under investigation by the author, but space does not permit the detailed documentation of the findings, and the figures I give must be regarded as provisional. It is worth emphasising that the fiscal pressures of the 1590s were less serious than those of the 1540s, even when the extra proportion of taxation borne by local assessments rather than parliamentary subsidies in the later period is taken into account. The £12,246 p.a. paid in direct taxes (including local military rates and the loans which the Crown failed to repay) arising from the royal demands between 1585 and 1603 compares with £12,090 p.a. paid between 1540 and 1559. In real terms this represents a drop of 40 per cent. Nor were the fiscal pressures as serious as those on the continent, in particular because subsidy was paid only by the top one-third of the city's householders.[62]

Nevertheless, although this research suggests that things were not quite as bad as was previously thought, it does not mean that they were rosy. The poor presented the City's rulers with an increasingly acute problem. Although the fragmentary statistics on poverty, discussed in chapter 5, are difficult to interpret, the mere fact that so much of the population growth was located in the extramural parishes suggests that the poor were increasing as a proportion of the total population. Whereas inner-city parishes regis-

[60] Rappaport, *Worlds Within Worlds*, ch. V. For other powerful critiques of the real wage series, see D. Woodward, 'Wage Rates and Living Standards in Pre-Industrial England', *Past and Present*, 91 (1981), 28–46; D. M. Palliser, *The Age of Elizabeth: England Under the Later Tudors, 1547–1603* (1983), pp. 156–9.

[61] A. B. Appleby, *Famine in Tudor and Stuart England* (Liverpool, 1978), pp. 137–40; Power, 'A "Crisis" Reconsidered', pp. 137–43.

[62] Sources and method as outlined in n. 53 above. For the continent, see M. Greengrass, 'The Later Wars of Religion in the French Midi', in *European Crisis*, ed. Clark, pp. 115–22, 124–5; I. A. A. Thompson, 'The Impact of War', in ibid. pp. 261–84.

tered modest levels of growth, over the same period the population of many extramural parishes more than doubled. Thus while St Michael Cornhill registered only a very small increase (844 to 898, or 6 per cent), and St Lawrence Jewry remained static at around 720, St Botolph Aldgate mushroomed from 2,570 to 5,640 (119 per cent), and St Giles Cripplegate from 3,730 to 7,745 (108 per cent). The extramural parishes were overwhelmed with immigrants crammed into the proliferating alleys whose insanitary conditions made them bastions of crisis mortality. London society was 'filling out at the bottom'.[63] An ever higher proportion of its inhabitants was constituted by the labouring poor, described by the preacher to the Virginia Company in 1622 as people who rose early, worked all day, went late to bed, and yet were 'scarce able to put bread in their mouths at the week's end and clothes on their backs at the year's end'.[64]

The perspective from which we view the statistical evidence for hardship affects our interpretation of it. The new index for real wages gives a credible scale to a deterioration in living standards which historians always had difficulty in accepting at face value. The data derived from the parish registers can only give the crudest indication of the extent of suffering because there are many degrees of human suffering short of death by starvation. Most Londoners faced impoverishment rather than death.[65] Although the absolute level of taxation was lower in the 1590s than in the 1540s, the relative burden on the poorer sections of society was increasing both because a higher proportion of taxation was being levied in the form of fifteenths, which were much wider in their incidence than the subsidy, and because the richer taxpayers were disproportionately the beneficiaries of the widespread under-assessment of the subsidy in the Elizabethan years.[66]

We are never going to arrive at a satisfactory index of human deprivation for the 1590s for the simple reason that there are too many unknown variables. We have no way of telling, for example, whether the number of

[63] Below, pp. 150–4, 188–9; E. Jones, 'London in the Early Seventeenth Century: An Ecological Approach', *London Journal*, 6 (1980), 126–33; R. Finlay, *Population and Metropolis: the Demography of London, 1580–1650* (Cambridge, 1981), pp. 70–82; Slack, *Impact of Plague*, pp. 170–3; G.L., MSS 9220/1; 6419/1; *The Parish Registers of Saint Michael Cornhill, London*, ed. J. L. Chester (Harleian Society Registers, VII, 1881); *The Register of Saint Lawrence Jewry, London*, ed. A. W. Hughes Clarke (Harleian Society Registers, LXX, 1940). In estimating the population of individual parishes here and elsewhere, I have averaged baptisms over five-year periods, and assumed 5 per cent under-registration and a birth rate of 37 per 1,000.
[64] K. Wrightson, *English Society, 1580–1680* (1982), p. 139.
[65] Cf. D. J. Oddy, 'Urban Famine in Nineteenth-Century Britain: the Effect of the Lancashire Cotton Famine on Working-Class Diet and Health', *Ec.H.R.*, second series, 36 (1983), 68–86.
[66] R. Schofield, 'Taxation and the Political Limits of the Tudor State', in *Law and Government Under the Tudors: Essays Presented to Sir Geoffrey Elton on his Retirement*, ed. C. Cross, D. M. Loades, and J. J. Scarisbrick (Cambridge, 1988), pp. 238–41, 253–4.

productive niches expanded at the same rate as the city's population, and therefore we have no measure of the extent of unemployment or under-employment, without which the data on real wages can only give a partial indication of the nature of living standards. Moreover, as far as the nature of social relations is concerned, it is people's perception of their situation, rather than the relativities in which historians so often deal, that matters. Londoners in the 1590s would have given short shrift to historians who pointed out that their suffering was not as acute as that of people on the continent, or that their tax burden was relatively low. There is, as we have already seen, a strong case for asserting the reality of a *perceived* crisis in the 1590s. The perception may have been out of line with realities, but it was nevertheless important in effecting changes in social relations.

EXPLANATIONS FOR STABILITY

It is not just over the question of the severity of the problems of the 1590s, however, that the 'revisionists' differ from earlier historians. They are also generally much less convinced by the emphasis on social polarisation and oligarchic rule which characterised the so-called 'doom and gloom' school of urban history of the 1970s. Their work has several salient features. First, they are drawing our attention away from the court of aldermen dominated by the city's mercantile elite, and redirecting it to the substructures of government, the parishes, wards, and companies, the cooperation of whose rulers was essential to the successful implementation of the elite's policies. At this level of government the opportunities for participation were much broader. Valerie Pearl has calculated that in any year about one in ten of London's householders held some kind of office in local government in the capital, while Steve Rappaport has emphasised the involvement of artisans at the middle tier of company government.[67] Secondly, a more sensitive under-standing of urban social structure is emerging. Steve Rappaport and Jeremy Boulton have both questioned the value of impressions of social structure derived from profiles of tax-payers. Rappaport has shown that company assessments were paid by a wider group than those assessed to the subsidy, and therefore that non-payment of the subsidy should not be taken as an indication of poverty, while Boulton has pointed out the existence of an economically self-sufficient group outside the rate-paying householders, shown by their ability to keep servants or leave something for their burial.[68] Moreover, tax records give a static picture of social structure, obscuring the

---

[67] V. Pearl, 'Change and Stability in Seventeenth-Century London', *London Journal*, 5 (1979), 3–34; Rappaport, *Worlds Within Worlds*, ch. VI.
[68] Ibid. pp. 166–71, 273–82; J. P. Boulton, *Neighbourhood and Society: a London Suburb in the Seventeenth Century* (Cambridge, 1987), pp. 104–19.

reality of mobility within an individual's life-time. Rappaport's study of a group of men who became free in 1551–3 concludes that 'for the man who sweated out his years of apprenticeship and then journeywork, the odds were seven to one that he would become a householder and have his own shop and then were roughly one in three that one day, if he remain alive and in London, he would wear the livery and thus enter the elite of his company'.[69] Thirdly, Pearl has drawn attention to the sensitive and apparently successful social policies pursued by London's rulers, poor rates supplementing the philanthropic bounty of the wealthy to provide a wide range of benefits and often a high level of care.[70] London's citizens therefore could reasonably expect to be masters of their own households free from domination by capitalist entrepreneurs; their aspirations for a role in government were catered for by office-holding in the companies, parishes, and wards; and they could expect the support of their fellow citizens for themselves in the event of sickness or old age or for their children in the event of their own premature death.

These are important findings and any explanation of the capital's stability must incorporate them. However, it is arguable that the reaction has been pushed too hard. Because the stability of the city is always in view, these writers tend to be biased towards the success stories. Their attention is focused on upwardly mobile Londoners and the recipients of poor relief, usually in the wealthier inner-city parishes. Pearl fails to discuss social policy with reference to the social topography of poverty, and important dimensions of the city's social problems, in particular vagrancy and criminality, are not discussed. Consensual explanations are always favoured over those which recognise a degree of coercion, so that there is no discussion, for example, of the repressive side to social policy. There is a tendency to adopt the most optimistic interpretation of the available evidence. Rappaport's favoured explanation for the extremely high drop-out rate among apprentices is that openings became available at home rather than that apprenticeship was fraught with tensions and that the drop-outs may have contributed to the vagrancy problem of the capital.[71] Tensions in the society and shortcomings in government thus remain under-explored. Part of the explanation for stability is likely to lie in the unfocused nature of grievances rather than their absence: in other words artisans might be divided according to the particular point at issue, or the poor subject to the internal divisions produced by godly protestantism or immigration.

The degree to which one is convinced by the stability thesis depends in part

[69] Rappaport, *Worlds Within Worlds*, ch. VIII, with quotation from p. 387.
[70] V. Pearl, 'Social Policy in Early Modern London' in *History and Imagination: Essays in Honour of H. R. Trevor-Roper*, ed. H. Lloyd-Jones, B. Worden and V. Pearl (1979), pp. 115–31.
[71] Rappaport, *Worlds Within Worlds*, pp. 311–15.

upon the kind of records which one is using. Rappaport's vision is that of the
members of the courts of assistants of the livery companies, the problems of
whose records as a guide to the attitudes of the artisans are barely discussed.
While he recognises that London faced some serious problems his repeated
use of Stow to illuminate them is rather unsatisfactory because that author's
primary intention was to celebrate the City's traditions rather than to
provide a detailed analysis of social ills.[72] That Pearl should find surprising
the absence of references in churchwardens' accounts to the gangs of
vagrants and street arabs which characterised the literature of the time is
suggestive of a similar source-bound myopia.[73] None of the advocates of
stability have examined the admittedly difficult records of urban criminality
to determine the dimensions of a problem which much exercised the rulers.
As a depiction of social relations in the city their accounts have serious
limitations.

Furthermore, in drawing out the salient features of the society which are
thought to have contributed to stability, these historians have tended to
produce a rather static account. It is static in the sense that it often fails to
explore the dynamics of interaction between rulers and ruled. Rappaport's
preferred view of stability as lying in the opportunities for social mobility
makes his analysis of the responses of company rulers to the demands of
artisans somewhat superficial. The achievement of householder status
emphatically did not remove people's grievances, and by heightening their
self-esteem, it may have made them less inclined to be pushed around. There
were types of dependence other than the straightforward relationship of
employer and employee, such as the control exerted by wholesalers over
craftsmen, and these might arouse powerful resentments. Workers in the
leather trades resented the control of dealers in leather over their raw
material; feltmakers resented exploitation by haberdashers who dealt in the
imported Spanish wools from which hats were made. All were householders.[74] Explanations of stability should therefore consider how grievances
were dealt with by the authorities. It is not enough to point to wider than
expected levels of participation in government, and to assume that this
guaranteed sensitivity to popular grievances, because the formal structure of
power might be a rather inadequate guide to its informal distribution. Some
people clearly had more weight in the decision-making process because of the
economic power they wielded. Rappaport's conclusion, that rulers usually
responded effectively to the demands of the artisans, is unsatisfactory
because he fails to recognise that there were some issues, such as the need for
restrictions on non-free labour, on which a greater level of consensus

---

[72] Ibid. pp. 16–17, 159–60.   [73] Pearl, 'Social Policy', p. 126.
[74] G. Unwin, *Industrial Organization in the Sixteenth and Seventeenth Centuries* (Oxford,
1904), pp. 128–36.

prevailed, than on others, such as the demands of artisans that profiteering by wholesalers be restricted. On some grievances the artisans were indeed promised redress, but soothing words were not always followed by sustained enforcement; and on other issues the artisans were largely ignored.[75] The loyalties of the artisans were essentially conditional, dependent on the rulers being sufficiently responsive to their demands to ensure their continuing obedience. Explanations of stability must therefore start with a sense of what people expected from their rulers.

The recent contributions have also been static in the sense of paying insufficient attention to chronological change. How well did the City respond to the challenges of its growth? Did the prospects for mobility remain as bright after 1560 as they were for those becoming free in the early 1550s, who form the core of Rappaport's study? Did the growth in the suburbs make London less governable? How well did the machinery of poor relief cope with the changed conditions? In what ways did the impoverishment of the later sixteenth century alter the pattern of social relations? Did the Reformation in London produce that clash of value systems that has been seen as so pervasive in provincial England? The 'revisionists' have not yet tackled these questions.

Finally, there is a risk that all of us who stress the importance of social relations in explaining a society's stability will neglect the role of contingent circumstances. The stability of local communities depended to a large extent on the stability of national politics, and the latter might be upset by forces extraneous to the social system. Thus many historians have questioned whether the breakdown of the mid seventeenth century reflected social conflicts, and have rather emphasised the contingent and unforeseen, the role of key personalities, and failures of communication.[76] A comparison of sixteenth-century London with earlier less stable periods has convinced me first, that the solidarity of the elite was a crucial variable in stability because when the elite divided its members were likely to start competing for support in other social groups, thereby radicalising politics, and, secondly, that the nature of national politics and particularly the relationship between London and the Crown played a key role in sustaining that solidarity. The solidarity of the elite, and the relationship with the Crown in sustaining that solidarity, therefore form major themes in the next chapter.

[75] Rappaport, *Worlds Within Worlds*, pp. 380–3.
[76] R. Cust and A. Hughes, 'Introduction: after Revisionism', in *Conflict in Early Stuart England: Studies in Religion and Politics, 1603–42*, ed. R. Cust and A. Hughes (1989), pp. 3–10.

—————————————— ≪ 2 ≫ ——————————————

The framework of social relations: the City elite

THE STABILITY OF THE CITY IN HISTORICAL PERSPECTIVE

The government of the corporation of London was formally oligarchic.[1] Executive authority lay with the court of aldermen, consisting of twenty-six men, one for each of the City's wards, and holding office for life. Apart from responsibility for much of the routine of City administration, the aldermen disposed of considerable judicial authority, managing the estates of minors in their capacity as the City's court of orphans, presiding over the mayor's court, the court of hustings, the sheriffs' court, and, in conjunction with representatives of common council, over the court of conscience with jurisdiction over petty debts.[2] The senior aldermen, those who had passed the chair, together with the recorder, constituted the commission of peace in the City, and sat on gaol deliveries and at City sessions.[3] The aldermen were able to exercise control over recruitment into their own ranks because, although vacancies were filled from among nominations from the wards, the court had the right to reject nominees. The high cost of office-holding, which resulted from the aldermen's duty of subsidising the round of civic feasting, meant that it was the preserve of the wealthy. In 1582, twenty-four of the aldermen were recruited from among the seventy-five householders assessed to the subsidy of that year at over £200.[4] In the early Elizabethan period almost all the aldermen belonged to the cloth-exporting Merchant Adventurers' Company. By custom they also had to be members of one of the twelve great livery companies, and any person from a lesser craft guild who was elected to the court had to change his company affiliation by translation,

---

[1] The best account remains V. Pearl, *London and the Outbreak of the Puritan Revolution: City Government and National Politics* (Oxford, 1961), pp. 45–68. Cf. F. F. Foster, *The Politics of Stability: a Portrait of the Rulers of Elizabethan London* (1977).

[2] C.L.R.O., Jour. 19, fo. 121ʳ⁻ᵛ; Jour. 22, fos. 193–4.

[3] *London Sessions Records, 1605–85*, ed. H. Bowler (Catholic Record Society, XXIV, 1934), p. ix.

[4] A. Beaven, *The Aldermen of the City of London* (2 vols., 1908–13); P.R.O., E179/251/16. The other two, William Allen and William Webb were assessed at £100 and £160 respectively.

18

so that the range of economic groups with formal representation on the court was quite narrow.

Responsibility for legislation and the right to approve civic taxation rested with common council. But its legislative initiative was circumscribed by the control of the aldermen over the matters discussed, by the presence of aldermen on its committees, and by the right of veto which rested with the aldermen. Its power to authorise civic assessments was limited to those made on the wards rather than through the livery companies. Although there were 212 common councillors, the pattern of elite recruitment was not significantly broadened. Once elected, common councillors tended to remain in office for long periods. Thus in Cornhill ward the average term of service seems to have been eight years in the later sixteenth century. They also tended to be the wealthiest men of their wards. Of 186 common councillors (88 per cent of the total) active in or around 1582, 80 per cent were assessed to the subsidy of that year at over £50, placing them in the top 4.8 per cent of London householders. 84 per cent belonged to the twelve leading companies, which in 1551–3 accounted fo 51.4 per cent of freedom admissions; the poorer crafts were often not represented at all.[5]

Although common councillors were formally elected at the wardmotes by all freemen, they were often the nominees of the sitting alderman. The right to participate in the election of the lord mayor, sheriffs, and members of parliament was confined to liverymen in meetings of common hall. There were probably 2,500 liverymen in late Elizabethan London, constituting about 10 per cent of householders in the capital.[6] Even their rights were

---

[5] Common councillors identified in M. Benbow, 'Index to London Citizens in Government, 1558–1603' (copy deposited with Centre for Metropolitan History, Institute of Historical Research, London), and from our own research on parish and ward records. 151 were definitely active in 1582; a further 35 active some time in the period 1580–5 can be traced for wards where the panel of 1582 remains incomplete. The calculation of the proportion of Londoners paying subsidy at specified rates is based on a population figure for the city (excluding Southwark and the Middlesex portions of the extramural parishes) of 83,000 and a mean household size of 4.5. Calculations of the population of Southwark parishes based on their parish registers, and of the Middlesex portions of the extramural parishes on the basis of relative numbers in these parishes assessed to the subsidy in Middlesex and London applied to population totals. R. A. P. Finlay, *Population and Metropolis: the Demography of London 1580–1650* (Cambridge, 1981), p. 155; P.R.O., E179/251/16; E179/269/41; G.L.R.O., P92/SAV/2001; P71/OLA/9; G.L., MSS 6419/1; 9220/1; 10342; 6667/1; Bodl., Rawlinson MS D796B, fo. 86.

[6] Calculation of number of liverymen based on quarterage lists and assessments in seven of the twelve great companies (average 73) and thirteen of the forty-five lesser companies (average 37), using the averages as multipliers: Rappaport, *Worlds Within Worlds*, p. 269 (seventy-one liverymen in Grocers' Company, 1580–99, eighty-nine in Clothworkers, 1590–99); C. M. Clode, *Memorials of the Guild of Merchant Taylors* (1875), pp. 590–1 (100 in Merchant Tailors, 1603); A. H. Johnson, *The History of the Worshipful Company of Drapers of London* (5 vols., Oxford, 1914–22), II. 195 (fifty-five in Drapers, 1598); Mc. Co., C.M. III, listing at front (seventy-four in Mercers, 1562); G.L., MSS 5578A/1 (sixty-seven in Fishmongers, 1610); 16986/1 (fifty-seven in Ironmongers, 1596–1600); 12085 (thirty-eight

limited because their choice was constrained by the conventions which dictated that one of the men nominated to be sheriff should be the junior alderman who had not served, and that one of the nominees for the mayoralty should be the senior alderman beneath the chair who was invariably elected. Meetings of common hall were therefore often dumb shows in which the process of choice had an illusory quality.

This structure of authority and the hierarchical principles which underpinned it were unchallenged in the Elizabethan period. It is true that individual policies pursued by the aldermen were regularly criticised. Petitions from the wards, for example, attacked the monopoly of sand held by Bridewell Hospital in 1579, and criticised the mayor for his failure to make regular inspections of weights in 1594.[7] There were undoubtedly tensions between the common council and the aldermen, usually because of suspicions that the aldermen were not sufficiently diligent in protecting the City from the demands of the royal court for patronage. It was, for example, pressure from the common council which lay behind the seven-year ban on admissions to the City freedom by redemption without the permission of common council in 1590.[8] The aldermen's use of the livery companies to raise loans to finance the purchase of grain in years of dearth without the authority of common council was often the occasion for grumbling. Their reluctant acquiescence shows through in the Grocers' agreement to pay up in 1566 'albeyt inordinate use of doing things therein is done which they hope hereafter may be amended'.[9] But although individual policies might be questioned, the right of the aldermen to rule was not challenged. In reality the aldermen were sufficiently responsive to criticism to defuse opposition. For example, when the patience of the companies snapped in 1575 after the loss of £2,032. 19s. 9d. of the money provided for grain stocks, as the markets fell unexpectedly, the aldermen brought the common council into discussions which led to the overhauling of the arrangements for providing grain.[10] Nor do controversies

in Armourers, 1606); 2883/3 (thirty-three in Blacksmiths, 1597–9); 7351/1 (thirty-four in Cordwainers, 1597–8); 7094 (fifty in Pewterers, 1597–99); 14346/1, p. 222 (twenty-seven in Curriers, 1591); 2210/1 (eighteen in Plumbers, 1594); 6152/1 (twenty-six in Tallow Chandlers, 1579–87); 6127/1, fos. 16–18 (thirty-five in Plasterers in 1608); Br. Sr. Co., MS 5255/1 (sixty-three in Barber-Surgeons in 1604); Rappaport, *Worlds Within Worlds*, p. 260 (fifty in Brewers, 1580–99, thirty-seven in Butchers, 1590–9, forty-five in Coopers, 1590–9); *Wardens' Accounts of the Worshipful Company of Founders of the City of London, 1497–1681*, ed. G. Parsloe (1964), p. 178 (twenty-six in Founders, 1569).

[7] C.L.R.O., Rep. 19, fo. 418ᵛ; G.L., MS 4069/1, fo. 62ᵛ.
[8] C.L.R.O., Jour. 22, fo. 408. For the sensitivities of the common council on this issue, see J. Kennedy, 'The City of London and the Crown, *c.* 1509–*c.* 1529' (Manchester M.A., 1978), pp. 40–7; Gronquist, 'London and the Crown', pp. 69–78.
[9] G.L., MS 11588/1, fo. 144ᵛ. Cf. ibid., fos. 71ᵛ, 83, 116, 148ᵛ; Mc. Co., C.M. III, fos. 18, 88ʳ⁻ᵛ, 95, 103ᵛ, 116ʳ⁻7, 239ʳ⁻ᵛ, 243ᵛ⁻4.
[10] C.L.R.O., Rep. 18, fo. 367ʳ⁻ᵛ; Jour. 20, fos. 436–7ᵛ, 440ᵛ⁻2, 444–6; Gs. Co., Reg. L, p. 248.

over policies appear to have become entangled with elections. There was no opposition to the convention by which the senior alderman below the chair was normally elected mayor. In elections for the sheriffs more problems were caused by the reluctance of men to take on the burdens of office than by factious electioneering. Between 1559 and 1579 fifteen men refused the office of sheriff, but thereafter until the end of the reign there were no less than fifty-six such refusals.[11] The only sign of politicisation in these elections is the possibility that the commons sometimes used the election as a means of punishing those of whose behaviour they disapproved, in the knowledge that the £200 fine for refusal of office was steep. John Bird, draper, claimed that his election in 1587 had proceeded from the 'malice of the inferior companies'. But such popular sanctions against individuals hardly represented a threat to the structure of authority.[12]

The course of City politics had not always been so undisturbed. In the fourteenth century London had been subject to frequent constitutional change, factionalised politics, and disorder involving members of the elite. The struggles revolved around such fundamental questions as the length of the terms to be served by the mayor and aldermen, the mode of election of common councillors, and the powers of common council and the frequency with which it was to be consulted. Thus the reforming regime associated with the draper, John of Northampton, in the years after 1376 supported a programme which had the effect of making the City's governors more accountable to the populace, and was bitterly opposed by other elements of the mercantile ruling group, led by the grocer, Nicholas Brembre. Both sides resorted to strong-arm tactics, purging the court of aldermen of their rivals, packing elections, and using armed force to intimidate opponents. Northampton was accused of 'inflaming the small people of the town against the great or worthy persons', and he lay behind the several days of rioting which followed Brembre's election as mayor in October 1383. Brembre's re-election the following year was in turn backed by the use of force.[13] Although the conflicts of the later fourteenth century were the most serious of the late medieval period, some of the issues were again ventilated in the radical agitation associated with the repeatedly rebuffed candidature of the tailor, Ralph Holland, for the mayoralty in the later 1430s and 1440s. Once again the authority of the elite was contested in rioting, as craftsmen felt themselves

[11] Based on records of common hall in the Elizabethan Journals of common council and of the fines levied in the Repertories of the court of aldermen.

[12] C.L.R.O., Rep. 21, fos. 455, 535, 553^v; Rep. 22, fos. 37^v, 331^v; Jour. 23, fo. 11^v; Jour. 25, fos. 76^v–7, 98; C. Wriothesley, *A Chronicle of England During the Reigns of the Tudors*, ed. W. D. Hamilton (2 vols., Camden Society, new series, XI and XX, 1875–7), II. 71–6.

[13] S. Thrupp, *The Merchant Class of Medieval London* (Chicago, 1948), pp. 60–80; R. Bird, *The Turbulent London of Richard II* (1949); C. M. Barron, *Revolt in London: 11th to 15th June 1381* (1981).

excluded from power. At the height of these struggles a tailor alleged that the craftsmen, not the merchants, were the basis of the City's prosperity.[14] Likewise, the earliest years of the sixteenth century saw widespread disaffection with the elite, on this occasion because of its marked internal divisions.[15]

By looking at the reasons for this earlier instability we can obtain some clues to the reasons for London's stability in the Elizabethan period. First, major difficulties were caused by the fact that the precedents on the disputed questions were vague: in the words of Sylvia Thrupp, the constitutional framework of the City was 'little better than a confused accumulation of ambiguous precedent and privilege'. The early City charters, while conceding that the citizens had the right to appoint their own mayor and sheriffs, had not defined citizenship nor prescribed the methods by which the officers were to be elected, so that it was open to the elite to manipulate elections.[16] There was a general recognition of the need for a balance between the principles of rule by the better sort and of the amending authority of the community. Both were necessary to effective government, the former because only the better sort had the resources to bear the costs of office, and the latter because members of the community were essential to the implementation of decisions in the absence of a highly developed formal apparatus of control.[17] But although groups of citizens had been summoned to aid the mayor and aldermen, there was no sense in which a regular council had been established by the early fourteenth century. Even in 1312, when it was ordained that the aldermen must obtain the unanimous consent of a citizen assembly before using the common seal, the reformers failed to specify how such an assembly was to be chosen. Londoners remained divided over the respective merits of election to common council by wards or by crafts. Experiments with the latter method of representation were made in 1312, 1326, 1351, 1352, and 1371, but mercantile interests were suspicious because of the threatened dilution in their own power if the representation of the lesser crafts expanded.[18] The latitude left to the aldermen in the interpretation of the constitution meant that it could be manipulated to their advantage. The absence of effective restraints created a potential for abuse which was fully realised by the corrupt regime of the closing years of the reign of Edward III.

The reforms of 1376 instituted sweeping changes in the government of the City. Common councillors were henceforth to be elected by the crafts rather

[14] C. M. Barron, 'Ralph Holland and the London Radicals, 1438–1444', in *A History of the North London Branch of the Historical Association, Together With Essays in Honour of its Golden Jubilee*, ed. A. L. Rowse and C. M. Barron (1971), pp. 60–80.

[15] Below, pp. 24–7.   [16] Thrupp, *Merchant Class*, pp. 60–1.

[17] S. Reynolds, 'Medieval Urban History and the History of Political Thought', *Urban History Yearbook*, 1982, 14–23; S. Rigby, 'Urban "Oligarchy" in Late Medieval England', in *Towns and Townspeople*, ed J. A. F. Thomson (1988), pp. 63–6.

[18] Thrupp, *Merchant Class*, pp. 66–73.

than by the wards, potentially widening the representation of the lesser crafts; the council's role in City government was more closely defined as it was to be summoned at least twice a quarter and was to approve all leases of City property; and it was to form the electing body for the mayor, thereby lessening the opportunities for the partisan packing of an electoral assembly traditionally constituted at the discretion of the mayor and aldermen. Finally, aldermen were to be elected annually, and not eligible for re-election until a year had passed.[19] But most of these changes were undone by the forces of reaction associated with Brembre and his successors. In 1384 Brembre restored the election of common council by the wards and secured a ruling that aldermen might be re-elected for successive terms, and the annual elections of aldermen were completely abolished in 1394. In 1397, with modifications in 1402, was established the procedure for the election of aldermen which prevailed in the sixteenth century. Assemblies in the wards were to nominate candidates for vacant posts from which the existing aldermen would make their choice.[20] But the question of the constitution of the electorate for the mayoralty remained controversial, a major bone of contention between Holland and the establishment in the 1430s and 1440s. Holland's reputation as a radical was acquired when he questioned the validity of a writ of 1315, invoked by the aldermen in 1426 to restrict attendance at the elections for the mayor and sheriffs. Although passed over for the mayoralty for the third time in 1441, his tenacious populism alarmed the aldermen, who in the following year obtained another writ to the effect that none but discreet and powerful citizens should attend the election. The outraged freemen counter-attacked in September 1443 by deposing the chamberlain who had served since 1434, but the mayor voided the election, turning away all who had not been personally summoned. These disputes generated some radical sentiments about the basis of authority: the popular candidate for the chamberlainship in 1443 was reported to have declared that the mayor was not mayor of those who had not elected him.[21]

Another factor which sustained instability was the tendency for conflicts of economic interest in the city to divide the elite to a far greater extent than was later the case. The struggles of the later fourteenth century reflected the tensions aroused by the domination of the court of aldermen by the wool-exporting Staplers, particularly prominent in the Grocers' and Fishmongers' Companies. Companies like the Drapers regarded the restoration of the franchise (that is the citizens' monopoly of retail trade, eroded by royal concessions to the aliens) as a more important issue than the rescinding of the licences granted by the Crown to evade the Staple. Northampton's

[19] Bird, *Turbulent London*, pp. 30–43; Barron, *Revolt in London*, pp. 14–16.
[20] Ibid. pp. 15–16; Beaven, *Aldermen*, I. 242.
[21] Barron, 'Ralph Holland', pp. 64–75.

breach with the Grocers occurred when the latter, having secured their victory over the licences in the Good Parliament of 1376, refused to support the wider demands of the Drapers and others for the restoration of the franchise. He was primarily concerned with the decaying position of his own guild rather than with achieving representation for the city's craftsmen, but he was able to draw on other fissures within the civic polity to achieve his objectives. Thus the proscription of his political opponents in the statute of 1382, which barred victuallers from political office, was achieved by mobilising popular hostility towards the Fishmongers' monopoly. Increasingly, he sought to shore up his position by populist measures such as the campaign against usury, which drew on the tensions between the ruling merchant group and the craftsmen. But these tensions would not have taken on the form they did were it not for the already existing conflicts within the elite arising from the domination of the Staplers.[22]

In the fifteenth century the court of aldermen was divided by the contest between the Drapers' and Tailors' Companies. Ralph Holland's efforts to become mayor were thwarted by the Drapers who were currently challenging the Tailors over the rights of search they had secured under their controversial charter of 1439.[23] Likewise, it was the opposition of the Drapers 'ffor malyce which they awgth unto the Taylours', which explains the repeated failure of the nomination of the tailor, John Percival, for the mayoralty in the 1490s. In the event only Henry VII's personal intervention in 1498 secured him the post.[24] But the king's favour towards the Tailors resulted in the escalation of conflict. Under their charter of 1503 they were incorporated under the pretentious name of Merchant Tailors and given authority to admit any Englishman to their fellowship in clear contravention of the rights of other companies.[25] The hostility felt within London towards the Tailors was intensified by Henry's foisting of the tailor William Fitzwilliam as sheriff on a reluctant city in 1506. Revenge came early in the new reign, in September 1510, when Fitzwilliam against all precedent was elected to serve a second term in the burdensome office of sheriff on the grounds that his first term had been invalid. It was rumoured that this had been done by the procurement of the draper mayor, Sir William Capell, at whose election there had been rumblings of discontent from the tailors. When Fitzwilliam refused to serve the second term, he was removed from the bench, disfranchised, and fined. Although he secured a favourable ruling from the council,

---

[22] Bird, *Turbulent London*, pp. 75–81; P. Nightingale, 'Capitalists, Crafts and Constitutional Change in Late Fourteenth-Century London', *Past and Present*, 124 (1989), 3–35.
[23] Barron, 'Ralph Holland', pp. 60–4, 67–8, 74–5.   [24] *Great Chronicle*, pp. 245–6, 288.
[25] Ibid. p. 323; H. Miller, 'London and Parliament in the Reign of Henry VIII', *B.I.H.R.*, 35 (1962), 130–6; *The Charters of the Merchant Taylors' Company*, ed. F. M. Fry and R. T. D. Sayle (1937), pp. 34–9.

his position within the city was untenable, and he left London soon afterwards.[26]

The king's role in the conflicts between the Tailors and the Drapers reminds us that the relationship between the Crown and the City, and the nature of national politics, was crucial to stability. Back in 1376, as at other times in London's history, it was instability in national politics which resulted in the factionalisation and radicalisation of City politics. The constitutional changes of 1376 came in the wake of the discrediting of the elite because of the impeachment of three of its members in the Good Parliament, victims of the anti-court campaign led by the earl of March. Richard Lyons, John Pecche, and Adam Bury were the beneficiaries of royal licences and monopolies and prominent in Crown finance and were therefore natural victims of a drive against court corruption. Moreover the campaign against them seems to have derived additional strength from the fact that it was supported by the City's members of parliament. William Walworth, representing the interests of the Staplers, was particularly incensed by the licences for the evasion of the Calais Staple associated with Richard Lyons and Lord Latimer. But the events in parliament seem to have focused the attention of citizens on the failings of the elite in general rather than on the shortcomings of individuals. The meeting of 1 August 1376 which initiated the programme of constitutional reform was called 'because of the great slander in the city because of the misbehaviour of persons convicted in full parliament and others which were still under great suspicion and because of the oppressive and unjust manner in which the magistrates and aldermen had lately governed the city for their own profit'.[27] It was this feeling which Northampton was able to mobilise in his campaign against the Staplers. Moreover, the attitude of the Crown remained a crucial variable in the political conflicts which ensued because, as Pamela Nightingale has recently shown, Northampton's power was based on his relationship with John of Gaunt, who supported the reformers in 1376, as part of his efforts to reverse the humiliations inflicted on the court in the Good Parliament, and again in 1382–3, as a means of pressurising the Staplers who were refusing to lend the Crown money.[28] Divisions within both the national and local elites therefore provide the key to explaining the instability.

The relationship between Henry VII and the City also shows the way that clumsy royal interventions destabilised City politics. The Merchant Tailors' charter was just one of several inflammatory actions taken by the king in the closing years of his reign. In 1504 a statute undermined the City's control

[26] *Great Chronicle*, pp. 332–3, 366–7, 378; C. M. Clode, *The Early History of the Guild of Merchant Taylors* (2 vols., 1888), II. 46–9; Kennedy, 'London and the Crown', pp. 60–3.
[27] Barron, *Revolt in London*, pp. 13–14; Bird, *Turbulent London*, pp. 17–22; G. Holmes, *The Good Parliament* (Oxford, 1975), pp. 108–14.
[28] Nightingale, 'Capitalists, Crafts and Constitutional Change', pp. 20–35.

over the livery companies by requiring that all their ordinances be approved
by the Crown's officers, and the City's own charter of 1505, for which the
king extorted 5,000 marks, did not specifically guarantee the City's right to
appoint to certain key offices granted by Edward IV in 1478.[29] But most
remarkable was the tightening of the machinery of law enforcement for
essentially fiscal objectives associated with the king's henchmen, Richard
Empson and Edmund Dudley. Dudley's regime was bitterly resented in
London:

whoo soo evyr hadd the sword born beffore hym, Dudley was mayer, and what his
pleasure was, was doon, thowth the auctoryte of the Cyte and ffraunchyse of the same
stood clerely agayn It, That the Cytyzyns were soo awyd wyth yll custumys & soo bett
wyth many Injuryes & wrongys doon to theym & theyr lybertees, that they were wery
of theyr lyvys & suffrid all thyng to Ren at myschieff, And undougthid It is to
presuppose, that If he hadd contynuyd In that maner any seson, The honour of that
Cyte hadd been clene ovyr turnyd, ffor soome off his affynyte were not a fferd to saye
opynly that he trystid to se the aldyrmen were clokys of Cotton Russet, In stede of
Clokys of Scarlet.

Three former mayors, Sir William Capell, Thomas Knesworth and Lawrence
Aylmer, were imprisoned for offences done during their terms of office. In the
most notorious case, Capell, found guilty by a jury 'ffastly boundyn to the
gyrdyllis of dudley & Empson' for failing to punish coining offences, ended
up in the Tower when he refused to pay the £2,000 fine.[30]

The result of this royal interference was that the respect of the commons
for the elite took a heavy battering. Fitzwilliam's election as sheriff in 1506
was met with 'grete dysdayn & obloquy of many of Þe comons of the
Cyte'.[31] Some citizens opposed Capell's second term as mayor in 1510, their
exchanges at the election in the Guildhall showing clearly the impact on
popular attitudes of controversy among companies combined with royal
pressure on the City. George Harward, tailor, 'went through the yeld hall to
every company incensyng and stirring theym rather to a scysme thanne
otherwise', claiming that Capell was unacceptable because he was not 'a
clere man ... for he ys farre in daunger to the king', and because 'his tyme by
the lawe and consticions of this Citie ys not come'. William Louth,
goldsmith, replied, 'there was a greatter breche of the lawe whanne there was
a shireff chosen and sworne and by the meanes and sute of oon of your
company meanyng mr Fitzwilliam'.[32] The Repertories of the court of
aldermen show a significantly large number of cases of lewd words against

---

[29] G. R. Elton, 'Henry VII: Rapacity and Remorse', in G. R. Elton, *Studies in Tudor and Stuart
Politics and Government* (3 vols., Cambridge, 1974–83), I. 45–65; J. P. Cooper,
'Henry VII's Last Years Reconsidered', *Historical Journal*, 2 (1959), 103–29; G. R. Elton,
'Henry VII: a Restatement', in G. R. Elton, *Studies*, I. 66–99; C. J. Harrison, 'The Petition of
Edmund Dudley', *E.H.R.*, 87 (1972), 82–99.
[30] *Great Chronicle*, pp. 334–5, 336, 348; *The House of Commons, 1509–1558*, ed. S. T.
Bindoff (3 vols., 1982), I. 569–70.
[31] *Great Chronicle*, pp. 332–3.   [32] C.L.R.O., Rep. 2, fos. 80, 86ᵛ–7, 100ᵛ.

members of the elite in the early years of Henry VIII's reign. One William Brownyng described Capell as a 'horeson churle & usurer', while Christopher Markham told Alderman Coppynger that 'men have lost their heads that have nott done so much harm to this city as ye have done'. Such was the anxiety of the aldermen that they sought legal advice on the precedents for the punishment of sedition.[33]

The mid-Tudor period illustrates a slightly different constellation of problems, but underlines once more the importance of national politics to an understanding of the reasons for the stability of the City. Divisions among the national politicians, now complicated by ideological considerations as the Reformation assumed greater importance in political alignments, posed difficult choices for the citizenry, choices for or against Somerset in October 1549, and for or against Lady Jane Grey and the Duke of Northumberland in July 1553. A wrong decision, as George Tadlowe, haberdasher, warned the common council at the meeting on 6 October 1549 when the City was approached by the lords of the privy council for aid against the isolated Protector, might be disastrous: rebellion against Henry III had resulted in the loss of the liberties of the City, 'and strangers appointed to be our heads and governors'.[34] Some tried to avoid the choices. Thus Alderman Richard Jervis appealed to his company, the Mercers, in June 1553 to save him from serving as mayor 'until the world be better established'.[35] In the event, the aldermen responded to the crises pragmatically, backing whichever side could bring greatest force to bear upon them, whatever their personal inclinations. Hence the aldermen's extraordinarily difficult position in the first year of the reign of Mary Tudor, who regarded them with intense suspicion for their acquiescence in the nine days' rule of her rival. When a dagger was thrown at Dr Bourne at a Paul's Cross sermon, the aldermen were summoned before the privy council and warned that if they could not keep the City safely then the mayor should yield up its sword.[36]

This discussion of earlier periods of instability in London politics helps establish a strategy for analysing the reasons for the lack of controversy in the Elizabethan period. The sections which follow therefore look in turn at the evolution of the City constitution and the establishment of a workable balance between the aldermen and the common council, the relationship between the City and the court, the reasons for the homogeneity of the elite, and the values which structured the relationship between elite and commons.

[33] Ibid. fos. 90ᵛ, 100ᵛ, 151ᵛ, 155ᵛ, 169.
[34] R. Grafton, *Chronicles* (2 vols., 1809), II. 523. London politics in this period are brilliantly reconstructed by Susan Brigden in *London and the Reformation* (Oxford, 1989), chs. XII–XIII.
[35] Mc. Co., C.M. II, fo. 261.   [36] *Wriothesley's Chronicle*, II. 38–9; *A.P.C.*, IV. 319.

THE DEVELOPMENT OF THE CITY CONSTITUTION

The achievement of stability was in part a matter of clarifying the disputed points in the City's constitution to realise a workable balance between the ascending and descending principles of political authority. It was generally recognised that rule by the rich should be tempered by some form of assent by the commons as a means of ensuring that their rule remained in the interests of the commonweal, that is to say, 'aristocratic' rather than 'oligarchic', according to the prevailing Aristotelian analyses of the forms of government. The difficulty in the fourteenth century had lain, as we have seen, in determining where that balance lay and in what form and precisely by whom assent should be expressed. In the course of the fifteenth and sixteenth centuries such a workable balance appears to have emerged.

A series of changes discouraged faction in City elections. The previously hotly contested issue of the composition of the electorate for the mayor and sheriffs was resolved. The measures of 1467 and 1475, which successively allowed the wardens of the livery companies and then all liverymen to attend the meetings of common hall at which the mayor and sheriffs were elected, reduced the opportunities for the partisan packing of meetings which had characterised the elections of the 1380s and 1440s.[37] It became more difficult for particular interests to become entrenched in City government as mayors no longer served successive terms. In 1424 it was ruled that no one was to be elected to the mayoralty a second time until after a lapse of seven years, and in 1435 that no one should ever serve more than two terms.[38] Moreover, it became customary to elect the senior alderman beneath the chair to the mayoralty, a practice which was rare in the fifteenth century, but near-universal in the Elizabethan period.[39] This procedure acted as a safeguard against ambitious men like Holland and Percival, strongly identified with particular interest groups, who openly strove for election. As James Dalton, the City's common pleader and probable author of the *Apologie of the Citie of London* put it, 'every man rather shunneth then seeketh the Maioraltie which is the best marke amongst them, neyther hath there been any strong faction, nor any man more popular then the rest, forasmuch as the government is by a Paterne, as it were, and alwayes the same, how oftensoever they change their Magistrate'.[40] The successful depersonalisation of magistracy is one of the most striking features of popular attitudes towards the rulers in the sixteenth century. Popular respect for the elite could

---

[37] Thrupp, *Merchant Class*, p. 83; Beaven, *Aldermen*, I. xxiv.   [38] Ibid. p. xxvii.
[39] Ibid. p. xxv.
[40] Stow, *A Survey of London*, ed. C. L. Kingsford (2 vols., 1908), II. 206, 386, 387.

be sustained as long as its members were not identified with competing policy options in contested elections.[41]

The balance between elite discretion and 'popular' participation was expressed in election procedures for offices in which the powers of nomination and election were divided between elite and more popular gatherings. Thus candidates for common council were usually nominated by vestry meetings, often after consultation with the local alderman, and elected by an assembly of all freemen resident in the ward at the annual wardmote.[42] In the election of the mayor the liverymen nominated two candidates both of whom had served as sheriff, and by the later sixteenth century always including the senior alderman beneath the chair, from which the aldermen chose one.[43] From 1492 the chamberlain and two bridgemasters were chosen by the liverymen from two candidates for each post presented by the aldermen.[44] Two members of parliament were simply nominated by the aldermen for approval by the liverymen, while the other two were elected by the liverymen from anything up to twelve candidates nominated by the aldermen.[45] These arrangements were designed to keep faction and disorder to a minimum. As the common council explained when introducing the new election procedures for the chamberlain and bridgemasters in 1492, 'every man there beyng at the tyme off the said eleccion, hath namyd ffor Chambyrlayn or Bridge mastyr such as they have ffavouryd Not Regardyng the comon weale of the cyte wherby many tymys nedy men & unhable for Pᵗ offycys have been admyttid.'[46] The effect of the order is illustrated by the chronicler Wriothesley's account of the election of the chamberlain in 1550:

there were divers persons that laboured to my Lord Mayor for the office and to the aldermen and the whole Commens; but, accordinge to an ould Act of Common Counsell made the vjth yeare of king Henry the VIIth, which was that my Lord Mayor and his brethren should nominate 2 persons sad and wisemen, of which the Commons had free election to chose one of the 2 persons to be theyr Chamberlaine, which lawe was read to the whole Commens, and there was appointed by my Lord Mayor and th'aldermen John Sturgeon, haberdasher, and Henry Fisher, grocer, for the sayd election ... [and] when they came to tryinge of handes quietly and without noyse or disturbance, th'ellection rested on John Sturgeon, haberdasher.[47]

It was preferable that candidates should be screened by the aldermen rather than that widespread canvassing should take place among the commons.

[41] Below, pp. 39–49.
[42] Pearl, *Outbreak*, pp. 53–5. Cf. below, pp. 68–9. In 1536 the wardmote inquest of Walbrook petitioned that the inhabitants might enjoy the free election of their common councillors and was answered by the court of aldermen that the election belonged to the alderman of the ward whose choice was then to be confirmed by the wardmote: C.L.R.O., Rep. 9, fo. 233.
[43] Beaven, *Aldermen*, I. 242; Pearl, *Outbreak*, p. 51.   [44] *Great Chronicle*, p. 245.
[45] *House of Commons, 1509–1558*, I. 140; *The House of Commons, 1558–1603*, ed. P. W. Hasler (3 vols., 1981), I. 201.
[46] *Great Chronicle*, p. 245.   [47] *Wriothesley's Chronicle*, II. 44.

Although the procedures are not quite the same as those described by Mark Kishlansky for avoiding strife at parliamentary elections, because the commons had more than one candidate to choose from rather than simply approving the man nominated by the elite, the intention to maintain consensus as far as possible was the same.[48] Another feature of the electoral arrangements deserves comment, and that is the emphasis in all the accounts of common hall on the separation of the nominating and electing assemblies between the council chamber and the great hall of the Guildhall. As Susan Reynolds has pointed out this was intended to prevent intimidation from either elite or commons.[49]

Another stabilising factor was the regularisation of the role of common council. Although the radical reforms of the Northampton era had been reversed, certain lessons had been learned. The conservative regime of 1384 had confirmed the elective basis of the council and admitted the need for four meetings a year.[50] In the fifteenth and sixteenth centuries common council underwent an increase in size, from 96 to 187 by 1460 and 212 by the Elizabethan period.[51] Although difficult to measure it would appear that its status was enhanced also. In the mid fifteenth century petitions were addressed to 'the right sad and discreet commoners of the city of London in this council assembled'.[52] Nowhere were the council's pretensions more clearly marked than in the claim produced by the 1527 committee for the commonweal that acts of common council 'ar of noo lesse strength then actes of the high court of parliament having this high libertie and large prehemynence'.[53]

Such claims were not always taken seriously by the citizenry. When in 1585 Jocelyn Turner, an alehouse keeper in Castle Baynard ward, heard that it was by authority of an act of common council rather than a statute that John Stow, aleconner, was proposing to fine him for false measures, 'he made a pufe' to show his contempt for common council.[54] And, as we have seen, there remained very real limits to the council's authority because of its dependence on the aldermen. Nevertheless its role in finance was sufficiently well established to make the aldermen's failure always to consult it in ordering loans and assessments from the livery companies a matter of grievance in the Elizabethan period.[55] And the aldermen recognised that the

---

[48] M. Kishlansky, *Parliamentary Selection: Social and Political Choice in Early Modern England* (Cambridge, 1986), pp. 3–9.

[49] H.M.C., *Hatfield House*, II. 116–17; S. Reynolds, *An Introduction to the History of English Medieval Towns* (Oxford, 1977), p. 175.

[50] Thrupp, *Merchant Class*, p. 81.

[51] C. M. Barron, 'The Government of London and its Relations with the Crown' (London Ph.D., 1970), p. 53.

[52] Thrupp, *Merchant Class*, p. 82.   [53] C.L.R.O., Jour. 13, fo. 23[v].

[54] Stow, *Survey of London*, I. lxv.

[55] Above, pp. 19–20.

failure to consult common council on important matters might sow the seeds of future discord. Thus when confronted by the privy council's proposal that strangers should be allowed to buy cloth at Blackwell Hall during the 1587 export crisis, the aldermen emphasised the need to consult common council, 'not to reason and dispute upon Her Maiesties good pleasure ... but to take their consents who otherwise might be worse affected towardes us and the cause'.[56] Certainly at times of crisis the role of common council was enhanced as the aldermen sought a broader basis of consent. Thus Caroline Barron has pointed out the increased frequency of meetings in the mid fifteenth century because of the City's need of money.[57] Again, in the early sixteenth century when the authority of the aldermen seemed fragile because of acute pressure from the Crown, the aldermen adopted the practice of appointing panels of common councillors, usually one from each ward, to advise on enormities prejudicial to the commonweal. Such committees were at work in 1517, 1527, and 1535.[58] Nor were their recommendations disregarded. A series of legislative initiatives (on the regulation of alehouses, freer trade in fish within the city, the registration of protections granted by the king, and the setting up of a table of the fees to be charged by carmen) can be traced back to the work of the 1527 committee.[59] Although these committees were not a feature of the Elizabethan years, the aldermen were careful to ensure that leading common councillors were involved with aldermen on the committees they appointed to formulate policy. In the closing years of the century the increasing administrative burdens on the corporation, in particular because of the war and the scale of the social problems confronting the aldermen, gave another argument for the wider role of common councillors in City government. The establishment of the committee for martial causes and the City lands committee, standing committees with common council representation, may reflect this need for a spreading of the burdens of administration as much as any pressure from the common council itself for a wider role.[60]

It would be misleading to talk of these changes in terms of increasing 'democracy' in the capital. Common councillors were recruited from that tier of metropolitan society immediately beneath the aldermen and were therefore hardly representative of the citizenry in the wider sense. There is little reason to suppose that their outlook was fundamentally different from that of the aldermen because they came from similar backgrounds, traded in the

[56] P.R.O., SP 12/201/31, 32.   [57] Barron, 'Government of London', p. 56.
[58] B.L., Additional MS 48019, fos. 225ᵛ–30; C.L.R.O., Rep. 8, fo. 66; Jour. 13, fos. 21–4, 435; Letter Book 'O', fos. 47–52.
[59] C.L.R.O., Jour. 13, fos. 35ᵛ–6, 36ʳ⁻ᵛ, 90ᵛ; Letter Book 'O', fo. 52ᵛ.
[60] F. F. Foster, 'The Government of London in the Reign of Elizabeth I' (Columbia Ph.D., 1968), pp. 144–8, 258–9; Foster, *Politics of Stability*, pp. 17, 21–2; N. R. Shipley, 'The City Lands Committee, 1592–1642', *Guildhall Studies in London History*, 2 (1977), 161–78.

same companies and partnerships, worked together in parish vestries, livery company halls and on the boards of governors of the hospitals, and were linked to the aldermen by ties of marriage and apprenticeship. This meant that there were a variety of informal avenues through which common councillors might make their views known and it helps explain the relative lack of institutional friction between the courts of aldermen and common council. Rather than thinking in anachronistic terms of the emergence of a more democratic constitution, it would be better to see the successful reconciliation of the ascending and descending principles of political authority as lying in consultation with a council which, if not representative in the true sense, nevertheless enjoyed strong ties of patronage with local communities whose grievances might therefore be channelled through it.

There is, of course, something horribly whiggish about the analysis thus far, of a City gradually finding its way to an ordered harmony, reconciling the principles of rule by the better sort and responsibility to the wider community in a set of workable compromises. It is true that custom hardened in the fifteenth and sixteenth centuries so that the details of the constitution were much less contested, but this stability was vulnerable for two reasons. First, the underlying tensions in London society, between wholesalers and artisans, freemen and foreigners, servants and householders, all remained. The elite walked on the crust of a volcano, and it was essential to stability that mechanisms be provided to cope with these tensions. Secondly, the electoral procedures could only avoid damaging contests as long as the elite was relatively homogeneous in outlook. It was one of the lessons of sixteenth-century continental experience that the perpetuation of elite control depended on its solidarity. As Thomas White reminded his congregation, looking at the recent experiences of Paris and Antwerp in 1576, 'a city divided against itself cannot stand'.[61] Once the elite divided, its members were only too likely to begin to compete for support in other social groups, bringing their grievances into the political arena. The solidarity of the elite might be compromised by clumsy royal interventions, by divisions in national politics and the difficult choices they might pose, and by ideological division within the elite. The remainder of this chapter therefore looks at the relationship between the City and the Crown, the homogeneity of the elite, and the values with which it approached popular grievances.

THE CITY AND THE CROWN

Historians have been advised by Valerie Pearl to explore the development of the 'significant collaboration' that 'emerged in the sixteenth century between

[61] T. White, *A Sermon Preached at Pawles Crosse on Sunday the Ninth of December 1576* (1578), pp. 56–7.

governmental and municipal interests'. Such a relationship was founded ultimately on the realisation by London's governors that collaboration was advisable if their privileges, which rested on royal grants, were to be retained and, it was hoped, enhanced.[62] There were times, as under Elizabeth's father and grandfather, when the Crown exploited the vulnerability of the City to extend its patronage and financial resources, but the effects on the stability of City politics were not encouraging. By contrast, Elizabeth's approach to the metropolis, as to the localities in general, was relatively low key and non-interventionist, so that the relationship was more fruitful to the City.[63] The reasons for this lack of pressure are probably to be found in the regime's rather exaggerated perception of its own vulnerability. Elizabeth's councillors had reached political maturity during the fraught mid-Tudor decades, and the lesson that serious pressure on the localities might result in revolt had been learned. Thus Burghley always maintained that 'the English people be most inclinable to sedition when oppressed with extraordinary payments'.[64] To these fears was added their self-perception as a protestant minority confronting an unreformed multitude. London was the beneficiary of a monarchy more aware of its own vulnerability, and therefore reluctant to press any of its subjects too hard.

The queen's interventions in City elections were rare, and then usually motivated by the desire to spare her servants from office, rather than being politically or ideologically inspired. Thus, temporary discharges from the burdensome office of sheriff were secured by Richard Martin, the warden of the Mint, in 1578, and by William Hewishe, the queen's linen-draper, in 1589, while in 1584 Henry Campion, the queen's beerbrewer, secured an absolute discharge, on each occasion after a letter from the queen. Edward Gilbert and Philip Gunter were both discharged from their aldermanries after interventions from the court, although on both occasions after paying the customary fines.[65] Elizabeth appears to have interfered with the mayoralty only once, when in 1596 she successfully requested that the customs farmer, Henry Billingsley, be spared for one year.[66] There was nothing to compare with the actions either of her grandfather who had promoted the careers of Percival and Fitzwilliam, or of her father who, at Cromwell's instigation, had pushed Humphrey Monmouth, Tyndale's patron, as sheriff

[62] Pearl, 'Social Policy', p. 118; Barron, 'Government of London', chs. VI and VIII.
[63] P. Williams, 'The Crown and the Counties', in *The Reign of Elizabeth I*, ed. C. Haigh (Basingstoke, 1984), pp. 125–46.
[64] Palliser, *Age of Elizabeth*, p. 12. Cf. W. Camden, *The History of the Most Renowned and Victorious Princess Elizabeth* (1675), p. 555; P.R.O., SP 12/255/84.
[65] C.L.R.O., Jour. 20, fos. 424ᵛ–5, 522; Jour. 21, fos. 128, 370ᵛ; Jour. 22, fo. 293ᵛ; Rep. 15, fos. 356ᵛ, 365ᵛ, 366, 394, 510ᵛ.
[66] C.L.R.O., Remembrancia II, no. 165.

in 1535, and kept the ultra-conservative, William Holles, from the mayoralty for three years in 1535–8.[67]

It is true that the City came under considerable pressure from the court for grants of its patronage. The aldermen, the governors of the hospitals, and the wardens of City livery companies were subjected to a stream of petitions from courtiers for grants of freedoms, reversions to offices, and leases for their servants and connections. Burghley, by force of his longevity, was able to build up a body of clients in the London bureaucracy. James Dalton, Thomas Weekes, Thomas Wade, and Richard Wheeler all owed their offices as common pleaders to his patronage; the clerksitter, Jasper Cholmeley, and the attorney in the mayor's court, John Fludd, were also Cecil clients.[68] Sometimes the favours flowed still more directly to the courtiers. The records of the Mercers' Company show that Burghley not only backed petitions from his connections for leases, but also sought to cash in on the company's resources himself by securng a lease of their Long Acre site in 1578 on very favourable terms. Although they had been offered a better deal, 'howbeit to have his honors favor the company [were] well pleased to graunt it'.[69] Court interventions were sometimes highly irritating as when the Merchant Tailors found it necessary to lay out £66. 13s. 4d. to buy off Lady Harper, importuning them for a renewal of her lease with the backing of the lord treasurer.[70] The drain on the City's patronage was resented among the freemen, and the common council took measures to stem the flow. In 1572 it was required that all offices, except those relating to the practice of the common law, were to be granted to freemen by birth or service only, and in the following year that leases of hospital property should be made only to freemen. Concern was renewed in the later 1580s, and in 1590 the common council imposed a seven-year ban on grants of reversions to offices, and asserted its control over the admission of redemptioners for a similar period.[71]

But it would be unwise to see the court's quest for patronage as a purely extractive relationship because the aldermen appreciated the reciprocal favours that might flow from it. Moreover, one must not regard patronage entirely as a City–court issue, because this neglects the control over patronage exercised by City bureaucrats themselves, and the pressures the aldermen were able to exert on the system. An influential and long-serving officer like William Seabright, the town clerk from 1574 to 1613, secured reversions and

[67] Above, pp. 24–7; *Wriothesley's Chronicle*, I. 31–2, 67; *Letters and Papers, Foreign and Domestic, of the Reign of Henry VIII, 1509–47*, ed. J. S. Brewer *et al.* (21 vols., 1862–1910), IX. 273–4.
[68] C.L.R.O., Rep. 15, fo. 334; Rep. 16, fos. 78, 158ᵛ, 453; Rep. 18, fo. 161; Rep. 19, fo. 235; Rep. 20, fo. 59ᵛ; B.L., Lansdowne MS 77/31.
[69] Mc. Co., C.M. III, fos. 313, 337ᵛ, 450ᵛ; C.M. IV, fos. 12ᵛ, 16.
[70] MT. Co., C.M. II, fos. 8ᵛ, 9, 19, 22, 25ᵛ.
[71] C.L.R.O., Jour. 19, fos. 427ᵛ–8; Jour. 20, fos. 67, 78ʳ⁻ᵛ; Jour. 22, fo. 408.

offices in the City bureaucracy for an army of his servants and under clerks.[72] Outgoing lord mayors disposed of considerable patronage: in September 1575, as his mayoralty drew to a close, Sir James Hawes obtained the reversions of the collectorship of scavage for his son-in-law, John Smith, the measureship of cottons for William Astley, and the beadleship of the court of conscience for Ralph Knighton.[73] Londoners were perfectly capable of resisting court pressures: even Cecil was turned down on several occasions. When in 1572 the aldermen rejected a request from the privy council for the reversion of the keepership of any of the City prisons for Richard Hatchman, Cecil professed himself content with their explanation that such offices were reserved for poor freemen, and 'comended there good care for poor decayed citizens and wished them to contynewe the same'.[74] Only a minority of City patronage was yet within the court's grasp.

The Crown's fiscal pressures were also relatively moderate. Because the assessment of the parliamentary subsidy was left to the locality with diminishing conciliar interference, the yields fell dramatically. In 1602–3 a subsidy in London yielded only £4,870 compared to £18,206 at Elizabeth's accession. It is true that the multiple grants of the 1590s counterbalanced the falling yields of individual grants, and cumulatively taxation was burdensome in the war years at the end of the century. Nevertheless, the levels of parliamentary taxation in London were much heavier in the 1540s and 1550s than in the 1590s: an average of £9,482 p.a. between 1540 and 1559 compared to £6,553 p.a. between 1585 and 1603. The figures from parliamentary taxation do not, of course, give us a picture of the full impact of the Crown's demands because an increasing proportion of the costs of warfare was borne directly by the localities now responsible for equipping and apparelling troops. But my estimates suggest that even when the local military rates and the loans that the Crown failed to repay are taken into account, direct taxation arising from the Crown's demands was less burdensome in the 1590s than in the mid-Tudor decades: £12,090 per annum between 1540 and 1559 compared to £12,246 per annum between 1585 and 1603, a drop in real terms of 40 per cent.[75]

The frictions in the relationship between City and Crown should not, however, be underestimated. Some earlier conflicts, for example that over the right of appointment to the garbeller of spices, an office over which Henry VIII had attempted to assert his control in the 1520s, rumbled on. Although the City secured a favourable ruling from the Exchequer over its right to appoint to the office in June 1569, the royal patent of 1567 granting

[72] C.L.R.O., Rep. 18, fos. 215, 279, 338ᵛ; Rep. 19, fos. 251ᵛ; Rep. 20, fos. 128ᵛ, 131ᵛ; Rep. 21, fos. 95, 101ᵛ, 218ᵛ, 488, 492, 528; Rep. 22, fos. 232, 464ᵛ; Rep. 23, fos. 81ᵛ, 530.
[73] C.L.R.O., Rep. 18, fos. 446ᵛ, 453, 459.
[74] C.L.R.O., Rep. 15, fos. 13, 19; Rep. 17, fos. 359, 395ʳ⁻ᵛ; Rep. 18, fos. 161, 203.
[75] Above, pp. 10, 12.

it to Anthony White, which had renewed the controversy, was not cancelled, and doubt was cast upon the validity of the Exchequer decree because the aldermen had appointed the brother of the lord chief baron (chiefly instrumental in the verdict) to exercise the office. Shortly after the collapse of the Crown's negotiations to buy out the interest of White's widow in 1581, she sold out to Sir James Croft, controller of the royal household, confronting the City with a much more threatening challenger. The ensuing litigation in the Exchequer was only settled when the City agreed to pay Croft 1,000 marks (£666. 13s. 4d.) in 1586.[76]

Other disputes resulted from the efforts of some of the Crown's leading office-holders to maintain the dignity and enhance the profits of their offices. To the interminable clashes of the City with the lieutenant of the Tower over the extent of the Tower liberties, were added in the early 1580s disputes over his claims to levy tolls on victuals coming to London and over the jurisdiction of the court kept within the Tower. The City challenged the issue of grants of protection to debtors by the Tower authorities, turning a blind eye to the arrest of those with protections within London, but the lieutenant retaliated by arresting citizens at random. Although the lord chief justices and the master of the rolls ruled against the lieutenant on the issue of protections in 1585, the controversies concerning the boundaries of the Tower liberty and the tolls remained unresolved in spite of persistent litigation by the City to achieve a settlement.[77] The lord admiral was also frequently pitted against the aldermen on a variety of issues, of which the most serious were his challenge to the City's measurage of coal and his claim to the conservancy of the Thames beneath London Bridge, which he exercised throughout the Elizabethan period in spite of royal charters and an act of parliament vesting it in the City.[78]

As royal resources became increasingly tight and the demands on royal patronage more pressing, the methods used to reward courtiers were the

[76] Kennedy, 'London and the Crown', pp. 102–5; B.L., Lansdowne MS 38/9–11; *C.P.R., 1566–9*, pp. 76–7; C.L.R.O., Rep. 16, fos. 257ᵛ–8ᵛ; Rep. 21, fos. 268–9, 309; Jour. 19, fos. 172ᵛ–3; Jour. 22, fos. 9ᵛ–10; P.R.O., E112/26/73; *Chamber Accounts of the Sixteenth Century*, ed. B. R. Masters (London Record Society, XX, 1984), pp. 34, 66, 71–2, 87.

[77] P.R.O., SP12/157/22–3; C.L.R.O., Jour. 21, fo. 472ʳ⁻ᵛ; Rep. 15, fos. 482–3, 495, 514; Rep. 16, fos. 1ᵛ, 157, 201ᵛ, 363, 476; Rep. 17, fo. 280ᵛ; Rep. 18, fo. 160ᵛ; Rep. 19, fos. 221ᵛ–2, 259, 285, 382ᵛ, 422ᵛ–3, 429; Rep. 20, fos. 9, 21; Rep. 21, fos. 52, 94ᵛ, 106ᵛ, 126ᵛ, 134, 215ᵛ, 530; Rep. 22, fos. 154, 161, 315ᵛ; Rep. 23, fos. 100ᵛ, 292, 414, 545, 580ᵛ, 593; Rep. 24, fos. 130ᵛ, 157, 238ᵛ, 407; Rep. 25, fos. 68ᵛ, 162ᵛ.

[78] Thames conservancy: *Chamber Accounts*, pp. xx–xxi; B.L., Lansdowne MSS 145, fo. 11; 162, fo. 67; C.L.R.O., Rep. 14, fos. 161ᵛ, 471ᵛ; Rep. 15, fos. 372, 408ᵛ, 418, 515ᵛ; Rep. 17, fo. 109ᵛ; Rep. 19, fos. 498ᵛ–9; Rep. 20, fos. 155, 239ᵛ, 241, 260; Rep. 21, fos. 135, 207ᵛ; measurage of seacoals: H.M.C., *Hatfield House*, VII. 300–1; VIII. 223; C.L.R.O., Rep. 21, fos. 407ᵛ, 422, 524; Rep. 23, fos. 16ᵛ, 388; Rep. 24, fos. 70, 180; Jour. 22, fos. 182ᵛ–3, 332; Remembrancia I, nos. 589, 615, 619; II no. 92; Admiralty jurisdiction: B.L., Lansdowne MS 52/53.

more bitterly resented. By the 1590s patents of monopoly were being granted, not with the intention of fostering new trades as had generally been the practice in the earlier years of the reign, but rather of reforming abuses within existing ones on sometimes spurious grounds, and thereby alienating already established interests. For instance, Richard Drake's monopoly of the production of beer and ale for use in the distillation of vinegar, secured in 1594, was bitterly contested by the Brewers' Company. Other courtiers sought to establish offices to regulate supposedly neglected areas of the economy, inevitably accompanied by fees lacking statutory backing. Edward Darcy's patent for the searching and sealing of leather not covered by the 1563 statute regulating the leather trades encountered a storm of opposition from the Leathersellers' Company, strongly backed by the aldermen. Another use of the royal licensing powers was to evade the provisions of statutes banning the export of certain commodities, and these licences, for example those to export leather, were resented by the crafts, at whose instigation the statutes had been passed, because of the increased raw material costs they entailed.[79]

The City's governors were well aware how much the loyalty of the citizenry depended upon their being seen to act vigorously to protect the City's rights in all these areas. Writing of an inquiry into the City's right to the office of garbelling in November 1582, the lord mayor, Thomas Blanke, asserted that 'nothing can arise of this inquisition but matter of our discredit and public bringing our good fame and uprightness in question ... to the disabling of our good countenance amongst those that should obey under our government'.[80] Among the barrage of arguments directed against Darcy's patent for searching and sealing leather was the threat of popular tumults, a not unreasonable assertion in view of a riot directed against the starch patentees in October 1595.[81]

But there was nothing comparable to the assaults on the City's privileges that had characterised the later years of Henry VII's reign or the 1520s. The problems over garbelling were caused by the efforts of Anthony White, the assignee of Robert Cowper (who had been granted the office by Henry VIII in 1526, and subsequently confirmed in it by the City), to strengthen his title to the office by a new grant from the Crown, rather than being the result of a conscious bid by the Crown to dispute the City's title.[82] In other cases the offence that Elizabeth caused the City was largely the unintended consequence of her efforts to reward her courtiers rather than a deliberate assault on the City's franchises. Nor did Elizabeth's ministers necessarily

[79] I. W. Archer, 'The London Lobbies in the Later Sixteenth Century', *Historical Journal*, 31 (1988), 29–34.
[80] H.M.C., *Hatfield House*, II. 537.
[81] C.L.R.O., *Remembrancia* I, no. 651; II, no. 110; *A.P.C.*, XXV. 16.
[82] B.L., Lansdowne MS 38/9.

share a common attitude towards the disputed issues. Burghley's commitment to 'commonwealth' ideals and his determination that patents should
not be hurtful to the subject were appreciated by the opponents of the
patents. It was to Burghley as the 'very Cato of the commonwealth' that the
Leathersellers turned for support in their campaign against Darcy.[83] I have
shown elsewhere how by sustained lobbying and litigation the City was able
to secure the withdrawal of some of the more noxious patents. Darcy's
leather sealing patent was revoked after being declared void by the judges in
Star Chamber in 1596, while Drake's patent was among those cancelled in
1601.[84] The City managed to persuade the lord admiral to withdraw his
claims to the measurage of coal, and although the queen proved reluctant to
confirm the agreement, the City's claims were enshrined in the charter
secured from James I in 1605.[85] In other cases the privy council adopted a
mediatorial role, as with the conflicts between the City and the lieutenant of
the Tower, by referring the points at issue to special commissions or to the
judges.[86] Although on some issues, like its claim to the Thames conservancy
beneath London Bridge, the City appeared to make little headway in
Elizabeth's reign, its unwillingness to allow its case to go by default proved
important in the long run. The aldermen repeatedly pushed the City's rights
to the conservancy before the lord admiral, paving the way for their ultimate
victory in 1613.[87]

Moreover, there were several spheres in which the privy council's authority and the prerogative powers of the Crown were of great value to the
City. First, the council's support was essential in securing for the capital
vitally necessary foodstuffs: it was in response to lobbying by the City that
the council issued its instructions to release grain from the counties for
London and to restrict exports of beer and grain in time of dearth. It is
striking how closely the City cultivated relationships with successive lord
treasurers to ensure the council's cooperation in its victualling.[88] Secondly, it
was only with the backing of the council that the City could secure
favourable solutions to the problems of order and tax evasion posed by the
liberties in its midst. During the 1590s the court of aldermen frequently had
occasion to appeal to the privy council to force the residents of the liberties to
contribute to military rates in the City.[89] Thirdly, the council could bring
pressure to bear on the suburban authorities to comply with policies being

[83] Ibid. 74/42. Cf. G. D. Duncan, 'Monopolies Under Elizabeth I, 1558–1585' (Cambridge
Ph.D., 1976), chs. II–III.
[84] Archer, 'London Lobbies', pp. 41–3.
[85] Foster, *Politics of Stability*, pp. 136–7; C.L.R.O., Remembrancia II, no. 92.
[86] C.L.R.O., Jour. 21, fo. 472[r–v]; Rep. 24, fo. 130[v].   [87] *Chamber Accounts*, p. xx.
[88] C.L.R.O., Rep. 15, fos. 154[v], 167, 171, 178, 184[v]; Rep. 17, fo. 451; Rep. 18, fos. 16, 383;
B.L., Lansdowne MS 49/5–6; below, p. 201.
[89] A.P.C., XXIV. 30; XXIX. 414–15; XXX. 134–5, 149–50; XXXI. 119–21.

pursued by the aldermen: the necessity for coordinated action between the City and the Middlesex and Surrey justices of the peace on matters as wide-ranging as public order, vagrancy, plague, the regulation of the theatres, and even the length of swords is a constant refrain of correspondence between aldermen and councillors.[90]

Finally, the prerogative powers of the Crown proved useful to specific City interests. For example, the Crown granted the livery companies their charters and supervised their ordinances, and these powers could be used by the companies to extend their jurisdiction over the suburbs and increase their control over non-free labour. Companies which found a parliamentary solution to their problems difficult to achieve often turned to the prerogative for help. Thus in 1567 the Vintners secured a renewal of their dispensation from a statute of 1553 which had limited the number of taverns in London and imposed a ceiling on wine prices; the Curriers were the beneficiaries of a series of licences dispensing them from the legislation which prevented their participation in the leather trade as middlemen; and the Clothworkers strengthened the provisions of the 1566 statute requiring that every tenth cloth exported should be finished within England by securing a patent from the Crown in 1576 allowing them to appoint their own searchers to operate in the ports.[91] Moreover, the privileges of the chartered companies engaged in overseas trade also rested on the prerogative and, as restrictionism tightened in the Elizabethan decades, this dependence increased. It was only with the support of the Crown that the Merchant Adventurers could fend off the criticisms of the outport merchants for increasing their admission fees in defiance of a statute of 1497. As Robert Ashton comments, 'the Elizabethan economic settlement was ... in many respects the product of an intimate alliance between the commercial elite of London and the government'.[92]

This brief and necessarily schematic survey of relations between the City and the Crown suggests that the Crown was sufficiently respectful of the City's liberties and responsive to its complaints to ensure that the aldermen were not divided over the attitude that they should adopt towards the central government. Nor did the aldermen forfeit the respect of the commons that an apparently pusillanimous response to court pressures might threaten.

THE HOMOGENEITY OF THE ELITE

The fact that no challenge was mounted to City government in the Elizabethan period has much to do with the relative homogeneity of the elite and

---

[90] Below, pp. 229–30.   [91] Archer, 'London Lobbies', pp. 26–9.
[92] G. D. Ramsay, *The City of London in International Politics at the Accession of Elizabeth Tudor* (Manchester, 1975), pp. 46–50; R. Ashton, *Reformation and Revolution, 1558–1660* (1984), pp. 96–100.

the absence of divisive issues in City politics. However, this is a subject on which it is unwise to be dogmatic because the historian can be easily seduced by the formality of the minutes of the proceedings of the aldermen and common councillors into an acceptance of the myth of civic harmony they were designed to perpetuate. These records give no hint of the variety of opinions which, as the presence of a balloting box in the court of aldermen indicates, must have been expressed, and so the aldermen remain largely cardboard cut-outs.[93] Accounts of meetings from other perspectives are extremely rare but, where they survive, show that opinion was far more divided than the formal minutes suggest. Recorder Fleetwood has left an account of a highly charged meeting of common council in September 1587 to repeal an act of 1579 allowing the sheriffs to appoint their own undersheriff of Middlesex. It was alleged that the act had encouraged corruption because the sheriffs had accepted bribes from aspirants for the office, and it was therefore proposed that the act of common council of 1545, by which the post was to be filled in rotation by the town clerk, the two secondaries of the counters, and the controller of the chamber, should be revived. However, in spite of the apparently unanimous decision of common council in its favour, the measure was opposed by Alderman Richard Martin, very probably a puritan, on the grounds that the 'auncient Lawe' of 1545 had been made by papists. The lord mayor, Sir George Barne, took this as a personal affront because the 1545 act had been made when his own father was sheriff of London, '& affirmed that his father was of as good a Religion as mr Alderman himselffe was, & saieth for profe thereof I wilbe Judged by the Lord Treasorer of England'. Unable to get his own way, Martin threatened to resign rather than suffer the humiliation of defeat on the issue.[94]

None of these exchanges, of course, are recorded in the minutes of the meeting of common council concerned, a powerful warning that we should not underestimate the divisions and differences of personality among the elite. But it should be emphasised that there were several powerful forces pushing for consensus and uniformity on the bench. It is striking that Fleetwood responded to Martin's outburst on the occasion just described by appealing to a principle of collegiality and corporate decision-making binding on all: 'that it semes that he was never brought upp in the parliament of England for in the commen howse there the greatest Counsailor maye perswade as he shall thinke cause, but the howse will doe as they shall thinke it good, & yet noe disgrace at all'.[95] Individuals who refused to submit to the

[93] Pearl, *Outbreak*, p. 61.
[94] B.L., Lansdowne MS 52/51, fos. 135–6; C.L.R.O., Rep. 11, fo. 210; Rep. 21, fos. 471^v–2; Jour. 15, fo. 270; Jour. 20, fo. 517^v; Jour. 22, fo. 125^v. On Martin's puritanism see P. Collinson, *The Elizabethan Puritan Movement* (1967), p. 140; Gs. Co., Reg. 'L', pp. 277–8; B.L., Harleian MS 698, fo. 93; C.L.R.O., Rep. 19, fo. 423.
[95] B.L., Lansdowne MS 52/51.

will of the majority were excoriated for their wilfulness because such behaviour would encourage disobedience among the lower orders with probably dire consequences for the City's enjoyment of its liberties. This thinking emerges clearly in the rhetoric with which such offenders against the corporate will were confronted. For instance, Alderman Altham, absenting himself from the court and refusing to give a clear answer whether or not he would accept the office of sheriff to which he had just been elected in 1557, was pilloried in the minutes for

not offerynge or gentylly submittynge hyme self at any tyme to the good order of the saide Courte accordynge to the purporte and true meanynge of the good and polytyque lawes and orders of the saide Cytye to the pernycyous example of all other wilfull persones and the greate daunger of the forfeytinge of the Liberties of the said Cytye.[96]

The aldermen's last point in their indictment of their colleague underlines the most powerful argument for containing disputes, namely that London's privileges depended ultimately on the support of the Crown. It was a lesson Londoners well knew from their own history. In an appendix to his *Apologie*, Dalton analysed 'the causes as have heretofore moved the Princes, either to fine and ransom the Citizens of London, or to seize the Liberties of the Citty it selfe'. He identified four reasons for intervention: the City's support for rebels against the prince, the breakdown of order within the capital, abuses in the City's own government and justice, and straightforward extortion by the Crown on flimsy pretexts.[97] This consciousness of London's past relationship with the Crown appears to have informed much of the political discourse of the period. Recorder Fleetwood, in an oration to the commons in 1587 at the election for the sheriffs, after several men had refused to serve, reminded his audience of the City's forfeiture of its privileges under Edward II when a mayor cast off his robes and refused to come to commissions of oyer and terminer.[98] George Tadlowe reminded the common council in 1549 of the penalties imposed by Henry III on the City for supporting the wrong side in the civil wars of his reign.[99] London's rulers therefore were highly aware of their potential vulnerability before the Crown. As Recorder Croke somewhat unctuously explained, it was from the queen alone that the mayor received 'his allowance, his light, his life'. It was a dependence which the Crown's ministers occasionally underlined with blunt reminders that what the Crown had once given it might take away if the City's rulers failed to fulfil their obligation to maintain good order. Replying to the recorder's speech at the presentation of the lord mayor at Whitehall in April 1593, Lord Keeper Puckering emphasised that 'her maiestie taketh not your charters to bind her prerogative, but that by abuses the same are to be

[96] C.L.R.O., Rep. 13, fos. 540, 543ᵛ. Cf. ibid., fos. 245ᵛ–6; Jour. 12, fos. 346ᵛ–8.
[97] Stow, *Survey of London*, II. 214–17.
[98] Johnson, *Drapers*, II. 445–9. [99] Above, p. 27.

resumed'.[100] Open division among the aldermen would focus criticism of municipal policies by giving critics rallying points within the elite. The result would be disorder, and intervention by the Crown.

A further restraint on individual wilfulness was the expectation that the law be observed and City custom followed. Although the lord mayor enjoyed considerable discretionary power, he was restrained by the necessity that he obey the law and by his duty to take the advice of his colleagues on important matters.[101] Obedience to the law entailed obedience to City custom, and, as far as possible, custom guided the deliberations of the court. Appeals to custom, for example, were frequently deployed in the resolution of the most intractable conflicts between companies in the City, such as those between the Clothworkers and Merchant Tailors in the early 1550s and between the White Bakers and the Brown Bakers in the 1570s.[102] An insistence on the need for conformity to the 'good and polytyque lawes and orders of the Cyte' in which custom was embodied was a constant feature of the arguments directed at offenders like James Altham. It was one of the blessings of gerontocratic rule that the mayor's colleagues acted as a repository of custom, preserving a collective memory, transmitted from one generation to another.[103] But as the administrative burdens and the complexity of government increased, the aldermen felt the need for more formal means of access to past practice. Piers Cain has recently explored the efforts made by the City solicitor, Robert Smith, in the later sixteenth century to reform the City archives by improving the provision of indexes and calendars as a way of making the precedents more accessible and so preserving the 'corporate memory of the City government'.[104] The connection between good record keeping, the accessibility of custom, and orderly government was widely appreciated in the City. In St Mildred Poultry in 1601, for example, the vestry book is described as a document 'wherein all the orders and actes made for the good government of the said parishe weare entred and Registred to thende they mighte continue in memory to the benefit of thinhabitantes of the said parishe and there posteritie which was a thinge of great importance and consequence for the good and peaceable government of the said parishe'.[105]

---

[100] H.M.C., *Frankland-Russell-Astley*, p. 2; B.L., Harleian MS 6849, fos. 325ᵛ–6; 'The Journal of Sir Roger Wilbraham', ed. H. S. Scott, *Camden Miscellany X* (Camden Society, third series, IV, 1902), p. 5.

[101] T. Norton, 'Instructions to the Lord Mayor of London, 1574–5', in *Illustrations of Old English Literature*, ed. J. P. Collier (3 vols., 1866), III. item 8, pp. 12–13.

[102] C.L.R.O., Rep. 12, fos. 387ᵛ–9; Jour. 16, fos. 110ᵛ–11; Jour. 21, fo. 146ʳ⁻ᵛ; P.R.O., SP12/150/18.

[103] K. V. Thomas, 'Age and Authority in Early Modern England', *Proceedings of the British Academy*, 62 (1976), 210, 233–4.

[104] P. Cain, 'Robert Smith and the Reform of the Archives of the City of London, 1580–1623', *London Journal*, 13 (1987–8), 3–16.

[105] P.R.O., STAC5/A44/10.

Thus there were powerful forces to cause the aldermen to sink any differences they might have. But it is also true that the differences among them were probably less serious in the later sixteenth century than in earlier and later periods. This was in part a matter of the absence of sharp divisions in national politics. Reacting against the traditional accounts which tended to stress the opposition between moderates gathered around Burghley and godly ideologues enjoying Leicester's support, historians have recently come to stress the homogeneity of the Elizabethan political establishment. Although there were personal rivalries at Elizabeth's court, Burghley and Leicester shared a similar outlook on religion and agreed over the objectives of foreign policy, if not always the means to achieve them, while even Leicester and Sussex, who clashed sharply in the mid 1560s and early 1580s, were able to cooperate through the intervening years. Elizabeth's depoliticisation of the privy chamber, and the domination of her court by leading privy councillors, limited the opportunities for the kinds of conflict between the council and sections of the court which had characterised the ascendancy of Wolsey and Cromwell.[106] The aldermen therefore would not have found their solidarity compromised by the court ties they enjoyed. There is no evidence that members of the elite felt exclusive obligations to anyone at court. On the contrary, where patronage relationships can be traced, they show that leading Londoners maintained a broad range of contacts within the Elizabethan establishment. Thus, the patrons of Thomas Norton, the City remembrancer, who has emerged as a key figure in relations between the City and the court in the writings of Michael Graves, included men as diverse in outlook as Burghley, Walsingham, and Hatton.[107] Likewise, Recorder Fleetwood, while enjoying a special relationship with Burghley, also possessed links with Leicester such as to earn him denigration as 'Leicester's mad recorder' in the tract, *Leycester's Commonwealth*.[108] Sometimes councillors worked together to promote individual careers, as when in 1583 Burghley, Leicester, Hatton, and Walsingham all wrote on behalf of John de Cardenas, one of Walsingham's servants, in his quest for a reversion to several City offices.[109]

This picture of a broadly consensual Elizabethan establishment operative at both the national and municipal levels begs a major question about what happened to City politics during the 1590s when, it is generally agreed, the rivalry between the earl of Essex and Robert Cecil assumed a bitterness

---

[106] S. Adams, 'Eliza Enthroned? The Court and its Politics', in *Reign of Elizabeth I*, ed. C. A. Haigh (Basingstoke, 1984), pp. 55–77; J. Guy, *Tudor England* (Oxford, 1988), pp. 254–8.

[107] M. A. R. Graves, 'The Management of the Elizabethan House of Commons: the Council's "Men of Business"', *Parliamentary History*, 2 (1983), 18.

[108] *Leycester's Commonwealth*, ed. F. J. Burgoyne (1904), p. 79; *House of Commons, 1558–1603*, II. 133.

[109] C.L.R.O., Rep. 21, fo. 212.

hitherto unmatched in Elizabethan court politics. This is particularly a problem because Essex reckoned on a substantial City following which he attempted to mobilise in his attempted coup in 1601. The prayers of prominent London preachers on Essex's return from Ireland in 1599, the popularity of engravings of the earl, which aroused the jealousy of the queen, the conspiracy among apprentices to rescue him from the Tower after his coup failed, the libels which circulated after his execution, all provide eloquent testimony of the popular support Essex enjoyed.[110] This was dangerous, in the same way as sympathy for Buckingham in 1521 and for Somerset in 1552 had been dangerous, because of the threatened conjunction of aristocratic and popular grievances. But whether there was anything approaching an Essex faction in London is much more doubtful. The earl had a few clients in prominent positions in the City like Giles Fletcher, Norton's successor as remembrancer, and in 1601 he expected much of the sheriff, Thomas Smythe. One can observe him exploiting his London connections in the summer of 1596, when he used Fletcher to communicate to the aldermen his scheme for the recovery of Calais, using the troops just returned from the Cadiz expedition, together with reinforcements to be provided by the City. Fletcher intimated to the lord treasurer the 'general concurrence of the most earnest wishes of the citizens that her Majesty would think of the recovery of Calais to which he perceived a great readiness in the city to contribute'. The aldermen therefore appear to have supported this attempt to influence royal policy.[111] But support for the goals of the forward protestant policy with which Essex was associated by no means implied a full identification with the earl's interests. Members of the London establishment who owed their advancement to Essex were very thin on the ground. He secured several grants of the freedom for his servants, but the Repertories do not record any grants of office made at his request.[112] It should also be remembered that the London elite was less prone than county elites to politicisation because its members were elected by the citizens themselves rather than being appointed by the Crown. They were therefore not as vulnerable to the rivalry of court factions as the justices of the peace were.[113] In short, the rivalry of Essex and Cecil does not appear to have seriously

[110] M. James, 'At a Crossroads of the Political Culture: the Essex Revolt of 1601', in M. James, *Society, Politics and Culture: Studies in Early Modern England* (Cambridge, 1986), pp. 448–52; Collinson, *Elizabethan Puritan Movement*, pp. 444–7; H.M.C., *De L'Isle Dudley*, II. 435; H.M.C. *Hatfield*, XI. 50, 53, 57–8, 77–8, 88–9, 91, 104, 132, 148, 156, 170, 270, 321–2.

[111] T. Birch, *Memoirs of the Reign of Elizabeth from the Year 1581 till her Death* (2 vols., 1754), II. 77, 100–1.

[112] C.L.R.O., Rep. 21, fo. 536; Rep. 23, fos. 265, 510, 593ᵛ; Rep. 24, fos. 223ᵛ, 302ᵛ; Rep. 25, fo. 156ᵛ; Remembrancia II, nos. 7, 142.

[113] A. Wall, 'Patterns of Politics in England, 1558–1625', *Historical Journal*, 31 (1988), 947–63.

disturbed City politics in the 1590s because such support as Essex obtained within London was limited and conditional. As Mervyn James has put it, 'For the City the Essexian role, however glamorously heroic, was firmly contained within the ordered and religious framework of the realm; outside that framework, he could have no status or standing except that of a traitor.'[114]

It was crucial to the stability of the city that civic politics were undisturbed by religious controversy. This was in marked contrast to the situation of the later seventeenth century and of many sixteenth-century continental cities. The most explosive outbreaks in continental cities occurred where the elite divided over the issue of religion, and in provincial England disorder resulted where local elites divided over the godly Reformation.[115] That London escaped serious controversy was due to a combination of local and national factors. England's success in escaping religious civil war was a result of the way that the country had stumbled into the Reformation so that the choices for or against reform were never starkly put: in Haigh's words the English Reformation was peaceful because it was piecemeal.[116] Elizabeth's soft-pedalling on enforcement, particularly in the early years, gave people time to adapt to her changes, and ensured that those who were permanently alienated remained a minority.

There were, of course, differences in religious outlook within the London elite. In the 1560s the bench still contained an influential conservative minority.[117] But, as Elizabeth's reign progressed, the grip of advanced protestants on City government tightened. Puritanism was not a divisive force in City politics because the puritans appear to have had few opponents within the elite. Any popular hostility to the godly that there may have been lacked an answering echo among the rulers. This is not to say that London's elite had very much sympathy with the presbyterian movement, whose organisation within the capital was surprisingly weak. Rather, for many Londoners practical godliness was of greater importance than platforms of Church government.[118] Nevertheless because of the notorious difficulties of unravelling individual religious commitment, it remains difficult to tell just

---

[114] James, 'Crossroads', p. 453.

[115] D. Richet, 'Aspects socio-culturels des conflits religieux à Paris dans la seconde moitié du XVIe siècle', *Annales E.S.C.*, 32 (1977), 764–89; C. R. Friedrichs, 'German Town Revolts and the Seventeenth-Century Urban Crisis', *Renaissance and Modern Studies*, 26 (1982), 27–51; D. Underdown, *Revel, Riot and Rebellion: Popular Politics and Culture in England, 1603–60* (Oxford, 1985), pp. 55–63; P. Collinson, *The Religion of Protestants: the Church in English Society, 1559–1625* (Oxford, 1982), p. 145. For the divisive impact of religion on later-seventeenth-century metropolitan politics, see G. S. de Krey, *A Fractured Society: the Politics of London in the First Age of Party, 1688–1715* (Oxford, 1985).

[116] *The English Reformation Revised*, ed. C. Haigh (Cambridge, 1987), p. 17.

[117] Foster, *Politics of Stability*, p. 122, 126–7.

[118] Collinson, *Elizabethan Puritan Movement*, passim.

how united the elite were over religious issues. Perhaps the almost unanimous support of the assistants of the Grocers' Company for the Bond of Association in 1584 with its professed intention to protect the life of a monarch committed to the 'profession and observation of the true christian religion' should be taken as a token of wealthy Londoners' commitment to the Reformation, but the pressures at work in securing signatures were rather more complex because of the primary issue of loyalty to the queen.[119] There are suggestive signs of elite sympathies in the widespread adoption of the parish lectureship, and in the identity of the preachers of funeral sermons named by Londoners in their wills.[120] It is true that one cannot be sure whether this typified elite behaviour or represented a highly motivated and untypical minority. But the silence of lay conservatism and the failure of puritan initiatives to ignite the kind of vocal opposition that often characterised provincial England would remain puzzling had there been a substantial conservative element within the elite.

Fortunately there is a document which provides hard evidence of a strong puritan presence in the upper reaches of City government. In 1584, 119 citizens attached their signatures to a petition to the lord mayor requesting him to intercede with the privy council on behalf of Thomas Barber, the puritan lecturer at St Mary Bow, recently suspended for his refusal to subscribe to Whitgift's articles. The petition deploys a characteristically puritan rhetoric in claiming that a catastrophic collapse in obedience would follow the suppression of preaching. Forty-six of those on the list were among the leading figures in City government as common councillors, and they included active committeemen like Walter Fish, Andrew Palmer, Robert Brandon, Robert Aske, and Thomas Aldersey. Had the signatories been evenly distributed through the city then the document's value as a guide to the religious orientation of the elite in general would have been much reduced, but in fact the vast majority of the signatories came from areas immediately adjacent to the parish involved. Most of the common councilors of the wards in which the petition was circulated were prepared to put their names to this puritan petition. The elite therefore seems to have been

---

[119] G.L., MS 11588/1, pp. 359–60.

[120] P. Seaver, *The Puritan Lectureships: the Politics of Religious Dissent, 1560–1662* (Stanford, 1970); H. G. Owen, 'Lectures and Lecturers in Tudor London', *Church Quarterly Review*, 162 (1961), 63–76. For the popularity of Robert Crowley with the elite, see *The Diary of Henry Machyn, Citizen and Merchant Taylor of London, 1550–63*, ed. J. G. Nichols (Camden Society, old series, XLII, 1848), pp. 278, 291, 296; Bodl., Ashmole MS 836, p. 297; P.R.O., C24/134, Langley vs. Langley; PROB 11/49, fo. 19; PROB 11/52, fos. 110 (in last two instances in association with Gough and Philpot), 173. The influence of puritanism in the City is also discussed in H. G. Owen, 'Tradition and Reform: Ecclesiastical Controversy in an Elizabethan London Parish', *Guildhall Miscellany*, 2 (1961), 63–70; D. A. Williams, 'London Puritanism: the Parish of St Stephen Coleman Street', *Church Quarterly Review*, 160 (1959), 464–82 and 'London Puritanism: the Parish of St Botolph without Aldgate', *Guildhall Miscellany*, 2 (1960), 24–38.

united by the conviction that a preaching ministry was essential to social discipline.[121]

We have also to ask whether members of the elite were divided in their business interests. Looking at the London elite in the early seventeenth century, Robert Ashton has identified an increasing divergence between the domestic and foreign concessionaries of the Crown, that is between the holders of internal monopolies, patents, licences, and customs farmers on the one hand, and the members of the regulated and joint stock companies chartered by the Crown for the purpose of conducting overseas trade on the other. This was because members of parliament began to discriminate in favour of the commercial concessionaries in their agitation against monopolies, and because the trading companies came to distrust the Crown as a result of its increasingly burdensome financial demands, its repeated infringements of company charters, and its failure to protect merchants in the wars of the 1620s. Robert Brenner has suggested that splits existed *among* the trading companies. He argues that tensions between the Levant/ East India Company interests and the newer colonial trades to the Americas played a role in determining civil war allegiances because of their differing relationships with the Crown and divergent attitudes to foreign policy.[122]

Whatever may have been the case by the second quarter of the seventeenth century, tensions within the elite over commercial questions do not appear to have been significant in the Elizabethan period. At the outset of the reign this was probably because of the domination of the court of aldermen by members of the Merchant Adventurers' Company which controlled the export of cloth to the Low Countries, then easily the dominant sector in English trade. George Ramsay has calculated that in 1564, twenty-four of the twenty-nine men who served as aldermen were Adventurers.[123] The other traditional trading interest, the Merchant Staplers who controlled wool exports, with whom the Adventurers had clashed earlier in the century, had been totally eclipsed.[124] The Adventurers, of course, did not always speak with one voice. Only a minority shared the enthusiasm with which influential godly big-wigs within the company, like Thomas Aldersey and Governor John Marsh, greeted the breakdown of the Antwerp mart in 1564. Indeed in December 1568 the company petitioned the government against a break with Spain.[125] But these tensions were ultimately contained because of

121 *The Seconde Parte of a Register*, ed. A. Peel (2 vols, Cambridge, 1915), II. 219–21. For Barber, see Collinson, *Elizabethan Puritan Movement*, pp. 253, 266, 320.
122 R. Ashton, *The City and the Court, 1603–43* (Cambridge, 1979); R. Brenner, 'The Civil War Politics of London's Merchant Community', *Past and Present*, 57 (1973), 53–107.
123 Ramsay, *City of London in International Politics*, p. 41.
124 P. Bowden, *The Wool Trade in Tudor and Stuart England* (1962), pp. 160–3.
125 G. D. Ramsay, *The Queen's Merchants and the Revolt of the Netherlands* (Manchester, 1986), pp. 67, 117, 131–2.

the way in which the outlook of the godly came to be more widely shared as the Spanish bogey took shape in 1569–72 with the rising of the northern earls, the pope's excommunication of Elizabeth, the Ridolfi plot, and the second revolt of the Netherlands. By the mid 1570s the Adventurers were increasingly lukewarm towards the idea of settlement with the Alva regime, not least because the new north German marts were proving workable.[126]

It is true that by the early seventeenth century the court of aldermen was much more variegated in its composition. In 1603 probably only one third of the aldermen belonged to the Adventurers; others were involved in the increasingly important new trades represented by companies like the Levant and East India Companies; and R. G. Lang has shown that at least half the aldermen of James I's reign owed the bulk of their fortune to the domestic trades.[127] There was not necessarily much overlap in membership between the new companies and the Adventurers. Only three of the thirteen merchants named in the Turkey Company charter of 1581 were Adventurers; and only eleven of the 150 Merchant Adventurers active in 1606 were among the 118 Levant Company charter merchants of 1605.[128] Moreover, tensions existed between the new companies and the Adventurers. The negotiations for the establishment of the Spanish Company in the 1570s were threatened by the hostility of the Adventurers to a proposal that membership be restricted to merchants who were not members of other companies and who had traded to Iberia since 1569, and the early years of its existence were dogged by disputes with the Adventurers over the shipment of goods direct from Germany to Spain.[129] The Levant Company's claim to a monopoly over the import of currants was unwelcome to the Adventurers who were thus unable to import currants from Germany.[130] Sometimes the new companies clashed with each other. For instance, the Venice Company, from 1583 enjoying a patent granting a monopoly to import currants for six years, clashed with the Turkey traders over the import of currants from Crete.[131] Nor were merchants necessarily united over foreign policy. The Spanish merchants were among the most vocal advocates of the return of Drake's treasure to Spain because of the threat a further deterioration in Anglo-Spanish relations would pose to their trade.[132]

However, these conflicts were not sustained, and usually resolved through compromises arranged by the Crown. When the Spanish Company charter was issued in 1577, twenty-four members of the Merchant Adventurers'

---

[126] Ibid. pp. 159–60, 179–82.
[127] Ashton, *City and the Court*, pp. 87–8; R. G. Lang, 'The Greater Merchants of London in the Seventeenth Century' (Oxford D.Phil., 1963).
[128] Brenner, 'Civil War Politics', pp. 57–8.
[129] *The Spanish Company*, ed. P. Croft (London Record Society, IX, 1973), pp. xii–xv.
[130] Ashton, *City and the Court*, p. 86.
[131] A. C. Wood, *A History of the Levant Company* (Oxford, 1935), pp. 18–19.
[132] S. Adams, 'The Lurch into War', *History Today*, 38 (May 1988), 21; *Spanish Company*, ed. Croft, pp. xxiv–xxv.

Company were admitted, and the subsequent differences between the two companies were sunk in the face of their common hostility to the pretensions of the Eastland Company and the outports.[133] The rivalry between the Levant and Turkey Companies was resolved through their union in 1592.[134] Some potential divergences of interest were unrealised. For example, Robert Ashton has suggested that the commercial and domestic concessionaries were united because of the common hostility of the House of Commons revealed in the monopolies and free trade debates of 1601 and 1604 respectively.[135] As far as the differences over foreign policy were concerned, Philip II obligingly removed any doubts the Spanish merchants may have felt about the wisdom of war when he seized all English shipping in Spanish ports in May 1585.[136] Finally, the edge of conflict was blunted because key individuals, like Sir Thomas Pullison, a member of both the Spanish and Merchant Adventurers' Companies, had interests shared between companies in dispute and therefore worked for compromise, and because the requirement that members of the chartered trading companies should also be members of a City livery company meant that merchants with different trading activities enjoyed a shared social life within the City.[137]

The ruling elite in Elizabethan London therefore showed an extraordinary level of cohesion, and there was little prospect of popular grievances becoming matters of controversy within the elite. Nevertheless this does not mean that the elite could rule in total disregard to those grievances. To have done so would have been to act against the prevailing ideals of magistracy, the force of which should not be underestimated in a Christian society. Such behaviour would also have been imprudent because of the relatively under-developed apparatus of coercion available to the elite. However great the informal sanctions they could apply to secure compliance, ultimately they were dependent for the maintenance of order on an unpaid constabulary, recruited from the middle tier of city society, whose members could not always be relied on to share elite perceptions and who sympathised with, if they did not actively promote, some popular grievances. The next section therefore considers some of the forces shaping the relationship between elites and people, which later sections of this book will explore in greater detail.

ELITES AND PEOPLE

The homogeneity of the elite is not sufficient to account for the stability of the capital because the aldermen could only count on the loyalty of the populace

[133] Ibid. pp. xii–xiii, xvi–xx.   [134] Wood, *Levant Company*, p. 20.
[135] Ashton, *City and the Court*, pp. 28–36.
[136] Adams, 'Lurch into War', p. 22.
[137] *Spanish Company*, ed. Croft, p. xvi; G. D. Ramsay, 'Clothworkers, Merchant Adventurers and Richard Hakluyt', *E.H.R.*, 92 (1977), 513.

so long as they were perceived to be committed to the interests of the citizenry as a whole rather than the narrow self-interest of a clique. Failure to fulfil popular expectations might strain loyalties. As we saw in the previous chapter, the riots of 1595 represented an indictment of magisterial failures to act in the markets.[138] There were very real tensions in metropolitan society between wholesalers and artisans, freemen and foreigners, householders and servants. While the solidarity of the elite was important in containing these tensions, it alone could not guarantee a stable polity, which depended also on the degree to which the elite was responsive to pressures from below.

It needs to be emphasised that the elite was not as out of touch with the realities of life for the city's lowlier inhabitants as some of its continental equivalents. Among the conventional praises heaped upon the queen for her favour to the City, Londoners lauded the Crown's good will in allowing the City to be self-governing, choosing its own magistrates from among its own citizens.[139] Some explicitly recognised the peculiarity of London by reference to continental contrasts, albeit with some patriotic hyperbole: thus the anonymous author of a tract defending the City's orphanage custom pointed out that London was governed 'not by cruell viceroyes, as is Naples or Millaine, neither by proude Podesta, as be most cities in Italie, or insolent Lieutenantes or presidentes, as are sundry Cities in France . . . but by a man of trade or a meere marchant, who notwithstanding, during the time of his magistracie, carieth himselfe with . . . honorable magnificence in his port, and ensignes of estate'.[140] Venality, hereditary office-holding, and the domination of a landowning patriciate were not features of London's government, as they were of so many continental cities. Nor was the power of the aldermen challenged by corporate bodies of lawyers in the way that French municipal authorities faced competition from the *parlements*. Nor was London subject to the control of officers lacking connections wth the locality like the *corregidores* in Spain.[141] Although London harboured many gentlemen residents, their role in City government was heavily circumscribed. They lacked any representation on the common council, and only in parishes like St Botolph Aldersgate, where they were particularly thick on the ground, did they enjoy fixed quotas of places on the vestry.[142] London's elite was therefore recruited from within the body of freemen, 'an incouragement', as Recorder Croke put it, 'to the one to governe well, a

---

138 Above, pp. 1–9.   139 *H.M.C., Frankland-Russell-Astley*, pp. 2, 4.

140 *A Breefe Discourse, Declaring and Approving the Necessarie and Inviolable Maintenance of the Laudable Customes of London* (1584), pp. 15–16. Cf. *Calendar of State Papers, Venetian*, X. 503; XV. 58–9.

141 Ramsay, *City of London in International Politics*, pp. 11–13, 33–4; J. H. Elliott, *Imperial Spain, 1469–1716* (Harmondsworth, 1970), pp. 93–6; V. G. Kiernan, *State and Society in Europe, 1550–1650* (Oxford, 1980), pp. 20, 46, 55, 57.

142 G.L., MS 1454/75.

provocacion to the other to obey well, the band of love & societie knitting both together, banishing discord, the poison of all commen weales'.[143]

It is true that the freedom masked great disparities of wealth, that the aldermen were recruited predominantly from the greater companies dominated by merchants and larger retailers, and that they were invariably the wealthiest members of City society. But there were very few urban dynasties in London: most of the City's rulers were first generation inhabitants recruited from relatively modest provincial backgrounds.[144] The result was that members of the elite had relatives in the country of lower social status than themselves. The evidence of their wills suggests that the aldermen did not forget their obligations to their poorer kinsmen, and the knowledge of the lowlier circumstances from which they had escaped may have helped condition their paternalistic responses to the problems of their fellow citizens.[145] Secondly, a high level of mobility into the elite helped sustain popular confidence in the idea of metropolitan opportunity which was so potent in the popular literature of the period.[146] The elite may therefore have been popularly perceived as open to men of talent.

Another feature of rule by freemen was the involvement of the elite in local and company offices, which gave them some experience of the problems of the less advantaged. Although some of the companies from which they were recruited, like the Mercers and Grocers, were cosy associations of merchants and large-scale retailers, others like the Haberdashers, Clothworkers, Skinners, and Merchant Tailors, had restless artisan majorities whose members needed careful handling. Likewise the *cursus honorum* of local office meant that most members of the elite had served in the positions of constable and churchwarden.[147] Many continued to be active on their parish vestries even after attaining a position on the aldermanic bench.[148] This gave them familiarity with the minutiae of local administration, an insight into the outlook of the men of middling status who attended vestries, and some contact with the poor, whose petitions for relief constituted an important segment of vestry business. Because of their preference for residence in the wealthy inner-city parishes, few aldermen had much close familiarity with

[143] Bucks. R.O., D138/22/1.
[144] R. G. Lang, 'Social Origins and Social Aspirations of Jacobean London Merchants', *Ec.H.R.*, second series, 27 (1974), 31–40.
[145] P.R.O., PROB 11/46, fo. 302; PROB 11/48, fo. 258; PROB 11/53, fo. 74.
[146] The legend of Dick Whittington achieved wide currency at this time: *The History of Sir Richard Whittington. By T. H(eywood)*, ed. H. B. Wheatley (Chap-Books & Folk-Lore Tracts, first series, V, Villon Society, 1885), pp. vii–ix; A. M. Hind, *Engraving in England in the Sixteenth and Seventeenth Centuries; a Descriptive Catalogue with Introductions* (3 vols., Cambridge, 1952–64), II. 192–3.
[147] Foster, *Politics of Stability*, ch. IV.
[148] For example, Anthony Ratcliffe and William Rider appeared regularly in the vestries of St Christopher-le-Stocks: *Minutes of the Vestry Meetings and other Records of Saint Christopher-le-Stocks*, ed. E. Freshfield (1886), pp. 13–19.

conditions in the poorest extramural areas, but they were emphatically not cut off from the practical problems of company and parochial government.[149]

The government of the City provided opportunities for respectable inhabitants of middling status to make suggestions on priorities for action by the elite through the annual petitions presented by the wardmote inquests to the aldermen. Those of Cornhill ward provide some indication of popular expectations of their magistrates. Many of the petitions reflected the perennial problems of life in the city, as the inquestmen demanded better measures to fight fires and the stricter enforcement of traffic regulations.[150] But others touched on more sensitive areas. Both in the early 1570s and in the later 1580s they petitioned for action against alien immigrants.[151] The dearth conditions of the 1590s were accompanied by requests that the aldermen take action against market offences and suppress defective weights and measures, and by the demand that they provide for the poor lying in the streets.[152] Their practical suggestions were informed by a strong sense of municipal corporatism, as they recommended that the aldermen establish brewhouses to supply beer of decent quality at reasonable prices, and mills to grind corn cheaply for the poor.[153] There are hints that some issues were the subject of city-wide campaigns. In 1574 most wards made presentments about the decay of the Thames through the ballast discharged into the river, while in 1579, as the corporation's policy of requiring the use of Thames sand in building came under attack, the aldermen demanded investigations into how the petitions had been 'procured'.[154] But it is striking in how many cases the aldermen took action in response to wardmote petitioning. Fire regulations were tightened in 1589, a yarn market established in 1600, and the municipal brewhouse built in 1594, in all cases after several years' petitioning.[155]

The character of sixteenth-century government cannot be understood without reference to the ideals which shaped magisterial performance. These ideals were most frequently articulated by the clergy. The primary obligation of the magistrate was to ensure that the word of God be set forth in preaching, and this usually involved a broad agenda, as it was essential that magistrates remove the obstacles to preaching in the form of idle pastimes. But rulers also had wider obligations to their subjects. The rich in general

---

[149] P.R.O., E179/251/16 for residence of aldermen.
[150] G.L., MS 4069/1, fos. 29ʳ⁻ᵛ, 38, 40, 42, 49; C.L.R.O., Samuel Barton's Book, fos. 46ᵛ, 47, 47ᵛ.
[151] C.L.R.O., Samuel Barton's Book, fo. 47; G.L., MS 4069/1, fos. 11ᵛ–12.
[152] G.L., MS 4069/1, fos. 65, 67, 71ᵛ.
[153] Ibid. fos. 33ᵛ–4, 36, 67.
[154] Ibid. fo. 14ᵛ; C.L.R.O., Samuel Barton's Book, fos. 44–3ᵛ; Rep. 18, fo. 151ᵛ; Rep. 19, fo. 418ᵛ.
[155] C.L.R.O., Jour. 22, fos. 370–1; Jour. 23, fo. 189ᵛ; Jour. 25, fos. 220ᵛ–1.

were constantly reminded that they held their wealth as stewards and therefore that they had an active duty to care for the poor, in giving alms, in not rack-renting their tenants, and in showing forbearance to poor debtors. Addressing the magistrates directly, William Cupper emphasised their obligations to pursue a vigorous policy in relieving poverty, as well as to take action to remove some of its perceived causes: 'usurers, brokers, badgers, hucksters, and such like locusts that eat up the poor and cause the markets to be inhaunced should be bridled so the poor may have things better cheap'.[156] The aldermen could not afford to ignore the pulpit, and they were sometimes explicit about the role that it played in formulating their policies, as when among the reasons deployed to persuade the privy council to outlaw all plays in the city and suburbs was the embarrassment caused to the elite by 'preachers daily railing upon the lord mayor'.[157] Nor should we underestimate the political sensitivity of City preaching, particularly when the preachers descended from generalities to specific policies or even individual cases. In 1603 Richard Stock denounced the regressive nature of the fifteenth, through which much war taxation was raised, in a St Paul's Cross sermon:

I have lived here some few years, and every year I have heard an exceeding outcry of the poor that they are much oppressed of the rich of this city, in plain terms of the Common Council. All or most charges are raised by your fifteenths, wherein the burden is more heavy upon a mechanical and handicraft poor man than upon an alderman.[158]

A major scandal occurred in1586 when George Closse, the minister of St Magnus', charged the lord mayor personally with injustice, and was made to confess his fault at Paul's Cross.[159] Sometimes aggrieved citizens attempted to exploit the power of the pulpit to bring their case to a wider audience. In 1580, Thomas Millington, grocer, found himself in Newgate after he had delivered a bill against the magistrates of the City to the Paul's Cross preacher.[160] These cases attracted attention because the personal nature of the attacks was so scandalous, but there was very much more preaching that delivered its criticisms implicitly and conditioned the notions of acceptable behaviour from magistrates. The legitimation of the hierarchy by the Church was therefore partial and conditional.

Many of the emphases of clerical commentators on magisterial roles were

[156] W. Cupper, *Certaine Sermons Concerning Gods Late Visitation in the Citie of London* (1592), pp. 341–6; C. Hooke, *A Sermon Preached in Paules Church in Time of Plague* (1603); sig. C iii^v; R. Crowley, *A Sermon Made in the Chappel at the Gylde Hall in London* (1575); T. Drant, *Two Sermons Preached, the one at S. Maries Spittle 1570 and the other at the Court at Windsor the viij of January, 1569* (?1570), sigs. H i–H iii.

[157] B.L., Lansdowne MS 20/11.   [158] H.M.C., *Hatfield House*, XII. 672.

[159] *Holinshed's Chronicles*, IV. 888–91; C.L.R.O., Rep. 21, fos. 273, 282, 287; A.P.C., XIV. 60–1, 188–9.

[160] C.L.R.O., Rep. 20, fo. 104^v.

echoed by influential laymen. Thomas Norton, in his *Instructions*, underlined the mayor's duties of protecting widows and orphans and ensuring
cheap supplies of victuals and fuel for the poor: 'Do justice with discretion,
execute lawes uprightlie and kepe order: have ever still a pitifull eye to the
poore.'[161] Similar sentiments emerge in the speeches of the recorder on those
set-piece occasions which punctuated the civic calendar, such as the assembly
of liverymen at the mayor's election, and his presentation at Westminster.
Commentators drew on the analogy between the mayor's responsibilities to
the citizenry and a father's responsibilities to his children. In exhorting the
mayor to take action to deal with dearth in 1596, Recorder Croke pointed to
the danger that the poor might perish 'which as no natural father can induer
to behold in his child, so the magistrate the father of the people [is] to be
touched with compunction of hearte [and is] to use all possible indevor to
prevent it'.[162] The official pronouncements of the aldermen were suffused in
a commonwealth rhetoric. For example, in calling for cuts in feasting in a
period of food shortage in 1579, the aldermen sought to tap the 'charitable
regarde to the maintenance of the whole socyetye'. In dealing with the abuses
of the poulterers in 1561, they attacked men 'so farre addicte and gevyn to
the onelie study care and desier of the unreasonable and unlawfull augmen-
tynge and avauncynge of their owne private and singuler gayne welthe and
proffytt ... that they do not onely forget and neglecte theire bounden duties
towardes almightie god and the charitable usinge of their neighbours But
also the common welthe of this Cytie'.[163]

The reciprocal rights and obligations articulated in this rhetoric were also
expressed in civic rituals. It was still customary for the poor to lead funeral
processions clothed at the expense of the deceased. They also played a
prominent role in the processions on lord mayor's day. Poor men, nominated
by the bachelors (that is, the leading members of the yeomanry, who lacked
the right to wear the livery) of the lord mayor's company, and wearing gowns
provided by subscription among the wealthy men of the company, would
march at the front of the procession, acknowledging their dependence by
carrying shields bearing the arms of past and present mayors of the
company.[164]

This was no empty rhetoric and ritual because it provided a set of values to
which the disadvantaged could appeal, and because it shaped popular
expectations of their rulers. Humble citizens appear to have enjoyed relatively easy access to the mayor. According to Strype, the mayor had the
power to summon any inhabitant of the City on the complaint of another

[161] Norton, 'Instructions', p. 12.
[162] Bucks. R.O., D138/22/1. Cf. *H.M.C., Hatfield House*, II. 117.
[163] C.L.R.O., Jour. 17, fo. 255^{r-v}; Jour. 18, fo. 271; Jour. 19, fo. 428; Jour. 20, fo. 467^v.
[164] *Lord Mayors' Pageants of the Merchant Taylors' Company*, ed. R. T. D. Sayle (1931),
pp. 21, 24, 26, 36, 47. For funeral gowns, see below, p. 175.

citizen, and to determine the controversies between them on his own authority. In the words of Thomas Wilson, the mayor was 'as it were the Chancellour for his tyme to compromitt matters and to mittigate the rigor of the lawe'.[165] The informality with which this jurisdiction was exercised means that it is only infrequently glimpsed in the documents. Ellen Harman tells us how when prevented from exercising her deceased husband's trade by the Horners' Company after her remarriage out of the craft, she approached Sir Martin Bowes, carrying her child in her arms, 'and my Lord Maior called the childe unto him and said yt was pitie that he shoulde have annie wronge nor she should have none duringe the time that he ruled the Citie and sett all things in good order'.[166] Members of the elite were sensitive to criticism for harsh treatment of the disadvantaged. Sir Baptist Hickes gave up his efforts to secure a lease of property in Saint Lawrence Jewry over the head of a widow 'for as much as there grew exclamations in the behalfe of the widow wherein he thought his reputation to be touched', and so 'he verye earnestly spake of the widow'.[167]

However, members of the elite did not act according to entirely abstract notions of 'charity' or 'paternalism'. Rather their practice was shaped by social conventions which limited its scope. It will be noticed from the instances cited above that their sympathies were most often mobilised in the support of widows and orphans, conventionally the most impotent groups in society. Because of the loss of the records of the lord mayor's informal jurisdiction, it is difficult to probe the nature of the power relationships that might decide whether a petitioner was heard or not. It is highly likely that the ability of petitioners to secure redress depended upon the character of the men prepared to testify in their behalf, and in particular on their relationship with the local elites, the rulers of their wards and parishes. Paternalistic ideals were always refracted through the hierarchy. Cupper complained that magistrates were 'ever climing with aspiring minds ... bent for the most part to their own private commodity', failing to execute justice with severity for fear of offending the powerful.[168] There was always a temptation to follow the line of least resistance: in the 1590s the aldermen were more ready to discipline marginal groups like fishwives and other hucksters than they were to restrain the wholesaling interests at which much popular anger was directed as the circulation of libels accusing the magistrates of involvement in a *pacte de famine* indicates.[169]

---

[165] J. Strype, *A Survey of London* (2 vols., 1720), II. 38; T. Wilson, 'The State of England Anno Dom. 1600', in *Camden Miscellany XVI* (Camden Society, third series, LII, 1936), p. 21. Cf. S. Macfarlane, 'Studies in Poverty and Poor Relief in London at the end of the Seventeenth Century' (Oxford D.Phil., 1982), ch. V.

[166] G.L., MS 9065A/1A, fos. 88–9. Cf. G.L.R.O., DL/C/210, fo. 140ᵛ; DL/C/213, fo. 298.

[167] G.L., MS 2590/1, p. 144.   [168] Cupper, *Certaine Sermons*, p. 217.

[169] *Hugh Alley's "Caveat"*, p. 23; T.R.P., III. 182–3.

Moreover, the existence of such paternalistic values and procedures does not mean that all mayors adhered to them with equal success. It was a frequently reiterated complaint that mayors who began with the best of reformist intentions rapidly ran out of steam. Christopher Hooke urged the mayor 'to double the care, to double the courage, to double the zeale and diligence of all your Predecessors, and that not for the first quarter, or for a while, as it were, *quinquennium Neronis*, the first five years of Nero, but during the time of your whole Maioraltie, even to the last houre thereof'.[170] Perhaps there is more than a hint of conventional preachers' rhetoric here, but it is clear that some magistrates were more in need of the warnings than others. The severity of the crisis of 1595 had much to do with the personal failings of Mayor Spencer, a notoriously mean-minded individual, 'a sparer, no spender' as Sir Thomas Tresham put it. In the wake of the riots he was criticised for corruption in allowing the sale of offices, for failing to consult with his colleagues, for keeping too loose a rein on City administration, and for insatiable avarice.[171] However, the ideals were an important restraint on individual self-seeking, and proved sufficiently strong in practice to ensure that there was no generalised disillusionment with the elite. One of the libels which circulated in 1595, for example, praised Sir Richard Martin at Spencer's expense. Martin was at that date engaged in negotiations to fund a new scheme to provide work for the able-bodied poor in Bridewell.[172] In fact, there seems to have been considerable respect for the mayoral office, if not always for the individual incumbent. The lewd words of Robert Finrutter, clothworker, are significant in this respect: 'he himself was as good a man as my lord maior was setting his office aside. And that when my lord Maior was owte of his place he woulde care noe more for him then for the worst Beadell in this Towne'.[173] It is a tribute to the degree to which ideals of magisterial behaviour were translated into action that many of the cases of lewd words against the elite come from victuallers who were the victims of the policies to control prices, reflecting the fact that some of the most bitter disputes in the City arose from the mayor's attempts to enforce the assizes. Thus, in July 1573, Elizabeth Ford, a poulterer's servant, told a man wishing to buy a rabbit at the price recently fixed by the lord mayor, 'that he shold go to my lord maior and bid hym saddell a catt and Ride into the contrye to bye Rabettes hym selfe'.[174]

It would be wrong to present the elite as an oligarchy of rapacious

---

[170] Hooke, *Sermon Preached in Paules Church*, sig. A iii.

[171] H.M.C., *Various*, III. 85; *Hatfield*, V. 250; L. Stone, 'The Peer and the Alderman's Daughter', *History Today*, 11 (1961), 48–55.

[172] B.L., Lansdowne MS 78/64; Huntington Library, Ellesmere MS 2522, fos. 10–13.

[173] C.L.R.O., Rep. 23, fo. 229ᵛ; P.R.O., KB9/686/248.

[174] C.L.R.O., Rep. 14, fo. 178ᵛ; Rep. 18, fos. 47, 98, 323, 352; Rep. 19, fo. 201; Rep. 20, fo. 161ᵛ.

extortioners ruling entirely in their own interests. 'Commonwealth' ideals clearly played a part in their approach to the government of the City. Their rule was shaped by the prevailing religious rhetoric, particularly the idea that wealth was held in stewardship, a consideration which secular-minded twentieth-century historians are apt to downplay. On the other hand the aldermen were not entirely the disinterested servants of the people. In falling in with the preachers' agenda, the aldermen were to some extent merely acknowledging the realities of power and the relatively limited coercive resources available to them. Moreover, they were the beneficiaries of the economic and social changes of the sixteenth century and they wished to perpetuate their enjoyment of their wealth. Conflicts between their own goals and the well-being of the commonwealth were frequent. As products of a particular social milieu as well as a religious culture, their responsiveness to popular pressure was therefore limited and conditional. The exploration of these tensions is one theme of the ensuing chapters, which look at the interactions between rich and poor in the frameworks of local government and the livery companies.

❊ 3 ❊

The framework of social relations: local government, neighbourhood, and community

INTRODUCTION

In the last chapter we saw how important the solidarity of the elite was in maintaining stability. But it has also been argued that the limited formal coercive powers available to the aldermen meant that the perpetuation of elite control depended on a degree of responsiveness to popular grievances. It will be one of the major contentions of the next two chapters that the substructures of government, the livery companies, and the parishes and wards played crucial roles in containing tensions by providing channels of communication between rulers and ruled and institutional frameworks within which the redress of grievances could be pursued. Thus, for example, the acute tensions between freemen and strangers, which lay behind so much of the aldermen's anxieties about the fragile fabric of order were largely contained because artisans pursued their campaigns against the strangers by lobbying the authorities for ameliorative action rather than by taking to the streets. They chivvied the rulers of their livery companies into suing aliens in the law courts and promoting legislation in parliament to tighten restrictions on non-free labour, and they promoted petitions through the wardmotes to pressurise the aldermen into supporting their campaigns.[1]

The success of these institutions in channelling popular grievances depended to a large extent on the degree to which they focused loyalties, integrating their members by creating communities. Community is here defined as a locality or social organisation (that is not necessarily defined by locality) characterised by social interactions, the density and frequency of which will determine the degree to which a community exists. Such inter-actions do not take place within an institutional framework alone, but institutions like the parish and the company can play an important role in the creation of a community particularly when, as in Elizabethan London, so many of the interactions between the wealthier and poorer members of

[1] Below, pp. 131–40; G.L., MS 4069/1, fos. 11ᵛ–12; C.L.R.O., Samuel Barton's Book, fo. 47.

58

society take place within those institutions. In well-developed communities the interactions are such as to create a sense of belonging among members. This might be drawn upon by community leaders in order to mobilise resources for common goals, but might also involve the development of obligations and expectations between members which might be drawn upon by the less advantaged in their quest for patronage or relief.[2]

In order to understand the ways in which institutions foster a sense of community, the historian must look at a wide range of variables. First, the functions of the institution need to be examined to determine the ways in which they foster loyalties, for example through dispensing charity, providing for the arbitration of disputes, organising business life, or promoting grievances before a higher authority. The conflicts which might develop with other communities in the discharge of those functions might also work to reinforce identity. Secondly, the level of participation in government needs to be determined, because such participation is important in shaping identity, and in keeping open the channels of communication between the wealthier and poorer sections of society, particularly where social status attaches to office-holding. But the historian must distinguish carefully between the formal and informal structures of power because initiative usually rests with much smaller groups of men than the formal pattern of office-holding might suggest. It is therefore necessary to bear in mind the less formal side of the relationships between rulers and ruled, the patterns of patronage, employment, debt and credit, and landlordship, which help provide individuals with access to the elite, as well as strengthening the power of the latter. Finally, the nature of the values and attitudes which shape the performance of the rulers of the institution also affect the attitudes of the less advantaged towards them. The ideals of magistracy and the traditions of communal responsibility which informed elite behaviour in Elizabethan London have already been illuminated in the previous chapter. We must also look at neighbourhood values, in particular the degree to which they might have transcended social divisions; and we must examine the role of society's rituals in sustaining communal values, reinforcing the sense of responsibility of the wealthy for the poor, and giving the poor a sense of their position in the hierarchy and the obligations of others towards them.

There is, of course, a danger of falling prey to the prevailing rhetoric of community and assuming a cohesive society united in the pursuit of the same goals. Elites show a tendency to insist upon such a rhetoric precisely as a means of concealing real divisions in the society, and they might manipulate the ideal so as to demand conformity to the will of the more powerful

[2] M. Stacey, 'The Myth of Community Studies', *British Journal of Sociology*, 20 (1969), 134–47; D. Garrioch, *Neighbourhood and Community in Paris, 1740–1790* (Cambridge, 1987), pp. 4–6; Boulton, *Neighbourhood and Society*, pp. 229–31.

sections of society. Moreover, the expressed attitudes of the poor towards their rulers might be shaped by the coercive dimension of social relations flowing from the unequal distribution of power in the community.[3] I have emphasised that the formal means of coercion in Elizabethan London were weak because the aldermen relied on unpaid locally elected officials in the maintenance of order. But there were less formal means by which subordination might be ensured. The necessity of having supporters among the elite to ensure a sympathetic hearing to requests for leases, salaried offices, and the promotion of grievances meant that the poorer members of the community had to show restraint. The patronage disposed of by the aldermen in licensing alehouse keepers, fishwives, hucksters, and porters kept aspirants for their favour in check. The bureaucratisation of poor relief in the sixteenth century offered greater opportunities for its discretionary management to mould the behaviour of the poor. The deferential values expressed in the petitions to the authorities might therefore have been instrumental rather than fully internalised. In other words, the 'meaner sort' might have recognised that it was only by the use of such a rhetoric that they stood any chance of achieving their objectives. The loyalties of the poor towards their rulers might therefore have been much more conditional than at first appears to have been the case. Deference could not be taken for granted, and social tensions emerged when the governors failed to meet popular expectations. It is perhaps rather in the ambiguity in the attitudes of the 'meaner sort' towards their rulers than in their unquestioning obedience that the reasons for the containment of tensions are to be sought.[4] Institutional loyalties underpinned that ambivalence because the frustrations the poor felt about their rulers were counterbalanced by the appreciation of the other benefits, like poor relief, the arbitration of disputes, or the promotion of grievances (albeit usually selective) which flowed from membership of a particular institution.

An individual's membership of one community should not be regarded as creating an exclusive hold on his loyalties. Most sixteenth-century Londoners were members of several communities: neighbourhoods, parishes, wards, livery companies, and even, in spite of its size, the City; all might create allegiances. The different institutions of government overlapped in their functions. Poor relief was available not only through the livery companies and parishes but also through the corporation itself, which ran the hospitals and administered buffer-stocks of grain and fuel to benefit the poor. When engaged in disputes Londoners could turn to their neighbours,

[3] L. Roper, 'The "Common Man", "the Common Good", "Common Women": Gender and Meaning in the German Reformation Commune', *Social History*, 12 (1987), 1–21.

[4] Cf. K. Wrightson, 'The Social Order of Early Modern England: Three Approaches', in *The World We Have Gained: Histories of Population and Social Structure*, ed. L. Bonfield, R. M. Smith and K. Wrightson (Oxford, 1986), pp. 177–202.

the assistants of their companies, or even the aldermen to arrange for arbitration. Alternatively, they could pursue litigation in the City courts. Popular grievances, as we have seen, were promoted through the wardmotes or the livery companies, and sometimes backed by the aldermen before the privy council or parliament. Likewise, in governing the City the aldermen saw the companies and wards as alternative instruments of rule. Thus troops could be raised either through the companies or the wards, and proclamations, for example those on apparel, could be enforced by householders chosen alternatively by the rulers of the companies or by the leaders of the wards.[5] It is probably mistaken to attempt to draw up a hierarchy of loyalties, to determine which were the most important, because the answer would doubtless vary from one individual to another. Londoners drew upon their membership of different communities for different purposes. The obligations of neighbourhood were important in many forms of social cooperation, and it was probably first to his parish that an individual turned in the quest for relief. But in the pursuit of craft grievances, his company affiliation and the privileges that citizenship brought became matters of some importance to him. The degree of identity felt with particular institutions varied according to context.

This stress on the integrating functions of communities poses some problems. Because communities defined themselves partly by means of exclusion, many Londoners did not fit so well into that matrix of overlapping communities that was so important to stability. The most basic division in the City was that between those who enjoyed the freedom and those who did not. The freedom entailed economic, political, and legal privileges. Freemen enjoyed the right to engage in retail trade, the privilege of pleading and being sued in the City courts for offences committed within the City walls, and the right to vote in elections for ward officials and, if liverymen, for the mayor and sheriffs.[6] Although Rappaport has demonstrated that the freedom was enjoyed by probably 75 per cent of males aged over twenty-eight in mid-sixteenth-century London, a much higher proportion than was previously appreciated, nevertheless a substantial minority of the inhabitants endured a subordinate status and were denied participation in the City's livery companies and the benefits that derived from membership.[7] A major component of this marginalised group were the subsistence migrants who thronged the city, particularly in times of dearth. They lacked the membership of the households of established citizens that apprenticeship entailed, and therefore access to a key instrument of socialisation was denied them.

[5] C.L.R.O., Jour. 21, fo. 19; Jour. 22, fos. 166^v-7^v; Rep. 15, fos. 76, 415^v.
[6] Rappaport, *Worlds Within Worlds*, pp. 29–36; N. L. Adamson, 'Urban Families: the Social Context of the London Elite, 1500–1603' (Toronto Ph.D., 1983), pp. 50–3.
[7] Rappaport, *Worlds Within Worlds*, pp. 49–53.

Rather they found themselves eking out an existence on the margins of
economic life, regarded with intense suspicion by local authorities, who
often harried them out of the parishes for which they were responsible. In
circumstances of contracting employment opportunities, such as characterised trade crises or dearth, these people faced the difficult choice
between impoverishment and petty crime.[8]

Nevertheless, those who lacked the freedom of the City often enjoyed
membership of other institutions which fulfilled integrating roles similar to
those provided by the livery companies and parishes. Andrew Pettegree has
shown how the stranger churches administered their own system of poor
relief and provided through the consistories a forum within which disputes
could be arbitrated. It is striking that when the City attempted to promote
legislation against the strangers they proved to be quite resourceful in
defending themselves in the law courts and before the privy council and
parliament.[9] And the principle of guild organisation applied even to some
groups in what we might otherwise be tempted to think of as the more casual
sectors of the labour market. Fraternities existed in the early modern period
among waterbearers, street porters, and labourers, performing functions
similar in many ways to the livery companies. Thus the orders for the good
government of the labourers, formerly called by the name of brethren of the
Holy Trinity, drawn up in 1605, included provisions for their direction by
twelve rulers and twelve assistants, for the restriction of non-licensed
labourers, and for the levying of a fund to provide poor relief. Although such
organisations were intended at least partly as instruments through which the
aldermen could control potentially threatening groups – two aldermen were
appointed to hear all controversies within the labourers' guild and no orders
for their government could be made without the consent of the elite – these
guilds at least provided non-free groups with bodies through which they
could negotiate with the authorities. Labour was not fully casualised, nor
defenceless before market forces.[10]

The following chapters develop the themes outlined above with relation
first to the local communities formed by parishes and wards, and then to the
livery companies. The current chapter first assesses the degree of participation in local government and the role of the local authorities as mediators
between the elite and people. It then tackles the nature of neighbourhood

[8] P. Clark, 'The Migrant in Kentish Towns, 1580–1640', in *Crisis and Order in English Towns,
1500–1700*, ed. P. Clark and P. Slack (1972), pp. 138–45; Beier, *Masterless Men*, pp. 40–7;
P. Clark, 'Migrants in the City: the Process of Social Adaptation in English Towns', in
Migration and Society in Early Modern England, ed. P. Clark and D. Souden (1987),
pp. 267–91.
[9] Pettegree, *Foreign Protestant Communities*, ch. VII; below, pp. 137–8.
[10] C.L.R.O., Rep. 27, fos. 98–100ᵛ, 163ᵛ. Cf. G.L., MS 9171/8, fos. 138–9ᵛ; C.L.R.O.,
Rep. 13, fos. 63ᵛ, 299, 300ᵛ, 405ᵛ, 427ᵛ–8; Rep. 16, fo. 504ʳ⁻ᵛ (waterbearers); Rep. 26,
fos. 521ᵛ–4 (street porters).

values and their capacity to transcend the widening social divisions that characterised Elizabethan London.

Although the aldermen enjoyed the services of a large number of officials responsible for the collection of tolls and the enforcement of economic regulations, for almost all other areas of City government, in particular the levying of troops, the collection of taxes, and the enforcement of the whole gamut of social regulation, they were dependent on the cooperation of unpaid locally elected officials. The officers of the mayor's household might have performed a wide range of functions in City government, but they were too few to serve in anything more than a coordinating capacity.[11] Much was therefore left to the discretion of the local community. It was, for example, only through the representatives of the local community that the aldermen could hope to obtain knowledge of offences. In addition to their Christmas presentments the wardmote inquests were regularly instructed by the aldermen to give information on specific offences such as breaches of the assize and defective weights and measures, and it is also clear from the certificates returned to the court of Chancery that they were engaged in searches for the detection of infringements of Lenten regulations as a matter of routine.[12] To some extent, these communities were self-regulating. The inquest undertook the policing of moral offences, examining offenders, instructing them to leave the ward, presenting them to the Bridewell authorities, or arranging for their indictment at sessions for bawds and scolds.[13] Alehouse keepers were licensed by the aldermen on the recommendations of local vestries and inquestmen.[14] Parish vestries enjoyed considerable power over local resources. They jealously guarded their control over the assessment and collection of local taxes.[15] Although control of expenditure from the poor rate rested with the governors of Christ's Hospital, they acted in response to petitions from the vestries, and vestries controlled decisions about expenditure from legacies.[16]

This begs a question about just how representative those who controlled parish and ward affairs were. It is one of the crucial insights of the revisionist

[11] B. R. Masters, 'The Mayor's Household Before 1600', in *Studies in London History*, ed. A. E. J. Hollaender and W. Kellaway (1969), pp. 95–114.

[12] C.L.R.O., Rep. 16, fo. 433^{r-v} (assize of tallow); Rep. 19, fo. 63^v (wine prices); Rep. 20, fo. 136 (new buildings); Rep. 22, fo. 341^v (weights); Jour. 24, fo. 191^v (brewers); Jour. 25, fo. 124^v (foreigners); P.R.O., C265/1, C203/1 (Lent searches).

[13] C.L.R.O., Rep. 15, fo. 59^v; Rep. 18, fo. 44^v; G.L.R.O., DL/C/210, fo. 96; DL/C/211, fo. 14; DL/C/213, p. 511; G.L., MSS 3018/1, fo. 66, 4069/1, fo. 3^v; B.C.B. III, fo. 265.

[14] *The Vestry Minute Book of the Parish of Saint Margaret Lothbury in the City of London, 1571–1677*, ed. E. Freshfield (1887), p. 32; G.L., MSS 9234/4, fo. 257; 4069/1, fo. 3^v.

[15] *Vestry Minutes of Saint Margaret Lothbury*, p. 24.   [16] Below, pp. 96–8.

case on early modern London that the City enjoyed a large number of elected officials: as many as one in three householders in a wealthy inner-city ward like Cornhill might expect to hold some kind of office in any one year.[17] Because there was an established *cursus honorum* the lowlier positions were often held by those who were to become leaders in parish and ward government. As the vestrymen of St Saviour Southwark explained when turning down the request of a newcomer to the parish to be immediately admitted to the vestry, it was their custom 'to make tryall of other offices before they truste them with matter of chardge'.[18] Even minor office-holding therefore helped to define local status. Deponents in church court cases often mentioned the offices they had held in order to establish their credibility.[19] Office-holding therefore served to identify individual citizens with the regime.

However, the arguments about popular participation in the substratum of local government need to be qualified from several directions. This was not simple rotatory office-holding by Buggins' turn, for the hierarchy of office reflected the hierarchy of wealth. Table 3.1 offers a profile of the wealth of those serving in the various parish and ward offices of Cornhill in the early 1580s by linkage to the 1582 subsidy, which was paid by the top 50 per cent of householders in this prosperous ward. It is clear that the payment of the subsidy was a major criterion for office-holding: only on the lowest rung was the proportion not assessed significant. The greater status of the offices on the higher rungs of the hierarchy was reflected in the greater wealth of those serving them. Linkage of the 1599 subsidy to office-holders in Portsoken suggests that in the extramural wards the correlation between office-holding and payment of subsidy was weaker (Table 3.2). It held true for the position of inquestman and for the constableship, a higher status office in Portsoken than in Cornhill and held after service as collector for the poor, but was much weaker for the lowlier offices of scavenger and collector. Subsidy was only paid by about 20 per cent of householders in Portsoken, and unfortunately there are few local assessments which might carry the analysis very much further down the social scale. Jeremy Boulton found that in early-seventeenth-century Southwark vestry offices were generally held by subsidy payers, while the holders of manorial office represented a wider group, although still from the upper echelons of the society.[20] It would therefore appear that in inner-city wards office-holders came from the top half of the inhabitants and in the extramural wards from the top quarter.

17 Pearl, 'Change and Stability', pp. 15–16. Cf. A. M. Dingle, 'The Role of the Householder in Early Stuart London *c.* 1603–1630' (London M.Phil., 1975); A. E. MacCampbell, 'The London Parish and the London Precinct, 1640–60', *Guildhall Studies in London History*, 2 (1976), 107–24; Boulton, *Neighbourhood and Society*, pp. 138–45.
18 G.L.R.O., P92/SAV/793.   19 G.L., MSS 9056, fo. 64; 9065A/2, fo. 186ᵛ.
20 Boulton, *Neighbourhood and Society*, pp. 139–42.

Table 3.1. *Tax assessments of Cornhill office-holders, early 1580s*

	n	£3	£5	£6	£8	£10–19	£20–9	£30–9	£40–9	Over £50	Not assessed	Less than £8 (%)	More than £8 (%)
Scavengers	20	5	5	3	2	1	1	0	0	0	3	75	10
Petty jurymen	38	10	13	3	2	2	2	0	1	0	5	74	13
Constables	28	8	5	2	0	6	0	0	1	4	2	54	39
Wardmote inquestmen	32	5	6	4	1	6	0	0	2	7	2	50	47
Collectors for poor	15	0	3	3	1	4	1	0	0	2	1	47	47
Churchwardens	13	2	1	2	1	4	1	0	0	2	0	46	54
Grand jurymen	35	7	4	2	1	9	2	1	2	8	0	40	60
Auditors	16	1	2	0	0	3	0	1	0	7	1	25	69
Common councillors	6	0	0	0	0	0	0	1	0	5	0	0	100

Sources: G.L., MSS 4071/1; 4072/1; 4069/1; P.R.O., E 179/251/16.

Table 3.2. Tax assessments of Portsoken office-holders, late 1590s

	n	Poor rate only	£3	£4	£5	£6	£8	£10–19	£20–9	Over £30	Not assessed	Less than £4 (%)	More than £4 (%)
Scavengers	20	5	7	0	2	0	0	0	0	0	6	55	10
Collectors for poor	11	3	3	1	0	2	0	0	0	0	3	63	18
Constables	21	4	8	2	2	3	1	0	0	0	1	66	29
Wardmote inquestmen	47	6	22	2	5	2	2	0	0	1	7	64	21
Churchwardens	14	1	3	1	3	1	2	1	0	0	2	36	50
Vestrymen	36	2	7	3	8	3	5	3	1	1	3	33	58
Common councillors	6	0	0	0	1	0	4	0	0	1	0	0	100

Warning: Comparisons of wealth of Cornhill and Portsoken office-holders on the basis of the above are invalid because of the erosion in the level of subsidy assessments between 1582 and 1599.

Sources: G.L., MSS 9234/2–7; P.R.O., E 179/146/382; Bodl., Rawlinson MS D 796B, fo. 86.

Moreover, initiative in local government was not evenly spread among the office-holding group. Some offices did not carry much clout. Scavengers were responsible for the collection of the rate for the raker and the supervision of street cleaning. The collectors for the poor were essentially rate collectors because decisions about eligibility to relief rested with the churchwardens. The wardmote inquest, it should be noted, tended to contain a broad cross-section of the upper half of Cornhill society, wealthy merchants and retailers sitting with middling artisans. But the higher positions on the inquest, particularly that of foreman, tended to be monopolised by the wealthier households. Stow emphasised the considerable discretionary power held by the foreman over the inquest's proceedings.[21] In parochial government too the lead tended to be taken by the wealthier members of the community. It was they who served as feoffees, sat on the most important parish committees, audited accounts, and authorised discretionary payments in poor relief; 'the worshipful of the parish', or the 'elders of the parish' as they are identified in the documents.[22]

The reaction in the direction of the self-regulating community has been pushed too far. It is striking that none of the recent discussion of local government in London has touched upon the role of the alderman's deputy, the real workhorse of local administration. In the fifteenth century deputies were temporary arrangements, but by the mid sixteenth century they were permanent features of local government.[23] Because the deputies were resident in the wards whereas the aldermen almost invariably were not, they became responsible for much routine government. The majority of precepts from the lord mayor recognised this in calling for action by the alderman or his deputy. The deputies were by no means alien to the communities they served. Leading common councillors, they were long-term residents of their wards, and often served as deputies for long periods.[24] Moreover they often acted in response to pressure from below, for example in arbitrating disputes between neighbours.[25] But they also enjoyed very considerable discretionary powers, most frequently brought to bear against the poor. They arranged for the punishment of vagrants, hustled inmates out of the ward, undertook the examination of pregnant single women, brought delinquents before the governors of Bridewell, and bound others over for appearance at the sessions.[26] They were also active in poor relief administration, authorising

[21] Stow, *Survey of London*, I. 191.   [22] G.L., MSS 1176/1; 4824, passim.

[23] Barron, 'Government of London', p. 72.

[24] Deputies can be identified from the Bridewell records and from stray references in church court depositions and parochial records.

[25] G.L., MSS 4524/1, fo. 83ᵛ; 9056, fos. 9ᵛ, 11; G.L.R.O., DL/C/214, fo. 71.

[26] Bodl., Rawlinson MS D796B, fos. 19, 108, 112ᵛ (vagrants); G.L., MSS 4072/1, fo. 84 (inmates); 9064/13, fo. 11ᵛ; 9064/14, fos. 12, 13ᵛ; G.L.R.O., DL/C/211, fos. 14–15ᵛ (pregnant women); B.C.B. I–IV, passim (offenders brought to Bridewell); *Vestry Minutes of Saint Margaret Lothbury*, p. 41 (binding to sessions).

payments by the collectors, and receiving monies collected for the relief of plague victims.[27] The increasing prominence of the deputy in local government was paralleled by a withering in the functions of the wardmotes. If presentments of the fifteenth century are compared with those of the sixteenth century, it is clear that the proportion of regulative and moral offences with which they were dealing was declining, leaving local nuisances as the most typical object of the wardmote's concern.[28]

How were local officers selected? The role of the assembly of inhabitants for the election of officers at the December wardmotes was limited because most nominations had been determined in advance by parish vestries. In St Botolph Aldgate, for example, the vestrymen nominated two candidates for each of the positions of constable and scavenger, but the wardmote was given no choice at all over the members of the inquest. Because the position of inquestman constituted one of the lowest stages in the *cursus honorum* this practice gave the vestry considerable power to filter out undesirables. The nominating assemblies were sometimes afforced by the presence of non-vestrymen or 'assistants' as they were called, but no nominating body wider than twenty-three persons has been found in this ward of 500 households.[29] Nevertheless, in making their nominations vestries were sensitive to local opinion. In 1606 the vestrymen of St Botolph Aldgate rejected the candidacy of James Demetrius, brewer, for the churchwardenship 'because of doeing other men wrong'.[30] Humphrey Gonson, whose term of office as scavenger had been marred by bitter disputes over a new scavenger's rate, failed to secure nomination to the position of constable from the vestry of St Sepulchre 'because the crie of the poore came unto their eares'.[31] The balancing of elite discretion and sensitivity to local opinion to achieve a rough consensus is nicely illustrated by another episode from St Botolph Aldgate, where in May 1590 Alderman Gourney called a meeting of 'dyveres parishioneres' to choose a deputy to replace Richard Casy, then engaged in an acrimonious controversy with a fellow vestryman. Casy, whose career exhibits a streak of populism, in fact secured 'most voices', but the alderman 'persayvinge that it would make no quyetnes' desired Henry Conway to take the office. Deferring to the alderman's wishes, Casy and the other parishioners present gave 'theire concent and good wyll' to his choice.[32] It should be emphasised that these electoral procedures were designed to keep

27 G.L., MSS 4071/1, fo. 110; 4524/1, fo. 100; C.L.R.O., Rep. 22, fos. 430, 431ᵛ, 438, 446ᵛ.
28 K. Anderson, 'The Treatment of Vagrancy and the Relief of the Poor and Destitute in the Tudor Period, Based on the Local Records of London to 1552, and Hull to 1576' (London Ph.D., 1933), pp. 395–404; *Calendar of Plea and Memoranda Rolls of the City of London, 1413–1437*, ed. A. H. Thomas (1943), pp. 115–41, 150–9; G.L., MSS 4069/1; 3018/1.
29 G.L., MSS 9234/1–7. Twenty-three were present at the nominating meeting in December 1588. Cf. G.L., MS 3505, fo. 19.
30 Bodl., Rawlinson MS D796B, fo. 31ᵛ.   31 P.R.O., STAC 8/160/6.
32 G.L., MS 9234/2B, fo. 61. On Casy, see below, p. 190.

controversy to a minimum. It was better that a consensus about the merits of particular candidates should emerge at a vestry meeting than that men should openly strive for election. The system would hold up so long as the society was not subject to deep ideological fissures and local politics remained as non-controversial as they appear to have been in the Elizabethan period.

The vestry therefore emerges as the cockpit of local government and the level of participation in the vestry is crucial to the assessment of the degree to which that government was representative and responsive. Many vestries in London confined attendance to a select group, usually those who had served certain offices, the ex-constables in St Sepulchre's, ex-scavengers in St Dunstan in the West, ex-churchwardens in St Bride's.[33] Occasionally a two-tier system was in operation, either where a general vestry elected the select body, or where certain aspects of parochial government, such as church repair, were reserved for wider assemblies.[34] All the heavily populated extramural parishes had select vestries by Elizabeth's reign. By the time of Laud's survey of parochial government in 1638, 59 out of 109 London vestries were select.[35] But in answering Laud's queries there was much room for ambiguity over the authority which established the select vestry. Many parishes had formally sought episcopal sanction for their select vestries, but others claimed select status by prescription alone. Often an episcopal licence sanctioned an already existing arrangement. Thus the parish of St Margaret New Fish Street passed a series of resolutions limiting eligibility to serve on the vestry to ex-office-holders long before it sought formal sanction for a select vestry in 1612.[36] Thus confusion over whether episcopal sanction was necessary to the establishment of a select vestry led some parishes to describe as open vestries where attendance was in practice limited. The ambiguities are captured in the answer of the churchwardens of St Bartholomew Exchange that their parish was governed 'by the auntientes of our parish in generall and not by a vestry of selected persons'.[37] Attendance was in many cases determined by those whom the churchwardens saw fit to call to a meeting: in this way a select vestry might be established informally. Although the vestries of St Bartholomew Exchange and St Margaret Lothbury were formally open, and the minutes regularly record attendance by 'the most of

---

[33] L.P.L., Cartae Miscellanae VII.
[34] Ibid. Cf. Thomas Earl's distinction in his description of parish government between 'an Assistance of churchwardens and constables before passed' and 'a vestry of the whole parish': Cambridge University Library, Mm. 1.29, fo. 21[v].
[35] G.L., MSS 1454/75; 9236, fo. 9[v]; 3016/1, fo. 43; 4249, fo. 5[r–v]; G.L.R.O., P92/SAV/449–50; Southwark Archives, St Olave's V.M. As for St Sepulchre, St Botolph Bishopsgate, St Giles Cripplegate, and St Bride Fleet Street, their parishioners claimed select vestries by prescription in 1638; L.P.L., C.M. VII.
[36] G.L., MS 1175/1, fos. 13[v], 37, 45, 50.
[37] L.P.L., C.M. VII; *The Vestry Minute Books of the Parish of Saint Bartholomew Exchange in the City of London 1567–1676*, ed. E. Freshfield (1890), p. 53.

the parisheoners', the attendance lists suggest that less than twenty actually appeared in parishes with 80 and 115 households respectively.[38] This may reflect a lack of interest in what many saw as only routine government, and, in meetings where the assessment of taxation was at issue, attendances might move up to between thirty and thirty-five. At one such meeting in St Bartholomew Exchange in 1593 for the reassessment of the parish rate paid by all householders, thirty-three were listed as present. 66 per cent of the thirty-nine male householders assessed at 20d. or above appeared, and 19 per cent of the thirty-two assessed below 20d.[39] This was the widest level of participation in local government one might expect to find in Elizabethan London.

It is also significant that the trend was in the direction of select vestries and a narrowing in the basis of consent thought appropriate for the conduct of parish affairs.[40] One might dispute the reality of this phenomenon on the grounds that the increasing number of episcopal licences to hold select vestries reflects tightening episcopal control rather than changes in the nature of parish government which, as we have seen, might have been select before the bishop's grant, while the crop of references in parochial sources might simply reflect a mushrooming in the availability of these sources in the later sixteenth century. Thus the novelty of the select vestry might be in doubt. Secondly, one might question whether the move to select vestries, if it did occur, was the result of a feeling of greater social exclusiveness. Sometimes the reasons alleged apparently had little to do with any consciousness of the social divide. The parishioners of St Margaret New Fish Street claimed that without a select vestry and the clearly defined duties of attendance it entailed, no one would turn up to the meetings.[41] Even more prosaically, in St Botolph Billingsgate it was alleged that the vestry house was too small to hold all the parishioners.[42] But the rhetoric which attends some of the grants is suggestive both of a new departure and of a perception of social divisions. Thus the order of 1592 establishing the select vestry in the parish of St Martin Ludgate asserts that 'through the generall admittance of all sortes of parishoners unto theire vestries theire falleth out great hinderaunce to good proceedinges by the dissent of the inferiour & late inhabitantes being for the most part the greater number and more headye to crosse then either discreet or hable to further any good order for the benefitt of the church & parish'.[43] And in one of the most extraordinary wills of the period, Thomas Lane, writing in 1594,

---

[38] *Vestry Minutes of Saint Margaret Lothbury; Vestry Minutes of Saint Bartholomew Exchange.* Number of households calculated from rate assessments for St Bartholomew's, and given in C. M. Pendrill, *Old Parish Life in London* (1937), p. 183 for St Margaret's.
[39] *Vestry Minutes of Saint Bartholomew Exchange*, pp. 28–9.
[40] Foster, *Politics of Stability*, p. 43.
[41] G.L., MS 1175/1, fo. 45.   [42] L.P.L., C.M. VII.
[43] G.L., MS 1311/1, fo. 86; Foster, *Politics of Stability*, p. 43.

brings to light frictions in his local vestry which could never have been inferred from the staid vestry minutes of the period:

And forasmuche as heretofore I have seene in the vestryes holden in the churche of Saint Mildred in the Pultrye every one of the parrishe be he never so Base or quarrelling a man being by some termed the maior parte hathe had equall voyce and hearing and borne lyke swaye as the chiefest man of the parrishe and some time overtaunted the chiefest man of the parishe althoughe such Chiefe man hath bene a very quiett man and of that Accompte that he hath fyned for the Sherifaltye of London.

Indeed so wound up was Lane by the disruptions of the 'maior parte' that he insisted that the parish establish a select vestry if it was to enjoy a bequest from his property for the purposes of poor relief.[44] We can easily understand the motives which might cause the leaders in the extramural wards to restrict admission to the vestry, but it is particularly striking that the desire for exclusivity should have been felt even in the small and relatively prosperous inner-city parishes where the poor were not so threatening.

However, select vestries were not necessarily unrepresentative of their communities. In inner-city parishes, communities typically of about eighty households, the establishment of a select vestry of twenty men hardly represented the imposition of a tiny elite. These parishes were small enough to give the vestrymen many connections, whether through friendship, employment, landlordship, credit, patronage, or poor relief, with those householders not represented on the vestry. Most householders could therefore count on the advocacy of some member of the vestry. The same may have been true to a lesser extent even of extramural parishes like St Olave Southwark where thirty vestrymen governed 1,800 householders.

In St Olave's the vestrymen were drawn not just from the subsidy-paying group, itself confined to less than 27 per cent of the householders in 1589, but from the upper echelons of that group. None was assessed to the 1589 subsidy at less than £10. Only fifty-nine householders in the whole parish, less than 5 per cent, were assessed at that rate and, of these, twenty-two were members of the vestry.[45] The vestry was clearly the preserve of the parish elite. Their dominant position in local life was enhanced by their monopoly control of the governorships of the parish school and the positions of jurors before the commissioners of sewers, and by the relative freedom of Southwark from outside interference.[46] They were a close-knit group. Sixteen of the twenty-two vestrymen dying in the period 1581–1609, whose wills have been traced in the Prerogative Court of Canterbury, included other vestrymen among the overseers of their wills. Several of the families intermar-

[44] P.R.O., PROB 11/84, fo. 115ᵛ.
[45] Southwark Archives, St Olave's V.M.; P.R.O., E179/185/335; 251/16. Number of households estimated from G.L.R.O., P71/OLA/9.
[46] St Olave's School, Orpington, SOI/1/1; G.L.R.O., SKCS 18.

ried. Two of the daughters of Charles Pratt, leatherseller, were married to other vestrymen. Others were linked by godparentage. Their self-consciousness emerges in the way they attended the funerals of their colleagues as a body. A strong puritan commitment runs through many of the wills. Perhaps the bequests for sermon cycles by William Lande, Thomas Harper, Charles Pratt, and William Dasset are not unusual. More suggestive are Dasset's bequest to a daughter of the preacher, Thomas Edmunds, Thomas Bates' lengthy self-congratulation for having avoided the perils of popery for most of his life, Robert Feltham's bequest to named ministers of the French church, Thomas Bulman's bequests to the poor 'suche as can say the Lordes prayer the tenne commaundements and the Articles of the christian faithe', and to the imprisoned preachers about London, in which he was followed by Helen Harrison, the widow of another vestryman.[47] This was the parish which provided employment for Robert Browne, the separatist, as schoolmaster when he fell foul of the ecclesiastical authorities.[48]

One might interpret their elite status, their inter-connectedness, and their espousal of a minority religious position, as indications of their alienation from the mass of the parishioners. But the complexion of the vestry did reflect the nature of local society to some extent. Although there was a sizeable group of merchants and retailers resident on the Bridge, most of the vestry's members were prosperous artisans representing the main occupational groupings in the parish. In 1589 there were two joiners, three metal workers, a cooper, a hatmaker, a fellmonger, a carpenter, and a dyer. The importance of brewing to the local economy was reflected in the presence of a few brewers, and the victualling trades in two innkeepers and a tallow chandler. Two major sectors in the economy were apparently severely under-represented: the unskilled sector accounting for 19.4 per cent of the workforce in the early seventeenth century, and the textile sector accounting for 35.6 per cent and represented by just one hatmaker.[49] But many of the

---

[47] P.R.O., PROB 11/67, fos. 108ᵛ–9 (Richard Harrison, white baker), 168ᵛ–9 (Thomas Harper, carpenter); PROB 11/68, fos. 325ᵛ–6ᵛ (Olyffe Burre, coppersmith); 377ᵛ–8ᵛ (William Lande, joiner); PROB 11/69, fo. 127ᵛ (Thomas Bates, haberdasher); PROB 11/70, fos. 103–4 (Thomas Pinden, tanner); PROB 11/71, fos. 91–3 (George Fletcher, hosier); PROB 11/73, fos. 370ᵛ–1ᵛ (John Audley, grocer); PROB 11/79, fo. 108ʳ⁻ᵛ (Richard Pinfold, tallow chandler); PROB 11/80, fos. 86ᵛ–8ᵛ (Robert Feltham, vintner), 187ʳ⁻ᵛ (Peter Metcalfe, clothworker); PROB 11/81, fos. 242–3 (Thomas Westwray, brewer); PROB 11/84, fos. 248–9 (Thomas Bulman, draper); PROB 11/88, fos. 218ᵛ–9 (William Dasset, merchant tailor); PROB 11/89, fos. 275 (John Selby, woodmonger), 440–1 (Thomas Rookes, leatherseller); PROB 11/98, fos. 23ʳ⁻ᵛ (Richard Bratell, grocer), 238ᵛ–9 (Anthony Leather, cutler); PROB 11/105, fos. 157–9 (John Palmer, grocer); PROB 11/107, fos. 3ᵛ–5 (Anthony Fawkes, clothworker), 114ᵛ (George Swayne, cooper); PROB 11/108, fos. 198ᵛ–9ᵛ (Richard Sampson, blacksmith).

[48] St Olave's School, Orpington, SO I/1/1, pp. 10–11.

[49] Occupations from parish records in Southwark Archives, especially St Olave's C.W.A., parish register in G.L.R.O., P71/OLA/9. Cf. Boulton, *Neighbourhood and Society*, p. 66.

unskilled were employed by vestrymen. The draymen, for example, were clearly linked into the brewers' establishments. Landlordship was another means by which the vestrymen built up contacts through the society. John Fox, dyer, owned Legg Alley, tenements in Maze Lane and Mill Lane, and two dyehouses near Battle Bridge, and leased the Signs of the Fox and Goose and Seven Stars.[50] On the one hand, the dominant position of the vestrymen as employers and landlords might be seen as a way in which they might perpetuate their control; on the other hand, it also provides evidence of the kind of contacts which the less advantaged might hope to mobilise in the quest for patronage or relief.

It is one of the great problems of the formality of parish records that it is difficult to tell how the vestrymen were perceived by those whom they ruled. The neighbouring vestry of St Saviour's, which was of similar complexion to that of St Olave's, was heavily criticised within the parish during the first decade of the seventeenth century. A reformist group demanded that vestry membership be widened to bring in another ten persons assessed to the subsidy at £5, and that these men be chosen, and the accounts of the churchwardens audited, by all £3 subsidymen. The vestrymen were accused of wasting parish revenues on feasting, profiteering by granting leases to each other on favourable terms, and 'maintaining State and Precedence'. Although the vestrymen were able to offer a detailed and convincing defence of their management of parish affairs, the accusations demonstrate the kind of suspicions that might be aroused by bodies as exclusive as these extra-mural vestries. But there were limits to the breadth of support that the reformers could call upon. It was no movement for parish democracy as the subsidy qualifications for the new vestrymen were high and the demand for election by all the £3 men was soon dropped. Moreover, according to the vestrymen, 142 out of the parish's 195 subsidymen had expressed their preference for the existing course of government; the opposition, they claimed, could only count on the support of thirty. The agitation had apparently originated in a pewing dispute, as about twelve parishioners complained to the bishop of Winchester and then to the court of Chancery that they lacked the pews in church that their status demanded.[51] What the dispute therefore seems to indicate is that the greatest threat to the stability of select vestry constitutions came not from the poor but from the middling householders who found themselves denied the place in parish government and the status going with it to which they thought they were entitled.

We owe our knowledge of these events in St Saviour's to the chance survival of papers outlining the vestry's case: there is no mention of it in the

---

[50] P.R.O., PROB 11/125, fos. 227ᵛ–9.
[51] G.L.R.O., P92/SAV/787–97. It is perhaps worth emphasising that the documents in the parish archive reflect the vestry's version of events.

formal parish records which, by the standards of other parishes, are otherwise quite full. It is therefore possible that further research in documents outside parish archives, in particular the records of the equity courts, might unearth more evidence of controversies of the kind which disturbed this Southwark vestry. However, for the time being, the argument from silence is tempting. It would appear that local government usually allowed for a degree of participation by the middling sort sufficient to contain controversies. Parish and ward authorities performed the task of mediating between locality and elite quite effectively. But participation, as we have seen, had its limitations because office was confined to the upper levels of the society. The question of the means by which humbler citizens were integrated remains open. The following sections explore the formation of community consciousnesses in London, and the ways in which they aided the processes of social integration.

NEIGHBOURHOOD VALUES

The multi-layered structure of City government through companies, wards, and parishes set up a complex of interlocking loyalties which helped identify many Londoners with the regime. The loyalties were differently felt at different social levels: the wealthy participated in government, civic ritual, and shared feasting to a much greater degree than the poor whose identification with the institutions of the City was more often related to their roles as administrators of charity and dispensers of patronage. This meant that integration was much weaker at the lower levels of society because the degree of loyalty was related to the success of the relief system, and because there was no guarantee that the deferential values the system sought to inculcate were fully internalised. But all found themselves appealing to communal and neighbourhood values at some time, the more substantial inhabitants in their roles as arbitrators of disputes and enforcers of communal norms, and the poorer in their quest for charity and in their efforts to mobilise support for the redress of grievances.

To some extent the City itself provided a focus for the loyalties of its inhabitants. These loyalties were probably stronger for the wealthier sections of the population because their political rights and the level of their participation in civic ritual were much greater. Only liverymen enjoyed the right to participate in the election of the lord mayor and sheriffs, and usually only liverymen filled the barges which accompanied the mayor to his oath taking at Westminster, and lined the route to Guildhall on his return.[52] But

[52] Rappaport, *Worlds Within Worlds*, pp. 250–61; *Lord Mayors' Pageants*, ed. Sayle, pp. 2–3; 'A Journey through England and Scotland made by Lupold von Wedel in the years 1584 and 1585', ed. G. von Bulow, *T.R.H.S.*, new series, 9 (1895), 252–3; *C.S.P. Venetian*, XV. 58–63.

civic loyalties were not absent among the poorer sections of the population. The fact that most Londoners adopted the title 'citizen' when describing themselves in their wills suggests that the freedom was valued. The continual skirmishing between freemen and foreigners in the courts shows that their economic privileges were highly regarded. City customs, like that which governed the disposal of the moveable property of freemen, reserving a third for the widow and a third for minors, were widely respected. A high proportion of testators cited City custom in their wills: 57 per cent of London freemen who left minors and whose wills were proved in the commissary court during the 1590s specifically instructed that the custom of London was to be followed in the division of their estates.[53] Because the freedom was so valued those jurisdictional disputes between the City and outside authorities in which the aldermen became embroiled often had resonances at a popular level. For example, the wardmote of Tower ward petitioned against the lieutenant of the Tower's practice of retaliating to the arrest of any of his officers within the city by arresting several citizens. They thereby fuelled the interminable conflict between the City and the Tower liberty.[54] Moreover the multifarious responsibilities of corporation government meant that many citizens availed themselves of its services, like the hospitals and the stocks of grain and fuel.[55] In tackling the social problems confronting London the aldermen frequently had occasion to draw upon the rhetoric of the commonweal of the City and the obligations on the wealthy that it imposed. Thus profiteering poulterers were accused in 1561 of neglecting not only 'theire bounden duties towardes almightie god and the charitable usinge of their neighbours But also the common welthe of this Cytie'. Such a rhetoric, frequently articulated in proclamations and the public punishment of heinous offenders, conditioned the expectations of the poor regarding their rulers within a specifically civic context.[56]

Nevertheless the City was unlikely to have enjoyed a primary hold on the loyalties of its inhabitants. This was partly because access to civic benefits was often mediated through some other organisation. Thus recipients of the charity of Christ's Hospital required backing from their parish authorities, and it was only through the livery companies that the aldermen could be mobilised into supporting craft grievances against the non-free. Moreover the majority of social interactions appear to have taken place within a particular locality. This is one of the central messages of Jeremy Boulton's

---

[53] Below, pp. 133–40; G.L., MS 9171/18; C. Carlton, *The Court of Orphans* (Leicester, 1974).

[54] C.L.R.O., Samuel Barton's Book, fo. 47^v; P.R.O., SP12/157/22. Cf. B.L., Lansdowne MS 52/53 (Admiralty jurisdiction); C.L.R.O., Remembrancia I, no. 662 (Marshalsea jurisdiction).

[55] Below, pp. 200–1.

[56] C.L.R.O., Jour. 17, fo. 255^{r-v}; Jour. 18, fo. 271; Jour. 19, fo. 428; Jour. 20, fo. 467^v.

work on Southwark, which has established the existence of a wide range of relationships in which neighbours interacted with each other. Neighbourhood exercised a significant influence over the choice of marriage partners and overseers of wills, while kinship links strengthened the relationships between many householders in the area studied.[57]

The anonymity of life in the city can easily be exaggerated, for there is every indication that the obligations of neighbourhood were taken seriously. The existence of a rich cycle of neighbourhood feasting is hinted at by the orders of the aldermen in 1565 for the curtailment of the celebrations at lyings-in, christenings, and churchings in their campaign against extravagance.[58] Neighbours also regularly visited each other when sick. As one witness explained before the church courts, she had 'saluted and comforted the said testatrix as neighbours comonlie doo'.[59] Depositions in testamentary causes record respectable gatherings even at the death beds of plague victims.[60] Neighbours proferred advice on the making of the will, often acting as brokers between conflicting interests within the family. The wife of Thomas Johnson, worried by her husband's stipulation that a brother receive £40 on her death because she feared that she might not be worth so much when she died, was persuaded by the neighbours present that she had been adequately provided for, whereupon the assembled family wept for joy.[61] Pressure might be brought to bear on testators to appoint executors and overseers acceptable to the local community. Anne Rigby, a fairly prosperous widow of Aldgate, was requested to appoint 'such of her neighbors that were good & honest men', and persuaded to remove one Brown from the executorship of her will because he was 'disliked by the neighbors'.[62] When offenders were presented to the authorities, their misdeeds were often articulated in terms of their breach of neighbourhood values. Thus among those presented by the wardmote inquest of St Dunstan-in-the-West in 1566 were six wives 'being persons of evyll name and lyving & not worthy to dwell amongst honest neybowres', and three men being 'very unquiet persons & brabblers with their neighbours and not fit to dwell among neighbours'.[63]

Neighbours were well-informed about each other's behaviour because so much popular sociability took place within the street. Depositions in defamation cases leave one with the impression that London housewives spent much of their leisure hours standing in their doorways exchanging views on the doings of their wayward neighbours. Nor were workers insulated from the street because so much trade was carried on from shop boards pushed down into the street. Foreigners regularly remarked upon the

[57] Boulton, *Neighbourhood and Society*, ch. IX.   [58] Cw. Co., C.M. II, fo. 70ᵛ.
[59] G.L., MS 9065A/1A, fo. 65ᵛ.
[60] G.L., MS 9065A/2, fo. 1ᵛ.   [61] Ibid. fo. 138. Cf. G.L., MS 9065A/1A, fos. 124, 128.
[62] G.L., MSS 9065A/2, fos. 104ᵛ–110ᵛ; 9171/18, fo. 30.   [63] G.L., MS 3018/1, fo. 15ᵛ.

apprentices and journeymen at the doors of their masters' shops and on the streets distracting passers-by.[64] Behaviour was therefore constantly being evaluated within the community. A house might quickly gain an unsavoury reputation if strangers were seen to be frequenting it. James Armes, an alien resident of St Katherine Cree, found himself before the alderman's deputy because his neighbours 'marvelled at' the resort of one Francis Kenninghall, 'being a gentleman', and his wife 'an evell and suspected person'.[65] The need to defuse the suspicions of neighbours explains why they were called in to witness marriage contracts. John Washe explained that he summoned the neighbours so that 'they shold understand for what occasion ... John Pursidge did frequent his house ... to avoid evell report that may ensue'.[66] It is true that historians, among them myself, have misinterpreted the cases of spying by neighbours through windows, doors left ajar, cracks in floor-boards, and holes in walls, as normal neighbourly behaviour rather than the planned and legally purposeful activities to satisfy the prevailing modes of proof they often were.[67] Nevertheless, once neighbours decided that they wanted such proof, the cheek-by-jowl conditions in which most Londoners lived meant that it was easy to obtain. Tenements were crowded into narrow streets and linked by alleyways and courtyards. Buildings were densely populated with chambers in separate occupation accessible only by common stairways. It was clearly a society with a much less developed sense of privacy than our own.[68]

As we have seen, the disapproval of the neighbourhood was effected in the first instance through the sanction of gossip. But in many cases members of the community went further and intervened directly in an attempt to reform behaviour in breach of its norms. Thus the wife-beater Ralf Pollard, 'a very bedlam and a hasty fellowe, sone & for nothing sett in fury and radge', was 'divers tymes' rebuked by 'ye neighbors'.[69] The wife of John Farmer of St Clement Dane's complained on several occasions to her neighbours about her husband's behaviour, so that 'all the whole parishe did speake againste hym', and eventually secured the arbitration of their landlord.[70] In another case it was the headstrong wife who was subject to community disapproval. Thomas Sharpe explained that, having observed the strife between Joyce

[64] 'The London Journal of Alessandro Magno, 1562', ed. C. M. Barron, C. Coleman, and C. Gobbi, *London Journal*, 9 (1983), 146; 'A Description of England and Scotland by a French Ecclesiastic in the Sixteenth Century', *The Antiquarian Repertory*, 4 (1809), 503, 511.

[65] G.L., MSS 9056, fos. 33–5ᵛ; 9064/13, fo. 147ᵛ.   [66] G.L., MS 9056, fos. 27ʳ⁻ᵛ, 44–5.

[67] M. Ingram *Church Courts, Sex and Marriage in England, 1570–1640* (Cambridge, 1987), pp. 242–5; I. W. Archer, 'Governors and Governed in Late Sixteenth-Century London, *c*.1560–1603; Studies in the Achievement of Stability' (Oxford, D.Phil., 1988), p. 65.

[68] J. Schofield, *The Building of London from the Conquest to the Great Fire* (1984), pp. 144–8, 158–62; *The London Surveys of Ralph Treswell*, ed. J. Schofield (London Topographical Society, 1987), esp. pp. 79–82.

[69] G.L., MS 9056, fos. 17ᵛ, 21ᵛ.   [70] G.L.R.O., DL/C/213, fos. 25–30ᵛ.

Griffith and her husband, he 'being an olde man gave her good counsell and willed her to obey her husband and not to fall forth with him and fight & chyde that all the neyghbors spake thereof'.[71] The ritual humiliation of offenders through charivari, though not absent from London, seems to have been uncommon. I have encountered a few instances in the mid-century chronicles, but nothing in the later Elizabethan period. More widespread may have been libelling, the response of a more literate culture. In 1613, for example, Ellen Gresham of St Saviour Southwark was libelled as a whore in a ballad pinned to her door and dispersed about Southwark whose inhabitants, she complained, were 'laughinge scoffinge and iestinge thereatt and takinge greate pleasure & disporte in the same'.[72] Community sanctions against behaviour in breach of its norms remained powerful in London.

Should a delinquent fail to comply with these neighbourhood pressures, various more formal courses of action were available to the residents. It was often at the initiative of neighbours that delinquents were brought to the attention of the authorities, usually represented in the first instance by the alderman's deputy. The deputy could arrange an arbitrated settlement, or he could take the matter before a higher authority, usually either Bridewell or the sessions of the peace.[73] An alternative, and sometimes supplementary, route to an appearance before these awe-inspiring bodies was through a summons before the wardmote inquest during its Christmas sitting. In addition to the formal presentment of delinquents prior to proceedings at sessions, the inquests disposed of the power to order offenders out of the ward.[74] The inquestmen were usually acting in response to often well-organised pressure from the neighbours. Thus in 1614 John Burrell, haberdasher, was presented for barratry by the wardmote inquest of Farringdon Within after thirty of his neighbours put their signatures to a petition against him.[75] Yet another sanction lay in the presentment of delinquents to the church courts by the churchwardens and sidesmen.[76] Sometimes an offender could find himself pursued by several of these strategies simultaneously: those appearing before the church courts often alleged that they had already been punished for the offence in Bridewell.[77]

It should be clear that my emphasis on the strength of the ties of neighbourhood is not intended to suggest that the communities to which Londoners belonged were harmonious. On the contrary the same conditions

[71] G.L.R.O., DL/C/210, fo. 139.
[72] M. Ingram, 'Ridings, Rough Music and the "Reform of Popular Culture" in Early Modern England', *Past and Present*, 105 (1984), 79–113; *Machyn's Diary*, pp. 278, 301; *Three Fifteenth-Century Chronicles*, p. 132; P.R.O., STAC8/156/29; STAC8/41/12.
[73] Above, pp. 67–8.   [74] G.L.R.O., DL/C/210, fo. 96; DL/C/211, fo. 14.
[75] P.R.O., STAC8/62/8.
[76] G.L., MS 9236, second foliated section, fos. 10ᵛ, 12ᵛ, 13, 13ᵛ; G.L.R.O., DL/C/301, passim.
[77] Ibid. pp. 111–12, 135.

which made neighbours so aware of each other's shortcomings multiplied the occasions of conflict. This was because many disputes originated in the cramped conditions of the urban environment. The community's more substantial residents were often annoyed by the unsavoury practices of its lowlier members. Doctor Doyley, resident of the hospital close at St Bartholomew's, complained about neighbours who hung out their bedding and emptied stools at his window, and used the well to wash clothes at unreasonable hours.[78] Powerfully placed residents might threaten poorer inhabitants who competed with them. James Carter was suspected of abusing his position as a principal lessee in the Blackfriars to establish a monopoly of victualling there, undermining the competition from his sub-tenants by stopping the gate through which draymen had to pass in order to make deliveries.[79] But there were also many occasions of conflict within the ranks of the wealthy and among the poor themselves. Building activity by the wealthy was likely to threaten access to light that was so valued in the overcrowded city, while within alleys tenants might feel as irritated as Doyley by neighbours who, for example, swept puddles in front of their doors.[80] Although they are not well documented, the conflicts between freemen and foreigners must have had resonances at the local level. The conflict between the free and foreign joiners was a dispute between residents of the parish of St Olave Southwark.[81] Disputes between companies, like that between the Coopers and the Brewers, must also have led to neighbourhood tensions since these occupations lived in such close proximity.[82]

However, various mechanisms were available to defuse neighbourhood conflicts. In the first place, there was the sanction of organised religion, which emphasised that neighbours must be in charity with each other if they were to receive communion. Some of those summoned before the church courts for failure to take communion gave as their reason the fact that they were in dispute with neighbours.[83] Occasionally we encounter evidence that ministers would suspend from the communion those who were in flagrant breach of charity.[84] If the communion was valued, suspension may have been a strong incentive to seek a settlement of differences. Another sanction lay in the hostility of the community to those disruptive individuals who were too frequently in dispute with their neighbours. One's reputation and credit in the neighbourhood could be damaged by involvement in too many disputes.

[78] S.B.H., Ha 1/3, fos. 107, 136.   [79] P.R.O., C24/120, Rey vs. Moore and Bradshaw.

[80] *A.P.C.*, XXIX. 37–8; P.R.O., STAC8/59/12; STAC8/126/10; G.L., MS 9065A/2, fo. 24; *London Viewers and their Certificates, 1509–1558*, ed. J. S. Loengard (London Record Society, XXVI, 1989).

[81] *Returns of Aliens Dwelling in the City and Suburbs of London*, ed. R. E. G. and E. F. Kirk (Huguenot Society Publications, X, 4 vols., 1900–8), II. 321–3; G.L.R.O., P71/OLA/9.

[82] H.M.C., *Third Report*, p. 8; H.M.C., *House of Lords*, XI. 30–1.

[83] G.L., MSS 9064/12, fo. 25; 9064/15, fos. 43ᵛ–4, 52, 186; G.L.R.O., DL/C/301, p. 216.

[84] G.L., MSS 9234/1, fo. 55; 9064/13, fos. 62ᵛ–3ᵛ.

Individuals described as 'of no creditt or estimacion, but a contensious scoffinge and brablinge fellowe', 'one that most uniustly seketh the vexacion of her neighbours', 'a contentious person sowing suits among the neighbours' had clearly lost standing.[85] Finally, and most importantly, members of the community were ready to negotiate arbitrations. Clergymen, the wardmote inquest, the alderman's deputy, landlords, and vestrymen all intervened. In 1564 the vestry of St Mary Magdalen Milk Street determined on monthly meetings with their vicar 'to hear matters of variance'. Inquests negotiated settlements and took sureties of disruptive parties for their good behaviour.[86] Moreover, in cases where the parties did go to law, proceedings were often brought to a close by a locally negotiated arbitration. Thus we are told that a defamation suit in the court of arches between Anne Pridgen and Christopher Thompson was taken up by 'earneste intreatie of neighbors and freendes', and settled at a local tavern where damages were agreed by the friends on both sides.[87]

Enough has been said to qualify the notion of 'urban anomie' and to demonstrate the strength of neighbourhood ties. But it is not clear whether the obligations of neighbourhood were differently perceived and regarded at different social levels. How far did cooperation transcend the social divisions within the community? It is easy enough to demonstrate that neighbours visited each other when sick, but much more difficult to determine whether wealthy parishioners felt an obligation to visit their poorer neighbours. The poor certainly laboured under strong prejudices about their worth. These emerge clearly in the efforts of poor witnesses to establish their credibility before the courts: 'he is a poore labouring man viz a carman and therby getteth his living honestlie and trulie but he is litle or nothing worth'; 'her husband is a poore man, but an honest man'.[88] The existence of such prejudices surely affected the pattern of social relations within the neighbourhood. It is easy enough to show the sanction of neighbourhood opinion against what was regarded as deviant behaviour, but more difficult to be sure whether one is capturing the sanction of the whole community or merely one section of it which had appropriated the rhetoric of neighbourhood. Such distinctions are occasionally hinted at as when we are told of the 'common fame among the substanciall men and wymen', or of the 'honest' parishioners making complaint.[89] On some offences there undoubtedly was a

[85] G.L., MSS 9065A/2, fos. 177ᵛ–8, 179; 9064/13, fo. 2; 9056, fos. 63ʳ⁻ᵛ, 83ᵛ; G.L.R.O., DL/C/213, p. 394.
[86] G.L.R.O., DL/C/213, p. 506 (clergy); G.L., MSS 4570/2, pp. 434, 438, 440; 2590/1, p. 16 (vestry); G.L.R.O., DL/C/213, fo. 30ᵛ; Stow, *Survey of London*, I. lxi. (landlords); G.L., MS 4069/1, fo. 31ᵛ (wardmote inquest); above n. 26 for deputies.
[87] G.L.R.O., DL/C/211, fo. 155; DL/C/213, p. 445.
[88] G.L., MS 9065A/1A, fo. 31; G.L.R.O., DL/C/211, fo. 187ᵛ.
[89] G.L.R.O., DL/C/213, p. 293.

consensus. Although the hostility of the substantial parishioners to deviant sexual behaviour was intensified by fears about the burden on the rates and often by a keenly felt religious ideology, their disapproval was echoed lower down the social scale where the preoccupation of humble citizens with sexual reputation emerges in the language of defamation suits. But where the prosecution of offences directly affected the economy of the poor, as in alehouse keeping or the taking of inmates, the reality of social distinction was more apparent.

The consciousness of the poor as a group apart threatening respectable society was enhanced by their tendency to cluster together in alleys, forming small sub-communities, only partially integrated with the rest of the parish. A common identity might be fostered by a common landlord, by shared facilities like privies, and by the 'chafer' system whereby tenants were sometimes obliged to make their purchases at particular victualling establishments.[90] The frequent assessments for the cleaning of privies were predicated on the assumption of some capacity for common action among the residents of alleys.[91] Sometimes they displayed a remarkable self-consciousness. The tenants of an alley in St Botolph Aldgate petitioned the lord mayor to get their parish to provide them with privies, while the tenants of Christopher Alley demanded to be discharged by the Armourers' Company of assessments to the scavengers' rate, 'orelles they wold exclayme of the company either to the Quene or to the lordes of her Majesties counsell'.[92] This self-consciousness was further focused by the hostility of the local establishment to alleys because of the threat they posed to public health, the morals of the people they attracted, and the prospect of an increasing burden on the poor rates. Katherine Wheel Alley in Thames Street, where nine good tenements formerly inhabited by 'honest citizens' had been converted into forty-three tenements shortly after 1584, was soon the object of local resentment. 'The waie and passage of the same alley', the parishioners complained, was

so streighted, as that two persons canne hardly passe thone by the other whereby the Aire is greatelie pestered, which maye breede daunger in the tyme of Infeccion. The poore tenementes beinge highlie rented, receave many Inmates and other base and poore people of badd condicions to the great trouble and annoiaunce of the honest neighbours that inhabite there and the whole warde who have made very earnest and importune sute for reformacion of the said ally by pluckinge down such unnecessary buildinges.

[90] *T.E.D.*, III. 427; G.L., MS 12806/2, fo. 224; C.L.R.O., Southwark Manor Court Book, 1539–64, fo. 276.
[91] S.B.H., Ha1/2, fo. 232ᵛ; Ha1/3, fos. 122, 167; G.L.R.O., SKCS 18, fo. 285ᵛ.
[92] G.L., MSS 9234/7, fo. 154; 12071/2, p. 521.

Examples of such sentiments can be multiplied from all over the city.[93] Wardmote presentments frequently identified alleys as the source of local nuisances.[94] Those with an interest in the administration of poor relief like John Howes looked with alarm on the spread of alleys because of the volume of charity they consumed.[95] The proliferation of alleys which was so much a feature of the later sixteenth century therefore contributed to the heightened profile of poverty in the capital and the rising consciousness of social distinctions.[96]

Impoverishment therefore might have contributed to the corrosion of the sense of community. But the alley did not establish an exclusive hold on loyalties any more than did a company, parish, or the City, and there remained ways in which the poor might feel they had common interests with the wealthier residents of their parish. Community might survive in spite of intensifying social stratification, although social interactions would now be shaped more by relationships of patronage and deference. The remainder of this chapter attempts to assess the degree to which the parish set up loyalties which might to some extent transcend social divisions, by looking at the services the parish provided for its residents, the level of religious observance in London parishes, and the ways in which community values were affected by the developing sense of social stratification.

THE PARISH AND IDENTITY

There are serious problems involved in regarding the parish as defining the boundaries of the local community, particularly in an urban context. No geographical area will satisfactorily describe the boundaries of a local social system in the sense of the area within which the social relationships of inhabitants were constructed because it will not include all the termini of the social relationships involved.[97] This is especially true of London because of the existence of non-territorial communities in the form of the livery companies. Occupational solidarities could produce common action among artisans from different quarters. The feltmakers' riot in Southwark in 1592 united inhabitants of the borough with residents of the Blackfriars liberty on

---

[93] Mc. Co., C.M. IV, fos. 8–9; Cw. Co., C.M. II, fos. 193ᵛ–4, 201ᵛ, 219, 222ᵛ; G.L., MS 4072/1, fos. 71, 84; S.B.H., Hc 9/1, fos. 28ᵛ, 33ᵛ.

[94] G.L., MS 3018/1, fos. 39ᵛ, 41ᵛ, 43ᵛ, 53a.

[95] *Contemporaneous Account of the Foundation and Early History of Christ's Hospital, and of Bridewell and Saint Thomas' Hospitals by John Howes* (privately printed, 1889), pp. 32–3.

[96] C.L.R.O., Jour. 16, fos. 120ᵛ–1; Jour. 19, fos. 255ʳ⁻ᵛ, 325ʳ⁻ᵛ; Boulton, *Neighbourhood and Society*, pp. 170–5; Stow, *Survey of London*, I. 124, 128–9, 149, 163, 237, 284; II. 60, 65, 71, 72, 79.

[97] Boulton, *Neighbourhood and Society*, pp. 228–31. For the parish as a unit of identity, see N. Alldridge, 'Loyalty and Identity in Chester Parishes, 1540–1640', in *Parish, Church and People: Local Studies in Lay Religion*, ed. S. Wright (1988), pp. 85–124.

the other side of the river.[98] Hence the sense of common identity need not necessarily flow from geographical proximity. Moreover some parishes were so large that they might include several neighbourhood communities; others were so small that it is hard to envisage their residents making a majority of their social contacts within that parish.

The identification between neighbourhood and parish is further muddied by the fact that the parish was not the only local administrative division, for the City was divided into wards and precincts whose boundaries did not coincide with those of the parishes. Several parishes therefore found themselves split between two wards. These divisions had real meaning to citizens. Attendance at the December wardmotes was compulsory and freedom certificates registered there. All citizens were subject to ward taxes like the scavenger's rate and the assessment for the beadle's wages, while the main national tax, the subsidy, was assessed and collected on a ward basis. The more substantial residents served in the ward offices, while ward officials like the alderman's deputy played a key role in the life of the neighbourhood. It was on a ward basis that the rotation of householders to serve in the City watch was determined. Moreover, the sitting of the wardmote in December was the occasion for feasting among the inhabitants: accounts from Bassishaw ward commencing in the mid seventeenth century show contributions towards a feast from between sixty-five and eighty householders, possibly one third of the total, although it is hard to envisage such widespread participation in the overcrowded extramural wards.[99]

But there is a strong case for asserting the primary importance of ties to the parish in the local context. The 'average' parish in London was relatively small by continental standards, and therefore a meaningful unit of identity.[100] It was by reference to their parish and only very rarely to a ward that Londoners defined where they lived. Hardly anyone but a few aldermen bequeathed money to the poor on a ward basis. As we have seen many vestries had appropriated the functions of the precinct meetings in nominating ward officials, and these officials often acted on the instructions of

---

[98] C.L.R.O., Remembrancia I, no. 662.

[99] Pearl, 'Change and Stability', pp. 15–26; C.L.R.O., Jour. 22, fo. 318 (subsidy); G.L., MS 3505, fos. 3 (proceedings at wardmote), 22ᵛ–3 (watch); above, pp. 63–8 (office holding and deputies); G.L., MSS 2505/1; 3461/1 (feast accounts).

[100] Rouen with thirty-six parishes had a population of between 71,000 and 78,000 in 1600, Lyon with nine parishes 65,000 in 1555, Toledo with twenty-one parishes 62,000 in 1571, London with 114 parishes 140,000 in 1595: P. Benedict, *Rouen During the Wars of Religion* (Cambridge, 1981), p. 3; N. Z. Davis, 'The Sacred and the Body Social in Sixteenth-Century Lyon', *Past and Present*, 90 (1981), 43, 52; L. Martz, *Poverty and Welfare in Habsburg Spain: the Example of Toledo* (Cambridge, 1983), pp. 95–6; Finlay, *Population and Metropolis*, pp. 155, 168–71. Cf. J. Shakespeare and M. Dowling, 'Religion and Politics in Mid-Tudor England Through the Eyes of an English Protestant Woman: the Recollections of Rose Hickman', *B.I.H.R.*, 55 (1982), 101.

vestrymen.[101] Although the share of each parish to ward taxes was determined by the inquest, the task of assessing parishioners usually fell to the vestry.[102] The wardmote met only once a year, whereas the parish was supposed to be united in prayer at least once a week. After the disappearance of the Midsummer watches the ward's role in civic ritual withered, whereas rituals identifying the parish, though much attenuated after the Reformation, persisted in Rogationtide processions.[103]

Parish records are soaked in the rhetoric of neighbourly unity. In doggerel of embarrassing awfulness the parish clerk of St Botolph Billingsgate composed the following verses:

Even as stickes may easselly be broken
So when neighbours agre not then ther is a confucion
But a great many of stickes bound in one boundell will hardly be broken
So neighbours being ioyned in love together can never be severed.[104]

Parish funds subsidised dinners so that 'the unitie and neighborlie meeting might be contynewed'.[105] Vestrymen addressed each other as 'your loving neyghbors and friendes'.[106] It was 'in regard of Neyghbourhood' that the vestrymen of St Botolph Aldgate expressed their reluctance to press for full sanctions against defaulters in an assessment to church repair.[107] The desire to increase brotherly love and unity was even cited in support of the establishment of select vestries as at Allhallows Staining.[108]

But how far was the community of the parish realised in practice? The very insistence with which the rhetoric was pressed may in itself be a sign of the failure to measure up to its demands. Lane's will warns us that the impression of harmony and consensus conveyed by the parish records might conceal the existence of very real tensions within the parish. Parish clerks were careful to conceal the existence of controversies: the sharp words that passed between two churchwardens in St Alphage Cripplegate have been carefully scrubbed out of the record.[109] Furthermore, the parochial community in sixteenth-century London was subject to strains which might have eroded the sense of common identity. Population increase and impoverishment, particularly in the extramural wards, sharpened the awareness of social distinctions, and the Reformation introduced potentially divisive forms of religious doctrine and practice. Thomas Bentley's early chronicle of

[101] Above, pp. 68–9.
[102] *Vestry Minutes of Saint Bartholomew Exchange*, pp. 8, 20, 33.
[103] M. Berlin, 'Civic Ceremony in Early Modern London', *Urban History Yearbook*, 1986, 15–27; for Rogationtide see below, p. 87.
[104] G.L., MS 943/1, flyleaf.   [105] G.L., MSS 1175/1, fo. 44; 1311/1, fo. 98ᵛ.
[106] G.L., MS 9236, fo. 78.
[107] G.L., MS 9234/5B, fos. 221ᵛ, 264ʳ⁻ᵛ, 266ᵛ.
[108] G.L., MS 4957/1, ordinances of 1574.
[109] G.L., MS 1432/3, fo. 34ᵛ.

parochial life in St Andrew Holborn might on the one hand be taken as evidence of the strength of parochial consciousness in Elizabethan London; on the other hand its message was that the coherence of the community was being eroded. He looked back nostalgically to the days when church repair had been financed by plays, shooting matches, church ales and drinkings, and commented bitterly on the increased litigiousness of the parishioners who failed to settled their disputes before the vestrymen but turned out of the local community to the justice of the peace.[110] The discussion of the parish's role in the life of its inhabitants which follows, therefore, seeks to bear in mind the tensions to which the community was subject and the changes it was undergoing.

Parish vestries controlled a wide range of resources for the benefit of the community. The vestrymen of St Olave Southwark owned a considerable amount of property locally, available for leasing to a wide range of parishioners. At one end of the spectrum were the chambers in the church-yard leased at low rents to the poor; at the other lay choice tenements leased by vestrymen themselves.[111] The vestry also managed commons on Horsey Down, regulating the digging of gravel by parishioners on the common and the number of cattle they might keep.[112] Four pumps maintained by the parish supplied water to the inhabitants.[113] Recreational facilities were also provided by the parish as the churchwardens regularly repaired the butts on the down.[114] With the help of a bequest from Henry Leake and the benevolence of parishioners, St Olave's had been provided with its own school in 1561 'to teche the cheldarne of the sayd parryshe to wrete and rede and caste accoumptes'.[115] In addition to administering the income from their own poor rate, they disbursed substantial sums in legacies, and by the first years of the seventeenth century managed small loan stocks for the benefit of parishioners and a stock of £30 to provide coal at below market rates for the poor.[116] St Olave's was perhaps exceptional in the range of its parochially managed resources, but all parishes controlled resources for the poor, and most owned some property. Although there were few parochially managed endowed schools in London, many vestries were prepared to support

---

[110] E. Griffith, *Cases of Supposed Exemption from Poor Rates Claimed on Grounds of Extra-Parochiality, with a Preliminary Sketch of the Ancient History of the Parish of St Andrew Holborn* (1831); C. M. Barron, *The Parish of St. Andrew Holborn* (1979), p. 31; G.L., MS 4249, fos. 13, 222ᵛ.

[111] Southwark Archives, St Olave's C.W.A., rentals; Society of Antiquaries, MS 236.

[112] Southwark Archives, St Olave's V.M., fos. 4ᵛ, 26, 66ʳ⁻ᵛ, 71ᵛ, 94ᵛ.

[113] Ibid. fo. 39.   [114] Ibid. fo. 66.

[115] Ibid. fos. 18ᵛ, 21; P.R.O., PROB 11/43, fo. 180; C.P.R., 1569–72, p. 298; R. C. Carring-ton, *Two Schools: a History of the Saint Olave's and Saint Saviour's Grammar School Foundation* (1971).

[116] Society of Antiquaries MS 236, fo. 46; Southwark Archives, St Olave's V.M., fos. 111, 113ᵛ.

education by allowing a schoolmaster the use of the vestry house or the church porch to teach in.[117] Many undertook the maintenance of pumps or conduits, the vestry of St Margaret Moses, for example, levying 1d. a year from every householder towards the maintenance of the pump.[118] Where parishes did not have access to endowed loan stocks, they sometimes, as in St Andrew Wardrobe, loaned out the church stock from year to year.[119]

In managing these resources parishes discriminated against the outsider. Preference was to be given in the parish schools to the children of parishioners; the parishioners of St Martin Ludgate ordered that waterbearers using the parish's conduit were not to carry water out of the parish; the vestry of St Dunstan in the West ordered that non-parishioners washing bucks at the Whitefriars Bridge, recently repaired at the parishioners's expense, should pay higher rates; and non-parishioners were debarred from keeping animals on the commons in St Olave's.[120] The most interesting consequences of discrimination against the outsider derived from the application of residence qualifications in the distribution of poor relief. Vestries required three years' residence in the parish before they would consider applications for regular relief, and more exacting conditions were sometimes applied in access to the more generous kinds of relief such as the six years' continual residence required by the parish of St Botolph Aldgate of applicants for places in its almshouses.[121] Residence qualifications opened a split in the ranks of the poor because the pensioner poor had an interest in keeping down the number of immigrants. This was harnessed by parish authorities in their use of the poor to keep out vagrants in posts such as the staff bearers introduced in 1557 and the salaried warders for vagrant persons which emerged in the 1570s.[122] The boundaries of the community were thus defined partly by means of exclusion, and in such a way that unwelcome newcomers were left stranded, and divided from the rest of the poor by discriminatory social policies.

Another means by which community consciousness might be enhanced was through the experience of conflict with other communities or individuals outside the community over resources. The interest of the community in the

[117] G.L., MSS 3016/1, fos. 37, 45; 1175/1, fo. 38ᵛ; 3570/1, fo. 48ᵛ; 2596/1, fo. 209ᵛ; 4165/1, pp. 7, 21, 24, 26 etc.
[118] *The Records of two City Parishes: A Collection of Documents Illustrative of the History of St Anne and St Agnes Aldersgate, and St John Zachary, London*, ed. W. McMurray (1925), p. 76; G.L., MSS 4415/1, fo. 14; 1431/1, fos. 9ᵛ, 10ᵛ; 3476/1, fos. 107ᵛ, 110, 114; P.R.O., E117/4/89; L.P.L., Holy Trinity Minories C.W.A., fos. 43, 48.
[119] G.L., MS 2088/1, 1588–9 acct.
[120] G.L., MSS 1311/1, fo. 72; 3016/1, p. 25; Southwark Archives, St Olave's V.M., fos. 4ᵛ, 36.
[121] G.L., MSS 9236, fos. 71, 77ᵛ; 4072/1, fo. 76.
[122] G.L., MS 12806/1, fo. 6; C.L.R.O., Rep. 13, fos. 531ᵛ–2; Anderson, 'Treatment of Vagrancy', p. 416.

collection of taxes, some of which, like the fifteenth and scavenger's rate were assessed on a lump sum basis among parishes, made vestrymen particularly sensitive over boundaries. Clashes between parishes over the question of their entitlement to collect rates from particular properties occurred regularly. The parish of St Peter Cornhill, for example, was involved in controversies with both St Michael Cornhill and St Martin Outwich over particular properties.[123] The importance of boundaries gave parishes an incentive to maintain their Rogationtide processions in spite of their tiny size.[124] Their ownership of property and charitable functions meant that many parishes were involved in litigation with adversaries as varied as the Crown's patentees for concealed lands, tight-fisted executors, and other parishes with whom they disputed entitlement to charitable resources. Thus the parishioners of St Olave's clashed with their neighbours in St Saviour's over payments from the will of Henry Leake in 1567, with its absentee parson over the collection of tithe in 1570, with the alien brewer, John Powell, over the stopping of a mill pond in 1584–7 and, in over twenty years' litigation, with the executors of one Dowsett's will.[125] Litigation was often financed by means of assessments on or loans from the more substantial parishioners,[126] but the implications for the availability of charity in the community that the lawsuits often involved, and the continual deployment of the rhetoric concerning the parish's obligations to relieve the poor, meant that litigation might have wider resonances among the poor themselves.[127]

The level of religious observance in early modern London is a crucial variable in determining the degree of identity with the parish and of the capacity for local loyalties to transcend social divisions. How far was the ideal of each local society united in prayer and communion realised? This is one of the most intractable problems confronting the social historian because of the ambiguity of much of the evidence relating to popular religion and because of disagreements among historians over the perspective from which they view popular behaviour. Replying to those who cite the stream of complaint from preachers about their sleepy congregations as evidence of popular apathy, Margaret Spufford has rightly emphasised the dangers of

[123] G.L., MSS 4165/1, pp. 30, 46, 52, 94, 109, 116; 951/1, fo. 10; 4072/1, fo. 80; C.L.R.O., Rep. 24, fos. 152, 177ᵛ, 203, 362ᵛ; Rep. 25, fos. 130ᵛ–1.
[124] G.L., MSS 4165/1, p. 30; 1176/1, accts. for 1590–1, 1591–2, 1592–3 etc.
[125] Southwark Archives, St Olave's V.M., fos. 31ᵛ, 35; C.W.A., p. 192 (for litigation over Leake bequest costing parish £39. 6s. 3d.); V.M., fo. 37 (parson), 67ᵛ, 78ᵛ, 79 (litigation with Powell costing parish £65. 3s. 7d.), 80ᵛ, 90ᵛ, 97; Society of Antiquaries MS 236, fos. 62ᵛ, 63ᵛ–4 (Dowsett). There was also recurrent litigation over the parish's title to Horsey Down: Carrington, *Two Schools*, p. 42.
[126] *Accomptes of the Churchwardens of the Paryshe of St. Christofer's in London, 1575 to 1662*, ed. E. Freshfield (1885), pp. 18, 22, 24.
[127] P.R.O., C2, Eliz. I, S25/60; C2, Eliz. I, C24/13; C24/135, Barker vs. Powntney.

adopting the highly demanding standards of the godly preachers to measure popular attitudes.[128]

There is no doubt that the Protestant Reformation was more successful in London than in any other part of the kingdom. The capital boasted an extraordinary wealth of sermons, up to three a week in a parish like St Botolph Aldgate.[129] High literacy rates meant that protestantism enjoyed a favourable environment.[130] The presses poured forth a torrent of religious literature much of it, like the plague sermons, of specific relevance to Londoners. Within a few weeks of an earthquake in London in 1580 the Stationers' registers record licences to print seventeen pamphlets drawing on the recent experience as a token of divine wrath and the need for speedy repentance.[131] As far as one can tell the duty of catechising was taken seriously, even in the extramural parishes. Churchwardens' accounts include payments for boards to carry the rota of householders whose members were to be catechised. The vestry of St Botolph Aldgate arranged for the division of the manor of East Smithfield into four so that servants and children could be catechised in rotation.[132] Preachers coming up to the city from the provinces felt that they were moving from darkness into light 'for here the word of God is plentifully preached'.[133] In London one encounters that extraordinary phenomenon of a minister expressing some satisfaction with the spiritual state of his congregation. In spite of a ministry in the difficult extramural parish of Saint Olave's James Balmford had occasion to commend his parishioners 'for in sundry things ye shew the obedience of faith. Amongst the rest, ye attend the Sacrament of Baptisme, from which in most places people runne away most contemptuously.' He also noted that his church was full on days of fasting and at his Friday lecture.[134]

Moreover, there is little evidence of the positive rejection of the Church by Londoners. Parishioners were frequently cited before the church courts for

128 M. Spufford, 'Can We Count the "Godly" and the Conformable in the Seventeenth Century?', *Journal of Ecclesiastical History*, 36 (1985), 428–38; E. Duffy, 'The Godly and the Multitude in Stuart England', *The Seventeenth Century*, 1 (1986), 31–55; P. Collinson, *Religion of Protestants*, ch. V; C. A. Haigh, 'The Church of England, the Catholics and the People', in *Reign of Elizabeth I*, ed. Haigh, pp. 195–219.
129 H. G. Owen, 'The London Parish Clergy in the Reign of Elizabeth I' (London Ph.D., 1957), pp. 91, 102, 112–14, 122–5, 150, 185–6, 389, 455.
130 D. Cressy, *Literacy and the Social Order. Reading and Writing in Tudor and Stuart England* (Cambridge, 1980), pp. 72–5, 120–1, 128–9, 134–5.
131 M. Spufford, *Small Books and Pleasant Histories. Popular Fiction and its Readership in Seventeenth-Century England* (1981), ch. VIII; *Stationers' Registers*, II. 367–75.
132 G.L., MSS 1013/1, fos. 23ᵛ, 67; 1046/1, fo. 2ᵛ; 2895/1, fo. 233; 5090/2, fo. 95; 4241/1, pp. 25, 103, 139–40; 9236, second foliated section, fo. 1ᵛ; 4249, fo. 235ᵛ; 3016/1, fo. 2ᵛ
133 E. Bush, *A Sermon Preached at Pauls Crosse* (1576), sig. F ii; W. Fisher, *A Sermon Preached at Paules Crosse* (1580), fo. 2.
134 J. Balmford, *A Short Dialogue Concerning the Plagues Infection* (1603), sigs. A iii – A iv. It remains true that a full church in a parish the size of St Olave's does not indicate universal attendance.

failure to attend church or to receive communion, but the reasons they gave for their delinquency do not suggest a fundamental disrespect for the Established Church. They often explained that it was a matter of economic necessity that they work on the Sabbath, because as tailors they had to satisfy a sudden surge in demand, or as clothworkers they needed to take advantage of fair weather after several days' rain to stretch their cloths.[135] The most constantly reiterated reason for not receiving communion among Londoners was a fear of arrest for debt if they ventured out of doors. Thus William Croft of Wapping explained that 'he kepeth his howse for feare of execution that is owte againste him for debte ... that he doth not forbeare to receave the communion for conscience and that he is contented to receave the same when his trobles be past'.[136] Others claimed that they were reluctant to receive while out of charity with their neighbours, and this, as Don Spaeth has argued, might be taken as a sign of the strength of popular religious feeling, as people adopted a more literal interpretation of the prayer book rubrics than their ministers intended.[137] Besides such explanations as these, cases of blasphemy are rare.[138]

However, comparison with the standards of rural England does not necessarily mark a high level of observance in absolute terms. Nor does the lack of evidence for popular blasphemy tell us much about the *kind* of religion experienced by the ordinary parishioner, whose outlook may have been very different from that demanded by the godly. The occasionally flattering remarks of preachers about the quality of their London congregations have to be set against their vociferous denunciations of those who neglected attendance at church for Sunday pleasures.[139] And the discussion so far has made no allowance for the possibility of variations in the level of religious observance in different parts of the capital. *Prima facie*, it is likely that standards were higher in the small inner-city parishes of between sixty and eighty households than in the extramural parishes with upwards of 1,000 households, whose churches could not contain the whole population. Although practices such as staggered communions meant that religion might touch in some sense upon the lives of a majority of the inhabitants in the extramural parishes, there was no way in which they could truly realise the community at prayer, which was a regular possibility in the inner-city parishes. The realities of church space meant that only substantial householders could enjoy a pew in the more populous parishes. In inner-city parishes, on the other hand, nearly all householders might have access to a

---

[135] G.L., MSS 9064/13, fos. 146, 228ᵛ; 9064/14, fos. 36ᵛ, 51.

[136] G.L., MS 9064/15, fos. 9ᵛ, 30ᵛ, 105ᵛ, 106, 118, 141ᵛ-2.

[137] D. Spaeth, 'Common Prayer? Popular Observance of the Anglican Liturgy in Restoration Wiltshire', in *Parish, Church and People*, ed. Wright, pp. 125–51.

[138] G.L., MS 9064/15, fos. 34ᵛ, 64ᵛ.   [139] Collinson, *Religion of Protestants*, p. 204.

pew.[140] This would have made it immediately apparent which families were failing in their duties of weekly church attendance. The fact that vestry minutes from inner-city parishes record complaints of non-attendance, whereas those of the extramural parishes tend to be silent on the issue, probably reflects the greater practicability of regular attendance in the smaller units.[141]

The statistical evidence for religious observance is extremely sparse and, where it does exist, difficult to interpret. Jeremy Boulton has established from the token books of St Saviour Southwark that a very high proportion of the population (between 80 per cent and 98 per cent) of this extramural parish attended Easter communion in the 1620s.[142] Unfortunately the impact of this conclusion is blunted by two considerations. First, attendance at Easter communion represents a minimal level of commitment, as parishioners were required by law to attend three times a year.[143] London parishes followed the best reformed practice in celebrating communion monthly.[144] It is clear that while large numbers may have communicated at Easter, the monthly communions were attended by only a minority. In St Botolph Aldgate, the *total* number of communicants at the non-Easter communions in 1598 was 507, compared to 1,758 attending Easter communion. In other words, only a minority of parishioners communicated more than once a year.[145] Secondly, the evidence from St Botolph Aldgate in the 1590s also suggests a much lower level of overall attendance (between 38 per cent and 56 per cent depending on assumptions about population) than that found in Southwark thirty years later.[146] Likewise, attendance levels were lower in St Stephen Coleman Street in the later Elizabethan period, where in 1602 there were 685 communicants out of a potential 908, an attendance rate of 75 per cent.[147]

It is not easy to explain these variations. Perhaps some London parishes were operating closed communion systems where applicants were screened for their worthiness, as recommended by some puritan critics of the church. If this did happen then it is an indication of the divisive impact of puritan ideology and practices on parish life. But there is in fact little evidence for closed communions. Particularly scandalous individuals may have been

---

[140] G.L., MS 1175/1, church seating plans for 1582, 1593, and 1597; Southwark Archives, St Olave's V.M., fo. 41.

[141] G.L., MS 1175/1, fos. 7, 40ᵛ; *Vestry Minutes of Saint Margaret Lothbury*, p. 27.

[142] J.P. Boulton, 'The Limits of Formal Religion: the Administration of Holy Communion in Late Elizabethan and Early Stuart London', *London Journal*, 10 (1984), 135–54.

[143] Ibid. p. 138.

[144] Ibid. p. 141; G.L., MSS 1013/1, fos. 33, 34ᵛ, 37ᵛ, 40, 42; 1176/1, accts. for 1585–6, 1586–7, 1591–2.

[145] Boulton, 'Limits of Formal Religion', p. 141.   [146] Ibid. p. 153, n. 56.

[147] G.L., MS 4457/2, fo. 70: £17. 11s. 4d. due in Easter offerings from parishioners; £1. 16s. 10d. not received.

barred, but there is little sign of general screening. If the practice was more widespread, one would have expected more evidence in the form of complaints against it, both in the church court material and in sermons. Moreover, it would remain difficult to explain why two puritan parishes, St Botolph Aldgate and St Saviour Southwark, of similar social complexion, behaved in different ways.[148] Alternatively, one might explain the variations in attendance rates as a reflection of variations in administrative practice, the difference between an active and a passive system for the distribution of tokens.[149] If this was the case, then the relatively low levels of attendance in Elizabethan London suggest a lack of spontaneous enthusiasm for the communion service. However we explain the low levels of attendance in Elizabethan London, it is clear that they provide some evidence of the failure of the Established Church to integrate all its parishioners in the metropolitan environment.

Did the lines of religious commitment follow the lines of social stratification? It is certainly tempting to assume that a high level of religious commitment prevailed among the more substantial parishioners and that the hold of organised religion on the poor was weak. The gulf may have been reinforced by the puritan commitment of the rulers. We know that the godly in London regarded themselves as a minority, and we also have evidence of the advanced protestant commitment of many of the rulers.[150] However, such an argument is vulnerable to the silence of the sources on the religious commitment of the poor. There are no lists of those attending communion in Elizabethan London which might be linked to local rate assessments. It is dangerous to assume a lack of commitment among the poor in general, for it is possible that they were divided by religion, that the contemporary discrimination between the godly and the unregenerate poor had some foundation in reality. Richard Turnbull, minister at St Pancras Soper Lane, warned his congregation against overmuch regard for the wealthy and 'contempt of the poore, which are religious, zealous, vertuous & honest'.[151] Some paupers may have been among the most diligent attenders of church because receipt of poor relief was often conditional upon it. Regular attendance at church was required of almsmen. David Smith expected the inmates of his almshouses in Castle Baynard ward to attend services in St Benet Paul's Wharf every Sunday, Monday, Wednesday, and Friday, subject to penalties of 2d. for non-attendance.[152] Many parishes arranged for

148 Boulton, 'Limits of Formal Religion', pp. 139, 142; above, n. 84.
149 Boulton, 'Limits of Formal Religion', pp. 142–3.
150 Above, pp. 45–7; P. Seaver, *Wallington's World. A Puritan Artisan in Seventeenth-Century London* (1985), pp. 22, 62–3, 104, 143.
151 R. Turnbull, *An Exposition Upon the Canonicall Epistle of Saint James* (1606 edn), pp. 96–7.
152 *Holinshed's Chronicles*, IV. 549–50; Boulton, *Neighbourhood and Society*, p. 144.

weekly distributions from the revenues of endowed charities to be made in church, while others made piecemeal distributions from legacies every week at the church door.[153] It is difficult to determine in what state of mind the poor attended these services. Attendance may have been constrained but, if it ran at the levels envisaged by the benefactors, it is likely that the prevalent religious values became internalised, if they were not already. In this sense, at least, the godly poor existed.

The parish therefore, subject to some important qualifications, was an important unit of identity, creating mutual ties among its members, rich and poor alike. The poorer members did not feel completely alienated from the institutions of local government because they benefited from some of the services vestries provided. The wealthier members acknowledged that their power within the local community imposed paternalistic obligations upon them. It is true that local loyalties could not entirely transcend the implications of social and cultural polarisation, but it should be appreciated that these two processes were not necessarily mutually reinforcing, given that the lines of religious division did not always follow those of social stratification. The complexity of the divisions helps explain the resilience of parochial identity in a period of considerable stress. The following section takes further this discussion of the persistence of community consciousness, stressing the ways in which it was adapted in the course of the later sixteenth century.

SOCIAL CHANGE AND THE LOCAL COMMUNITY

One of the problems with the concept of community as it has been deployed by many historians is that it does not readily accommodate social change. Communities tend to be seen as enduring sources of cohesion and resilience, and are vested with the sentimental hues of 'merrie England'. Although there was no seismic shift in the pattern of social relations in Elizabethan London, the slow pace of change should not blind us to the fact that it was taking place. I have just pointed out the divisive implications of the Protestant Reformation, and elsewhere I have emphasised the development of social polarisation as society filled out at the bottom, particularly in the rapidly expanding extramural parishes.[154] These changes did not result in the disappearance of the sense of community, but it came to be articulated in different ways, as the reality of social stratification began to shape more aspects of social relations. The expression of communitarian sentiments in the form of shared activities like feasting and recreations weakened as the vertical relationships strengthened. This does not mean that the more

[153] Society of Antiquaries MS 236, fos. 1ʳ⁻ᵛ, 7ᵛ–8; G.L., MS 2596/1, fo. 156ᵛ; *Vestry Minutes of Saint Bartholomew Exchange*, p. 5.
[154] Above, pp. 12–13.

substantial parishioners had withdrawn from the community, rather that their relationship with their inferiors was more consciously shaped by the extraction of deference in return for patronage, in particular through the exercise of poor relief. Community sentiments and the rhetoric of neighbourhood were still important because they continued to provide a framework of values to which the poor could appeal. But they were qualified by a strengthening of the rhetoric of the godly, an insistence that the poor conform to godly ideals.

Community in the sense of people of different social status doing things together was being eroded. We have seen how the move towards select vestries represented a narrowing of the basis of consent that was thought appropriate in decision-making at the local level. Secondly, we have seen how the role of religion in providing a common bond across the social spectrum may have been weakened by the more intellectually demanding, and, to some, more theologically unwelcome, protestantism, even in a favourable environment like London. Office-holding, recreational activities, and the pattern of parish feasting were other areas affected by social stratification.

There are some signs that the wealthier inhabitants were more reluctant to serve in the lowlier positions of local government in the later sixteenth century. In 1600 the vestrymen of St Dunstan in the West expressed their concern about the inconveniences arising from the fines taken to dispense the 'better sort' from the positions of constable and scavenger, which had caused the aldermen to complain that the queen's service was neglected.[155] Because fines sometimes went to the poor box, they do not consistently appear on churchwardens' accounts so that it is difficult to measure the extent of the avoidance of office, but receipts for dispensation from office are undoubtedly more common later in the reign.[156] The most extensive treatment of the phenomenon, by A. M. Dingle, found that the problems it posed can be exaggerated: of 616 positions filled in St Dunstan in the West in the period 1603–30, only 91 offices were fined for, and many of those who fined for one office subsequently served in others.[157] But although fining did not signal the breakdown of ward administration, it did mark a perception among some of the more substantial inhabitants that certain offices were beneath their dignity, and should be left to humbler people. This breach in the *cursus honorum* may have contributed to a reduction in the status attached to the lower offices and weakened the identification of incumbents with the regime.

Members of the community were less likely to participate in shared recreational activity after the middle years of the sixteenth century as

---

[155] G.L., MS 3016/1, fo. 33; C.L.R.O., Jour. 25, fos. 223ᵛ–4.
[156] G.L., MSS 2088/1; 2895/1; 1279/2.
[157] Dingle, 'Role of the Householder in Early Stuart London', pp. 127–34.

traditional festivals came under attack. Stow mourned the loss of the Midsummer watches when 'the wealthier sort also before their doores neare to the Bonefiers, would set out Tables on the Vigiles, furnished with sweete breade, and good drinke, and on the Festivall dayes with meates and drinks plentifully, whereunto they would invite their neighbours'.[158] In a similar mood Thomas Bentley recalled the church ales, shootings, and suppers which had financed the repair of his parish church, St Andrew Holborn, before the Reformation. Whereas in the later medieval period the repair of the church had been a matter for the whole community, by the later sixteenth century, like so many other parish services, it was financed either by rating or by the benevolences of the more substantial parishioners.[159] May Day celebrations, according to Stow, had formerly been supported by 'the governors and Maisters of this Citie', and parishes had set up their own maypoles, and arranged for the performance of plays and the provision of diversions such as archers and morris dancers. May Day, however, came under increasing suspicion because of its associations with attempted insurrection in 1517, and because of the vituperative preaching of protestants who saw May Day festivities as pagan survivals and enticements to lust. By the later sixteenth century May Eve was regularly accompanied by orders for a doubling of the city watch. In the face of this hostility the Mayings withered: in 1575 a London apprentice, asked what sports there were in London on the holidays, said 'he knewe of none but two or three dromes & Awnsientes and suche like showes in Southwarke'.[160] One must be careful of exaggerating the divorce which this opened up between popular and elite cultures; popular values were themselves evolving under the impact of widening literacy. The public theatre and bear baitings which loomed prominently in the leisure activities of Londoners united spectators from a broad cross-section of society and contributed to interpenetration between elite and popular values.[161] But they were very much more anonymous forms of recreation than the parochially based activities of the pre-Reformation period, and allowed for little direct face-to-face social bonding.

The disappearance of the religious fraternities which had often united

---

[158] Stow, *Survey of London*, I. 101; C.L.R.O., Jour. 12, fo. 329.
[159] G.L., MS 4249, fo. 222ᵛ; G. Rosser, 'The Essence of Medieval Urban Communities: the Vill of Westminster, 1200–1540', *T.R.H.S.*, fifth series, 34 (1984), 101–3; Pendrill, *Parish Life*, pp. 62–3, 102–3. For assessments to church repair in the later period, see G.L., MSS 2593/1, fos. 46–7ᵛ; 2590/1, pp. 145, 151; 943/1, fo. 21ᵛ.
[160] Stow, *Survey of London*, I. 98–9; C.L.R.O., Rep. 7, fo. 172ᵛ; Rep. 11, fos. 61ᵛ, 322ᵛ, 326, 327ᵛ; Rep. 12, fos. 91ᵛ, 223; Rep. 13, fos. 41, 155ᵛ; Jour. 16, fos. 251ᵛ–2, 277ᵛ; B.C.B. II, fo. 114ᵛ.
[161] P. Burke, 'Popular Culture in Seventeenth-Century London', *London Journal*, 3 (1977), 143–62. For a sophisticated exploration of the relationship between popular and elite cultures in an urban context, see J. Barry, 'The Cultural Life of Bristol, 1640–1775' (Oxford D.Phil., 1985).

people of differing social status in shared feasting contributed to the widening of social distances. They had been particularly prominent in the extramural wards, providing integration in ways that the parish, because of its size, could not.[162] It is true that there were occasions of commensality in the Elizabethan parish. Accounts regularly record allowances to the church-wardens for dinners at the bishop's visitation, the auditing of accounts, and the election of churchwardens. Any costs incurred above the allowance were paid for by the churchwardens out of their own pockets. It is also probable that some of these dinners were introduced in the mid century to compensate for the loss of the commensality enjoyed in the fraternities. Bentley records that in St Andrew Holborn, drinkings at the election of the churchwardens did not occur until 1564.[163] But attendance at these feasts was very much more restricted than in the fraternities. The large sums expended in some inner-city parishes, £3–£4 in St Margaret New Fish Street, might be taken as indicating a wide attendance, but most of the records refer rather unhelpfully to the presence of the parson, churchwardens, sidesmen, and 'other parish-ioners'.[164] In 1583 the parishioners of St Michael Querne spent £8. 5s. 3d. on a meeting of the whole parish 'aswell of the poore as of the ryche at a supper', but it was clearly exceptional, the clerk noting that it was held 'in Respete of other metinges which weere omytted'. As this expenditure occurred at the end of a plague year, it can be seen as an effort to reaffirm the bonds weakened by recent experiences.[165] Such wide participation was rare in inner-city parishes, and unheard of in the extramural areas. The one parish which does provide us with regular lists of those attending the parish dinners shows that they were confined to the minister, lecturer, sidesmen, clerk and sexton, and guests invited by the churchwardens who were almost invariably fellow-vestrymen and their wives.[166] This represents a very much more exclusive clientele than would have been the case in many fraternities.

An awareness of social differentiation also surfaces among the bequests of testators for funeral dinners. Anne Bressie was exceptional in demanding that her executors 'shall invite and have to dinner & suppar as the tyme and case shall requier all my neighbours inhabitantes in the parishe of St Dionis Backechurche ... as well poore as riche without exception or partialite'.[167]

[162] C. M. Barron, 'The Parish Fraternities of Medieval London', in *The Church in Pre-Reformation Society*, ed. C. Harper-Bill and C. M. Barron (1985), pp. 13–37; S. Brigden, 'Religion and Social Obligation in Early Sixteenth-Century London', *Past and Present*, 103 (1984), 94–102; *Parish Fraternity Register: Fraternity of the Holy Trinity and SS Fabian and Sebastian in the Parish of St Botolph Without Aldersgate*, ed. P. Basing (London Record Society, XVIII, 1982).

[163] G.L., MS 4249, fo. 230ᵛ.   [164] G.L., MS 1176/1, accts. for 1585–9.

[165] G.L., MS 2895/1, fo. 222ᵛ.

[166] G.L., MSS 9234/2A, fo. 19; 9234/2B, fo. 17; 9234/5A, fo. 22ʳ⁻ᵛ; 9234/5B, fos. 30–1; 9234/7, fos. 49ᵛ–50, 165ʳ⁻ᵛ.

[167] P.R.O., PROB 11/88, fo. 188ᵛ.

Her very insistence on the point is a sign that practice generally diverged from this neighbourly ideal. Likewise, John White, haberdasher, appears to indict the prevailing practices in leaving 10s. to the poor in every ward in London 'which I shalbe instead of my spice bread used to bee given to riche folkes'.[168] Some recognised their obligations to their poorer neighbours in leaving money for two dinners, but keeping the poor apart from their betters. Thus Katherine Waddington requested that a dinner be held for the wealthier and more substantial parishioners and a supper for the poorer sort.[169] Others provided a meal only for the 'chiefest and ancientest parishioners', or the 'ancient and substantial parishioners', or simply the 'honest inhabitants'.[170] It is true that in these cases the funeral dinner was accompanied by a bequest to the poor, sometimes explicitly to be distributed at the same time as the better sort tucked into their generous meals. The obligations of community clearly had meaning to these people, but their arrangements made the expression of the social bond a much more hierarchically articulated one than the older practices of commensality among neighbours.

The operation of the poor law in the later sixteenth century also served to emphasise the dependence of the poorer members of the community on the wealthy who therefore also enjoyed greater opportunities to mould the behaviour of the poor. Proclamations, statutes, and sermons pushed ever more vociferously the binary classification of the poor into the categories of the deserving and undeserving. Such a system of classification offered a means of defining the boundaries of acceptable behaviour among the poor, fitting well with the ambitions of the godly to reform popular manners.[171] Although, as we shall see in chapter 5, informal methods of poor relief persisted longer than is customarily acknowledged, the increasing bureaucratisation of relief in the sixteenth century offered vestrymen numerous occasions to manipulate it to secure compliant behaviour. As John Walter suggests, the fact that the observance of the traditional practice of charity was being made discretionary rather than obligatory gave the elites scope for greater control.[172] Decisions about eligibility for relief seem in practice to have rested with a small group of the more substantial vestrymen who authorised extraordinary disbursements. Thus the alderman's deputy and the churchwardens in St Botolph Aldgate, the churchwardens and constables in St Botolph Bishopsgate, the 'masters of the parish' in St James Garlickhithe

[168] P.R.O., PROB 11/68, fo. 236.
[169] P.R.O., PROB 11/53, fo. 20ᵛ; G.L., MS 9171/16, fos. 333, 442ᵛ.
[170] P.R.O., PROB 11/88, fos. 276, 310; PROB 11/89, fo. 334; PROB 11/90, fo. 30ᵛ.
[171] P. Slack, *Poverty and Policy in Tudor and Stuart England* (1988), pp. 23–6, 149–52.
[172] J. Walter, 'The Social Economy of Dearth in Early Modern England', in *Famine, Disease and the Social Order in Early Modern Society*, ed. J. Walter and R. Schofield (Cambridge, 1989), p. 126.

were responsible for the distribution of legacies.[173] Sometimes the practice
was formalised in a vestry order as at St Olave Southwark, whose vestrymen
in 1557 instructed the churchwardens and eight of their number 'to vewe see
& appoynte suche as to be poore, layme, feable and wayke to have the
charytie & almes of the parryshe and to put owt and avoyde all them that be
strong & able to worke'.[174] In applying for relief the poor needed a voice on
the vestry, so that each disbursement contributed to a reinforcement of the
hierarchy.[175] Pensioners in St Bartholomew Exchange were expected to give
thanks for the charity they had received at each Sunday service.[176] There is
little sense in which the poor were able to regard relief as a right. Because
pensions were inadequate those who received them also had to seek
numerous hand-outs from legacies, each occasion offering the possibility of
the exercise of discrimination by the parish leaders.

Charity, of course, had always been exercised by the wealthy, and they had
long enjoyed the option of exercising discretion about eligibility on the basis
of their local knowledge.[177] But the sanctions became more effective as an
increasing volume of relief was channeled through the churchwardens and as
the introduction of pensions made the threat of removal from relief a
powerful one. Because of the lack of data for the earlier period and because
of the difficulty of determining practice where the testator left money
without an indication of whom he expected to distribute his bequest, it is
difficult to provide firm statistical evidence in support of the argument that
an increasing proportion of private charity was actually distributed by the
parish officials rather than by the executors. But receipts of such money are
increasingly common on the churchwardens' accounts of the later sixteenth
century: in St Margaret Westminster no less than 80 per cent of total receipts
for poor relief handled by the parish bureaucracy in the 1590s came from
private charity.[178] Moreover, churchwardens administered an increasing
volume of endowed charity. Particularly common were the weekly distributions of loaves or pennies, usually to twelve parishioners.[179] Decisions
about eligibility for relief therefore became a matter for frequent discussion
among the leaders of the parish so that an 'official' viewpoint on the
worthiness of potential recipients might emerge. Guilt about the refusal of
relief was much less likely in the security of collective decision-making.

Poor relief was increasingly used as a form of social control. Vestries are

---

[173] G.L., MSS 4824, fos. 6, 7, 8ᵛ; 4524/1, fo. 21; 9234/7, passim; 2088/1.
[174] Southwark Archives, St Olave's V.M., fo. 12ᵛ. Cf. L.P.L., Holy Trinity Minories C.W.A.,
fo. 50ᵛ.
[175] G.L., MS 9234/7, fo. 131.
[176] *Vestry Minutes of Saint Bartholomew Exchange*, p. 5.
[177] J. A. F. Thomson, 'Piety and Charity in Late Medieval London', *Journal of Ecclesiastical
History*, 16 (1965), 178–95.
[178] W.P.L., E147, accts. for 1590–9.   [179] Below, pp. 179–80, 199.

found removing disorderly pensioners from their almshouses or temporarily depriving them of relief in hope of the 'amendment' of their behaviour.[180] The preoccupation with the regulation of the poor was a feature of schemes for the reform of poor law administration in later-sixteenth-century London. The City's orders of 1579 required that the poor be visited every day by a member of the vestry to determine whether or not they were working, and the vestries were to make monthly presentments to the wardmotes of the disorderly poor and their children.[181] A proposal for reform in 1595 emphasised the need for officers 'to take uppon them the charge of the poore not as by collections to receave onely that which is leveied of the parishioners for the use of the poore butt as providers overseers & correctors of ye poor as weare the deacons in the prymitive church'. The introduction of an additional tier in poor law administration in the form of the overseers of the poor in 1598, an office served by men of higher social status than the collectors of the poor they supplemented, was a further move towards the realisation of these ambitions.[182] But it was a suggestion which many vestries were already implementing either through the informal gatherings of leading vestrymen or through new officials like the surveyors of inmates in the Southwark parishes who snooped into the morals of the poor.[183]

To conclude, the acquiescence of the middling householders is to be explained in terms of the opportunities for participation in local government, the considerable discretionary power in the hands of local administration, and the ways in which they could make clear their priorities for action by the elite. Greater subtlety is necessary to explain the acquiescence of the poor, not least because of the absence of sources as to their attitudes, and the consequently inferential nature of the arguments concerning them. In the first place, it is necessary to emphasise that however homogeneous they appear to have been in official sources, they are likely to have been divided, in particular by religion, occupational rivalries, and their status as free or non-free, and long-term resident or newcomer. Secondly, it is dangerous to assume from their invisibility in much of the source material that they had no sense of identity with local institutions: it was within a parochial context that so much relief was available; and, for many, the parish remained an important focus for religious sensibilities. Thirdly, although it is true that

[180] G.L., MSS 4887, fos. 162, 171ᵛ, 174; 594/1, pp. 14, 38; 9234/1, fo. 27; 2590/1, p. 93; MT. Co., C.M. III, fo. 437; G.L.R.O., P92/SAV/450, p. 357; *Vestry Minutes of Saint Margaret Lothbury*, p. 33.

[181] *Orders Appointed to bee Executed in the Citie of London, for Setting Roges and Idle Persons on Work and for Relief of the Poor* (1582). For implementation see G.L., MSS 4249, fo. 7ᵛ; 4415/1, fo. 7; 877/1, p. 14; *Vestry Minutes of Saint Margaret Lothbury*, pp. 12, 13.

[182] C.L.R.O., Remembrancia II, no. 87. Cf. C. Hill, *Society and Puritanism in Pre-Revolutionary England* (1964), pp. 271–3.

[183] Below, pp. 184–5; G.L., MS 2590/1, pp. 39, 40; Slack, *Poverty and Policy*, pp. 205–8.

social distances were widening in the Elizabethan period and that there was a greater insistence on the need for conformity with godly ideals, this does not mean that community had collapsed. As Keith Wrightson puts it, the poor law 'provided in its balance of communal identification and social differentiation a powerful reinforcement of habits of deference and subordination'.[184] Although the wealthy might seek to manipulate relief to secure conformist behaviour, the poor could themselves, within the limits set by a more restrictive definition of the eligible groups, attempt to manipulate the ideal of community and the obligations it imposed on the wealthy towards the poor. But they were cast in the role of petitioners, each act of petitioning and receiving serving to reinforce their dependence on their wealthier neighbours.

[184] Wrightson, *English Society*, pp. 181–2.

4

The framework of social relations: the livery companies

INTRODUCTION

The livery companies remained key institutions in the City because they controlled access to the freedom and the political, legal, and economic privileges it entailed. They were central to the organisation of business life, providing a framework within which the conditions of employment could be regulated, standards of production maintained, and legislation for the benefit of the craft promoted. The bonds between members were reinforced by the conviviality fostered in a rich cycle of feasting, by the charity provided by the companies, and by the availability of a framework within which disputes could be reconciled. Membership of a company was therefore a crucial component of a citizen's identity, and the companies generated those institutional loyalties which, I have argued, were important in ensuring that the pursuit of the redress of grievances remained institutionally focused. Nevertheless, to concentrate on the goals shared by members of the same trade and the social round which bound them together would only give one side of an often complex picture. Not all companies were equally successful in achieving the identification of the rank and file of the membership with the institution. Because of the unequal distribution of power within the companies, the aspirations of the artisans were often neglected by the rulers, or, worse still, the companies became instruments for the exploitation of the artisans, institutions through which wholesaling interests could ensure the dependence of producers on them. In the first decade of the seventeenth century the artisan skinners were complaining with great bitterness that among their rulers it was 'a matter disputable whether we be members of the said company or not'.[1] Clearly the Skinners' Company was failing in its integrating role. Companies might therefore become battlefields between groups with divergent interests.

These two perspectives are not adequately reconciled in the existing literature. Historians have created an exaggerated impression of either

[1] Sk. Co., C.M. I, fo. 88ᵛ.

conflict or consensus by their rather selective treatments. George Unwin's highly influential account written at the turn of the century, which reflects a rather whiggish quest for the origins of the trade union movement, stressed the conflicts between the artisans and the wealthier trading element which used the company to exercise some control over production. These conflicts, he argues, became more acute in the sixteenth century as the commanding positions in the leading companies were taken over by merchants benefiting from the expansion in the cloth trade. Companies like the Clothworkers, Haberdashers, and Skinners were increasingly split between liveries dominated by wholesalers and yeomanries comprising the bulk of the artisans. Their interests often diverged, as when clothworkers agitated for restrictions on the export of undressed cloth, skinners for limits on engrossing by middlemen, and feltmakers for controls on the delivery of untrimmed hats to country chapmen, in each case encountering the opposition of powerful interests on the ruling courts of assistants.[2] Steve Rappaport, on the other hand, writing in the 1980s, and reflecting the paradoxical preoccupations of that decade, the quest for a balance between an individualistic, competitive, market-orientated society and more traditional 'community' values, has found a realisation of that harmony in sixteenth-century London. His account stresses both the opportunities for social mobility within the companies and their fulfilment of integrative functions through poor relief and dispute arbitration. Against views of company government which stress the monopoly of power in the hands of the assistants he has underlined the need for a degree of consent in government which led to the delegation of certain functions to the yeomanry and made the assistants responsive to pressures from below: 'the companies functioned rather well as flexible institutions within which conflicts could be resolved'.[3]

As well as reflecting the different preoccupations of historians at either end of the twentieth century, these contrasting emphases are the result of real difficulties with the evidence. In the first place it is difficult to do full justice to the sheer variety of experience among companies. They varied greatly in size, in the heterogeneity of their membership, and in the degree of penetration by mercantile interests. Members would be less likely to identify with a huge company of possibly upwards of 2,500 members like the Merchant Tailors than with an intimate association of just 58 like the Plumbers. It was not just that the company hall could not possibly accommodate all the merchant tailors; it was also the case that the custom of London, which allowed a freeman to pursue any trade, had made inroads into craft identity.[4] Because

---

[2] Unwin, *Industrial Organization*.
[3] Rappaport, *Worlds Within Worlds*, Cf. Rappaport, 'Social Structure and Mobility in Sixteenth-Century London: Part I', *London Journal*, 9 (1983), 107–35 and 'Social Structure and Mobility in Sixteenth-Century London: Part II', *London Journal*, 10 (1984), 107–34.
[4] Below, pp. 114–15.

the penetration of mercantile interests was most marked in the twelve great companies, Unwin's model of conflict between traders and handicraftsmen, based on the experiences of the Skinners, Clothworkers, and Haberdashers, is not applicable to the lesser companies where a much greater community of interest between rulers and ruled prevailed. Secondly, it has to be recognised that it is extraordinarily difficult to recover the authentic voice of the artisans because the surviving records are overwhelmingly biased towards the perceptions of the ruling assistants. One should be sensitive to the danger of inferring from the court minutes a harmony which was part of the myth the rulers sought to perpetuate. A wider range of sources can alter our perceptions. Thus Rappaport cites the rejection by the assistants of the Clothworkers' Company of a labour-saving device for the rowing of cloth in 1560 as evidence of the sensitivity of rulers, but is apparently unaware of the evidence from the Repertories of the court of aldermen of a combination between the journeymen of the Clothworkers' and Merchant Tailors' Companies for better wages in the same year, on which the company records are silent.[5] On the other hand we should be wary of using those few documents that were generated by the artisans themselves as the only evidence for their attitudes because they beg questions concerning authorship and representativeness, and because the polemics into which men are drawn in the heat of a particular conflict are not necessarily typical of their normal positions. It is easy enough to string together isolated instances of conflict to create an impression of polarisation, neglecting the issues, such as quality control and the regulation of non-free labour, on which a greater degree of consensus existed. The accounts of both Unwin and Rappaport have their limitations. Although Unwin is weak on the companies' integrative functions, Rappaport is perhaps too ready to assume that they were equally successfully fulfilled at all levels of the company, and he is inclined to neglect the selectivity which characterised the governors' response to the grievances of the artisans. Both accounts fail to bring out the confusing variety of experiences, and the variables which explain those differing outcomes. Nor do they do justice to the ambiguities that characterised the attitudes of the artisans: the hostility they sometimes felt towards their rulers over their failure to take up craft grievances was blunted by a consideration of the advantages derived from company membership such as poor relief and the arbitration of disputes. It was a delicate balance.

COMPANY GOVERNMENT

The most common criticism levelled at the rulers of the companies, it has long been recognised, was that they were unrepresentative of the interests of

[5] Rappaport, *Worlds Within Worlds*, pp. 374–5; Cw. Co., C.M. II, fo. 13ᵛ; C.L.R.O., Rep. 14, fos. 224ʳ⁻ᵛ, 225, 226ᵛ–7, 228, 233.

the whole membership, being engaged in economic activity, usually as merchants or retailers, unrelated to that of the rank and file of artisans. Thus the artisan skinners complained in 1606 that the wardens were 'men of other professions whereby they have no compassionate feeling of abuses in the said art'. Hugh Williams, fishmonger, expressed characteristic frustration at the results of the 1604 election in his company: 'What two Lynnen drapers gonne out of office and two come in a poxe of god on them all.' Sometimes the sense of isolation was accompanied by the suggestion that the assistants were exploiting their positions for their own gain. Thomas Lateware, clothworker, hitherto a respectable artisan who had served as warden of the yeomanry and was frequently employed to view faulty cloths, was dismissed from the livery of his company in 1601 for his lewd words to the effect 'that the Assistantes of this Companie were Pellicans & did sucke out the blood of theire dam, & weed out the profitt of the Companies landes, which of right belongeth & was given to them of the handitrade of this Companie'.[6] Sometimes resentments of these kinds surfaced in the lesser crafts. For example, the attempt of the artisan cutlers to secure a provision in their new charter in 1606 that the wardens should always include an artisan reflects their fear that they were in danger of losing a voice in company affairs.[7] Most historians have accepted such criticisms at face value, laying stress on the way in which the companies were submerged by the cloth exporting interests in the mid sixteenth century and therefore ruled by men lacking connections with the trade.[8] How valid was this critique? What was the character of these ruling bodies?

The formal electoral procedures of the companies demonstrate clearly the limits of participation. The composition of the nominating and electing bodies was extraordinarily varied, but only very rarely did the yeomanry enjoy any role in the choice of the company's rulers. It is true that in the Goldsmiths' Company the yeomanry nominated two of the four 'choosers' who joined the ex-wardens and any aldermen members of the company to elect the officers, but their role was circumscribed by the fact that the choosers had to be assistants, in other words to have held senior office already.[9] More frequently participation was confined to the livery, and even then the arrangements were such that their power was diluted by dividing the responsibility for nominations and elections between the livery and the

---

[6] Sk. Co., C.M. I, fo. 88; G.L., MS 5570/2, p. 404; Cw. Co., C.M. III, fo. 211. For Lateware's earlier career, see ibid. II, fos. 244ᵛ, 250ᵛ; III, fos. 91ᵛ, 96, 106ᵛ, 142ᵛ, 167.
[7] C.L.R.O., Rep. 27, fos. 218ᵛ–9. Cf. G.L., MS 12071/1, pp. 368–9.
[8] Unwin, *Industrial Organization*, ch. IV; G. D. Ramsay, 'Victorian Historiography and the Guilds of London: The Report of the Royal Commission on the Livery Companies of London, 1884', *London Journal*, 10 (1984), 155–66.
[9] Gs. Co., Reg. K, p. 483. For the discussion which follows, cf. Rappaport, *Worlds Within Worlds*, pp. 245, 252–3.

assistants. Sometimes the livery was the nominating body and the assistants the electing body (Fishmongers' Company); sometimes it was the other way round (Cordwainers' and Butchers' Companies).[10] Elsewhere the livery were involved in the election of only some of the officers. In the Armourers' Company, for example, the livery elected the junior warden only, the master and first warden being chosen by the outgoing master and the new master respectively.[11] But in many companies the livery were entirely excluded from elections. Thus in the Clothworkers' and Merchant Tailors' Companies nominations to the wardenships were taken from the outgoing wardens and presented to the assistants, while the right to elect to the mastership was further confined to the small group of men who had already held the office (although in the case of the Merchant Tailors the ex-masters were joined by the current master and wardens).[12] Many of the lesser crafts, such as the Saddlers', Blacksmiths', Plasterers', and Tallow Chandlers' Companies, also confined electoral rights to the wardens and assistants.[13] Moreover the vagueness of some company ordinances on electoral procedures may have given an opportunity to wardens to curtail the rights of the livery. The livery of the Coopers' Company was complaining in the 1590s that elections were not free because the master and wardens acting with the consent of only three or four of the ancientest of the livery had appropriated the right to make nominations: in the subsequent arbitration it was ruled that the master and wardens should act with the consent of the greatest part of the livery in making nominations.[14]

Nevertheless, such procedures did not inevitably result in rulers who were alienated from their membership. In the lesser companies mercantile domination of the craft was scarcely ever an issue. On the contrary, artisan involvement in the government of the craft was commonplace. For example, although the rulers of the Coopers' Company included a sprinkling of wine importers and vintners, analysis of the lists of those fined for shoddy workmanship shows that the assistants were dominated by craftsmen: at least twenty-seven of the thirty-eight men entering the court between 1567 and 1602 were working coopers.[15] Likewise, an analysis of fines and building accounts shows that fourteen of the sixteen assistants in the

---

[10] G.L., MSS 5570/1, pp. 42, 336; 8033, p. 23; A. Pearce, *The History of the Butchers' Company* (1929), p. 204.

[11] G.L., MS 12071/1, p. 490.

[12] *The Ordinances of the Clothworkers' Company* (privately printed, 1881), pp. 38–42; Clode, *Memorials*, pp. 204–6.

[13] G.L., MSS 5385A, 1561 ordinances, no. 1; 2943, 1572 ordinances, no. 2; 6132, 1586 ordinances, nos. 3–4; 6174/1, 1588 ordinances, nos. 3–4.

[14] G.L., MS 5633, controversies concerning disorders of those bearing office. The arbitration did not settle the disputes: G.L., MS 5602/1, 3 May 1597.

[15] G.L., MSS 5606/1–2. The names of those fined were indexed.

Plasterers' Company in 1582 were artisan plasterers.[16] Elsewhere retailing interests were most prominent on the ruling bodies. We can use the documents generated by the aldermen's efforts to regulate the price of candles in the 1570s to show that at least eleven of the twenty-four Tallow Chandler assistants in 1582 sold candles, and that many of these were engaged in production as well. Others, like Hugh Ingram, were involved in the coastal trade in butter and cheese; others, like Robert Atkinson, alebrewer, or Michael Blake, the wine importer, made their fortunes in the victualling trades. They were a mixed bag, but generally engaged in activities related to their company affiliation, and they were therefore competent judges of the misdemeanours of the smaller fry.[17]

Mercantile domination can be exaggerated even on the courts of assistants of leading companies like the Clothworkers. Only twelve of the thirty-five Clothworker assistants in 1582 can be shown from the Port Books and the charters of the trading companies to have been engaged in overseas trade.[18] Many of the others presumably made a living out of the retail trades. The clothworkers named in a survey of 1562 as men 'trading and occupying silks' who were not apparently engaged in overseas trade were probably retailers.[19] But the Clothworker assistants also included nine men of more modest fortunes assessed to the subsidy at less than £50. Some of these were in fact artisan clothworkers. They can be shown to be such by analysing the lists of those fined for shoddy workmanship of cloths or serving as viewers of faulty cloths, since the viewers seem almost always to have been artisans.[20]

---

[16] G.L., MS 6122/1. The following were identified through building accounts in company records: Cornelius Hand, Simon Betaugh, Thomas Warbish, Edward Jackson: G.L., MS 16988/2, fos. 177ᵛ, 212; *Records of the Worshipful Company of Carpenters*, ed. B. Marsh, J. Ainsworth and B. Millard (7 vols., 1914–68), IV. 138.

[17] C.L.R.O., Rep. 18, fos. 43ᵛ, 44, 70ᵛ, 71, 213ʳ⁻ᵛ, 221, 320 for the regulation of traders in candles; Rep. 15, fos. 44, 244 for Anthony Alderson and Michael Booth, dealers in butter and cheese; P.R.O., E190/6/8; E163/15/5 for Hugh Ingram; G.L., MS 5442/4, 1563–4 acct. for Robert Atkinson; *The Port and Trade of Early Elizabethan London*, ed. B. Dietz (London Record Society, VIII, 1972), pp. 12, 15, 17, 36; C.P.R., 1553–4, p. 313 for Michael Blake.

[18] Clothworker assistants in 1582 who were engaged in overseas trade: Thomas Altham, Robert Coggan, John Hawes, Henry Hewett, William Hewett, Rowland Heyward, Lawrence Mellowe, Nicholas Moseley, John Oldham, Edward Osborne, John Spencer, Richard Staper. The following sources have been consulted for overseas trade: C.P.R., 1563–6, pp. 178–9 (charter of Merchant Adventurers, 1563); C.P.R., 1575–8, pp. 317–18 (charter of Spanish Company, 1577); P.R.O., C66/1185, mm. 21–4 (charter of Eastland Company, 1579); P.R.O., SP 12/6/52 (cloth exports, Sept. 1559); *Port and Trade of Early Elizabethan London*; F. E. Leese, 'A Calendar and Analysis, with Introduction of two Elizabethan Port Books' (Oxford B.Litt., 1963); T. S. Willan, *Studies in Elizabethan Foreign Trade* (Manchester, 1959), ch. IV; P.R.O., E190/6/3; E190/6/4; E190/7/8; E190/8/1; E190/8/4.

[19] P.R.O., SP 12/20/63; Thomas Blackwey (cf. P.R.O., SP 12/34/69), Thomas Bayard, Robert House (cf. G.L., MS 12806/2, fo. 168), John Lacy, John Maye (cf. ibid., fos. 187, 201ᵛ, 210ᵛ), Lawrence Palmer, Thomas Skinner.

[20] P.R.O., E179/251/16; Cw. Co., C.M. II–III: those fined and serving as viewers have been indexed. See C.M. III, fo. 166ᵛ for artisans serving as viewers.

Of the 1582 assistants, Clement Devike, Thomas Gilborne, Robert Heron, and John Robotham were artisan clothworkers. They were differentiated from their less prosperous colleagues partly by the greater scale of their operations and partly by the diversification of their interests beyond cloth finishing. In 1574, Devike and Gilborne, for example, were in trouble for keeping large numbers of apprentices.[21] Moreover, artisans with some spare capital made small profits by participating in the cloth markets, appearing regularly before the governors of Christ's Hospital for their failure to pay dues on cloth sales. Clement Devike, for example, was fined £3 in 1577 for selling, in his house, cloths not presented at Blackwell Hall.[22] The ruling bodies of the main companies were thus pluriform in character. Merchants may have been the wealthiest members and those most prominent in civic government, but their power was diluted by a strong retailing element and a sprinkling of artisans. The courts of assistants were not therefore closed bodies; artisans had some opportunity of making their grievances heard through their own representatives.

However, it was not only through their occasional presence on the ruling bodies of the companies that the artisans acquired influence, but also through the middle tier of company government in which they were much more prominent. Wardens of the yeomanry, sometimes called masters of the bachelors, and in the Merchant Tailors' Company, wardens substitute, were usually elected each year by the assistants of the livery from a panel of names prepared by the yeomanry. It is unclear whether the slate of candidates was drawn up by an assembly of the whole yeomanry or by co-option by the existing yeomanry wardens or assistants, although the latter seems more likely.[23] In some companies, notably the Skinners and Pewterers, those chosen as wardens of the yeomanry were often already members of the livery, and this may have had the effect of reducing the capacity of the yeomanry organisations to satisfy the aspirations of artisans.[24] It should also be remembered that the yeomanry was not an exclusively artisan organisation since all freemen began their company careers as members of it: the yeomanries therefore included young merchants and retailers, building up their businesses and standing in civic society prior to their admission to the livery.

The career structure of the Clothworker wardens of the yeomanry has

---

[21] Cw. Co., C.M. II, fo. 182.
[22] P.R.O., SP 14/133/36; G.L., MS 12806/2, fos. 197, 233, 318ᵛ; C.L.R.O., M.C.1/8/80.
[23] Johnson, *Drapers*, II. 297–9, 320–2; J. Nicholl, *Some Account of the Worshipful Company of Ironmongers* (1866), pp. 125–8; *Clothworkers' Ordinances*, pp. 125–8; Rappaport, *Worlds Within Worlds*, pp. 219–32.
[24] Sk. Co., C.M. I, fo. 11ʳ⁻ᵛ; II, fo. 215; C. Welch, *History of the Worshipful Company of Pewterers of the City of London* (2 vols., 1902), II. 26–7.

been reconstructed from the freedom records and company accounts.[25] Analysis of the careers of the forty-six men who served as wardens of the yeomanry in the twelve years after 1593 suggests that the average time-lapse between freedom and service was about fifteen years (15.3). But the career structure was less regular than that of the livery wardens in that the yeomanry rulers consisted both of young men destined for the livery who achieved the yeomanry wardenships in less than ten years, and older men who achieved office after more than twenty years. Service as yeomanry warden was neither a necessary precondition for admission to the livery, nor did the latter follow inevitably on the former. Of the seventy-nine men admitted to the livery of the Clothworkers' between 1583 and 1600, forty-one had not held yeomanry office, while of the thirty-eight men who did hold yeomanry office in the 1560s only twelve subsequently entered the livery. Thus the yeomanry rulers included men who had passed the age at which they would normally expect to enter the livery. They were not all 'birds of passage', impatient for the privileges of livery membership and the kudos of higher office, regarding service in the yeomanry as menial drudgery, men who, as the Merchant Tailors put it in 1598 'reccon it a kind of disparagement to be called to the said place'.[26] Rather, for many, their primary loyalty was to the yeomanry and the craft. This conclusion is underlined by linkage once more to lists of those fined for shoddy workmanship. Of the 113 men who can be identified as serving as wardens of the yeomanry in the period 1560–1600, twenty-eight can be identified as artisans because they were fined at some time for poor workmanship. A further twenty-three acted as viewers or overseers of workmanship. So at least 45 per cent of the yeomanry wardens of the Clothworkers' Company in the Elizabethan period were artisans. The instance in 1559 when all the yeomanry wardens lacked skill in the trade appears to have been exceptional, and it is noteworthy that on this occasion the assistants took measures to ensure that they were assisted by artisans.[27] It was expected that there would always be representatives of the handicraft among the yeomanry rulers.

The relatively low level of participation by artisans on the ruling courts of assistants therefore may not necessarily have been damaging to their interests given their greater role in the middle tier of the companies. But the success of the yeomanry wardens in fulfilling the aspirations of the artisans depended on the degree of independence the ruling assistants allowed them and the resources available to them. It is therefore crucial to assess the role of the

[25] Cw. Co., C.M. III for names of wardens of yeomanry; Book of Freedoms for dates of freedom; Wardens' Accounts for dates of admission to livery and indications whether the individual concerned had served in yeomanry office.
[26] MT. Co., C.M. III, fo. 371.   [27] MT. Co., C.M. II, fo. 10ᵛ.

yeomanry organisations in the government of the companies. Common to all was their role in the collection of quarterage dues, a time-consuming and often thankless task, particularly when the wardens were expected to chase up the recalcitrant who failed to turn up at the quarterly assemblies.[28] But the collection of the dues was important to the yeomanry because they formed the bulk of their available income in most cases. In 1588–9 quarterage dues accounted for 77 per cent of the income of the Merchant Tailors' yeomanry; the proportion in the Haberdashers' Company in 1600–1 was 40 per cent.[29] The Merchant Tailors were fortunate because their yeomanry were able to keep all the quarterage dues collected, providing a sound financial base, but this was not universal practice. Often a portion of the dues went to the wardens of the livery: the yeomanry of the Haberdashers, for example, paid a fixed rent of £22 p.a. in the earliest years of the seventeenth century.[30]

In circumstances such as these the yeomanry found themselves acting merely as delegates of the livery wardens, a potentially disruptive arrangement because of the likelihood of disputes between the different wardens over what was their due. Yeomanry wardens were naturally enough reluctant to collect money over the expenditure of which they had little control. Indeed the subordination of the yeomanry wardens could become a live issue even in companies where we would not expect there to have been much tension. The social distance between the liverymen and yeomen of the Barber Surgeons' Company cannot have been that great, but the company's history in the sixteenth century is peppered with disputes over the status of the yeomanry wardens. The yeomanry organisation was suppressed for three years between September 1552 and October 1555, and further suspensions were threatened in 1557 and 1590.[31] The orders re-establishing the yeomanry in 1555 are particularly revealing of the rulers' conception of the organisation.[32] The subordinate position of the yeomanry wardens was continually emphasised. They were to pay all quarterage to the master and wardens of the livery; they were to pass on matters of general import decided by the master and wardens of the clothing to the whole company; they were not to engage in searches to see how many apprentices or journeymen company members kept, this being the proper sphere of the wardens of the livery. Subordination was to be ceremonially emphasised by the presence of the yeomanry wardens bearing cups before the wardens of the clothing at feasts. The yeomanry wardens had clearly been guilty of appropriating greater authority than their elders thought their due. They were henceforth to call themselves 'Wardens of the Yeomanry and no other'. Likewise an

[28] MT. Co., C.M. I, p. 568; III, fos. 156, 157; G.L., MS 7094, fo. 21ᵛ.
[29] MT. Co., W.A. VI, fo. 283ʳ⁻ᵛ; G.L., MS 15868.
[30] G.L., MS 15868; Br. Sr. Co., MSS 5257/2, fos. 51, 52, 237; 5257/3, p. 240.
[31] Br. Sr. Co., MSS 5257/1, pp. 15, 29; 5257/2, fos. 41, 42ᵛ, 44ᵛ, 51, 51ᵛ, 52.
[32] Br. Sr. Co., MS 5257/1, pp. 29–35.

order of September 1558 reflects the ruling assistants' jealousy of yeomanry wardens who gave themselves airs: the four wardens were not to presume to be waited on home, nor to go anywhere in the city with trains, 'but every person quietlie to departe'.[33] For their part the yeomanry wardens clearly resented the high-handed action taken by the rulers of the company. Not only were they unable to spend the quarterage dues they had collected as they wished, but also the rulers had regarded the yeomanry box as a cash reserve to be raided for general company purposes. As part of the 1555 agreement the yeomanry secured a promise from the assistants that they would not borrow money from the yeomanry without giving a bill specifying the date of repayment. It was also agreed that although the yeomanry had to submit their accounts to annual audit, they were to have control of expenditure. Nevertheless, in subsequent years the wardens of the livery intervened to criticise the yeomanry for taking more in quarterage than they were allowed, for spending too much on the corporate account at election dinners, and in 1579 for impoverishing themselves by quarter dinners.[34]

The Barber Surgeons were not the only company to have doubts about the benefits of a yeomanry organisation at this time: the Clothworkers also temporarily suppressed their yeomanry in 1549.[35] Possibly elite sensitivities about order were peculiarly heightened at this time because in other respects the assistants, particularly in the greater companies, saw advantages in the yeomanry organisations. It is true that the artisan clothworkers were a notoriously troublesome lot. They had been behind riots about the export of wool in 1484 and 1486; their agitation at the outset of Henry VIII's reign had earned a serious rebuke from Bishop Fox; they were continually harassing the Merchant Adventurers about the export of undressed cloth; and in Edward VI's reign their struggle with the Merchant Tailors over the merchant tailor clothworkers raged at fever pitch.[36] But it is likely that their agitations would have been more threatening but for the existence of the yeomanry organisation. The yeomanry wardens, being relatively prosperous and as status conscious as anyone else in the sixteenth century, many hoping for entry into the livery, had every reason to strive for quiet rule. The yeomanry organisations also served to reinforce hierarchical values because they inserted further refinements into the social hierarchy (the wardenships were one more honour to be striven for, one more distinction a man could

[33] Ibid. p. 79.

[34] Ibid. fo. 82, 6 June 1577, 9 Oct. 1579; MSS 5257/2, fo. 35; 5257/3, pp. 151, 181, 210.

[35] Cw. Co., C.M. I, fo. 209. It appears to have been restored in December 1552; ibid. fo. 241.

[36] *Acts of Court of the Mercers' Company, 1453–1527*, ed. L. Lyell and F. D. Watney (Cambridge, 1936), pp. 159–60, 292, 364–71, 472–3; G. R. Elton, *Reform and Renewal* (Cambridge, 1973), pp. 113–14; G. D. Ramsay, 'Industrial Discontent in Early Elizabethan London: Clothworkers and Merchant Adventurers in Conflict', *London Journal*, 1 (1975), 227–39.

enjoy above his fellows), and because the service of their wardens before the wardens of the livery in ceremonial, both at feasts and at public events like the lord mayor's show, emphasised the bonds of patronage and deference which helped to cement the society. Moreover the yeomanry had a more strictly utilitarian function since the tasks of governing a company were multifarious and the time available to the ruling wardens was limited by their own business concerns and often by the holding of office elsewhere. It was to the advantage of the livery to delegate some of the tasks of company government to the yeomanry wardens. As the yeomanry wardens were more likely to be better informed about the financial circumstances of individual members, it was convenient to use them in making assessments for civic or company purposes. Moreover the yeomanry would be useful in the detection of infringements of company regulations. The rulers of the yeomanry of the Brewers' Company were expected to make weekly or monthly searches presenting offenders to the wardens of the livery. The Drapers instructed their masters of the bachelors to make quarterly searches of those keeping foreigners.[37] In most cases responsibility for punishment remained with the courts of assistants, the yeomanry wardens being used as inspectors. But sometimes the inferior body was allowed considerable independence. The wardens substitute of the Merchant Tailors' Company were meeting fortnightly in the first decade of the seventeenth century to coordinate measures against foreigners, employing informers on the company's behalf.[38] The wardens of the yeomanry of the Clothworkers' Company regularly prosecuted suits in parliament, often with relatively little involvement by the ruling assistants apart from their provision of instalments of cash for financing the suits. However, the assistants still expected to be kept informed of developments, expressing annoyance when the artisans initiated suits to the privy council without their assent.[39]

The yeomanry of the Clothworkers' and Merchant Tailors' Companies enjoyed a particularly favourable position. Elsewhere the relative inactivity of the yeomanry wardens may have led the yeomen to wonder whether the office and its attendant expenses was worthwhile. In 1600 the yeomanry of the Skinners' Company was assembled to be asked whether they wished to discontinue their wardens. The opinions voiced were apparently diverse and, although on further soundings and a promise from the assistants to allow increased funding for dinners the wardens were maintained, a petition was again received in 1606 for the wardens to be discharged.[40] It is difficult to tell whether this merely reflected annoyance at the cost of office on the part of

[37] Johnson, *Drapers*, II. 324–5; Consitt, *Weavers*, p. 145; Sk. Co., C.M. II, fos. 186ᵛ, 227ᵛ, G.L., MS 5496.
[38] Clode, *Memorials*, pp. 562–4; MT. Co., C.M. III, fos. 367, 401ᵛ, 437.
[39] Cw. Co., C.M. II, fo. 195; III, fo. 21.
[40] Sk. Co., C.M. II, fos. 317, 317ᵛ, 377ᵛ.

those who were expected to bear it, or whether it reflected a wider feeling among the handicraft that their wardens were not fulfilling a worthwhile role, particularly as in this company they were often already liverymen and therefore perhaps as uninterested in the handicraft as the members of the court of assistants were alleged to be. Certainly where the yeomanry were confined to a largely ceremonial role their exclusion from power might be as resented as it appears to have been in the Barber Surgeons' Company. As Thomas Walker, fishmonger, exclaimed: 'in other companies there wardens of the yeomanrye are suffred to kepe courtes & to take order for the benefitt of there severall yeomanries but in this companye they are not'.[41] The maintenance of harmony therefore depended on the achievement of a subtle balance between the aspirations of the lower ranks for some control over their own affairs, and the fears of company rulers that if unchecked artisans would behave in disorderly and irresponsible fashion. It did not work equally well in all cases.

Finally, appreciation of the yeomanry's role in company government and their ability to cater for some artisan aspirations should not blind us to the realities of power. The courts of assistants held most of the money bags: the suits of the handicraftsmen would stand much less chance of success without the release of company funds by the assistants. Only the wardens of the company had the authority to overrule those haughty individuals who withstood company ordinances, or to dissuade the wealthier members from practices which might hurt the interests of the handitrade. And it was the assistants who had the valuable contacts in central government, relatives at court, friends in the judiciary, and the 'countenance' and the money to make men in government think their goodwill worth cultivating. At many points the yeomanry were going to need the help of the assistants, and relations between artisans and assistants depended on the willingness of the latter to give them that support.

ASPECTS OF IDENTITY

How successful were the companies in generating loyalty through a sense of community that a shared social round might develop? Such loyalties might be important in helping to ensure that the expression of grievances remained institutionally focused. The creation of community might be important in giving the poorer members of the society another framework within which they could appeal to the sense of responsibility of the wealthy. As usual the problem is that there is very much more evidence for the identification of the wealthier members with the company. There are plenty of references to the obligation on members of the livery to turn up at the funerals of their

[41] G.L., MS 5570/1, p. 171.

deceased brethren, and we are deluged with material relating to the round of feasting in which livery members were regularly invited to participate. Wills apparently suggest a greater degree of identification with the company on the part of members of the livery. They regularly made provision for a dinner for livery members accompanying the corpse to the grave, and such instructions were often followed by the bequest of plate or napery to the company. Among the wills of the artisans there is much less evidence of this kind. Artisans were clearly aware of their company affiliations, usually describing their status with some company label, but there were few material demonstrations of their loyalty. Should this be taken as evidence of a very tenuous attachment, a sign that the company existed mainly for the gratification of its wealthier members? Or was it simply a reflection of the humbler resources of the artisans whose loyalty to the craft might be expressed in less extravagant and enduring forms?

When we turn to the fragmentary evidence surviving from the yeomanry organisations there are signs of a more vigorous social round. Their wardens were responsible for the organisation of a range of communal activities and the provision of welfare on a modest scale for decayed members.[42] Their accounts show drinkings at the quarterly gatherings of the company to hear the reading of the ordinances, and election feasts often involving an elaborate ceremonial which aped that of the livery.[43] Their minutes show that the yeomanry wardens undertook the arbitration of disputes among members, referring difficult cases to the wardens of the livery.[44] The yeomanry may have been denied the use of the rich hearse cloths available to the livery, but they had their own.[45] For example, in the mid 1590s the yeomanry of the Tallow Chandlers decided to buy a new hearse cloth for the use of their members. Half the company, 110 members, and a high proportion of the active membership (in the sense of those who regularly paid their dues), made a contribution towards its purchase.[46] The hearse cloths are one sign that the yeomanry appeared at burials, and that members regarded their company affiliations as worthy of memory at the moment of their departure from this world. This is confirmed by the inclusion of penalties for non-attendance at burials among orders relating to the government of the yeomanry.[47] Burial was not the only rite of passage to be marked by their participation. It also appears to have been customary for yeomen to be invited to contribute to a

[42] G.L., MSS 6155/1–2; 6156; 7094; 15868; 12073; 7885/1–2.
[43] G.L., MSS 12073, fo. 25; 6155/2, passim. For election garlands, see ibid. fo. 87ᵛ; 7885/2, 1582–3 acct.
[44] G.L., MS 12073.
[45] Sk. Co., C.M. I, fo. 7ᵛ; G.L., MSS 5602/1, 10 Aug. 1592 (cloths confined to livery); 7094, fo. 79 ('a buriall cloth of St. Michaell' in inventory of yeomanry); 7885/1, 1572–3 acct., expenditure of £9. 14s. 3d. on a hearse cloth for yeomanry.
[46] G.L., MS 6155/2, 1595–6 and 1596–7 accts., minutes for 9 Oct. 1595 and 21 July 1597.
[47] G.L., MSS 7094, fo. 21ᵛ; 7885/1, 11 Aug. 1572; 5177/2, fo. 257; Welch, *Pewterers*, I, 211.

wedding gift for any of their number getting married: in 1569 the Bakers ordered that the wardens of the yeomanry should go through the company accompanied by the beadle to collect at least ½d. from every member for a wedding gift.[48] Sometimes it appears that the yeomanry were expected to accompany the groom to the service, although the evidence for this comes from a minute in the Plasterers' Company making the attendance voluntary rather than compulsory.[49]

However, there were restraints on the capacity of the yeomanries to promote a sense of identity with the companies. Limited resources explain their rather restricted role in poor relief. It is true that the Merchant Tailors spent the bulk of their income from quarterage on welfare, paying out £52. 4s. 8½d. in 1561–2, £67. 16s. 0d. in 1587–8, and £90. 0s. 8d. in 1594–5.[50] But expenditure from regular yeomanry funds was rarely, if ever, on this scale. The surviving accounts of the yeomanries of the Drapers and Haberdashers indicate that these companies preferred to spend their monies on dinners or the accumulation of a stock to support the lord mayor's triumphs, the organisation and finance of which was the responsibility of the yeomanry. Their accounts record no expenditure on poor relief in spite of the large numbers of poor in these companies.[51]

Another constraint was the suspicious attitudes of the rulers towards the yeomanry organisations. It is striking that much of the evidence about yeomanry activities comes in the form of orders from the assistants curtailing them. Jollifications at weddings were particularly the target for censorious elders, especially where they involved the unsupervised disports of journeymen. The Pewterers in 1561 ordered that no journeyman was to go to offerings but 'duely to wayt uppon their masters uppon the Sondayes and hallydaies untill Evensong be donne, and they uppon lycens to goo where honestie shall require as to shooting and suche lyke'. The Tallow Chandlers were even more determined: a court order of 1588 was directed against the bidding of any offerings in the company. Such orders are another indication of the widening social distances and elite withdrawal from some aspects of the popular culture that we noted taking place in the parishes at the same time.[52]

But the most important constraint was the sheer size of many companies. Professor Rappaport's researches have revealed that a much larger proportion of the City's inhabitants enjoyed the freedom than has hitherto been

[48] G.L., MS 5177/2, fo. 70ᵛ.   [49] G.L., MS 6122/1, Jan. 1602.
[50] MT. Co., C.M. I, p. 47; W.A. VI, fo. 283ᵛ, 1594–5 acct.
[51] Dp. Co., Bachelors' Accounts, 1616–90; G.L., MS 15868. For poverty in these companies, see Dp. Co., Rep. E, fo. 256ᵛ; G.L., MS 15842/1, fos. 115ᵛ–16, 175.
[52] Welch, *Pewterers*, I. 222, 245; G.L., MSS 6155/2, 2 Apr. 1588; 5177/2, fos. 257ᵛ–8, 278ᵛ; 2881/1, p. 150; C.L.R.O., Rep. 20, fos. 190ᵛ–1; J. R. Gillis, *For Better, For Worse: British Marriages, 1600 to the Present* (Oxford, 1985), pp. 86–7; above, pp. 92–8.

recognised. His calculations, based on the surviving fragment of the City freedom registers dating from the mid sixteenth century, suggest that three-quarters of males in the City over the age of twenty-eight were freemen.[53] The corollary is that some of the London companies were enormous. Quarterage lists from the larger companies are rare, but surviving lists show that the Fishmongers' Company had 802 members in 1610, and the Drapers' 2,106 in 1617. The largest company was the Merchant Tailors', which was admitting an average of 157 freemen a year in the 1590s, and whose total membership in 1595 I have estimated at 2,673 by deflating previous freedom admissions according to a survivorship curve derived from the Model North life tables.[54] It is obvious that the communal life which could be sustained by groups of less than 100 was much more intense than that which could be enjoyed in the larger companies, many of whose members must have had only the most tenuous of connections with them. Participatory office-holding was clearly more meaningful in the smaller companies than in the larger. About eighty freemen were being admitted each year in the Clothworkers at a time when at most four new places opened up among the yeomanry wardens each year, whereas there was a greater prospect of the fifteen freemen admitted each year in the Tallow Chandlers' Company holding one of the two yeomanry wardenships appointed each year. Mobility into the livery was likewise a more realistic prospect in the smaller craft companies where the livery constituted between 10 per cent and 27 per cent of the membership (Coopers 10 per cent, Armourers 12 per cent, Plumbers 24 per cent, Founders 27 per cent – actual proportions) than in the greater companies where the proportions were much lower (Drapers 5.4 per cent, Clothworkers 6 per cent, Merchant Tailors 3.7 per cent – all estimates).[55] It is probably their size which explains the lack of evidence for communal activities among the yeomanry in some of the greater companies. Numbers over 1,000 could hardly have assembled in the halls to hear the reading of ordinances, let alone sit down to a common dinner.

The increasing size of the companies was accompanied by another development which contributed to the erosion of members' identity with them. This was the way in which the custom of London, by which a freeman could exercise any trade and not just the one to which he had been apprenticed, eroded the occupational cohesion of the companies. Originally this seems to have been intended to apply only to those engaged in wholesaling, but by the sixteenth century it was being cited in the crafts to

---

[53] Rappaport, *Worlds Within Worlds*, pp. 49–53.
[54] G.L., MS 5578A/1; Johnson, *Drapers*, III. 88; Rappaport, *Worlds Within Worlds*, pp. 69–71; Archer, 'Governors and Governed', pp. 127–30, 182, n. 64.
[55] Johnson, *Drapers*, II. 195; *Wardens' Accounts of the Founders*, pp. 178–9; J. E. Oxley, *The Fletchers and Longbowstringmakers of London* (1968), p. 20; Cw. Co., Q.W.A.; Clode, *Memorials*, pp. 590–1; G.L., MSS 5606/2; 2210/1; 12085.

justify the pursuit of trades other than those from which the relevant company took its name. It became especially common as employment opportunities began to contract with the stagnation in cloth exports in the later sixteenth century.[56] The result was that many companies were acquiring a very heterogeneous complexion. By the 1570s there were already more candle sellers outside the Tallow Chandlers' Company than within it. In the period 1553–8 no less than seventy-five freemen from companies other than the Vintners obtained licences to retail wines. During the first decade of the seventeenth century the Blacksmiths admitted at least three tailors, two hatmakers, two goldsmiths, a coachmaker, a pointmaker, an embroiderer, a carman, and a wheelwright, and it is unlikely that all cases were recorded. The erosion of occupational homogeneity made it more difficult for the companies to enforce their ordinances, and weakened the identity of some freemen with their companies. Members of the Blacksmiths' Company who were hatmakers were unlikely to feel much in common with their fellow companymen.[57]

It is, of course, extraordinarily difficult to measure the level of participation in company affairs. But the proportion of members who paid their quarterage dues provides one indication. Quarterage lists (lists of those eligible to pay together with an indication of whether they actually paid) survive for the Tallow Chandlers, Coopers, Brewers, and Fishmongers. These show that members were highly remiss in the payment of their dues, and that the situation was deteriorating.[58] Although 83 per cent of the Coopers' Company's householders were paid up in the 1560s, only 57 per cent were paying in the 1590s, while the figures for the journeymen coopers were only 38 per cent and 13.5 per cent, respectively. In the larger companies the situation was even more serious. By the time that listings commence in the Fishmongers' Company in 1610, of 668 members of the yeomanry organisation only 16 per cent paid in full, a further 18 per cent made a partial contribution, and no less than 66 per cent failed to make any payment at all. Quarterage was usually collected on the quarter days, the assembly of the company members to hear the ordinances read, and the high levels of default may well also be a sign that members were failing to turn up. Certainly, complaints of slack attendance on these occasions abound.[59] In the Haberdashers' Company this was a serious problem even among the livery, with

---

[56] S. Thrupp, 'The Grocers of London: A Study of Distributive Trade', in *Studies in English Trade in the Fifteenth Century*, ed. M. M. Postan and E. Power (1933), pp. 260–2; Rappaport, *Worlds Within Worlds*, pp. 110–17; Ashton, *City and the Court*, pp. 48–50, 58–61.

[57] C.L.R.O., Rep. 18, fos. 70ᵛ–2; C.P.R., *1553–4, 1554–5, 1555–7*; G.L., MS 2881/1.

[58] G.L., MSS 5606/2; 5578A/1; 6155/1–2; 7885/1–2.

[59] Sk. Co., C.M. II, fo. 274ᵛ; Mc. Co., C.M. III, fos. 161, 298, 308, 463; MT. Co., C.M. III, fo. 197; Cw. Co., C.M. II, fo. 116.

recurrent complaints about the small appearance of the 'younger sort' of livery. Only nine turned up at one quarter day in 1591.[60] Community spirit clearly had its limitations. How many shared the opinions of Richard Bradshaw called up before the assistants of the Skinners' Company to pay his fine for not appearing on the quarter day and exclaiming: 'What am I the better for the company?'[61] The high level of default suggests that at least there was little spontaneous enthusiasm for the company among a large section of its membership. It remains true, however, that there was an active core in the sense that the same members tended to pay up in successive years.

Another consequence of the increased size of the companies was an increase in the level of social differentiation which found one of its clearest expressions in company feasting. The social round of the London livery companies was punctuated by a series of dinners. Many companies enjoyed dinners on each of the quarter days, although sometimes this was cut to two in the interests of economy. A dinner was provided at each company hall for those livery members who did not dine at Guildhall on the day of the presentation of the lord mayor at Westminster. But the climax of each company's calendar was the election feast, usually held annually, sometimes biennially. The election feasts were characterised by extraordinary largesse: capons roasted and boiled, swans, venison pasties, all generously spiced, sturgeon, pike, marchpanes, washed down with prodigious quantities of claret. The splendour of the occasion was enhanced by the presence of distinguished guests, representatives of the aldermanic elite and of the court. The halls were often hung with rich tapestries specially hired for the occasion.[62] Music was provided for the entertainment of those present: 'all dinner time ye syngyng children of Paules played upon their vialles & songe verye pleasaunt songes to ye great delectacion & reioysynge of ye whole companie'.[63] Guest lists were less impressive in the smaller companies, but the fare was still lavish: bucks were regularly delivered to the Carpenters' and Armourers' feasts.

Feasting served various purposes within the companies. Commensality was widely recognised as promoting brotherhood. Appointing a feast for their bachelors, the assistants of the Drapers' Company looked forward to 'thincrease of love and amytie withe better knowledge amonge the Bretherne to be hadd of this company'.[64] Secondly, the obligations of individuals to the corporate body were underlined by the table service of the younger members and the part financing of the feasts by the wardens. The Drapers required the service of the four master bachelors of the yeomanry as dressers, supervising

---

[60] G.L., MS 15842/1, fos. 22ᵛ, 26ᵛ, 27, 53ᵛ, 69ᵛ, 90ᵛ, 126ᵛ–7.
[61] Sk. Co., C.M. II, fo. 163ᵛ.
[62] Dp. Co., Dinner Book; Gs. Co., Reg. K, p. 460.   [63] Gs. Co., Reg. K, p. 125.
[64] Johnson, *Drapers*, II. 75–6, 297; Mc. Co., C.M. III, fos. 130ᵛ–1.

another twenty of the bachelors being 'the best & comlyest that cold be founde and best apparrelled' who conducted the guests to their seats and actually served the food.[65] The feasts on the lord mayor's day were customarily provided by members of the livery nominated by the wardens. The fulfilment of obligations to the company brought reciprocal benefits: the service of the bachelors and younger members of the livery was generally a prerequisite for higher office.[66] Thirdly, the feasts celebrated the wealth and worship of the company and of its leading members. Among the guests at the feasts were nobles, privy councillors, judges, officers of the Exchequer and customs administration, household officials and privy chamber men.[67] It was not only before the powerful that the company's wealth was displayed, for at the Drapers' feasts venison pasties were delivered out also to quite humble people – to the kennel raker, the parish clerk and local parson, the company's four porters and labourers, the porters of Blackwell Hall, and no less than fifteen pasties to the 'neighbours afore our gate'.[68] Although occasionally resentment surfaces at the burden of paying for the feasts,[69] most wardens seem to have welcomed the opportunities to advertise their status. The biographer of John Isham, mercer, describes the large quantities of venison the merchant was able to procure through his gentlemen friends on the occasion of the company's feast in 1567. We are told how 'agaynst the tyme of the feast [he did] gather togeither 33 fatt and Large buckes, Which he showed to divers of his company, Lyinge alltogeither in a gallery ... yt was thought, that not one man before his time nor sens had the Lyke by a great many'.[70] Such competitive display yielded benefits to the warden or steward not only among his fellow companymen, but also in a wider society, for it was customary for large numbers of the venison pasties to be delivered to the wardens to bestow on their household servants, relatives, and friends.[71]

[65] Dp. Co., Dinner Book, fo. 16; Gs. Co., Reg. K, p. 125; G.L., MS 15201/1, p. 154.
[66] G.L., MS 2881/1, pp. 114, 140; 14789, 1582 ordinances, no. 12.
[67] Nobles: MT. Co., C.M. I, p. 403; III, fos. 32ᵛ, 93, 196ᵛ, 271; Mc. Co., C.M. III, fos. 61–2ᵛ; G.L., MS 5570/1, p. 106; Exchequer officials: Gs. Co., Reg. K, p. 460; Dp. Co., Dinner Book, fo. 28; Customs officials: Mc. Co., C.M. III, fos. 61–2ᵛ; Sk. Co., C.M. II, fo. 98ᵛ, 203ᵛ; privy council clerks: G.L., MS 5570/1, pp. 42, 106, 243, 313; household officials: G.L., MSS 5570/1, pp. 42, 243, 313, 466; 5174/2, fo. 179ᵛ; privy chamber men: Mc. Co., C.M. III, fo. 61.
[68] Dp. Co., Dinner Book, fo. 11ᵛ.
[69] G.L., MSS 5570/1, pp. 281–2; 11588/1, fo. 187ᵛ; Cw. Co., C.M. II, fo. 164ᵛ.
[70] *John Isham, Mercer and Merchant Adventurer. Two Account Books of a London Merchant in the Reign of Elizabeth I*, ed. G. D. Ramsay (Northamptonshire Record Society, XXI, 1962), p. 171. For the provision of venison by the wardens, see Dp. Co., Dinner Book, fo. 10ᵛ.
[71] Dp. Co., Dinner Book, fos. 10–11ᵛ. The description of the 1564 feast shows no less than 74 of the 162 pasties (baked from the 25 bucks provided by the wardens) being delivered to the wardens.

But there were real limits to the degree to which feasting might promote incorporation. This was because of the rather exclusive attendance at most company dinners. In almost all companies only members of the livery were eligible to attend the dinners at the election of new wardens and on the lord mayor's day.[72] It is true that in the smaller craft companies attendance at the dinners on quarter days was wider: the master of the Armourers' Company was instructed to make a drinking for the whole company with buns and spice cakes, beer, ale, and cheese. But even here social distinctions were to be maintained for it was to be followed by the election dinner which only the livery were eligible to attend.[73] In the greater companies there were indications that the yeomen departed after the reading of the ordinances to leave the livery to enjoy a drinking.[74] More significantly still, there are signs that in the past, when the companies were smaller and more intimate associations, attendance had been wider. As late as 1546 the election dinner in the Weavers' Company seems to have been open to the whole guild above journeyman status, but by the time of the ordinances of 1579 it is clear that the dinner was confined to the livery and their spouses.[75] The Brewers' accounts for the mid sixteenth century record dinners at which 'all the hooll Company aswell in Lyverey as owte of Lyverey' were present, but wider participation ended with the accession of Elizabeth.[76] In the later-fifteenth-century Drapers' Company it was customary to select members out of the bachelors, as many as sixty-seven in 1487–8, to attend the election dinner, but the practice was abandoned at the turn of the century.[77] It may well be that this contraction in participation was prompted more by reasons of escalating costs and the increased size of the companies combined with the constraints of hall space than by any real sense of greater social exclusiveness. However, the consequences were very much the same: a reduction in contact between yeomen and liverymen whose social rounds moved increasingly in separate spheres.

This is not to deny that there were occasions of convivial assembly on the part of the yeomanry. Their accounts show quarterly drinkings where the members consumed bread and cheese washed down with beer. But these

---

[72] For election dinners, see *Carpenters' Records*, V. 167, 178, 195; Consitt, *Weavers*, p. 301; Welch, *Pewterers*, I. 294; Gs. Co., Reg. K, pp. 125, 156; Sk. Co., C.M. II, fo. 323; Br. Sr. Co, MS 5257/1, p. 26; G.L., MSS 6152/1, fo. 125; 5445/4, 20 Aug. 1571; 5445/5, 9 Aug. 1576; 12071/1, pp. 493, 556. For lord mayor's feast, see ordinances: G.L., MSS 6132; 3308; 14789; 12071/1, p. 499; W. A. D. Englefield, *A History of the Painter-Stainers' Company of London* (1923), p. 70; Pearce, *Butchers*, p. 209; Mc. Co., Register of Writings II, fos. 142ᵛ-3. For quarter dinners, see Mc. Co., C.M. III, fos. 130ᵛ-1; Dp. Co., Rep. E, fo. 268; G.L., MS 11588/1, fo. 57ᵛ.
[73] G.L., MS 12071/1, p. 486.   [74] Gs. Co., Reg. K, p. 92; Reg. L, p. 162.
[75] Consitt, *Weavers*, pp. 123, 221, 301.
[76] G.L., MS 5442/3, 1552–3, 1559–60, 1560–1, 1561–2 accts.
[77] Johnson, *Drapers*, I. 149.

gatherings generally lacked the participation of the liverymen.[78] The yeomanry's election feasts customarily represented all sections of the company, but the danger then was that the feasts would be taken over by the livery. Extant lists of those attending the yeomanry dinners of the Armourers' Company include members of the livery; the accounts of the wardens of the Haberdashers' yeomanry include payments by the liverymen in dinner money; and descriptions of the Fishmongers' yeomanry feasts specify the presence of the guests at the high table and the ancients and livery at the side tables.[79] However, in companies the size of the Fishmongers' and the Haberdashers' it was clearly impossible to accommodate the whole company at the one dinner, so that the feasts tended to turn into gatherings of the wealthier bachelors and livery. The descriptions of the Fishmongers' yeomanry feasts explain that once the livery and the guests were accommodated 'there was rome but for few of the yeomanrye'.[80] This tendency was apparent even in some of the smaller crafts. On a couple of occasions the ruling body of the Pewterers' Company instructed its yeomanry wardens not to make a sumptuous feast but to provide meat and drink for 'the number of xxx of the best of the Yemandrie'. When this order was made for the second time in 1593 it was described as being 'accordying to an Ancyent order'.[81]

Conviviality among the yeomanry, particularly in the twelve great companies, was still further limited by inflationary pressures and the increasing profile of poverty in their companies. The cost of the yeomanry dinners gave cause for serious concern. Accounts from the Haberdashers' Company at the turn of the century show an expenditure of about £100 on each dinner. Contributions by diners amounted to between £30 and £45, support by the wardens of the yeomanry to £35–£55, and allowances from the yeomanry stock to £15–£20. Although the allowance from the stock was small, it represented a high proportion of yeomanry income.[82] There were increasing doubts in the later sixteenth century about whether the expenditure was justified. The Haberdashers held no yeomanry dinner between 1586 and 1595.[83] An even worse situation prevailed in the Merchant Tailors' Company where the contribution from corporate funds was even higher. In the 1560s the dinner was consuming between £40 and £50 of the yeomanry stock each year.[84] So, in 1570 the assistants, feeling that the money would be better spent on poor relief, took the decision that the dinner should be held

---

[78] Generally, but perhaps not universally. It is possible that in some companies, particularly the lesser crafts, the quarter days may have seen a drinking among the whole company. But attendance is difficult to establish.

[79] G.L., MSS 12073, fos. 25, 29; 6155/2, 28 June 1561, 12 Apr. 1565, 2 Apr. 1588, May 1598; 7094, fo. 212; 5570/1, pp. 105, 464–5; 15868; Dp. Co., Rep. B, fo. 127.

[80] G.L., MS 5570/1, p. 105.   [81] Welch, *Pewterers*, I. 233; II. 13.

[82] G.L., MS 15868.

[83] G.L., MS 15842/1, fos. 25, 31, 37v, 42v, 47v, 78v.

[84] MT. Co., C.M. I, pp. 47, 218, 286, 504.

only every third year.[85] But the curtailment of the dinners had its own cost because for many companymen they must have been one of the few tangible expressions of the benefits of company membership. In 1595 the wardens substitute were complaining that 'a greate nomber of the yonger sorte of the Bachelers either withhould or repyne and grudge to pay their quarteredge due to the company for that there is no generall calling together of them as hath ben in tymes past accustumed'.[86] In the same year the Haberdashers revived their yeomanry dinners because their suppression had 'growen to the greate dislike of the generalitie of this Company'.[87] Perhaps in this conflict between the claims on company funds of the needs of the poor and commensality, we see something of the changing conception of brotherhood in the sixteenth century. Whereas in the past the company had sat down to a general feast, now the social bond received its most frequent and tangible expression in the appearance of poor petitioners before the courts of assistants requesting pensions or in the wealthy bachelors' choice of those poor men who were to wear the gowns, for which the company had subscribed, in the lord mayor's procession.

There was nothing new in principle about the relief of the poor by the livery companies. From their inception the duty to support those who had fallen on hard times was accepted, but there was something peculiar about the volume and scope of later-sixteenth-century charitable activity. The fifteenth century had seen the foundation of some well-endowed almshouses administered by the companies for the benefit of their members, and more were established in the early sixteenth century.[88] However, apart from almshouses, company activity had been rather irregular. There were few grants of regular pensions from company stock, although much relief was doubtless distributed in the form of doles from poor boxes maintained by voluntary contributions and possibly fines, or after whip-rounds among company rulers. From the middle decades of the sixteenth century a major change, paralleling developments in the corporation's own involvement in the relief of the poor, is evident as the volume of relief administered by the companies increased markedly. This was partly as a result of the accumulation of endowments, but it also reflected the increasing number of pensions being granted from house stock. Thus in the early sixteenth century the Grocers' support of the poor was confined to the £10–£13 p.a. paid to the company's almsmen under the Keble benefaction, and miscellaneous payments at obits. From the 1550s, pensions from house stock appear. Initially the recipients were few, only two in 1552–3, but by the 1570s the

[85] Ibid. p. 458.   [86] MT. Co., C.M. III, fos. 302, 377^v.
[87] G.L., MS 15842/1, fo. 78^v.
[88] W. K. Jordan, *The Charities of London, 1480–1660: the Aspirations and Achievements of the Urban Society* (1960), pp. 135–41.

company was spending £18 p.a., and in the 1590s twenty pensioners received over £60 p.a.[89] The Carpenters were spending £1–£2 p.a. on pensions in the 1550s rising to £4–£5 p.a. in the 1570s and £13 p.a. in the 1590s. More individuals benefited from the grants, the recipients of Carpenters' Company charity doubling between the 1570s and 1590s.[90]

Using techniques elaborated in the next chapter, it has been possible to estimate the volume of poor relief directed at company members. The value of endowments for poor relief has been calculated from the charity commissioners' reports checked wherever possible against contemporary documentation. This shows that by the mid 1590s the companies were supporting at least 199 almsmen and almswomen, backed by pensions amounting to a total of £596 p.a., and that other endowments for the company poor amounted to £251 p.a. The total value of pensions disbursed out of house stock has been estimated by calculating the amount spent in the mid 1590s in twenty-two extant company accounts (listed in the bibliography), and inflating the total by a multiplier derived from the proportion of freedom admissions accounted for by these companies in 1551–3. Depending on whether generous companies like the Mercers or the Goldsmiths are included in the calculations the total lies between £644 p.a. and £862 p.a.[91] The results of the reconstruction for a sample of companies and the balance between endowments and contributions from company stock is shown in Table 4.1. Two caveats must be inserted. First, there must remain some uncertainty about the volume of relief granted by the yeomanry. As has been shown it was substantial in the Merchant Tailors, but much less elsewhere. However, the lack of documentation makes it difficult to be dogmatic on this point. Secondly, the figures cannot give any idea of the volume of *ad hoc* relief, which in some cases, particularly where the regular effort was nugatory as in the Tallow Chandlers' Company, may have been substantial.

It would appear that the companies were spending £1,647 p.a. on the relief of their poor in the mid 1590s (assuming £800 for pensions from house stock), suggesting that they were as important as the poor rate in outdoor relief: the poor rate, yielded £1,420 for the pensioner poor in the parishes, and £820 for the orphans in Christ's Hospital.[92] However the numbers supported by the livery companies were not as great as those relieved by the

[89] G.L., MSS 11571/4–8.

[90] *Carpenters' Records*, IV (accts. for 1552–5); V (accts. for 1570–3), VII (accts. for 1596–8).

[91] Below, pp. 164–7; 'Report of Her Majesty's Commissioners Appointed to Inquire into the Livery Companies of the City of London', *Parliamentary Papers*, 1884. XXXIX, parts IV–V. The following companies' accounts were examined for payments out of house stock: Armourers, Leathersellers, Brewers, Carpenters, Cutlers, Pewterers, Curriers, Barber Surgeons, Blacksmiths, Grocers, Skinners, Vintners, Ironmongers, Salters, Coopers, Merchant Tailors, Drapers, Clothworkers, Cordwainers, Butchers, Mercers and Goldsmiths. For freedom admissions in 1551–3, see Rappaport, *Worlds Within Worlds*, p. 92.

[92] Below, p. 181.

parish authorities because of the peculiarly large size of some company pensions. A typical pension in the parishes at this time was 6d. per week (26s. p.a.), but the average pension in the Goldsmiths was twice this (54s.).[93] This reflects the fact that the companies adopted a wider definition of poverty than the parochial authorities. Their efforts were not directed merely at the destitute, but also at 'decayed liverymen', formerly prosperous but fallen on hard times. This category of claimant was potentially wide. Richard Grassby's study of the personal estates of London freemen in the period 1586–1614 showed a large number of freemen registered as possessing no net estate, but more than £500 in gross assets (8 per cent of the sample).[94] One encounters many victims of business failures among the recipients of company charity. Sir Thomas Lodge was imprisoned in the Fleet for debts of £2,500 at the end of his mayoralty and sought loans from the companies.[95] Many, like Richard Grafton, a freeman of the Grocers, publishing entrepreneur, City M.P., and a leading light in the foundation of the City hospitals, ended their days in receipt of company charity.[96] Individuals in these categories received larger pensions in accordance with their former estate in the company. Richard Springham, mercer and Merchant Adventurer, was awarded a pension of £20 p.a. in 1576 'in consideracion of his necessity and losses susteyned by the prince of Sweden infortunity of the see evil dettors sickness and otherwise', and because he had formerly held high office in the company. Large pensions of up to £13. 6s. 8d. were relatively common in the greater companies.[97] In the Merchant Tailors' Company almshouses were specifically reserved for the liverymen in their old age.[98]

The large pensions granted to individuals were sometimes resented by the artisans. The artisan skinners complained in 1606 that their assistants had granted pensions to merchants' factors 'whereby aged persons past labour are deprived of theire due'.[99] But however revealing of the suspicions that could arise when artisan representation on the court of assistants was weak, this was in reality a rather jaundiced view. The assistants pointed out that all the almshouses 'except one or two' were occupied by artisan skinners and tawyers, that about thirty artisans had money in loan, and that although a pension of 3s. 1d. per week (£8. 0s. 4d. p.a.) had been granted to the relative of a benefactor this case was untypical.[100] The criticisms of the artisans doubtless reflected the fact that the pensions granted to the really poor were

---

93 Bodl., MS Eng. Hist. c. 479.
94 R. Grassby, 'The Personal Wealth of the Business Community in Seventeenth-Century England', *Ec.H.R.*, second series, 23 (1970), 224.
95 G.L., MS 11588/1, fo. 168; Mc. Co., C.M. III, fos. 117ʳ⁻ᵛ, 122ᵛ, 139ᵛ.
96 G.L., MS 11588/1, fo. 233ᵛ; *D.N.B.*
97 Mc. Co., C.M. III, fo. 292ᵛ. Cf. MT. Co., C.M. I, p. 756; Cw. Co., C.M. III, fos. 137, 167ᵛ; Gs. Co., Reg. K, p. 92; Br. Sr. Co., MS 5257/2, fos. 13ᵛ, 32, 49ᵛ; G.L., MSS 15842/1, fo. 41ᵛ; 11588/1, fos. 119ʳ⁻ᵛ, 413ᵛ, 417.
98 MT. Co., C.M. III, fo. 345ᵛ.   99 Sk. Co., C.M. I, fo. 88ᵛ.   100 Ibid. fo. 90.

Table 4.1. *Resources for poor relief in selected London livery companies,*
c. 1595

	Grocers	Clothworkers	Goldsmiths
Estimated size of company	1,048	1,456	less than 700
Number of almsmen and size of pension	7 @ 26s. 2 @ 34s. 8d. = £12.11s. 4d.	7 @ 32s. 6d. 1 @ 20s. = £12.7s. 6d.	67 pensions paid, 15 with accommodation in almshouses Total expend. on almsmen and other pensions:
Other pensions from company stock[a]	£62. 5s. 6d.	£48. 17s. 6d.	£182. 4s. 8d.
Number of other pensions[b]	20	20	52
Endowments for company poor	Nil	£24. 16s. 10d.[c]	£4. 9s. 2d.
Total	£74. 16s. 10d.	£86. 1s. 10d.	£186. 13s. 10d.

[a] Includes payments in occasional relief.
[b] Excludes recipients of occasional relief.
[c] Includes payments in clothing under Lambe's benefaction where it is not clear whether the recipients were company members.
Sources: Bodl., MS Eng. Hist. c. 479, fos. 173–92; Gs. Co., 'Register of Deeds'; P.R.O., PROB 11/84, fo. 270[v]; G.L., MSS 11571/8, accts. for 1594–6; 11616; Cw. Co., Q.W.A. and R.W.A., 1595–6; 'Wills Book'; 'Benefactors' Book'; *Parliamentary Papers*, 1884, XXXIX, parts IV-V. For sizes of companies, see Archer, 'Governors and Governed', pp. 127–30, and for Goldsmiths cf. Pearl, 'Change and Stability', p. 30.

never sufficient, nor ever could be, given the pressures on company resources. Indications of these constraints appear in the anxieties occasionally expressed that pensions were consuming house stock,[101] in the grant of lump sums to individuals 'on condition he is no more suitor'[102] and in petitioners being told to await vacancies.[103] Moreover it is clear that there was an imbalance in the distribution of resources among the companies (Table 4.1). For example, the Goldsmiths were spending £187 p.a. and the Clothworkers £86 p.a., although the Goldsmiths were half the size of the Clothworkers and

[101] Mc. Co., C.M. III, fo. 313[v]; G.L., MSS 15842/1, fo. 175; 15201/2, p. 18.
[102] G.L., MSS 11588/1, fos. 247, 265[v]; 5570/1, p. 5; 5445/9, 29 July 1591, 21 Mar. 1592; Br. Sr. Co., MS 5257/2, fo. 37[v].
[103] Gs. Co., Reg. L, p. 229.

their membership not so poor. And, because of the large pensions paid to individuals, £36.5s.10d. of the money spent by the Clothworkers was directed at just six people.

To varying degrees then the companies fulfilled valuable integrating roles in sixteenth-century London. In the largest companies their sheer size combined with the erosion of craft identity through the custom of London weakened the sense of loyalty felt by many members. But even in these companies there remained an active core for whom the company remained important as a vehicle for regulating the trade and promoting craft grievances as well as a source of poor relief. It is true that the communal bond was a more hierarchically articulated one at the end of the sixteenth century as commensality was eroded and the practice of poor relief more intensive. But in granting relief the rulers were acknowledging their responsibilities towards the poor, providing a rhetoric which could be exploited by lowlier members in their quest for the support of the elite in the enforcement of ordinances and the amelioration of craft grievances.

ORDINANCES AND THEIR ENFORCEMENT

The majority of the London livery companies were emphatically not merely 'social' organisations concerned only with feasting and the administration of charities.[104] Involvement in the regulation of production and the labour supply was still central to most. It is true that some companies lost their affiliation with particular trades at an early stage. The rise of the Merchant Adventurers eclipsed the domination of the Mercers' Company in the export of cloth and involved members of other of the leading companies in the export of cloth and the import of luxury fabrics with the result that the company lost its monopoly of the retailing of silks, still sufficiently recent a development for it to be resented in the 1560s and 1570s.[105] Merchant members of the Grocers' Company were still the largest importers of grocery wares in the 1560s but, with the disruption of the Antwerp mart and the multiplication of the sources of supply, other merchants became involved, weakening the company's control of the trade. It is noticeable that the company's vigorous exercise of its rights of search in the 1560s had lapsed by the later 1580s.[106] But these cases were untypical, and the erosion of the search should not be pre-dated. Although merchants were prominent on the ruling bodies of companies with large artisan representation, like the Merchant Tailors, Haberdashers, Clothworkers, and Skinners, they were

[104] J. Youings, *Sixteenth-Century England* (Harmondsworth, 1984), p. 351.
[105] Mc. Co., C.M. III, fos. 23ᵛ–5; Ramsay, 'Victorian Historiography', pp. 159–60.
[106] See *Port and Trade of Early Elizabethan London*, and P.R.O., E190/8/1 for grocery importers; G.L., MSS 11588/1–2 for trade regulation.

still expected to see that the search was maintained and the ordinances enforced, either by themselves or by delegation to others.

Ordinances were directed in the first place at maintaining standards of production.[107] The companies regulated admission to the craft by administering the apprenticeship system and by requiring masterpieces from those who had completed their terms. Common standards of production were often laid down and enforced by means of a system of trade marks and regular searches of the membership. The protection of the consumer was not the only consideration behind such ordinances because they were generally supported by artisans who recognised that those who produced shoddy goods were likely to profit at the expense of others. Moreover, artisans often took pride in their craft, particularly where companies were in dispute. Thus the Bricklayers' search book records the shoddy work of three members with the comment that it was 'founde to be very insufficiently done to the discreditt of the company which was scoffed at by the plasterers & therefore worthy of a great fyne'.[108] In some cases the skill of a particular craft could be a highly sensitive issue. Clothworkers were anxious to maintain standards to scotch the criticisms of those merchants who alleged the inferiority of English cloth-dressing techniques to those of continental artisans as an argument for exporting undressed English cloths.[109]

Other ordinances were unambiguously directed at the protection of the small-scale producer and journeyman. Limits were placed on the scale of individual enterprises through restrictions on the number of apprentices in each workshop and by confining members to one retail outlet. Further protection for journeymen was achieved by regulations requiring that masters with establishments of a particular size employ them and by the

[107] Much of the following is based on surviving company ordinances: G.L., MSS 12110 (Armourers, 1570); 2943 (Blacksmiths, 1572); 5496 (Brewers, 1580); 14789 (Broderers, 1562, 1582, and 1609); 5633 (Coopers, 1561); 8033 (Cordwainers, 1573); 8059 (Joiners, 1572); 184/2 (Pinmakers, 1606); 6132 (Plasterers, 1587); 2207 (Plumbers, 1520 and 1611); 5385A (Saddlers, 1561); 6174/1 (Tallow Chandlers, 1588); 3308 (Turners, 1608); 15364 (Vintners, 1594); C.L.R.O., Rep. 21, fos. 375–9ᵛ (Curriers, 1587); Rep. 22, fos. 389ᵛ–94 (Founders, 1592); Rep. 21, fos. 485–7 (Fruiterers, 1587); Rep. 20, fos. 157ᵛ–60 (Vintners, 1581); S. Young, *The Annals of the Barber Surgeons* (1890), pp. 117–20, 179–82, 579–86 (1530, 1566, 1606); H. H. Bobart, *Records of the Basketmakers' Company* (1911), pp. 31–41 (1569); Pearce, *Butchers*, pp. 201–39 (1607); *Clothworkers' Ordinances*, pp. 37–96 (1587); Johnson, *Drapers*, II. 304–30 (1578); T. F. Reddaway, *The Early History of the Goldsmiths' Company, 1327–1509* (1975), pp. 210–74 (1483); Nicholl, *Ironmongers*, pp. 116–24 (1581); *The Charters, Ordinances and Bye Laws of the Mercers' Company* (1881), pp. 67–92 (1504); Clode, *Memorials*, pp. 202–26 (1507, 1613); Englefield, *Painter-Stainers*, pp. 66–73 (1582); *The Book of Ordinances Belonging to the Company of the Tylers and Bricklayers Incorporated Within the City of London* (? date, 17th cent.); Consitt, *Weavers*, pp. 218–23, 285–308, 318–21 (1492, 1577, 1596).
[108] G.L., MS 3047/1, Oct. 1606.
[109] Cw. Co., C.M. I, fo. 254B; Ramsay, 'Industrial Discontent'.

careful licensing by the wardens of the employment of non-free labour. Efforts were made to protect craftsmen from exploitation by trading interests. For example, the Skinners legislated against members acting as middlemen between the country producers of skins and the artisans because this practice was regarded as causing increases in prices.[110] The Fishmongers attempted to restrain the forestalling of fish, maintaining twelve factors at Rye to make purchases on behalf of all members. The thinking behind this was that it would prevent engrossing by the wealthier members and keep prices down.[111]

In some cases the degree of intervention envisaged by the ordinances was high: several companies, like the Broderers, Armourers, and Pinmakers required that no goods be put to sale until they had been searched by the wardens, as well as enjoying powers of search over imported wares.[112] Others showed considerable flexibility in devising new mechanisms to improve the search. Thus in November 1567 the Clothworkers introduced searchers and sealers of cloth at the request of their artisans. Initially the office rotated among members of the yeomanry, but this sharing of responsibility probably resulted in some dilution of professional standards, so that when the machinery was tightened in the 1590s the sealers were given salaries.[113] When the Cordwainers secured new ordinances in 1612 they attempted to improve their search by arranging for the division of the city into four areas, each of which was to be represented by two overseers who were to join the wardens in the search.[114] At its most extreme the company's intervention involved the corporate purchase of raw materials. The charter of the Cordwainers in 1562 licensed the wardens to establish a fund for the purchase of leather in provincial fairs and markets by purveyors. The leather so obtained was to be distributed among the members according to the size of their contributions at cost price. Its intention was to eliminate forestalling and engrossing and prevent the increases in raw material costs to the small producer which followed.[115]

Moreover, it would be wrong to see the companies as hopelessly ill-equipped to the demands of enforcement. The existence of occupational concentrations within the city meant that the chances of detection were often high.[116] Companies disposed of a wide range of sanctions to deal with those in breach of their ordinances: offenders could be fined, publicly humiliated

---

[110] Sk. Co., C.M. II, fos. 225ᵛ–6, 284.

[111] G.L., MS 5570/1, pp. 191, 254, 300, 350, 404; H. Townshend, *Historical Collections* (1680), pp. 309–10.

[112] G.L., MSS 12110; 184/2; 14789.

[113] Cw. Co., C.M. II, fos. 78, 87ᵛ, 106, 111–12, 113, 120ᵛ, 122, 141ᵛ; III, fos. 115, 179ᵛ, 191ᵛ, 194ᵛ, 209ᵛ.

[114] G.L., MS 8033, pp. 68–9, 72.   [115] C.P.R., *1560–63*, pp. 262–3.

[116] Stow, *Survey of London*, I. 81–2; M. J. Power, 'The Social Topography of Restoration London', in *London, 1500–1700*, ed. Beier and Finlay, pp. 215–22.

by stocking, or briefly imprisoned on the word of the mayor. It is clear that wardens used considerable discretion in determining suitable punishments, taking into account the gravity of the offence, the previous reputation of the offender, and his material circumstances. It was customary to require offenders to bring in pawns to cover the full cost of the fine required by the ordinances, and, once the contrite offender was at the mercy of the court, to mitigate the fine according to circumstances. If offenders refused to bring in pawns, the wardens could apply the sanction of imprisonment.[117] Such a system was well calculated to secure obedience: submissive and contrite behaviour, a recognition that one was being justly punished, was encouraged by the knowledge that the wardens would be less favourable if the offender remained recalcitrant. Fines were also rendered more acceptable by an element of consensual policing as the wardens took care to draw on expert advice in the judgement of offences. Thus the Clothworkers appointed viewers from among the artisans to determine whether workmanship was worthy of a fine; the wardens of the Grocers were assisted in the trial of spices taken in their searches by 'ij Advocates skilfull in tryeng of the sayde powders'.[118] This involvement of a wider range of the company membership also served to give publicity to offences and thus to deter future infractions since a reputation for bad workmanship was not good for business.[119]

However, effective enforcement depended on the existence of a consensus within the company, and such a consensus was hardly ever present on all aspects of the ordinances. It is for this reason that we frequently encounter bitter outbursts from artisans that the ordinances remained unenforced. Thus Nicholas Walker, clothworker, complained in April 1570 'that what yll workemanshipp, or what mysorder soever was doon by any parson, yt was either maynteyned, or passed unponysshed by this table'. Thomas Walker, fishmonger, complained in 1598 that his wardens allowed 'all bad and naughtye fishe to be sold without controlement'. The wardens of the Skinners were alleged to have 'no compassionate feeling of abuses in the said art'.[120] The most contentious areas were the ordinances relating to apprentice recruitment and those which attempted to restrain the activities of the wholesaling interests.

The relatively controversial nature of ordinances limiting numbers of apprentices is suggested by the frequency with which they were reiterated, and the difficulties experienced in finding a suitable formula which balanced the claims of the poorer householders and journeymen to a fair share of work against the desires of the wealthier members to expand their enterprises.

[117] G.L., MSS 5570/1, pp. 94, 109, 185; 11588/1, fos. 52ᵛ, 53ᵛ, 58, 90, 120ᵛ–1; 6152/1, fo. 125; Sk. Co., C.M. II, fos. 71ᵛ–5; Archer, 'Governors and Governed', pp. 145–7.
[118] Cw. Co., C.M. II–III, passim, esp. III, fo. 166; G.L., MS 11588/1, fos. 82, 89, 102ᵛ, 147.
[119] Cw. Co., C.M. II, fo. 141ᵛ.
[120] Cw. Co., C.M. II, fo. 140; G.L., MS 5570/1, p. 170; Sk. Co., C.M. I, fo. 88.

Orders limiting apprentices were sometimes accompanied with the provision that anyone moving for a revision should be liable to a fine in recognition of their controversial nature.[121] Artisans were often sensitive about the privileges enjoyed by their assistants. On complaint from the 'young men' of the Plasterers' Company in 1587 about the excessive number of apprentices, the aldermen ruled that Ralph Bettes and Thomas Kelley might have three apprentices, but that no other company member should enjoy this privilege thereafter. In spite of the arbitration, disagreements on this point remained, for the company ordinances, obtained in the same year and renewed in 1596, allowed *any* man who had served as master to keep three apprentices after four years.[122] Moreover the restrictions were often difficult to enforce because of the practice of setting over apprentices: such was the substance of a complaint in the Bricklayers' Company in 1608.[123] In some companies there are signs that the ordinances were being waived and turned into a revenue raising device. Between 1561 and 1581 the Carpenters' Company levied an average of twelve fines a year (up to £5 each) from its more prominent members 'to have apprentices', presumably in excess of those prescribed by the ordinances.[124] Such practices are unlikely to have been popular with journeymen anxious about the level of apprentice recruitment. Elsewhere there is evidence that some of the more prosperous householders resented the necessity of keeping journeymen to match their apprentices. A statute of 1551 had required that one journeyman be set on work for every apprentice employed in excess of two. In 1563 the wardens substitute of the Merchant Tailors, accompanied by Walter Fish, Thomas Ludwell, William Phillips, and 'others using the handicraft of tailory', requested the aid of the company in the repeal of this statute.[125] Again it is likely that there were divisions of opinion among the handitrade about the advisability of this course of action which was not calculated to be popular among the journeymen. The records of the Merchant Tailors' Company afford little sign of an effort to restrict apprentice recruitment.

In responding to pressure from their poorer members for action the rulers often displayed a neurotic suspicion of their intentions. When the young men of the Grocers' Company petitioned in 1563 for an ordinance to limit apprentice recruitment, the assistants responded by demanding that those who had signed the petition be summoned before the court so that their 'personages' might be viewed, and interrogatories drawn up 'against everie

[121] G.L., MS 11588/2, fo. 38ᵛ; Welch, *Pewterers*, I. 185, 200, 237–8. For evidence of the difficulties of arriving at a suitable formula, see G.L., MS 5602/1, 28 Aug. 1571, 11 Nov. 1585, 3 Aug. 1590, 2 Mar. 1591; C.L.R.O., Rep. 22, fo. 199ᵛ.
[122] C.L.R.O., Rep. 21, fo. 395; G.L., MS 6132.   [123] G.L., MS 5043, p. 10.
[124] *Carpenters' Records*, IV–V: analysis of accounts 1561–81. Cf. G.L., MS 7090/2, fos. 214ᵛ, 215, 219, 237ᵛ.
[125] 3 & 4 Ed. VI c. 22; MT. Co., C.M. I, p. 43; *C.J.*, I, 66, 67.

Article mencioned in the said bill and so to be obiected unto them'.[126] The journeymen of the Clothworkers' Company who agitated in 1577 for measures to relieve their distress were criticised for failing to come to work.[127] Such prejudices worked to ensure that it required sustained pressure from the artisans to secure action. The difficulties of the journeymen were compounded by the fact that their petitions ran counter to the interests of the wardens of the yeomanry. Hence enforcement remained intermittent. Although in 1577 the Clothworkers began investigations into the size of workshops and fined several members for keeping apprentices without setting journeymen on work, thereafter there is little sign of further action on this issue until renewed pressure in the 1590s resulted in another crop of fines.[128] The response to the petitioning therefore has an air of tokenism about it. In other companies, like the Goldsmiths, Grocers, and the Haberdashers, it also appears that only the pressures of the 1590s created sufficient urgency for the assistants to take action: the Grocers, for example, had failed to respond to the petitions of 1564, and only passed the required ordinance limiting apprentice recruitment in 1595.[129] It is only in terms of a perceived lack of commitment among the assistants that we can explain the grievances of the artisan skinners in the early seventeenth century. The court minutes provide evidence of only intermittent enforcement of the ordinances with which the artisans were most concerned. In December 1593 the company ordered that the 'laws of forefathers' relating to forestalling and engrossing by wholesalers should be put into execution because 'the whole arte & handicrafte of skynners are growen to greate decaye in so muche that dyvers of the bodie of the same arte are become verye obstynate and contrarious to all good & Laudable ordynaunces'. Although in the following months several liverymen were hauled before the court for their dealings in the country, the assistants were reluctant to persist in the campaign because they were running the risk of alienating a powerful group among the liverymen. The kind of campaign the artisans wanted was therefore likely to produce tensions within the elite.[130] Similar considerations doubtless explain the reluctance of the assistants of the Haberdashers' Company to restrain the activities of wholesalers who sent untrimmed hats into the country to the detriment of the feltmakers.[131] Likewise the artisan clothworkers in the Merchant Tailors' Company experienced considerable frustrations in getting their assistants to ensure that the retailers of cloth put their cloth to dressing

[126] G.L., MS 11588/1, fo. 85.   [127] Cw. Co., C.M. II, fos. 182ʳ⁻ᵛ, 210ᵛ, 211ᵛ.

[128] Ibid. fos. 211, 212ᵛ, 213ᵛ, 214, 215 (1577); III, fos. 161, 176ᵛ–7, 177ᵛ, 178, 179 (for the late 1590s); IV, fos. 2ᵛ, 4ᵛ, 8ᵛ (for another crop in 1605–6).

[129] G.L., MSS 11588/1, fos. 88ᵛ, 90ᵛ; 11588/2, fo. 38ᵛ. Cf. Gs. Co., Reg. N, pp. 112, 115–16; G.L., MS 15842/1, fos. 17ᵛ, 72ᵛ, 74.

[130] Sk. Co., C.M. II, fos. 225ᵛ–6, 226ᵛ–7, 229, 230ᵛ.

[131] G.L., MS 15842/1, fos. 17ᵛ, 108ᵛ, 111ᵛ.

by members of the company. The company's rulers initially responded to petitioning in December 1568 by trying to pesuade the retailers of the plight of the artisans, and only granted an ordinance when the agitation was renewed in 1571. Complaints that the ordinance was not enforced surfaced on several occasions, and it was not until 1598 that the wardens entered into litigation in King's Bench with Edward Davenant to secure his obedience to the ordinance, and then their action proved inconclusive.[132] It is difficult to tell whether the artisans were satisfied with this degree of action. Could the assistants not have tried harder? Certainly the assistants were wary of their artisan body: the accounts in 1606 record the expenditure of 20s. for a copy of the skinners' patent 'to the end that our companie may forsee that our tailors do not do the like'.[133]

It should be emphasised that the friction over the enforcement of ordinances was not likely to produce outright and continuing resentments between rich and poor in the companies. Sometimes the conflicts reflected the divergent interests of artisans and rulers, but sometimes, particularly in the lesser companies, they were disputes among liverymen and personal animosities may have been more important. The attack sponsored by six liverymen on the wardens and assistants of the Pewterers' Company in 1572 'for injuries done' appears to reflect the tensions generated when personal animosities (in this case reflecting resentment at the Curtis family's domination of the company) were perceived as determining the pattern of enforcement.[134] Even where the battle-lines were more clearly drawn, the frustrations experienced by the artisans over the enforcement of ordinances were likely to be counterbalanced by other considerations. Retailing fishmongers were undoubtedly annoyed by the zeal with which their wardens enforced an ordinance against the watering of fish with lime, a practice clearly near-universal among the waterers but opposed by the wardens in the interests of the consumer. On the other hand they knew full well that the wardens were promoting suits for the benefit of the poorer brethren in attempting to secure the better enforcement of the Lenten fast and the repeal of the 1581 Act against the import of foreign-cured fish, and in restraining the exploitation of the market by wholesale dealers.[135] Likewise, journeymen clothworkers might have felt that the ordinances restricting apprentice recruitment were only half-heartedly enforced, but they were at

132 MT. Co., C.M. I, pp. 366–9, 553, 622, 691, 699, 701; III, fos. 110ᵛ, 187, 189ᵛ, 387ᵛ, 388ʳ⁻ᵛ, 391ᵛ, 392ᵛ, 402, 405, 413ᵛ, 414ᵛ–15, 426; W.A. VII, fos. 339ᵛ, 397ᵛ–8.
133 Ibid. 1606–7 acct.
134 Welch, *Pewterers*, I. 268–9, 270–1; C.L.R.O., Rep. 17, fos. 59ᵛ, 95ᵛ, 171; G.L., MS 7090/2, fos. 62ᵛ, 94ᵛ, 101, 108ᵛ, 115.
135 G.L., MS 5570/1, pp. 87, 88, 89, 90, 94, 102, 109, 169–71, 185, 197, 205, 232, 271, 314, 360, 376, 379; G. R. Elton, 'Piscatorial Politics in the Early Parliaments of Elizabeth I', in *Business Life and Public Policy: Essay in Honour of D. C. Coleman*, ed. N. McKendrick and R. B. Outhwaite (Cambridge, 1986), pp. 1–20.

one with the more prosperous artisans in wishing for the enforcement of the statutes requiring the dressing of cloth for export.[136] Another crucial issue which might work to solidify company loyalties was hostility towards strangers and foreigners practising the craft.

STRANGERS AND FOREIGNERS

Londoners encountered the problem of the non-free in two forms, the strangers or aliens, immigrants mainly from France and the Netherlands, and the English non-free who were termed 'foreigners'. The challenges they represented to London artisans were broadly similar and company regulations often treated them together, but feeling against strangers was more bitter because of xenophobia and the ease with which they could be identified. Anti-alien feeling sometimes threatened public order, whereas resentments against foreigners do not seem to have reached such dimensions. Aliens and foreigners were resented because they were thought to evade company regulations and produce substandard goods, and by taking on large numbers of apprentices they threatened the employment prospects of journeymen, and simply because they competed in the same market-place. Thus in 1575, the pursemakers, glovers, and other artisans working in the leather trades petitioned against foreigners for working in secret chambers, producing deceitful wares, and taking too many apprentices.[137] In 1595 the Weavers claimed that the aliens kept twice as many looms and apprentices as they ought to have done under company ordinances, that they had taught the craft to their fellow countrymen without requiring the seven-year apprenticeships the Englishmen had served, and that they set women and girls on work. The competition of the strangers led to price cutting: 'they must make things so cheap that it will not suffice to find the people bread'.[138] Craftsmen in the Armourers' Company criticised the strangers for engrossing wares; the Cutlers claimed that the aliens counterfeited the trade marks of respectable English artisans to pass off their shoddy goods.[139] Alien merchants were singled out for attack because they imported goods which competed with English products.[140] Aliens were also seen as forming an inward-looking society of their own deliberately cutting themselves off from their hosts: 'though they be demized or borne heere amongst us, yett they keepe themselves severed from us in church, in a government, in trade, in langauge and marriage'.[141] There was of course much that was irrational about such arguments. A survey of 1593 revealed that 1,665 stranger householders in

---

[136] Ramsay, 'Industrial Discontent'.   [137] C.L.R.O., Rep. 18, fos. 412ᵛ–13.
[138] Consitt, *Weavers*, pp. 313–14.
[139] G.L., MS 12071/2, p. 50; C.L.R.O., Rep. 21, fo. 280.
[140] Consitt, *Weavers*, p. 314; *T.E.D.*, I. 309.   [141] Ibid.

the metropolitan area employed 1,671 Englishmen, and the benefits of alien skills have long been recognised.[142] Nevertheless the perceptions were real and threatening enough.

It is difficult to make quantitative estimates of the scale of the competition represented by aliens and foreigners. We know that the alien population was around 5,000 in the later sixteenth century, in other words about 4–5 per cent of the City's population.[143] Rappaport's estimates of the size of the free population suggest that about three-quarters of adult males enjoyed the freedom in the mid sixteenth century, but it is worth emphasising that much of the competition was suburban in nature.[144] Particularly worrying were those crafts in which the non-free were well represented in Westminster close to the aristocratic clientele. The non-free cutlers of Westminster were a real challenge to the freemen of Fleet Street. The battles between the free and non-free cordwainers were largely battles between the shoemakers of London and Westminster.[145] It is also important to appreciate that some crafts were more seriously threatened than others. Quarterage lists suggest that the non-free accounted for a relatively high proportion of the work force in several occupations. The quarterage list for the Coopers' Company in 1571–2 shows that strangers alone accounted for 35 per cent of the work force (excluding apprentices); strangers and foreigners together for 42 per cent. In the Founders' Company the lists of the early Elizabethan period suggest that between 19 per cent and 26 per cent of the work force were aliens. Quarterage receipts in the Blacksmiths' Company in the period 1559–63 indicate that 38 per cent were probably non-free.[146] In some companies the competition was more clearly from foreigners than strangers. The surveys of the alien population show very few alien carpenters, and the company's regulative activity was directed predominantly at the English non-free.[147]

The large numbers of aliens in particular crafts reflects the fact that they had special skills to offer. Andrew Pettegree has shown how in the 1550s the Weavers' Company harnessed alien skills in new branches of the craft, particularly silk weaving.[148] In 1590 the wardens of the Armourers' Company claimed that they had learned new techniques from the aliens, but even so their products were in black rather than white armour.[149] The truth was that in many ways the services of the aliens were indispensable.

[142] *Returns of Strangers in the Metropolis 1593, 1627, 1635, 1639*, ed. I. Scouloudi (Huguenot Society Publications, LVII, 1985), p. 90.
[143] Ibid. p. 76; Finlay, *Population and Metropolis*, p. 68.
[144] Rappaport, *Worlds Within Worlds*, pp. 42–60.
[145] *Calendar of State Papers Domestic, Addenda, 1566–79*, p. 19; below, pp. 136–7.
[146] G.L., MSS 5602/2, 1571–2 acct.; 2883/1, 1559–63 accts.; *Wardens' Accounts of Founders*, pp. 152–4, 171–2, 178–9.
[147] Below, pp. 133–4.   [148] Pettegree, *Foreign Protestant Communities*, pp. 96–101.
[149] B.L., Lansdowne MS 63/5.

Although the English non-free cannot be said to have offered much in the way of new skills, attitudes towards them were ambivalent. When in 1556 common council passed an act forbidding freemen to employ foreigners, petitions for exemptions flowed in from the Bakers, Cordwainers, Blacksmiths, Joiners, and Dyers.[150] Sometimes the exemptions reflected alien skills as when Henry van Tynen was licensed at the suit of the Dyers' Company.[151] But most of the sixty foreign bakers and fourteen foreign blacksmiths who figured among the beneficiaries were Englishmen.[152] This reflected the fact that in spite of the complaints of the craftsmen about looming unemployment, the available freemen were not always sufficient to satisfy demand. Emergencies like war created an extra demand which free labour could not satisfy. In 1558 the Armourers were licensed to set foreigners to work for the duration of the war, and the Bakers to use non-free labour in the baking of biscuit.[153] But it was not only the pressures of suddenly increased demand that made the use of non-free labour attractive in some quarters. It also offered the opportunity of keeping wage costs down. Employers are found complaining that they could not get freemen to work at the wages assessed by proclamation: in April 1573 the aldermen empowered the lord mayor to grant discretionary exemptions from the 1556 Act on these grounds.[154]

The poorer artisans did not appreciate the benefits of alien skills, nor the necessity of a large pool of labour to keep costs down and satisfy irregular surges in demand. The truth is that the attitudes of the larger producers on the one hand and the smaller craftsmen and journeymen on the other diverged. For the former, the aliens might mean new skills and lower costs, but to the latter, they meant increased competition. Tensions within the companies over the employment and licensing of non-free labour are frequently encountered. In 1583 the privy council wrote anxiously to the aldermen about a libel circulating in the city which stated that the 'masters of the halles and companies' had taken money from strangers 'to set up what trade they lyst'.[155] The young men of the Carpenters' Company were angered by the lax attitude of their rulers in licensing the employment of foreigners for a small fine and in admitting foreigners as free journeymen to practise their craft under the company's protection. Their agitation resulted in a ruling from the court of aldermen in 1583 requiring that the wardens of the company should not give licences to foreigners to set up frames.[156] The

---

150 C.L.R.O., Letter Book S, fo. 93ᵛ; Rep. 13, fos. 427, 432, 444ᵛ, 445, 445ᵛ, 451.
151 Ibid. fo. 432.
152 Ibid. fos. 438, 445.   153 Ibid. fo. 516; Rep. 14, fo. 5.
154 C.L.R.O., Rep. 18, fo. 9.
155 C.L.R.O., Remembrancia I, no. 507.
156 *Carpenters' Records*, IV. 111, 121, 133, 157; V. 55, 65, 77, 134, 160; C.L.R.O., Rep. 20, fo. 449.

message seems in this case to have been taken to heart for the company's accounts reveal a fairly vigorous campaign against non-free labour in the 1590s and early seventeenth century: in 1595–6 twenty-one foreigners were sent to ward, and twenty-three in 1596–7.[157] It proved more difficult to defuse the tensions in the Weavers' Company whose rulers admitted in 1583 that they had licensed no less than seventy-three masters and eighty journeymen in the past six years. The frequency with which the aldermen were called upon to arbitrate the disputes between the yeomen and the assistants of this company over the employment of non-free labour – there were complaints in 1585, 1590, 1595, and 1599 – demonstrates the problems of finding a satisfactory and enforceable solution.[158] But however much disagreement there may have been over the employment of strangers and foreigners and the role they were allowed to play in company affairs, companymen were united in their determination to bring the non-free within the sphere of the company's control, and it is to these efforts that the discussion now turns.

Strangers and foreigners were already subject to many restrictions. By the terms of City custom the right to engage in retail trade was reserved to freemen, and any transaction between non-freemen was termed 'foreign bought and sold', the penalty for which was forfeiture of the goods. Non-freemen were entitled to pursue their trades provided that they placed lattices before their windows so that their wares could not be seen from the street.[159] City custom as regards the aliens was amplified by a series of Henrician statues, apparently passed in response to the agitation against the strangers which had assumed such threatening forms in the Evil May Day disturbances of 1517. Non-denizens were forbidden to set up workshops at all, and denizens limited as to the number of journeymen they could employ, and banned from employing stranger apprentices. All aliens within two miles of the City were to be subject to company jurisdiction which they were to acknowledge in regular searches and through payment of quarterage.[160] Although the position of the English non-free was unaffected by this legislation, they could be regulated under the provisions of the Statute of Artificers which required that no one exercise a trade without an apprenticeship of at least seven years, although this would not have covered all

157 *Carpenters' Records*, VII. 64, 80.
158 *Returns of Aliens*, II. 305–7; Consitt, *Weavers*, pp. 309–12, 318–21; C.L.R.O., Rep. 22, fo. 196ᵛ; Rep. 23, fos. 350ᵛ, 373ᵛ; Rep. 24, fo. 391ᵛ–2.
159 *Returns*, ed. Scouloudi, pp. 41–2.
160 14 & 15 Hen. VIII c. 2, 21 Hen. VIII c. 16, 32 Hen. VIII c. 16. The legislation is discussed by Pettegree, *Foreign Protestant Communities*, pp. 14–15, and in *Returns*, ed. Scouloudi, pp. 41–53. But neither have looked at the practice of company regulation. For the early sixteenth century, see D. Ransome, 'The Struggle of the Glaziers' Company with the Foreign Glaziers, 1500–1550', *Guildhall Miscellany*, 2 (1960), 12–20.

foreigners in London, some of whom would have served provincial apprenticeships.[161] Had these laws been properly enforced then the position of the non-free artisan would have been that of a dependent craftsman whose products were distributed through citizens, while alien merchants would have been dependent on freemen intermediaries for access to goods brought to London by provincial traders. Non-denizens would have been barred from any activity.

However, these restrictions were difficult to enforce. There was, for example, a body of opinion which held that the entire corpus of anti-alien legislation had been repealed by the Statute of Artificers on the grounds of the sweepingly incautious words of its preamble. Such was the plea of Richard Platt, when he was sued in the Exchequer for keeping more alien servants than he was allowed by statute, and the same argument was used by the Westminster shoemakers in 1576.[162] Doubtless this interpretation was disputed but it could only multiply the law's delays. It was also highly frustrating to the companies that the Henrician legislation placing the aliens under company jurisdiction did not apply to the foreigners.

It is therefore unsurprising that a considerable amount of company lobbying was directed to tightening the regulations. The easiest way of doing this was by exploiting the prerogative powers of the Crown to secure ordinances which extended the scope of company control.[163] One particularly important feature was the attempt to put the foreigners under the same restrictions as the 1529 Star Chamber decree had imposed on the aliens. Thus foreigners were expected to turn up on quarter days, to pay quarterage, and to be searched by the wardens. Some companies added the right to license strangers and foreigners only after their skills had been tested. Restrictions on the recruitment of apprentices, usually confining the non-free to no more apprentices than were enjoyed by the yeomen, were always included. The problem was that the status of the ordinances was disputable. When the free cordwainers demanded quarterage as required by their letters patent, the foreigners replied that the Queen 'can give no quarteredge by letteres patentes and so yt gyft is voyd to bynd the subiectes of this Realme to quarteredge'.[164] No taxation without consent. Others took a more direct line still. John Parker, a Southwark plasterer, sued in Star Chamber by the Plasterers' Company in 1598, when shown the company's letters patent which laid down that none should use plastering in London and Southwark but freemen of the company, is reported to have exclaimed:

---

[161] 5 Eliz. I c. 4. For provincial apprenticeships, see P.R.O., STAC 5/P11/24.

[162] P.R.O., E123/3, fo. 208ᵛ; B.L., Lansdowne MS 22/39, fos. 106–109; 5 Eliz. I c. 4 § 1. The foreign cordwainers alleged in Star Chamber that the 1529 Act had not received the royal assent: P.R.O., STAC 5/C59/38.

[163] For ordinances, see above, n. 107.   [164] B.L., Lansdowne MS 22/39.

'Letter me noe letters nor patent me noe pattentes. I care not a Turde for your letters nor patentes.'[165]

Companies therefore frequently found themselves forced to turn to the courts to test their rights. Refusals of quarterage by the foreigners led both Coopers and Cordwainers into protracted litigation in the central courts. Between 1566 and 1569 the Coopers' accounts record the expenditure of approximately £90 in suits relating to the refusal of strangers and foreigners to seal their 'round bonge barrels' (salmon barrels), and the foreigners' refusal to pay quarterage to the company. Strangers and foreigners appear to have been indicted at the Middlesex and Surrey sessions, but the company's enemies counter-attacked with litigation of their own. When the master and wardens of the company distrained two foreigners for non-payment of quarterage, they were indicted at the Surrey assizes for extortion. The case was removed to King's Bench and an arbitration, the details of which are not to my knowledge extant, negotiated by Justice Southcot and Sergeant Wray.[166] In the mid 1560s the free cordwainers were also asserting their rights vigorously with the result that the foreigners sued them in the court of requests. The aldermen, to whom the case was referred, ruled unusually harshly against the company, criticising its wardens for having exceeded their powers in demanding that quarterage be brought to the hall instead of being collected at the workplace, in taking quarterage of foreigners, and in failing to use the services of strangers in the search. The situation was further confused by the aldermen's subsequent reversal of this order, apparently because of the sympathies of the new lord mayor, Sir Roger Martyn, for the free cordwainers.[167] The free cordwainers turned to the Exchequer and, in what was later claimed to be a collusive action begun in 1569, secured a much more favourable agreement, which was registered by the court in November 1571. They obtained the crucial concession that quarterage was to be paid by all. The wardens were to examine all who wished to set up and test their workmanship. The search was to be exercised over foreigners, the wardens being accompanied by two or three representatives of the foreigners. Limits on apprentice recruitment were to apply to foreigners. Foreigners were to be liable to the payment of assessments for corn money to the City, though not to other assessments.[168] This proved to be the high-water mark of the free cordwainers' efforts, because they were soon challenged by the foreigners who turned to Burghley for support when the company tried to

[165] P.R.O., STAC 5/P61/22.
[166] G.L., MS 5606/1, fos. 292ᵛ, 300, 300ᵛ, 305ᵛ–7, 314ᵛ–5; *Calendar of Assize Records. Surrey Indictments. Elizabeth I*, ed. J. S. Cockburn (1980), p. 71.
[167] P.R.O., REQ 2/54/56; REQ 2/185/34; C.L.R.O., Rep. 16, fos. 294ᵛ–5, 298ᵛ, 316ᵛ, 324, 328ᵛ, 339, 342ᵛ, 353, 384, 385ᵛ.
[168] P.R.O., STAC 5/C59/38; G.L., MS 8033, pp. 9–20. New ordinances were granted to the company at the same time: ibid. pp. 21–43.

extract bonds of £5 for the payment of quarterage. The freemen launched a new offensive in 1576 by bringing informations in the Exchequer, commencing litigation in Star Chamber on the grounds that the foreigners were engaged in a conspiracy to make void the royal incorporation of the Cordwainers, and indicating the leaders of the foreigners for riot when they assembled with the intention of visiting their solicitor. Star Chamber's verdict, only reached in November 1579 after much hesitation by the judges, and even then admitting the ambiguity of the law, was that the agreement of 1571 should remain in force; hardly the firm line that the company had hoped for.[169]

The frustrations of the law meant that the companies' preferred solution was parliamentary legislation. Restrictions on retail trade, either barring aliens from retailing specific commodities such as linen or, more generally, from dealing in imported goods, were promoted in no less than four of the later Elizabethan parliaments, but none ever reached the statute book.[170] Another bill in 1589 sought to outlaw all non-denizens from plying their crafts, and required a seven-year apprenticeship from all denizens.[171] These bills, like the bill 'to avoid strangers' (1563), that 'for apprentices with artificers strangers' (1567), and the bills in 1571 and 1572 to compel the payment of quarterage by strangers (the latter probably related to the problems of the Coopers and Cordwainers just discussed), were doubtless the result of cooperation between companies.[172] Other measures, such as that of 1566 placing all cutlers within three miles of the City under the government of the Cutlers' Company, were promoted by individual interest groups.[173]

None of these measures passed into law. The reasons for the parliamentary failures were similar to those for the frustrations at law. The aliens formed a well-organised lobby of their own, and there was a considerable amount of sympathy in government quarters for their plight. Cecil wished to harness alien skills in his projects for import substitution; Grindal as bishop of London was a friend of the religious refugees. The privy council restrained the City authorities from shutting up the shops of non-denizens in 1561 and allowed large-scale denizations. It is true that the government became more

---

[169] B.L., Lansdowne MSS 21/30, 24/73, 26/25; P.R.O., STAC 5/C59/38; E159/372, Eas. 19 Eliz., recorda, rots., 41–2; SP 46/31, fos. 51ᵛ–2; G.L.R.O., MJ/SR/198/27–8.

[170] H.M.C., *Third Report*, p. 5 (for 1584–5); Northamptonshire Record Office, Fitzwilliam of Milton MS 147 (for 1587); C.L.R.O., Rep. 22, fo. 36; B.L., Lansdowne MS 55/63, fos. 186, 187ᵛ, 188–9; *L.J.*, II. 182, 184 (for 1589); H.M.C., *Third Report*, p. 8; B.L., Cotton MS Titus F II, fos. 67–77 (for 1593).

[171] H.L.R.O., Main Papers, 1586–8, fos. 17–18.

[172] *C.J.*, I. 63, 78; C.L.R.O., Rep. 16, fo. 134; Rep. 17, fos. 144, 323. Other attempts at legislation in the later 1570s and early 1580s, in particular those directed against the children of strangers, are discussed by Pettegree, *Foreign Protestant Communities*, pp. 289–91.

[173] *C.J.*, I. 75.

anxious about the alien problem in the 1570s as the pressures of the threat of religious heterodoxy, the deteriorating international situation, and the outcry of London artisans made themselves felt. These anxieties were shown in schemes for resettlement of the aliens and in a determination to get rid of those who were not religious exiles.[174] But as the pressures receded the government resumed its protective role. As high steward of Westminster Cecil was expected to protect the artisans who lived there: it was to him that the non-free cutlers turned in 1566, and the non-free shoemakers in 1575.[175] In the 1590s the council responded to petitioning from the Dutch church to restrain the activity of informers, and government spokesmen showed themselves lukewarm towards restrictive measures in the house of commons.[176]

The lack of formal craft-based organisations among the non-free did not prevent them from vigorous lobbying. They promoted a bill in 1572 complaining about the exaction of quarterage from foreigners outside the city and the taking of fees for the registration of letters of denization.[177] The Dutch church was quite ready to argue on behalf of artisan members. In 1572 they petitioned against the City's bill to strengthen the custom of London because by allowing a freeman to practise any trade it presented the prospect of Englishmen taking over the trades the aliens themselves had introduced.[178] In 1576 they promoted a bill of their own for the repeal of the recent act of common council against taking alien children as apprentices.[179] The struggles of the non-free coopers and cordwainers showed that they too appreciated the benefits of working through the courts.

Harassment and the obstruction of the non-free was the most the companies could hope to achieve. Companies launched indictments at the sessions against foreigners for exercising their trades without seven-year apprenticeships and against aliens for practising without letters of denization.[180] The services of professional informers were frequently drawn upon. It is hardly coincidental that the wave of informer actions against alien candlemakers in the early 1590s coincided with the City's appointment of committees to investigate the complaints of the candlemakers against the aliens.[181] Company accounts often make explicit the connection between

[174] Pettegree, *Foreign Protestant Communities*, ch. IX.
[175] C.S.P.D., *Addenda, 1566–79*, p. 19; B.L., Lansdowne MS 21/30. Cf. C.L.R.O., Rep. 15, fo. 50ᵛ for Cecil's intervention on behalf of the wherrymen of Westminster.
[176] *Ecclesiae Londino-Batavae Archivum*, ed. J. H. Hessels (3 vols., Cambridge 1889–97), II. 901, 905, 909; III. 939–40, 975, 1070–2; A.P.C., XXII. 502; B.L., Cotton MS Titus F II, fos. 76ᵛ–7.
[177] *Proceedings in the Parliaments of Elizabeth I, 1558–1581*, ed. T. E. Hartley (Leicester, 1981), p. 380; C.J., I. 97; C.L.R.O., Rep. 17, fos. 335, 337.
[178] Hessels, III. 125–8.   [179] Ibid. 272–3.
[180] G.L., MSS 2883/3, pp. 44, 45; 2881/1, p. 130; 6122/1, May 1598; G.L.R.O., MJ/SR/311/10; MJ/SR/359/18; MJ/SR/386/16, 18.
[181] C.L.R.O., Rep. 22, fo. 355ᵛ; Jour. 23, fo. 111ᵛ–12; Hessels, III. 939–40; A.P.C., XXII. 506.

company pressure and the activity of informers. The Plasterers paid money to Thomas Johnson, informer to the Chamber of London and active in the mayor's court; the Merchant Tailors and Curriers employed Gilbert Lillie in suits against foreigners; and in 1606 the Cutlers turned to Gilbert Whetstone for his help in the prosecution of aliens and foreigners.[182] Within the City liberties the companies could hope to lobby the aldermen into allowing the chamberlain to enforce regulations against the non-free engaging in retail trade and against strangers without denization working at their crafts. The chamberlain was periodically instructed to shut up shops.[183] But the corporation drew back from such radical solutions as were promoted at the turn of the century by the Merchant Tailors' Company, who agitated for a general expulsion of all foreigners from the capital, only to run into the now predictable hostility of the council and parliament.[184]

The impression one gets is of intermittent and faltering regulation. It is true that a high degree of pressure involving the continual harassment of the non-free could yield dividends. Thus the more vigorous search conducted by the Coopers' Company at the same time as their litigation against foreigners and strangers in the later 1560s resulted in much higher levels of quarterage payments by the non-free. In the accounting year 1567–8, thirty out of thirty-two Dutch householders are listed as paying, and eleven out of eighteen English foreigners. But there were limits to the control that could be achieved. Aliens and foreigners hardly ever appear among the lists of those fined for the production of defective vessels. Moreover, as the pressures relaxed, so the control weakened. By 1571–2 only one of the twenty-seven foreigners listed, and only twenty-four of the thirty-five stranger house-holders, paid their dues.[185] Suits against the foreigners continued through the 1570s as the company retained informers to prosecute them, but they had little effect. The action petered out after 1576.[186] Control tightened once more in the later 1590s as the company secured a warrant from the privy council to apprehend foreigners who refused to submit to the ordinances. Although foreigners had ceased to pay quarterage in recent years, in 1596–7, seventeen out of thirty-five foreign householders made a payment. But within five years only five were paying.[187] The same picture of intermittent and

182 G.L., MSS 6122/1, July 1584; 14346/1, fo. 195ᵛ; 7151/1, fos. 38, 39, 59ᵛ; MT. Co., C.M. III, fos. 367, 401ᵛ, 437. See also C.L.R.O., Rep. 19, fo. 180ᵛ for Lillie and Johnson.
183 C.L.R.O., Rep. 17, fos. 100ᵛ–1; Rep. 20, fo. 61ᵛ.
184 MT. Co., C.M. III, fos. 367, 388ᵛ, 392ᵛ–3, 394, 401ᵛ, 423ᵛ, 437, 439ᵛ, 440ᵛ; V, pp. 1–4; C.L.R.O., Rep. 24, fos. 379, 380ʳ⁻ᵛ, 382ᵛ–4, 386ᵛ–8ᵛ, 394ᵛ–5, 398ᵛ–9, 406, 411, 422ᵛ; Hessels, II. 899, 901.
185 G.L., MS 5606/1, 1567–8, 1571–2 accts.
186 G.L., MSS 5606/2, fos. 3ᵛ–4, 10, 21ᵛ, 22ʳ⁻ᵛ, 30ʳ⁻ᵛ, 42; 5602/1, 27 Oct. 1573, 11 Nov. 1573.
187 G.L., MS 5633, fo. 10ʳ⁻ᵛ; A.P.C., XXV. 60–2; G.L., MS 5606/2, fos. 217ᵛ, 221, 232, 235ᵛ, 254, 273ᵛ. Indictments were launched against foreigners who had not served apprentice-

faltering regulation emerges from the Cordwainers' Company accounts when they commence in 1595. In the later 1590s the company was arresting foreigners for non-payment of quarterage, suing strangers without denization in the Guildhall, and getting the chamberlain to shut up foreigners' shops. In 1598–9, when this action was at a peak, 212 foreigners paid quarterage compared to only seventy in the previous year. It was a success which could not be sustained for, in the next two years, payments were received from only 129 and 119 respectively.[188]

Several conclusions suggest themselves. Difficulties in the interpretation of the law, the sympathetic attitude of the government, and the resourcefulness of the non-free weakened the companies' position and prevented them from adequately enforcing their received powers or from securing new ones. Company control never reached the level envisaged by the ordinances and one's impression is that their powers were only intermittently exercised. Nevertheless the efforts that the companies did make were important and their timing significant. Efforts at company regulation were most energetic in the late 1560s and early 1570s, and again in the 1590s, both periods of considerable anti-alien tension and economic difficulties. There are two points to be made here. First, the aliens were blamed for problems the causes of which lay elsewhere. Anti-alien feeling was one means by which tension in times of crisis was earthed. The elite escaped criticism. As long as company rulers asserted themselves against the non-free, they too escaped criticism, and the homogeneity and self-consciousness of the guild was enhanced by the campaign against the outsider. Secondly, the form that anti-alien feeling took is significant. There were libels and reports of conspiracy against the strangers in both the periods of tension. Evil May Day haunted the consciousness of the sixteenth-century metropolitan magistrate, but there never actually was an anti-alien riot. Part of the explanation for this must lie in the fact that the energies of the London artisans were channeled into the harassment of the aliens and foreigners in parliament and the law courts rather than stoning them in the streets. The availability of legislation that the companies could attempt to enforce, the knowledge that statutes had been obtained in the past and might be in the future, encouraged artisans to work within the framework of the law.

CONCLUSIONS: CONFLICT AND COMMUNITY

This chapter has on the one hand pointed to the continuing vitality of many companies in the enforcement of their ordinances and the promotion of suits

ships: ibid. fos. 208ᵛ–9, 218ᵛ, 225, 227, 238ᵛ, 257; G.L., MS 5602/2, fos. 4ᵛ, 9ᵛ; P.R.O., KB9/705/26–7.
[188] G.L., MS 7351/1, accts. for 1596–1601.

for the benefit of their membership, contributing to Londoners' identification with their companies. On the other hand the limits of that sense of community have been emphasised and conflicts within the companies continually underlined. There is no contradiction here. In part it reflects the variety of experience among the companies: at the broadest level it is clear that 'community' was weaker and the potential for conflict greater in those companies like the Clothworkers, Haberdashers, Skinners, and Merchant Tailors with large artisan components ruled by merchants and retailers than in the smaller craft associations where the community of interest was greater. But the confusion also reflects the ambiguity of attitudes among the artisans themselves. The frustrations felt by artisans about the shortcomings of their rulers were often counterbalanced by an appreciation of other benefits, like poor relief and the arbitration of disputes, which flowed from membership of the association. The existence of a sense of identity with the company meant that artisans tended to pursue their grievances within the company framework, while the sentiments of community surrounding company membership could be manipulated by the rulers to build up obedience. Conflicts of interest within the companies were real enough but the battle lines never clearly drawn. Artisans might have felt frustration at the failure of their assistants to take up some of their grievances, but they also knew that on other issues they were at one with their rulers. The artisans themselves might have been divided between journeymen and the larger householders because their interests diverged on the issue of apprentice recruitment and possibly the employment of strangers. Disputes between companies splintered loyalties even when they had common grievances, as for example on the custom of London and the competition of strangers and foreigners. In this final section I want to explore further the nature of conflict within the companies in order to underline the reasons why tensions were contained.

The first point is that much conflict was political in nature, centering on disputes about the abuse of power, failures of administration, and the details of internal constitutional arrangements rather than reflecting conflicts of economic interest. Where disputes occurred about constitutional arrangements within the companies the point behind them usually appears to have been the suspicions of the younger and poorer members about the misapplication of company funds and partiality towards individuals rather than a sense that the court of assistants was an instrument in the hands of the wealthier members for the subjugation of the poorer craftsmen. The conflicts within the Barber Surgeons' Company over the constitution of the yeomanry organisation did not reflect underlying conflicts of economic interest, but rather were related to the clash between the desire of the yeomanry to control their own funds and the suspicions of the assistants about their competence for the task. It would likewise be hard to find much conflict of economic interest in the Cordwainers' and Coopers' Companies both of which were troubled by electoral disputes in the Elizabethan period. In both instances criticism of the assistants was generated among the liverymen who felt that their rights were being overlooked in the fixing of elections by the assistants.[189] Questions about the distribution of the tax burden on the membership repeatedly aroused controversy. In 1562 the poor of the Curriers' Company complained that the wealthier members of the company had charged them at unreasonable rates for the supply of soldiers.[190] The plasterers in 1608 felt that their wardens were too ready to resort to assessments on the membership to increase company funds.[191] The artisan skinners in 1606 attacked their wardens for laying taxes on the membership 'to keep them poore'.[192] The extra charges laid on new freemen in the form of breakfasts for the wardens or payments of silver spoons were criticised by the coopers in 1591 and the plasterers in 1608.[193] The management of company funds was also a target for attack. The skinners claimed that the assistants had 'broughte the hall indebted partlie by the purchase of a bad title of land at a farre higher rate then the same was tendered unto, partlie by unnecessarie buildings and partlie by letting leases to themselves at an undervalue'.[194] The demands made by the plasterers and coopers that their wardens keep proper accounts and observe the proper procedures in auditing them reflected suspicions that the goods of the companies had been 'vainly and inordinately spent'.[195] Sometimes criticism was directed at the administration of poor relief. The grievances of the skinners on this issue have already been discussed. The journeymen of the Curriers' Company complained in 1581 that not all the money taken out of the poor box had in fact been spent on the poor, in response to which the aldermen ordered that one of the three keys to the poor box be held by someone not in the livery and that four non-livery members be present at the distribution of funds.[196] Partiality towards individuals in the search was another sensitive area: the young men of the Plasterers complained in 1608 that some workmen escaped punishment. The aldermen's solution, that the company nominate twelve persons each year from among whom the aldermen would choose six to search without partiality the work done by the assistants, shows that the

---

[189] C.L.R.O., Rep. 14, fos. 151ᵛ, 325ᵛ–6; G.L., MS 5633, controversies concerning disorders of those bearing office.
[190] C.L.R.O., Rep. 15, fo. 108ᵛ.
[191] C.L.R.O., Rep. 28, fo. 165.
[192] Sk. Co., C.M. I, fo. 88ᵛ.
[193] G.L., MS 5633, controversies concerning disorders of those bearing office; C.L.R.O., Rep. 28, fo. 165.
[194] Sk. Co., C.M. I, fo. 88ᵛ.
[195] G.L., MS 5633, controversies concerning disorders of those bearing office; C.L.R.O., Rep. 28, fo. 165.
[196] C.L.R.O., Rep. 20, fos. 190ᵛ–1.

point of grievance was that the assistants were guilty of overlooking the failings of their colleagues.[197] In the Freemasons' Company there were complaints that the enforcement of ordinances was neglected because wardens remained in office too long.[198]

Thus the quality of the wardens' rule might be criticised, but rarely their right to rule. Paternalistic values were widespread in this society and shaped the ideal of company rule. This is rarely explicitly stated, but emerges occasionally in the homilies directed at offenders. When Nicholas Stalworth, armourer, attacked his wardens apparently on the grounds that they lacked skill in the craft ('It was never merye syns that tynkers bare so moche Rule'), he was subjected to a long eulogy on the benefits of company membership:

the company hath been benefycyall unto hym and others of the poore bretheren of the company and hath alwayes sought out by what meanes the poore bretheren myght be Relevyd nother sparing the losse of tyme nor yett there great industrye labor as now at thys tym we have a master god be praysed the weche hath taken as great payne as ever eny man dyd that was in offyce I thinke thys hundreth yeres And all for the common welth of his company not seking hys owne commodytie but the commodytie of the hoill company.[199]

It was an ideal which could be exploited by company members in seeking the support of their rulers. In 1568 the clothworker merchant tailors petitioned their assistants for measures to ensure that the merchants and retailers of the company put their cloths to dressing by their fellows. They pointed with some envy to 'the greate zeale and good will which the clothworkers beare unto them which be there brothers and members of the handy occupacion which ... with greate expens of monye do shewe for profitable lawes and liberties for the Advauncement of their handicrafte'. The implied indictment of their fellow merchant tailors becomes explicit: 'where wee hope to resceive helpe and frendshippe of oure owne companye wee have nothinge but disfrendshippe and slaunder'. The petition also carried a veiled threat. Exploiting their wardens' suspicions that they had encouraged the Clothworker agitation for the union of the two companies, they gave assurances that 'wee beinge lincked to you do beare you so perfecte love and earnest good will that onelesse necessitie dothe so constraine us as no lawe can restraine us we will never assent to them'.[200] In other words they would be loyal to the company provided that something was done to relieve them. Rule by the rich and powerful was acceptable so long as they took action in response to craft grievances.

It was not then an unquestioning obedience. If wardens were thought to be uninterested in the craft, opposition could develop. Thus the key to the

[197] C.L.R.O., Rep. 28, fo. 166ʳ⁻ᵛ.
[198] Ibid. fo. 35ʳ⁻ᵛ.
[199] G.L., MS 12071/1, p. 475.   [200] MT. Co., C.M. I, pp. 366–9.

agitation of the artisan skinners in the early seventeenth century was the sense that they 'coulde get no favoure at theire handes towards the good of the arte but we are dismissively used', a grievance which was focused by the half-hearted support the assistants had given to recent parliamentary campaigns.[201] It is striking that this company spent only £45 on the suits of the artisans in the quarter-century from 1580.[202] The Clothworkers spent this amount in 1604–5 alone, and a further £62 in 1605–6, neither particularly exceptional years for the company.[203] Even small crafts like the Coopers were spending large sums on suits. It is difficult to tell how common disaffection of the kind encountered in the Skinners' Company was because of the rarity with which the documents reflect artisan attitudes. Because of the lukewarm support given to their suits by their wardens some of the feltmakers who were members of the Haberdashers' Company overcame their normal antipathy for foreigners to support the controversial incorporation of a separate Feltmakers' Company secured by the latter in 1604.[204] We have also noted the doubts of the Merchant Tailors about the loyalty of their artisans at about the same time.[205]

The artisan skinners show an awareness of a separate identity, a sense that the company in its present form was no longer an organisation with which they could identify: 'their opression is growne to such a height that amongst some of them it is a matter disputable whether we be members of the company or not, and whether they prevaile against us or not they will never love us'.[206] But their critique had significant limitations. What worried them was the wardens' neglect of their responsibilities rather than a sense that the assistants used their control to further the economic subjugation of the artisans. Indeed so unrelated were the activities of most of the wardens to the fur trade that this issue could hardly have arisen. Very occasionally artisans did come close to the perception that their rulers abused their position in the company to further their hegemony in the trade. When the feltmakers sought a grant of the search of imported wools from the Crown in order to prevent deceits in the quality of the wool delivered to them, they pointed out that the Haberdashers' Company's search of wools was redundant because 'the chiefest and most parte of the merchantes that bringeth in and the ingrosers

[201] Sk. Co., C.M. I, fo. 88ᵛ. In 1605 the wardens only allowed half the costs of the parliamentary suit on the company's account; in 1606 they refused the request of the artisans for reimbursement for the costs of their second (and successful) suit on the grounds that when the artisans had first approached the assistants they had desired 'onely the countenance and ayde of the company in the seid suyte att their own charges' Sk. Co., C.M. I, fo. 85ʳ⁻ᵛ; C.M. II, fos. 35ᵛ, 370.
[202] Sk. Co., W.A. IV–V.   [203] Cw. Co., W.A. as stated.
[204] Unwin, *Industrial Organization*, pp. 130–6. I shall be discussing this episode in detail in my forthcoming history of the Haberdashers' Company.
[205] Above, pp. 129–30.   [206] Sk. Co., C.M. I, fo. 88.

of wolls are haberdasshers'.[207] The conflicts in the Stationers' Company in
the early 1580s between the holders of patents from the Crown giving them
the privilege of printing certain classes of books and the non-privileged
printers was sometimes represented in the petititions of the aggrieved parties
as a conflict with the 'governors' of the company.[208] And yet in neither case
does the point seem to have been pushed very hard, and this probably reflects
the complexities of the real position as opposed to the sweeping generali-
sations into which artisans might be tempted in the heat of propaganda. For
the truth was that the importers of wools included several merchants who
were not free of the Haberdasher's Company at all, and that those merchants
who did deal in wool and were rulers of the company probably only
represented a fraction of the ruling body of that company.[209] Again it was
neglect rather than direct exploitation which really troubled the critics of
company administration.

Grievances were unfocused and loyalties splintered. Journeymen and
householders were united over some issues, like the desire among artisan
clothworkers to restrict the export of undressed cloth, but the householders
were unenthusiastic about the agitation over wages in the early 1560s and
the periodic efforts of the journeymen to restrict apprentice recruitment.
The power of the journeymen clothworkers was probably further weakened
by the difficulties of concerting measures with the clothworkers free of the
Merchant Tailors, although on one occasion in 1560 there was a combination between the journeymen of the two companies, a threat which the
aldermen treated very seriously indeed.[210] The employment of aliens and
foreigners might, as we have seen, produce a divergence in attitudes between
wealthier householders and poorer artisans and journeymen, but both
groups might unite against non-free labour not subject to company control at
all. Moreover, companies sometimes witnessed conflict between different
groups of artisans engaged in different stages of the manufacturing process.
Thus the skinners and tawers, and fullers and shearmen, continued to
squabble after their formal union within the frameworks of the Skinners' and
Clothworkers' Companies respectively.[211] When groups of artisans did
criticise the rule of the assistants it is not always clear how strong the backing
was. Their opponents characteristically painted reform movements as self-
interested factions led by demagogues unrepresentative of the majority of
loyal artisans.[212] But there might have been some truth in this. The

[207] B.L., Lansdowne MS 28/28.   [208] *Stationers' Registers*, II. 770–1.
[209] Note the merchants signing B.L., Lansdowne MS 29/52, including Francis Bowyer, grocer,
William Hewett, clothworker, John Heydon, mercer, Thomas Pullison, draper, Austin
Foulkes, clothworker, Alexander Everie, clothworker.
[210] Above, p. 102.
[211] Sk. Co., C.M. II, fos. 115ᵛ, 163, 230ᵛ, 232ᵛ–3; Cw. Co., C.M. II, fo. 104ᵛ.
[212] B.L., Lansdowne MS 29/25.

feltmakers admitted in 1578 that the richer feltmakers were not as badly affected by the practices of the merchants because they were in a position to resell faulty wools to the poorer feltmakers.[213]

The generation of city-wide agitation across craft boundaries was difficult because of the inwardness of each company. This point will surely be clear from the many provisos for individual company experiences which have cluttered the foregoing arguments. Companies shared some grievances, for example over aliens and the custom of London, and there were attempts at a common approach as in the case of the bill to common council promoted by fourteen handicraft companies in 1571 for the reform of custom, and the bills against strangers prepared for parliament at the same time.[214] But the action was rarely sustained. There is no sign, for example, of organised opposition to the City's bills to strengthen City custom, except from the Mercers' Company in 1576.[215] Many companies were worried by monopolies in the 1590s. Their petitions often raised points of general constitutional principle, but never referred to the afflictions of other trades: in this sense it is the particularity of the opposition which is striking.[216] The victualling trades were frequently in conflict with the aldermen over the assizes, but they never made common cause. This was partly because the chronology of the pressure was different in each case. The years of most severe pressure on the brewers (1564, 1572, 1592) were not in fact dearth years, and the selection of the brewers in these years perhaps reflects the enthusiasms of particular lord mayors.[217] As a peculiarly unpopular group dominated by aliens, few were likely to make common cause with the brewers anyway. Much of the frustration of the Tallow Chandlers over the assize of candles was directed against the butchers who controlled tallow supplies rather than at the aldermen.[218]

Conflicts between companies were a major obstacle to common action. Demarcation disputes between closely related crafts were frequent. The Plasterers, for example, were regularly in conflict with the Painters and Bricklayers, the companies harassing each other with informations in the Exchequer, City courts, and at the Middlesex sessions, for using trades to which they had not been apprenticed, and binding infringers of their

---

[213] B.L., Lansdowne MS 28/28.

[214] C.L.R.O., Rep. 17, fo. 146ᵛ; MT. Co., C.M. I, pp. 519–21; Cw. Co., C.M. II, fo. 151ʳ⁻ᵛ; Mc. Co., C.M. III, fos. 184, 192ᵛ–3ᵛ; *Carpenters' Records* III, 133; G.L., MS 5174/3, fo. 180.

[215] Mc. Co., C.M. III, fos. 288–91ᵛ.   [216] Archer, 'London Lobbies', pp. 29–34.

[217] Based on study of the assize of beer, including the pattern of Exchequer informations against the brewers, which I hope to publish in due course. See especially, C.L.R.O., Jour. 18, fos. 271, 291; Jour. 19, fos. 428–30; Jour. 23, fo. 111ᵛ; Rep. 22, fo. 438ʳ⁻ᵛ.

[218] C.L.R.O., Rep. 15, fos. 63, 65, 66, 440, 459ᵛ, 468ᵛ, 477; Rep. 16, fos. 42ᵛ, 370ᵛ; Jour. 20, fos. 126ᵛ–7.

monopolies in recognisances not to use another's trade.[219] The Painters promoted bills in parliament against the Plasterers in 1597, 1601, and 1604, while the Plasterers themselves tried to use parliament against the Bricklayers in 1606 and 1614.[220] Likewise clashes over rights of search punctuated the history of the Armourers', Cutlers', and Blacksmiths' Companies in the Elizabethan period.[221] Such conflicts might have been resolved had the crafts united, but corporate pride was at stake here. Negotiations for a union of the Armourers and Cutlers in 1555 foundered because, as the Armourers' clerk self-righteously informs us, 'the Cutlers were mech weddyd to those thynges that be but a vayn glory in the world as to have the for part of a name & the preamynence of the furst offecers'.[222] The involvement of different companies in different stages of the manufacturing process produced conflicts over standards and prices for workmanship. The Cordwainers repeatedly clashed with the Curriers, on whom they were dependent for the dressing of their leather, on these issues and over the attempts of the Cordwainers to keep the Curriers out of the leather market.[223] Merchant Tailors, Clothworkers, and Drapers clashed with the Dyers' Company over their standards and prices, while the Dyers complained about the failure of members of the other companies to settle their debts.[224]

A final factor militating against sustained conflict was the opportunities

---

[219] Plasterers versus Bricklayers: C.L.R.O., Rep. 16, fos. 26–7, 284; Rep. 20, fos. 42^v, 46^v–7; Rep. 21, fos. 139^v, 154^v; G.L., MS 6122/1, accts. for May 1584, Oct 1584, Feb–July 1585, Nov. 1597, 1598. Plasterers versus Painters: P.R.O., E159/355, Mich. 9 Eliz., recorda, rots. 212–15; G.L., MS 6122/1, Sept. 1585.

[220] S. D'Ewes, *The Journals of All the Parliaments During the Reign of Queen Elizabeth* (1682), p. 571 (for 1597); G.L., MS 6122/1; Townshend, *Historical Collections*, pp. 191, 245, 270; *L.J.*, II. 248, 255, 257–8; *T.E.D.*, I. 136–40; H.L.R.O., Main Papers, 1597–1607, fos. 85–91 (for 1601); *L.J.*, II. 292, 294, 295, 297, 299, 305; *C.J.*, I. 228, 239, 246; 1 Jac. I, c. 20 (for 1604); G.L., MSS 3054/1, accts. for 1606 and 1614; 6122/1, accts. for 1606.

[221] Armourers versus Cutlers: G.L., MS 12071/1, pp. 424, 440–1, 442–3, 450–1 (1555: collapse of negotiations for union); C.L.R.O., Rep. 17, fos. 47, 190^v (1571: controversies over search at Bartholomew Fair leading to establishment of joint searching procedures); G.L., MSS 12071/2, pp. 458, 462; 12065/2, fo. 38; 7147/1, p. 7; C.L.R.O., Rep. 21, fo. 96 (1584: Cutlers reject joint search; aldermen reiterate earlier order); G.L., MS 12065/2, fo. 70; 7147/1, p. 118; C.L.R.O., Rep. 22, fos. 433^v, 436^v (1592: Armourers protecting Tilman Childe a stranger making swords); Armourers versus Blacksmiths: C.L.R.O., Rep. 18, fos. 136, 228; Rep. 19, fo. 354^{r-v}; G.L., MSS 12065/2, fos. 7, 10, 11^v, 12; 12071/2, p. 273 (1573–8: persistent controversies over search); G.L., MS 12065/2, fo. 45 (1585–7: order that Blacksmiths should not search until they show letters patent); G.L., MSS 12065/2, fos. 81^v–2, 85; 2883/3, p. 11 (1596–7: litigation in King's Bench over search); G.L., MSS 12065/2, fo. 91^v, 12071/2, pp. 635–6; 2883/3, pp. 37–41; C.L.R.O., Rep. 25, fos. 52^v, 69–70 (1597–8: lobbying of privy council, lord treasurer, and lord mayor; arbitration of aldermen establishes joint search).

[222] G.L., MS 12071/1, pp. 450–1.

[223] B.L., Lansdowne MS 63/5; D. M. Dean, 'Public or Private? London, Leather and Legislation in Elizabethan England', *Historical Journal*, 31 (1988), 525–48.

[224] C.L.R.O., Rep. 14, fos. 444^v, 450, 451^v, 461^v, 474^v, 478, 495^v–6, 517^v, 518; Rep. 15, fos. 227^v, 268; Cw. Co., C.M. II, fos. 9^v, 52, 241^v.

available to discontented artisans to appeal over the heads of their rulers to
the aldermen, or even the privy council. The interventions of the aldermen in
the affairs of the Cordwainers, Curriers, Weavers, and Plasterers have been
noted, and the signs are that their arbitrations were relatively impartial. On
the other hand all these examples come from the lesser crafts in whose
economic activities the aldermen had few personal interests at stake. Where
artisans touched more sensitive nerves the aldermen were rather more
partial: the lord mayor intervened against the feltmakers' suit for the search
of wool imports in 1580; and the aldermen petitioned against the skinners'
suit for a monopoly in the trade in skins in 1592.[225] But again artisans were
unlikely to be uniformly hostile towards the elite. Such disaffection as there
was would be sectional. Moreover, there was the possibility of an appeal to
the court or privy council. The council occasionally intervened in internal
company disputes: commissioners appointed by the council negotiated a
compromise in the conflicts in the Stationers' Company in 1583; and the
artisan skinners secured enough conciliar backing to come within a whisker
of successfully remodelling their company's constitution in 1606 to allow the
artisans more representation.[226] The accessibility of the institutions of
central government to groups with grievances, another sign of the collaboration that characterised relations between Crown and City in the Elizabethan period, was therefore another important factor in containing tensions.[227]

[225] B.L., Lansdowne MSS 29/27, 71/54.
[226] W.W. Greg, *A Companion to Arber* (Oxford, 1967), pp. 125–33; Sk. Co., C.M. I,
fos. 87–90.
[227] Archer, 'London Lobbies'.

5

Social policy

INTRODUCTION

A central element in the more optimistic view of social relations in early modern London is an emphasis on the impressive ameliorative social policies pursued by the capital's rulers. In a seminal article published in 1979, Valerie Pearl argues for an imaginative, sensitive, and apparently successful programme of poor relief. She writes of enormous sums raised from legacies, rents, and rates even in the extramural parishes. It was a flexible system, as mechanisms existed for redistributing resources from wealthy to poorer parishes, and care was taken to adjust payments to needs. Thus pensions were increased in years of crisis and supplementary payments made to meet special needs. Parishes are found paying medical bills, helping with rent and clothing in times of difficulty, and even giving pensioners Christmas bonuses. The humanitarianism of parish administrators is shown by the high level of care provided for foundlings, including support for their education. A strong sense of communal responsibility is suggested by the innovative policies pursued by vestries in seeking solutions to the problems confronting them, for example in encouraging subscriptions from parishioners to buy up housing, the income from which might be used to support the poor. Poor relief, it is suggested, sustained demand, and allowed some measure of economic growth, contributing to the development of the consumer industries whose growth has been charted by Joan Thirsk.[1]

Three basic criticisms of Pearl's case can be made. First, her discussion of social policy in early modern London makes no distinctions of chronology, so that it is not clear how policy evolved and to what pressures it responded. Some of the features she describes, in particular the large landed endowments of the extramural parishes and the adjustment of pensions in crisis years, are more characteristic of the seventeenth than of the late sixteenth century. It

[1] Pearl, 'Social Policy'; J. Thirsk, *Economic Policy and Projects: the Development of a Consumer Society in Early Modern England* (Oxford, 1978).

149

will be one of the arguments of this chapter that there were important changes in the scale and character of relief at the turn of the century as London's rulers responded to the experience of the recent crisis. Secondly, in confining her attention to poor relief, she is only considering one aspect of social policy and neglecting others, in particular the efforts to limit responsibilities and the link between relief and social discipline. Thirdly, and most fundamentally, there is no attempt to consider the balance between needs and resources. She does not explore the responses to crisis conditions like those experienced in the mid 1590s when the ranks of the urban poor were swollen by immigration and by the impoverishment of formerly self-supporting households. Nor does she examine the problem of poor relief with reference to the social topography of poverty. Most of the evidence for humanitarian poor relief comes from the inner-city parishes whereas the problems were most serious in the riverside and extramural parishes. As Figure 1 demonstrates these were the parishes where the rates raised from the wealthier households were inadequate to support the poor without support from other parishes. The aim of this chapter is to reconstruct the various sources of relief in London and to consider the contribution they made to family budgets and their distribution with reference to the location of the poor. Poor relief clearly played a role in the maintenance of stability but it is necessary to differentiate between effectiveness in the sense of making a contribution to stability by meeting what may have been limited expectations, and effectiveness in the absolute sense of relieving poverty and of achieving the policy's declared aim of eliminating begging.

THE DIMENSIONS OF POVERTY

As we saw in the introduction, many of the long-held assumptions of historians concerning the scale of poverty in sixteenth-century London are under attack. Exemption from taxation can no longer be correlated with poverty, and real wage indices on their own tell us little about levels of deprivation.[2] In the absence of detailed data concerning living standards, the quest for an 'absolute' level of poverty, by which the success of London relative to other societies in coping with its social problems can be measured, is a fruitless one. We are forced to rely on the way contemporaries defined and enumerated the poor. Surveys of the poor have been used to great profit by historians of provincial towns, and have illuminated the distinction between 'background' poverty and 'crisis' poverty, between those dependent on regular relief, and those able to support themselves in normal times who

2 Above, pp. 11–12, 14–15.

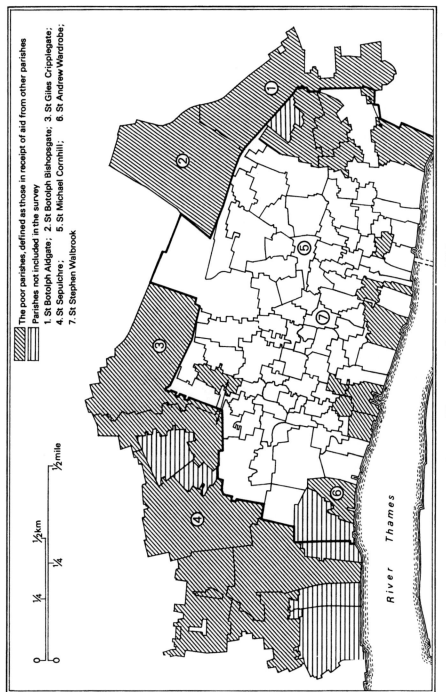

The poor parishes, defined as those in receipt of aid from other parishes

Parishes not included in the survey

1. St Botolph Aldgate; 2. St Botolph Bishopsgate; 3. St Giles Cripplegate;
4. St Sepulchre; 5. St Michael Cornhill; 6. St Andrew Wardrobe;
7. St Stephen Walbrook

¼   ½km
¼   ½mile

River Thames

Figure 1 The topography of poverty, 1598

topple over into poverty in the event of sickness, a hard winter, or sudden increase in prices.[3]

The main problem confronting the historian of Elizabethan London is that, although such censuses were regularly taken, few survive, and none in the kind of detail which would allow us to illuminate variables such as age structure, nature of employment, numbers of dependants, and so on. Every now and again the documents throw up stray figures relating to the number of poor, but we do not know how they were arrived at, nor therefore whether they are reliable or comparable. What appears to be a listing of the number of the poor arranged by parishes, and totalling 2,196 individuals, was drawn up as part of the reorganisation of 1598. But it would be unwise to place too much weight upon this document in the absence of reliable information concerning the kind of poor it covered. My own understanding, for what it is worth, is that, because it was drawn up to help target regular relief, it records the impotent poor eligible for pensions rather than the labouring poor who might qualify for relief in exceptional circumstances. This is an important distinction, not recognised in Steve Rappaport's discussion of the figures, which therefore downplays the extent of poverty.[4] Another figure from the 1590s is the 4,015 householders, probably 16 per cent of the City's total, recorded as 'wanting relief' in late 1595. But we do not know whether this represents the total number of poor in the capital or merely those whom the existing system was failing to relieve, nor is there any indication of family size. It is important that we know the size of the households of the poor because it will affect the calculation of the proportion of the population who were poor. Because the households of the poor were usually small, the proportion of poor in the population is almost always less than the proportion of householders who were poor. Another frustrating lacuna in our knowledge relates to change over time.[5] It is intriguing that there were said to be 1,000 poor in London in 1517 and 12,000 in 1594, perhaps an indication that the proportion of poor in the population was increasing, since this easily exceeded the probable doubling of the City population in the same

[3] Slack, *Poverty and Policy*, pp. 2–5, 38–40, 73–5; P. Slack, 'Poverty and Politics in Salisbury 1597–1666', in *Crisis and Order in English Towns 1500–1700*, ed. P. Clark and P. Slack (1972), pp. 168–78; A. L. Beier, 'The Social Problems of an English Country Town: Warwick 1580–90', in *Country Towns in Pre-Industrial England*, ed. P. Clark (Leicester, 1981), pp. 54–60; T. Arkell, 'The Incidence of Poverty in England in the Late Seventeenth Century', *Social History*, 12 (1987), 1–22.

[4] C.L.R.O., Jour. 24, fos. 322ᵛ–3.

[5] B.L., Lansdowne MS 78/66; C.L.R.O., Rep. 23, fo. 479ᵛ; Rappaport, *Worlds Within Worlds*, pp. 167–71; Slack, *Poverty and Policy*, pp. 71–2, 76–7. I have estimated the population of the area covered by the survey (the area under the City's jurisdiction north of the river) at 115,000. The recent estimate made by Shearer and Finlay of a population of 100,000 for the City within and without the walls excludes the parishes of St Giles Cripplegate and St Andrew Holborn: R. Finlay and B. Shearer, 'Population Growth and Suburban Expansion', in *London 1500–1700*, ed. Beier and Finlay, pp. 45, 58.

period.[6] But we do not know whether these figures were guesses, or whether they were based on comprehensive surveys, nor what criteria the surveyors may have used and therefore whether they are really comparable. We are forced back on the argument I made earlier, that the location of population growth in the parishes we know to have been deprived is a sign that the proportion of poor in the population was increasing.[7]

A few sources do make use of the distinction between background and crisis levels of poverty, and they are our best indication of the extent of poverty. In St Martin in the Fields in 1603 the parish authorities reported that 52 parishioners received weekly alms, and that there were a further 123 householders with 265 dependants 'that want relief and are likely to come to have relief.' The population of St Martin's at this date was about 2,950, so this represents 7.9 per cent of householders on regular relief and a further 18.8 per cent on the margins. The two groups together with their dependants account for 13.75 per cent of the population.[8] These figures are almost exactly the same as those calculated by Jeremy Boulton for the Boroughside district of Southwark in 1618: 7.4 per cent of householders received weekly pensions and 18.6 per cent stood in need of occasional relief.[9] The breadth of the group of those felt to be poor by some criterion as opposed to those thought eligible for regular relief emerges constantly in the large numbers of recipients at the distribution of legacies or funeral doles. Thus in St Michael Cornhill in 1570, 69 named individuals from 60 households received money compared to the no more than 14 pensioners in the same parish. Here, one third of householders were considered sufficiently poor to qualify for occasional relief, perhaps reflecting the more liberal definition of poverty that was possible in the inner-city parishes where the numbers of poor were less pressing.[10] It was presumably of this kind of occasional relief that the churchwardens of St Sepulchre's were thinking when, in their reply to the chantry commissioners in 1548, they claimed that out of 3,400 communicants, 900 poor were relieved, that is 17 per cent of the population.[11] The surveys are therefore consistent in suggesting that about 7 per cent of householders were dependent on regular parish support and a further 18 per cent in need of occasional help and threatened with destitution in crisis years. As a proportion of the population the poor were about 14 per cent. These figures are consonant with Paul Slack's conclusions relating to provincial towns, 'that 4 or 5% of the population of a town commonly received relief in

---

[6] Palliser, *Age of Elizabeth*, p. 123.   [7] Above, pp. 12–13.
[8] W.P.L., F 6039; *Register of Saint Martin in the Fields.*
[9] Boulton, *Neighbourhood and Society*, pp. 95–6, 115, 123.
[10] G.L., MS 4071/1, fo. 94; *Parish Registers of Saint Michael Cornhill.*
[11] *London and Middlesex Chantry Certificate, 1548*, ed. C. J. Kitching (London Record Society, XVI, 1980), p. 8.

the sixteenth century, and that another 10 or 15% was recognised to be "poor" and liable at some time to claim it'.[12]

Central to relief in the capital were the hospitals founded in the mid-Tudor period on a wave of godly enthusiasm and alarm about the growing dimensions of London's poverty. They represented a comprehensive approach to the problem, categorising the poor in terms of the sick and impotent who were to be cared for in St Thomas' and St Bartholomew's, orphaned children who became the responsibility of Christ's, the unemployed and work-shy who were to be set to work or disciplined in Bridewell, and decayed householders relieved by pensions raised through the poor rate. Royal endowment from the lands of the Savoy foundation, the Bridewell palace precinct, and the former hospital of St Bartholomew's and its properties was supplemented by the corporation's assignment of various dues and tolls deriving from its regulation of the City's internal economy: the Blackwell Hall hallage dues on sales of cloth went predominantly to Christ's, while St Bartholomew's enjoyed the profits of the City beams. Some effort to tackle the imbalance between needs and resources was made by Christ's which redistributed some of its receipts from the collections in the inner-city areas to the extramural parishes.[13]

The refounded hospitals did not provide as many beds as the medieval foundations they replaced. In her survey of hospital provision in late medieval London, Carole Rawcliffe estimates that the Savoy, St Thomas' Southwark, St Mary without Bishopsgate, and the Elsyng Spittle together provided 420 beds, and this figure does not include the unknown quantity of accommodation available at St Bartholomew's and St Thomas Acon. The refounded St Thomas' and St Bartholomew's could comfortably support only 220 in their earliest years, although numbers in excess of this are recorded.[14] However, the mid-century establishments represented new standards of medical care. Whereas the medieval hospitals offered, with the exception of the Savoy, itself a recent foundation, only food, shelter, and basic care, their successors adopted a much more ambitious approach, providing professional medical expertise to cure the poor of their ailments and make them fit for work in the commonweal. Both St Thomas' and St

[12] P. Slack, 'Poverty and Social Regulation in Elizabethan England', in *Reign of Elizabeth I*, ed. Haigh, p. 232.
[13] P. Slack, 'Social Policy and the Constraints of Government, 1547–58', in *The Mid-Tudor Polity c. 1540–1560*, ed. J. Loach and R. Tittler (1980), pp. 108–13; *Parliamentary Papers*, 1840. XIX; *T.E.D.*, III. 415–20.
[14] C. Rawcliffe, 'The Hospitals of Later Medieval London', *Medical History*, 28 (1984), 1–21; C.L.R.O., Rep. 14, fo. 465; S.B.H., Ha1/3, fo. 27.

Bartholomew's boasted a physician and three surgeons each, employing some of the best medical talent available.[15]

It was not only to the physical welfare of the inmates that the hospital authorities looked, for they were also determined to mould the morals of those in their care. Virtuous habits were to be inculcated by setting the patients to work. The governors arranged for the purchase of flax for use in spinning and provided a hand-mill for the grinding of corn within the hospital.[16] Inmates were expected to attend religious services within the precincts and threatened with loss of their meals if they defaulted. A special effort was made to prevent the poor leaving the precincts on Sundays.[17] Patients caught playing cards and dice were punished, and those who gadded to alehouses without the permission of the almoners were threatened with dismissal.[18] Those whose diseases could be linked to moral failings were punished by whippings once the cure was completed. In 1568 the governors of St Thomas' ordered that patients sent from Bridewell should be returned for punishment once cured; and thirty years later that all victims of the pox should be punished 'that by the terror therof others may be admonished for falling into the like vyce'.[19] This stern moralistic outlook made the governors unsympathetic towards some classes of patient. Pregnant single women were regarded with such great suspicion that the governors of St Thomas' ordered in 1562 that none were to be received into the hospital 'for that it is a house erected for the relefe of honest persons and not of harlottes to be maynteyned there'.[20]

Whether the hospital regime had much impact on the behaviour of inmates may however be doubted. This was because in the first place their stay was short. The average length of stay seems to have varied between two and three months.[21] Secondly, the repeated orders relating to the provision of work suggest a series of false starts rather than the achievement of a hive of industry. Thirdly, and most importantly, the hospital authorities faced serious staffing problems for the governors appear to have spent as much time disciplining the sisters as the inmates themselves. Complaints against the nurses were manifold: they were drunk on duty; they were of lewd speech

---

[15] T. Vicary, *The Anatomie of the Bodie of Man*, ed. F. J. and P. Furnivall (E.E.T.S., extra series, LIII, 1888), pp. 295–6; N. Moore, *The History of Saint Bartholomew's Hospital* (2 vols., 1918), II. 421–51, 586–617.

[16] G.L.R.O., H1/ST/A1/2, fos. 17, 27, 44ᵛ, 69ᵛ; H1/ST/A1/3, fos. 36, 105; H1/ST/A1/4, fo. 137; C.L.R.O., Rep. 18, fos. 310ᵛ, 368.

[17] G.L.R.O., H1/ST/A1/2, fos. 42, 52ᵛ; H1/ST/A1/3, fo. 206.

[18] G.L.R.O., H1/ST/A1/2, fos. 34ᵛ, 56ᵛ; H1/ST/A1/3, fo. 74ᵛ.

[19] G.L.R.O., H1/ST/A1/2, fo. 85; H1/ST/A1/4, fo. 147; S.B.H., Ha1/3, fo. 45ᵛ.

[20] G.L.R.O., H1/ST/A1/1, fos. 25ᵛ, 46; G.L., MS 12806/2, fo. 27.

[21] Based on statistics of admissions and discharges at St Thomas' in 1571–3, and at St Bartholomew's in 1595–6: G.L.R.O., H1/ST/A1/3, fo. 442ᵛ; B.L., Additional MS 12503, fo. 288.

and brawled; they neglected the care of the patients.[22] They were hardly effective instruments of social regulation.

It is also clear that however conscientious the management of the hospitals may have been, they were confronted by challenges that their resources were inadequate to meet. This is suggested by the constantly reiterated pleas of the governors that the number of poor housed in the hospitals be reduced, reflecting a sense that standards of care deteriorated as the hospitals filled up. Thus the governors of St Thomas' on several occasions stipulated that the numbers in care should be limited to 120, while in St Bartholomew's the limit was fixed at 100, and later at 150.[23] In practice these limits were frequently breached, the numbers in care usually expanding in the winter months. Thus in 1568–9 the average number of inmates in St Thomas' was 140, with a peak of 200 at the end of March.[24] It is also true that the hospitals could afford to maintain larger numbers in the 1580s and 1590s because the value of their endowments increased rapidly as leases fell in, more than compensating for inflation (Table 5.1). According to John Howes, former renter to St Thomas' and author of a dialogue on hospital administration, by the early 1580s St Thomas' harboured 200, and St Bartholomew's 140.[25] Nevertheless financial constraints continued to be acutely felt, and the demands for restrictions on numbers continued to be articulated.[26] Moreover the hospitals were not exclusively the preserve of the poor because some prosperous masters used the hospitals for the care of their servants, sometimes paying a maintenance fee towards their support.[27] Nor were they exclusively a London resource because in the 1590s they filled up with the maimed soldiers who congregated in the city as the place where they were most likely to obtain relief. St Bartholomew's claimed to have carried out 1,143 'cures' in 1595–6, compared with 442 and 602 in the peace-time years of 1582 and 1610 respectively.[28] A turnover of this level borne by a staff no larger than that of the hospital's original establishment, and in the context of a widely perceived need for specialist hospitals for maimed soldiers, suggests a deterioration in the level of care.[29]

The Italian traveller Ubaldini was critical of the hospitals in general claiming that they were small and badly maintained, but he made an exception of Christ's, and he was followed by other foreign visitors in his

[22] G.L.R.O., H1/ST/A1/1, fo. 72ᵛ; H1/ST/A1/2, fo. 80ᵛ; H1/ST/A1/3, fos. 95ᵛ, 102; H1/ST/A1/4, fos. 30ᵛ, 32, 47, 52.
[23] C.L.R.O., Rep. 14, fo. 465; Rep. 16, fo. 261ᵛ; G.L.R.O., H1/ST/A1/3, fos. 18ᵛ, 114; H1/ST/A1/4, fo. 77ᵛ; S.B.H., Ha1/3, fos. 27, 46ᵛ.
[24] G.L.R.O., H1/ST/A1/3.   [25] T.E.D., III. 424–5.
[26] G.L.R.O., H1/ST/A1/4, fo. 77ᵛ; S.B.H., Ha1/3, fos. 27, 46ᵛ.
[27] S.B.H., Ha1/2, fo. 53; G.L.R.O., H1/ST/A1/1, fo. 12ᵛ; H1/ST/A1/2, fos. 30ᵛ, 39ᵛ, 40.
[28] B.L., Additional MS 12503, fo. 288; T.E.D., III. 424–5; H. L. Collman, *Ballads and Broadsides, Chiefly of the Elizabethan Period* (Oxford, 1912), p. 222.
[29] G.L., MS 4069/1, fo. 42; C.L.R.O., Jour. 22, fo. 373; Jour. 23, fo. 189; Rep. 25, fo. 148.

praise.[30] In the 1580s and 1590s Christ's catered for between 550 and 650 children at any one time, representing an annual intake of between 60 and 90.[31] Although the children of freemen were clearly preferred, its admissions policy was reasonably broad. The hospital orders required three years' residence in the city by the parents, and the frequently expressed reluctance to admit illegitimates was regularly overcome as foundlings accounted for about 10 per cent of those admitted by the end of the century. The majority of the children, sponsored by the parish vestries, came from one-parent families of households overburdened with children. Sometimes Christ's actually put the children out to nurse to their own parents, providing a form of family allowance and access to the hospital facilities.[32] As with other aspects of the hospital scheme, careful attention was paid to ensuring that the children were brought up in virtuous habits. Elementary education was widely available in the petty school, and the more able were taught in the grammar school, from which several passed on to the universities.[33] Attempts were made to provide industrial training for others, as a needlemaker set up in the hospital.[34] In the 1580s an average of thirty-three children a year left the hospital for apprenticeship or service, sometimes in the households of prominent citizens.[35]

However, the hospital faced problems. Some of these stemmed from its very success as Christ's became a target for aristocratic patronage. Government officials and courtiers bombarded the aldermen with requests for the admission of children. By the quinquennium 1594–9, 16 per cent of admissions were at the suit of private persons or by order of the court of aldermen, usually acting in response to their petitioning.[36] Although some of these children would probably have been admitted from the parishes in any case, the practice represented a weakening of the bond between the hospital and the parishes, already under strain for other reasons, as we shall see. It was perhaps policies such as this which explain the outburst of one Goodman Jugger that 'rytche mens children be preferde here and poore mens children reiected'.[37] It was part of the price that had to be paid for the good-will of the great and influential, both in the form of legacies and of help in

[30] E. P. de G. Chaney, '"Philanthropy in Italy": English Observations on Italian Hospitals', in *Aspects of Poverty in Early Modern Europe*, ed. T. Riis (Florence, 1981), pp. 191–2; *Thomas Platter's Travels in England*, ed. C. Williams (1937), p. 179.

[31] Admissions figures are recorded regularly in the hospital accounts: G.L., MS 12819/2. Cf. the admissions register (G.L., MS 12818/1), printed as *Christ's Hospital Admissions, 1554–1599*, ed. G. A. T. Allan (1937).

[32] G.L., MS 12806/2, fo. 172; *Memoranda, References, and Documents Relating to the Royal Hospitals of the City of London* (1836), p. 83; *Christ's Admissions*. Concern for freeman status was occasionally expressed by the governors: G.L., MS 12806/2, fos. 254, 405; C.L.R.O., Rep. 17, fo. 415ᵛ.

[33] G.L., MS 12806/2, fos. 11, 27ᵛ, 210, 221ᵛ, 293.

[34] Ibid. fos. 25, 39ᵛ, 117ᵛ, 120, 126ᵛ, 135, 193.

[35] *Christ's Admissions*.   [36] Ibid.   [37] G.L., MS 12806/2, fo. 172.

those cases where the hospitals required their support, as in the promotion of parliamentary legislation, or against the attentions of Adams and Wood-shaw, patentees for concealed lands.[38]

The hospital's most critical problems centred on its finances. As the bulk of the royal endowment had passed to St Thomas' and St Bartholomew's, Christ's was left dangerously dependent on casualties (Table 5.1). In the early 1560s collections in the parishes, then still voluntary, accounted for 67 per cent of net income, while the Blackwell Hall hallage dues, vulnerable to fluctuations in the market for cloth and the corruption of inadequately salaried officials, provided a further 16 per cent. Most of the residue came from the benevolence of citizens in the form of legacies and life-time giving, lands only accounting for 1.7 per cent. By the early 1580s, income from all sources but collections had increased, and gifts to the hospital in the intervening period ensured that lands were accounting for a steadily increasing proportion of income (13 per cent). Confidence in the future was doubtless further boosted by the addition of the fees for licensing carmen to the revenues in 1582.[39] With 550 children in its care the hospital had expanded considerably from the original establishment for the relief of 380 children. But Howes felt that more could have been relieved.[40] Moreover, Christ's remained dangerously dependent on casualties. The hospital, the governors complained in 1586, 'doeth stande for the moste parte uppon benevolence and casualties havinge a verie small certen revenewe or Lyve-hood and yet mainteyned the greatest charge of all the reste of the howses'.[41] Bills soared in the later 1580s and 1590s just as the income from the hallage dues and collections slumped. Trade depression sent the Blackwell Hall dues spiralling downwards from 1586, at a time when the income from the rate was faltering as vestries were confronted by an increasing demand for outdoor relief and by the difficulties of the ratepayers themselves. The result was that Christ's remained in debt for all but two years in the period 1585–1602, leaving it ill-equipped to cope with the problems confronting London at that time. Indeed there were periodic attempts to restrict admissions. Alarmed by the growing numbers of abandoned children, which they felt their charity only encouraged, the governors imposed a one-year ban on the admission of foundlings in 1591.[42] In July 1595 it was ordered that no petitions for the admission of children be accepted 'betweene this & bartholomewtide next cominge or untill yt shall please god things are become more cheap'.[43] The consequences of such constraints appear clearly

[38] Ibid. fos. 74, 284, 341ᵛ, 342, 344, 344ᵛ.   [39] C.L.R.O., Rep. 20, fo. 320ᵛ.

[40] *T.E.D.*, III. 420, 425.

[41] G.L., MSS 12806/2, fos. 388, 390, 399, 415ᵛ; 12806/3, fos. 69ᵛ, 90, 92ᵛ, 93, 99ᵛ, 101, 101ᵛ, 107ᵛ–8, 110, 113ᵛ–14, 119; C.L.R.O., Rep. 23, fo. 2ʳ⁻ᵛ.

[42] G.L., MS 12806/2, fo. 416.

[43] G.L., MS 12806/3, fo. 72. Cf. ibid., fos. 90, 102ᵛ, 109ᵛ.

Table 5.1. *Analysis of income of Christ's, St Thomas', and St Bartholomew's Hospitals in the later sixteenth century (nearest £ p.a.)*

	1561–4	1570–4	1581–4	1595–8
Christ's				
Poor rate	876	937	975	828
Private charity	202	223	317	586
City tolls	205	231	704	474
Endowment	22	59	297	603
Miscellaneous	4	5	62	34
Total	1,309	1,455	2,355	2,525
St Bartholomew's				
Private charity		66		132
City tolls		333		265
Endowment		647		1,443
Miscellaneous		43		18
Total		1,089		1,858
St Thomas'				
Private charity		83		140
Endowment		814		1,412
Miscellaneous		88		49
Total		985		1,601

Figures given are net of deductions for administrative costs in collection, annuities and quit-rents payable by the hospitals, and expenditure of the poor rate on extramural parishes.
Sources: G.L., MS 12819/2; S.B.H., Hb1/2; Hb1/3; G.L.R.O., H1/ST/A24/1; H1/ST/E29/2.

in the petitions of the wardmote inquest of Cornhill in 1595 and 1596 about 'the poore lyenge in the stretes that they may be provided for', in the complaints of the aldermen about the 'lame and impotent people especiallye children who daylye lye under stalls and for want of necessarye releife do peryshe most miserrablye', and in the testimony of individual testators like Jasper Lambard leaving money in 1596 for 'such poor comfortles children as hath no friends and lieth in the streets'.[44]

This situation made for a tense relationship between the hospital and the parishes. This was because control of the poor rate was centralised in the hands of the governors of Christ's who were appointed to receive the metropolitan collections under the poor relief legislation of 1563 and 1572. It was they who determined the proportion of their collections that the

[44] G.L., MS 4069/1, fos. 65, 67; C.L.R.O., Rep. 18, fo. 122ᵛ–3; Rep. 22, fos. 173ᵛ, 210ᵛ; Jour. 19, fo. 191; Jour. 23, fo. 74; P.R.O., PROB 11/87, fo. 311ᵛ.

parishes retained in their own hands for outdoor relief. Most of the remittances from the inner-city parishes the hospital retained for its own needs, but Christ's also undertook the redistribution of resources to the extramural parishes, whose dependence on the governors was therefore even greater.[45] Pensioners were licensed by Christ's and presented to the hospital every Michaelmas.[46] The accounts of all the collectors for the poor in the city were audited by Christ's. The hospital could use its power to refuse to admit children from the parishes as a means of disciplining those which were recalcitrant in forwarding their contributions.[47] Some extramural parishes found their allowances from the hospital reduced as children were taken off their hands.[48] On the other hand incentives to parishes to increase their rates might be offered by allowing them to retain a higher proportion of the money collected for the support of their own poor.[49] But the relationship between hospital and parishes was often fraught. Vestries were always inclined to grant more pensions than Christ's, preoccupied both with its own needs and with those of the extramural parishes, was willing to grant. Thus in December 1572 the aldermen, at the hospital's instigation, required the local authorities 'to myttigate & abate of the somes allreadie allotted unto them ... for that the colleccion all readie appoynted will not serve to advaunce suche ample pencions'.[50] Parochial dissatisfaction with Christ's was doubtless exacerbated by the revelation in 1593 of the corruption of the hospital clerk, Richard Wilson, who handled many of their monies.[51] But the main cause of friction in the 1590s resulted from the difficulties vestries began to encounter in securing the admission of the children of their own parishioners, as the financial problems of Christ's forced it into more restrictive admissions policies. Tetchiness certainly resulted from the turning down of requests to take in children, the corollary of which was the necessity for parochial provision either by means of disbursement from the church stock or by special collections.[52] Thus after the rebuff of repeated efforts to secure the admission of a foundling in 1591 and 1592, the vestry of St Michael Cornhill determined on detaining the money for keeping it from their

[45] 5 Eliz. I c. 3 § 14; 14 Eliz. I c. 5 § 29; G.L., MS 12819/2.
[46] G.L., MSS 4958/2, fos. 110ᵛ, 111ᵛ–12; 1431/1, fo. 6 (for petitions for licensing of pensioners from parishes); 12806/2, fos. 29ᵛ, 260.
[47] Ibid. fos. 113, 201.   [48] Ibid. fo. 202ᵛ.   [49] Ibid. fo. 370.
[50] C.L.R.O., Jour. 20, fo. 32ᵛ; Jour. 24, fo. 306; Rep. 26, fos. 37ᵛ, 402ᵛ–3; G.L., MS 12806/3, fos. 117ᵛ, 119.
[51] G.L., MS 12806/3, fos. 59ᵛ, 60.
[52] Increased expenditure on foundlings is discernible in the churchwardens' accounts of many city parishes in the 1590s: G.L., MSS 2596/1; 6574; 1432/3; 5090/2; 6836; 4835/1; 1046/1; 2088/1; 2593/1; 1568; 4887; 3907/1; 959/1. For special collections to support foundlings and orphans, see G.L., MSS 4241/1, fo. 107; 819/1, fo. 7v; 9234/6, fos. 292, 295; *Vestry Minutes of Saint Margaret Lothbury*, pp. 33, 34, 35, 38; *Vestry Minutes of Saint Christopher le Stocks*, p. 17.

hospital contribution.[53] Parishioners had other grounds for disillusionment as the early hopes that the hospitalisation of the poor would end the problem of beggary were soon dashed. Some refused to pay their assessments to the rate on such grounds, and the sense of frustration is captured in Howes' comment on the paradox of the 'masse of moneye' given in relief, and 'the streates yet swarme with beggars'.[54]

Such factors explain the patchy success achieved by the hospital authorities in their efforts to get parishes to increase their collections.[55] We can use the date obtained from the Christ's Hospital accounts and the fragmentary accounts of the collectors for the poor from the inner-city parishes to estimate the volume of money raised by the rate. Inner-city parishes sent an average of 58 per cent of the money they collected to Christ's, retaining the remainder for the support of their own pensioners. We know that the hospital received £1,279 from the collections of 1573–4, so that the total collected in the contributing parishes would have been £2,205.[56] To this figure must be added the collections in the extramural parishes which sent no money to Christ's. Some information, shown in Table 5.2, is available for most of these, although sometimes at a date somewhat removed from 1573. The total amount collected in poor rate in 1573–4 was therefore about £2,500. This was probably the largest amount realised before 1598, for it came shortly after a major reassessment of the rate in 1572.[57] The pattern seems to have been that although an administrative drive might have increased collections substantially for a few years, in the long term the amounts raised tended to drift downwards once more. Thus the introduction of compulsory rating in 1572 appears to have resulted in immediate increases of between 20 per cent and 40 per cent, but the long-term improvement was only of the order of between 10 per cent and 20 per cent. Surveying the Elizabethan period as a whole it is true that in a few parishes apparently substantial increases were registered – 60 per cent in St Michael le Querne between the 1560s and 1590s – elsewhere the improvements were more modest – 22 per cent in St Mary Aldermanbury and 12 per cent in St Mary Woolnoth – and in some parishes like St Andrew Hubbard there was no

[53] G.L., MS 4072/1, fos. 51, 52ᵛ, 54ᵛ. Cf. G.L., MS 2590/1, p. 100.
[54] G.L., MS 12806/2, fo. 27; *T.E.D.*, III. 421.
[55] G.L., MSS 12806/2, fos. 300ᵛ, 413ᵛ; 12806/3, fo. 69ᵛ; C.L.R.O., Jour. 19, fos. 173ᵛ–4; Jour. 20, fo. 24; Rep. 17, fo. 35; Rep. 18, fos. 80, 108ᵛ–9, 151, 191ᵛ; Rep. 19, fos. 25ᵛ, 52ᵛ; Rep. 21, fo. 496; Rep. 23, fo. 2ʳ⁻ᵛ.
[56] For receipts from the poor rate, see G.L., MSS 1016/1; 2895/1; 959/1; 5090/1–2; 6836; 9234/1–7; 3556/1; 1002/1A; 1013/1; 1279/1; 1278/1. For less continuous series, see G.L., MSS 2596/1; 4415/1; 2088/1; 4791; 593/2, fo. 78; 4071/1, fo. 66ᵛ; 4072/1, fo. 73; 4810/1, fo. 114; 4957/1; 4249, fo. 137ᵛ; *Vestry Minutes of Saint Bartholomew Exchange*, pp. 3–4, 29, 38–9; *The Account Books of Saint Bartholomew Exchange*, ed. E. Freshfield (1895), pp. 4–5, 7, 8, 10–12, 15–17; *Vestry Minutes of Saint Margaret Lothbury*, pp. 3, 5, 6, 9, 11; *Vestry Minutes of Saint Christopher le Stocks*, pp. 2–3, 4.
[57] C.L.R.O., Jour. 20, fos. 15ᵛ, 24, 25, 32ᵛ; Rep. 17, fos. 373ᵛ, 389ᵛ; 425ᵛ–6.

Table 5.2. *Size of the poor rate in the extramural parishes*

	Amount	Date
Saint Sepulchre	£75	1573
Saint Giles Cripplegate	£85	1585
Saint Botolph Aldgate	£20	1589
Saint Dunstan in the West	£35	1577
Saint Andrew Holborn	£25–£30	1582
Saint Botolph Bishopsgate	£15	1561
Saint Botolph Aldersgate	£20	Half the assessment of 1620s
Saint Bride Fleet Street	£20	Guess

Sources: C.L.R.O., Rep. 17, fos. 425ᵛ–26; G.L., MSS 12806/2, fo. 346ʳ⁻ᵛ; 9234/1–2; 2968/1, fo. 304ᵛ; 4249, fo. 137ᵛ; 12806/1, fo. 45; W.A.M., 13550.

improvement at all or, as Stow complained of St Botolph Billingsgate, collections actually yielded less at the end of the period, than at the beginning.[58] The evidence in the form of the gross receipts from the rates at Christ's Hospital would appear to confirm this picture. Receipts at Christ's fell in the 1560s and recovered sharply in the early 1570s. But significantly, in November 1573, at the end of a year of high prices and plague, the governors were complaining that of £1,540 due to them £300 remained uncollected. Indeed, in spite of brief spurts, the receipts averaged £1,200 throughout the later sixteenth century. The achievement is not impressive in the light of price inflation of 43 per cent between the 1560s and 1590s.[59]

It was only after the legislation of 1598 that very substantial increases in the rates were achieved. Collections leapt by 250 per cent in the first decade of the seventeenth century over the 1590s in Allhallows London Wall, and doubled in St Bartholomew Exchange and St Andrew Wardrobe, increases which seem to have derived from a decision to double the existing rate of assessment at Easter 1599. An increase of this scale was not achieved without difficulty.[60] Some parishes had their collectors imprisoned because they withheld money from the treasurers on the grounds that they should be receiving support from other parishes rather than contributing.[61] Payments in accounts leave one with the impression that parish authorities were now

[58] Above, n. 56; Stow, *Survey of London*, I. 208. In the estimates of the yield of the poor rate incorporated into Table 5.8, I have therefore assumed total income of £2,250.

[59] C.L.R.O., Rep. 18, fos. 108ᵛ–9; G.L., MS 12819/2.

[60] G.L., MSS 5090/2, 2088/1; 2089; *Accounts of Saint Bartholomew Exchange*, pp. 4–5, 7, 8, 10–12, 15–17.

[61] G.L., MSS 12806/3, fo. 93ᵛ; 4241/1, fo. 161; 3570/1, fos. 57, 64ᵛ; C.L.R.O., Jour. 24, fo. 329ᵛ; Rep. 25, fos. 189, 397; Rep. 26, fos. 56ᵛ, 111ᵛ, 137ᵛ, 164ᵛ.

more ready to call in the aldermen in their capacity as justices to discipline defaulters.[62] This is impressive testimony to the City elite's responsiveness, albeit belated, to the problems they faced and the results that sustained administrative pressure could achieve, but it is significant that the reforms came only in the wake of the crisis, and the large sums then realised suggest the inadequacy of provision in the recent past.

PRIVATE CHARITY

Historians seeking to assess the role of private charity in the relief of the poor are confronted by the monumental labours of W. K. Jordan, who attempted to chart the changing patterns of London philanthropy in the sixteenth and early seventeenth centuries through a comprehensive survey of the surviving wills. He argued that the post-Reformation decades witnessed massive investment by all classes of civic society in the relief of the poor, that this represented a new rational philanthropy in its supposedly greater discrimination among the objects of relief than the haphazard catholic forms it replaced, and that private charity contributed more to social welfare than the poor rate.[63] These arguments have all proved controversial. The most frequently reiterated criticism is that he failed to take account of inflation. A deflated curve of giving produced by Bittle and Lane suggests a collapse in giving in the Elizabethan period. But the argument has not been without its defenders. In a relatively little noticed contribution to the debate J. F. Hadwin has pointed out that the application of the deflator to Jordan's crude totals is misleading because it fails to take into account the accumulated yield of previous endowments. Working on the assumption that about one-fifth of benefactions were absorbed in the decade in which they were made, while the rest yielded at 5 per cent, Hadwin's figures for the *yield* of charities for poor relief show a modest increase in the Elizabethan period even when deflated.[64]

Secondly, Jordan has been accused both of exaggerating the novelty of discriminating attitudes towards the poor in the post-Reformation decades and of underestimating the later-sixteenth-century continuities with the past. Thomson points out that many late medieval testators demanded that their executors discriminate between the deserving and the undeserving in distributing their doles, while Lee Beier's work shows the persistence of

---

[62] Society of Antiquaries MS 236, fo. 48ᵛ; G.L.R.O., P92/SAV/450, pp. 339, 343; P92/SAV/1463.

[63] W. K. Jordan, *Philanthropy in England, 1480–1660: A Study of the Changing Pattern of English Social Aspirations* (1959) and *Charities of London*.

[64] W. G. Bittle and R. T. Lane, 'Inflation and Philanthropy in England: a Reassessment of W. K. Jordan's Data', *Ec.H.R.*, second series, 29 (1976), 203–10; J. F. Hadwin, 'Deflating Philanthropy', *Ec.H.R.*, second series, 31 (1978), 105–17; Slack, *Poverty and Policy*, pp. 162–4.

traditional forms of giving in funeral doles.[65] Although these historians do not deny that attitudes changed, they tend to make the process of change a slower one than Jordan envisaged, and question his conclusion that it was protestant teaching which was responsible for the emergence of a more discriminating philanthropy. Many of his critics assert the primacy of the economic over the religious variable in explaining changes in attitudes. Attitudes to poverty changed as the problem increased in scale. The stereotypical polarity between the deserving and the undeserving was strengthened because contemporary understanding of the causes of poverty was, with a few exceptions, not sufficiently sophisticated to allow for the possibility that men could be unemployed through no fault of their own. Therefore as unemployment increased and more people took to the road in search of work, the existence of a subculture of the idle and work-shy, however illusory it may have been in reality, was more widely perceived. These perceptions were translated into a more discriminating philanthropy.[66]

A third front on Jordan's argument tackles the problem from the point of view of the recipient rather than the donor groups. How much support could private charity provide and what was its role in the economy of the poor in comparison with the poor rate? Jordan's argument rests on the comparison of the absolute amounts raised in different periods, but fails to consider the volume of resources in relation to the needs of the poor. Because he has focused on the donors, he disregards the problem of the degree to which charitable intentions were implemented, and neglects to raise the question of whether charities were established in areas of most need. His remarks about the relative balance of private charity and the poor rate are worthless because based on the astonishing fallacy that those few poor accounts which have survived represent all the rates levied in the counties under review.[67]

It is most unfortunate that faults in Jordan's methodology make it impossible to answer most of these questions from his data. The figures are shrouded in obscurity by his failure to disaggregate his data adequately. He tends to lump diverse forms of charity into misleading general categories. For example, the inclusion of such diverse forms of relief as loan stocks for young merchants, legacies to the hospitals, subsidies for apprenticeship of the poor and the marriage of poor maidens, and doles in the debtors' prisons, under the general heading of social rehabilitation, is not very satisfactory when we try to look at the volume of charity from the point of view of the recipient. Still more fundamentally, he fails to indicate the proportion of the invest-

[65] Thomson, 'Piety and Charity', pp. 182–3; Beier, 'Social Problems of an Elizabethan Country Town', pp. 69–73.
[66] Cf. B. Pullan, 'Catholics and the Poor in Early Modern Europe', *T.R.H.S.*, fifth series, 26 (1976), 15–34.
[67] Jordan, *Philanthropy in England*, p. 141.

ment which was in the form of capital endowments. Although we are told that 82.6 per cent of the benefactions were in the form of capital aggregates we are left wondering whether this was so at all times during the period under consideration and whether the remark applies equally to all kinds of relief. Finally the figures do not allow one to gauge the extent of participation in the philanthropic movement. Lee Beier, Susan Brigden, and J. A. F. Thomson have all emphasised the need to count the number of individual benefactions to estimate the proportion of testators participating in their relief, if we are to generalise about changing attitudes to the poor.[68]

We are thus faced with rather unsatisfactory data to answer the questions we wish to pose. Some attempt to recover the pattern of charity on the ground is necessary, and preferably by a more economical method than the survey of all surviving wills prior to and during the period of study which was Jordan's approach. My solution to this problem is a two-pronged strategy involving the use of the nineteenth-century charity commissioners' reports as a basis for calculations of the yield from endowed charities, combined with two samples of wills to estimate the volume of cash bequests at different points in the period under review.[69] Such a method requires some justification since it depends upon the commissioners having recorded all endowed charities in operation some 250 years before their investigations. First, it should be said that their survey of the evidence was impressive, involving the use of will books, deeds, and church memorial tablets, sources which are sometimes lost to the modern investigator. Their efforts were not confined to charities then in operation but sometimes involved the uncovering of funds which had been lost in the intervening period. Secondly, wherever possible, the data derived from the commissioners' reports have been checked against sixteenth-century documentation, and any necessary revisions incorporated in the data presented in Table 5.7. Such checks have involved the use of the wardens' accounts of twenty-seven livery companies, including ten of the twelve great companies which acted as trustees for a high proportion of city charities, and of the churchwardens' accounts of thirty-eight city parishes.[70] The accounts were invaluable in solving some of the problems left by the reports, in particular the pensions paid to almsmen. Although some additional charities were uncovered through the accounts, the level of inaccuracy of the reports was reduced by the time-lag in the implementation of other charities. Annuities and rent charges are almost

[68] Beier, 'Social Problems of an Elizabethan Country Town', pp. 72–3; Thomson, 'Piety and Charity', p. 181; Brigden, 'Religion and Social Obligation', pp. 104–5.
[69] The early-nineteenth-century surveys of parochial charities are conveniently collected in *Parliamentary Papers*, 1903. XLIX and *Parliamentary Papers*, 1904. LXXI. Surveys of company charities are recorded in *Parliamentary Papers*, 1884. XXXIX, parts IV and V. For the will samples, see notes to Tables 5.3–5.8.
[70] See accounts listed in bibliography.

always recorded, and, although parish loan stocks were likely to be missed, at this date most loan stocks went to the livery companies where they are well recorded in will registers and accounts. The level of accuracy of the reports suggested by these checks was 87 per cent by value. It might be objected that there is a degree of circularity in this argument: either charities were more likely to continue in operation in parishes and companies with good traditions of record keeping, or the commissioners' reports were more likely to achieve accuracy in parishes and companies where the contemporary documentation was good. There is, however, a means of checking the accuracy of the reports which is independent of these sources of bias. One can determine whether the endowed charities intended to be established by the testators in the will sample appear in the commissioners' reports. In the few cases where they did not, the explanation sometimes lies in difficulties encountered with the executors because the size of the deceased's estate did not measure up to expectations.[71] Indeed this demonstrates one possible advantage of the reports over wills, as they record implementation rather than intention. They also record the charitable trusts established in a donor's lifetime. All in all the level of error produced by this strategy is sufficiently slight, and certainly no greater than that obtained by working through wills, to justify the approach.

The will samples require less justification. Tables 5.3–5.5 chart changes in the proportion of testators supporting various forms of charity. All surviving wills for two four-year periods, 1570–3 and 1595–7, have been examined. We are fortunate in possessing wills from all probate jurisdictions, except for wills of testators of lesser social status in the thirteen city parishes which were peculiars of the archbishop of Canterbury, so that the picture is nearly complete. London testators in the sample are defined as any person living within the City or describing themselves as citizens of London though resident outside the City's jurisdiction. The value of bequests in City parishes north of the river has been separated from benefactions to the Middlesex and Southwark parishes for which the data is less complete.

Table 5.6 shows the results of an attempt to value the bequests, distinguishing between cash bequests and endowments, and between bequests which the testator intended should take effect in any circumstances and those which were contingent upon the death of other beneficiaries without issue. It has proved difficult to value some bequests, in particular those where the residue of the estate was directed to charitable works or those where property was bequeathed without an indication of its capital value. Rather than attempting guesses, the number of bequests which defied valuation in each category is indicated. Fortunately bequests of this nature were rare; they

---

[71] For example, John Wilkinsons's bequest to the poor in Saint Gregory's: P.R.O., PROB 11/54, fo. 10.

were most common among contingent bequests whose size may have been academic anyway, but they do pose real problems in bequests to the stranger poor to whom donations of the residue of the estate were common.

The figures presented in Tables 5.3–5.5 suggest that the surge in charitable giving accompanying the Reformation years identified by Susan Brigden was sustained into the 1570s, by which time 61.9 per cent of the wealthier testators whose wills were proved in the Prerogative Court of Canterbury made some bequest to the poor, and 34.9 per cent of the poorer testators whose wills were usually proved in the lesser probate jurisdictions. These figures compare with the mid-Tudor peaks of 51.6 per cent and 32.4 per cent for wealthier and poorer testators respectively.[72] By the mid 1590s participation in the relief of the poor was narrower, as giving to the poor among Prerogative Court of Canterbury testators fell back to 53.9 per cent, and among the craftsmen and shopkeepers to 23.5 per cent. In part this reflects a decline in the number of token bequests of sums as small as 1s. to the poor, which may have been a result of the weakening of ideas about the efficacy of prayers of the poor. The more restricted base to giving also probably reflects the difficulties experienced by the middling sort in the 1590s when economic pressures may have strengthened the sense of primary responsibility towards members of the immediate family who dominate bequests. Nevertheless, participation in charitable giving remained nearly as widespread as in the mid-Tudor decades.

This pattern of charitable activity in the years after the Reformation lends support to Jordan's perception of a shift from religious to secular objects of giving in which there was widespread participation. But it would be unwise to assume that the increased participation in giving arose simply from religious change. We must also entertain the possibility that Londoners were responding to dramatically increased needs. The 1540s have traditionally been regarded as a period of profound social dislocation as a result of the inflation caused by repeated debasement of the coinage. However, this view rests largely on the rhetoric of complaint of the commonwealthmen, protestant clerics who saw improvements in social welfare as part of the task of building the godly commonwealth.[73] Recent appraisals of the state of the mid-Tudor economy have been rather more optimistic than their jeremiads would suggest. In particular Rappaport has demonstrated that whatever temporary disruption the debasements caused, real wages soon returned to their pre-debasement levels. It is therefore unlikely that the impoverishment of this period was so massive as to explain the greatly increased participation

---

[72] S. Brigden, 'The Early Reformation in London, 1522–47: the Conflict in the Parishes' (Cambridge Ph.D., 1979), pp. 358–9 and 'Religion and Social Obligation', pp. 104–5.
[73] B. Bradshaw, 'The Tudor Commonwealth: Reform and Revision', *Historical Journal*, 22 (1979), 470–2.

in the relief of the poor.[74] But there is more to the question of needs than the evolution of the economy. The volume of need was undoubtedly greater in the 1540s for the simple reason that the dissolutions of the monasteries and religious gilds wiped out substantial charitable resources.[75] The Reformation therefore created a vacuum in charitable provision. Whether the reformers' ideology made a difference in the way that Jordan postulated is more doubtful. Protestants did not deploy very distinctive arguments and strategies relating to the poor. The novelty of the discriminatory attitudes which underpinned the 'pervasive secularism' characteristic of the sixteenth century according to Jordan must be doubted. Long before the Reformation testators had sought to confine their charity to worthy recipients and place them in almshouses where their behaviour could be more closely regulated.[76] Protestants were handed down the intellectual baggage of Erasmian humanism, which had developed the arguments for discrimination which would be intoned by the reformers over the next century.[77] And, as we shall see in a moment, a conservative outlook towards the poor continued to underpin much charity after the Reformation.

The Reformation is more likely to have played a role in the way in which it focused attention on the plight of the poor as yet another example of the failings of the traditional religion, and protestant preachers exhorted the faithful to acts of charity as a way of demonstrating their superiority over the foe. Susan Brigden has emphasised the way in which the passionate advocacy of early protestants for the cause of the poor earned them a reputation as dangerous social radicals.[78] Protestants in Mary's reign recalled with pride the participation of the citizenry in the establishment of the hospitals as an enterprise of protestant piety. It was a theme to be repeated many times in the course of the protestant polemic of later generations, culminating in Andrew Willet's *Synopsis Papismi*, the appendix to which set out to prove that sixty years of protestantism had brought forth more good works than twice as long of popery.[79]

It is clear that the transformation in patterns of charitable giving was not as dramatic as Jordan asserted. The very narrow basis of the more sophisticated forms of giving such as the revolving loan stock and other forms of

---

[74] Rappaport, *Worlds Within Worlds*, pp. 145–50.
[75] M. K. McIntosh, 'Local Responses to the Poor in Late Medieval and Tudor England', *Continuity and Change*, 3 (1988), 225–8.
[76] Thomson, 'Piety and Charity', pp. 182–3; McIntosh, 'Local Responses', pp. 217–25; M. Rubin, *Charity and Community in Medieval Cambridge* (Cambridge, 1987), ch. III.
[77] M. Todd, *Christian Humanism and the Puritan Social Order* (Cambridge, 1987).
[78] S. Brigden, 'Popular Disturbance and the Fall of Thomas Cromwell and the Reformers', *Historical Journal*, 24 (1981), 270–2.
[79] *Narratives of the Days of the Reformation*, ed. J. G. Nichols (Camden Society, old series, LXXVII, 1859), pp. 181–3; A. Willet, *Synopsis Papismi* (1613), pp. 1219–43; R. L. Greaves, *Society and Religion in Elizabethan England* (Minneapolis, 1981), p. 573.

endowment is immediately apparent. Moreover, to contrast a religious-minded fifteenth century with a secular-minded sixteenth is highly misleading. The line between religious and secular objects of giving is not easily drawn. Religious giving before the Reformation had often been associated with spin-off benefits to the poor such as doles at obits, and so-called 'secular' giving had its religious aspect because of the way any charity was thought to build up treasure in heaven.[80] Likewise, bequests to the poor in the sixteenth century long continued to have religious connotations. Testators still regularly insisted on the presence of the poor at their funerals. Of 168 Prerogative Court of Canterbury testators in the 1570s who left cash for poor relief in the parishes, 45 (26.8 per cent) requested that at least part of their bequest be distributed in dole form at their burial, and in the 1590s the proportion was 28.7 per cent (77 out of 268). Among those of lesser status the proportions were about the same, 24 per cent (31 out of 129) in the 1570s, and 30.2 per cent (38 out of 126) in the 1590s. In the earlier period, with a dash of catholic survivalism, a few testators expressed the hope that the prayers of the poor would aid the passage of their souls to rest.[81]

There was, however, no incompatibility between puritan commitment and a funeral dole. Helen Harrison of St Olave Southwark left £10 to the poor imprisoned preachers about London, but also asked that twelve dozen loaves of bread be distributed at her funeral. She also left 40s. to forty of the 'godliest poor' of her parish, and entrusted the distribution of her dole to the discretion of her executors and overseers, who included the Southwark vestryman, Richard Denman, and her good friend, the puritan preacher, William Charke.[82] It was perfectly possible to combine discrimination with a funeral dole. It is true that the numbers envisaged at some doles were so large as to make one doubt whether discrimination was possible in all cases. Ralph Eggerton, grocer, left £10 for a dole of 4d. apiece which would have meant 600 recipients.[83] Such doles sometimes produced alarming scenes as when beggars were crushed to death at Lady Mary Ramsey's funeral in 1600. The parish clerk of St Botolph Aldgate noted the 'multitude of other straundge disordered poore people' at a dole in 1592. His remark indicates, however, that it was usually expected that those present at a dole should not be strange to the parish.[84] It is striking that most testators who left money for doles also specified that recipients should be residents of their parishes: in these cases there would be no difficulty in filtering out undesirables. Thus the persistence

---

[80] C. Harper-Bill, *The Pre-Reformation Church in England, 1400–1530* (1989), pp. 71–2.
[81] P.R.O., PROB 11/55, fo. 220; G.L., MSS 9051/4, fo. 21ᵛ; 9171/16, fo. 102.
[82] P.R.O., PROB 11/85, fo. 25.
[83] P.R.O., PROB 11/84, fo. 230.
[84] *The Letters of John Chamberlain*, ed. N. E. McClure (2 vols., Philadelphia, 1939), I. 135; G.L., MS 9234/2C, fo. 31.

Table 5.3. *Patterns of philanthropy, 1570–3 and 1594–7 compared: Prerogative Court of Canterbury testators*

	1570–3 n = 391						1594–7 n = 635					
	1	2	3	4	5	6	7	8	9	10	11	12
Any poor relief	242	61.9					342	53.9				
Parochial poor (London)	174	44.5	168_4	7	7_2	0	275	43.3	268_{12}	13	0	2
Parochial poor (non London)	56	14.3	54_1	2_1	0	1	115	18.1	108	9	2	3_1
Gowns for poor	59	15.1	59	0	0	0	67	10.6	67	0	0	0
Hospitals	91	23.3					145	22.8				
Christ's	87	22.3	86	1	2	0	133	20.9	128	4	3_2	3_3
St Bart's	27	6.9	26_1	0	1	0	24	3.8	24	0	0	0
St Thomas'	31	7.9	30	0	1	0	27	4.3	27	0	1	0
Bridewell	4	1.0	4	0	0	0	17	2.7	15	1	1	0
Bethlem	5	1.3	5	0	0	0	6	0.9	6	0	0	0
Poor in companies	12	3.1	8	3	0	1_1	27	4.3	21	8	0	0
Almshouses	17	4.4	16	0	1	0	11	1.7	8	2	1	0
Prisons	71	18.2	70	0	1_1	0	91	14.3	86	4	1	1
Marriage portions	14	3.6	13	0	1	0	6	0.9	6	0	0	0
Ransoming captives	0	0	0	0	0	0	2	0.3	2	0	0	0
Maimed soldiers	0	0	0	0	0	0	5	0.8	5	0	0	0
Stranger poor	12	3.1	12	0	0	0	15	2.4	15	0	1	0
Companies: general purposes	28	7.2	27	0	0	1_1	39	6.1	37	3	0	0
Loan stocks	10	2.6	0	9	0	1	29	4.6	0	28	0	1
Education	28	7.2	20_1	5_1	2_1	1	38	6.0	28	11	2_1	1
Highways	6	1.5	5	1_1	1	0	9	1.4	9	1_1	0	0
Sermon cycles	38	9.7	37	0	0	0	28	4.4	25	3	0	1
Church repair	18	4.6	18	0	0	0	15	2.4	13	1	1	0
Forgotten tithes	3	0.8	3	0	0	0	0	0		0	0	0

Key
Columns 1 and 7   Number of testators making any bequest.
Columns 2 and 8   Percentage of testators making a bequest.
Columns 3 and 9   Number of testators making cash bequest.
Columns 4 and 10 Number of testators making endowment.
Columns 5 and 11 Number of testators making cash bequest (contingent on death of other beneficiaries without issue).
Columns 6 and 12 Number of testators making endowment (contingent on death of other beneficiaries without issue).
Note: Figures in subscript indicate number of bequests in each category which have defied attempts at valuation.

Sources:
Will sample, 1570–3: P.R.O., PROB 11/52–55.
             1594–7: P.R.O., PROB 11/83–90.

Table 5.4. Patterns of philanthropy, 1570–3 and 1594–7 compared: testators in lesser probate jurisdictions

	1570–3 n = 478						1594–7 n = 616					
	1	2	3	4	5	6	7	8	9	10	11	12
Any poor relief	167	34.9					145	23.5				
Parochial poor (London)	138	28.9	129_2	6	4_2	0	127	20.6	126_4	2_1	0	1
Parochial poor (non London)	7	1.5	7	0	0	0	8	1.3	8	0	0	0
Gowns for poor	4	0.8	4	0	0	0	7	1.1	7	0	0	0
Hospitals	17	3.6					29	4.7				
Christ's	13	2.7	13	0	0	0	28	4.6	28_1	0	0	0
St Bart's	1	0.2	1	0	0	0	2	0.3	2	0	0	0
St Thomas'	2	0.4	2	0	0	0	0	0	0	0	0	0
Bridewell	0	0	0	0	0	0	1	0.2	1	0	0	0
Bethlem	1	0.2	1	0	0	0	0	0	0	0	0	0
Poor in companies	2	0.4	2	0	0	0	3	0.5	2	0	1_1	0
Almshouses	1	0.2	1	0	0	0	2	0.3	1	0	1	0
Prisons	18	3.8	17	1	1	1	14	2.3	14	0	1	0
Marriage portions	5	1.1	3	0	1	0	0	0	0	0	0	0
Ransoming captives	0	0	0	0	0	1	0	0	0	0	0	0
Maimed soldiers	0	0	0	0	0	0	0	0	0	0	0	0
Stranger poor	18	3.8	18_4	0	1	0	30	4.9	30_6	1	1_1	0
Companies: general purposes	10	2.1	10	0	0	0	12	2.0	10_1	1_1	1	1
Loan stocks	0	0	0	0	0	0	3	0.5	0	2	0	1
Education	4	0.8	2	0	1	1_1	5	0.8	1	4	0	0
Highways	2	0.4	2	0	0	0	0	0	0	0	0	0
Sermon cycles	4	0.8	3	1	0	0	6	1.0	6	0	0	0
Church repair	2	0.4	1	1_1	0	0	2	0.3	2	0	0	0
Forgotten tithes	2	0.4	2	0	0	0	0	0	0	0	0	0

Key

Columns 1 and 7   Number of testators making any bequest.

Columns 2 and 8   Percentage of testators making a bequest.

Columns 3 and 9   Number of testators making cash bequest.

Columns 4 and 10 Number of testators making endowment.

Columns 5 and 11 Number of testators making cash bequest (contingent on death of other beneficiaries without issue).

Columns 6 and 12 Number of testators making endowment (contingent on death of other beneficiaries without issue).

Note: Figures in subscript indicate number of bequests in each category which have defied attempts at valuation.

Sources:

Will sample, 1570–3: G.L., MSS 9051/3–4; 9171/15–16; 25626/2; G.L.R.O., DL/C/358; W.P.L., Will Register Elsam.
           1594–7: G.L., MSS 9051/5; 9171/18; 25626/2–3; G.L.R.O., DL/C/359; W.P.L., Will Register Elsam.

Table 5.5. Patterns of philanthropy in sixteenth-century London: summary

	Wealthier testators (Prerogative Court of Canterbury)						Poorer testators (lesser probate jurisdictions)				
	1531–2	1537–9	1539–41	1553–8	1570–3	1594–7	1522–39	1539–47	1547–53	1570–3	1594–7
Relief of poor	21.0	31.3	29.6	51.6	61.9	53.9	13.4	11.9	32.4	34.9	23.5
Debtors in prisons	18.4	17.5	12.4	24.2	18.2	14.3	3.6	3.0	N/A	3.8	2.3
Poor in hospitals	2.6	1.8	3.5	28.4	23.3	22.8	0.6	0.4	N/A	3.6	4.7
Marriage portions	5.3	4.2	3.5	N/A	3.6	0.94	0.7	0.9	N/A	1.1	0.0
Education	2.6	3.6	1.8	3.2	7.2	6.0	0.1	0.2	N/A	0.8	0.8
Highways	N/A	1.8	3.0	5.2	1.5	1.4	0.0	0.2	N/A	0.4	0.0

Figures show percentages of testators making bequests for purposes specified.

Sources:
Will sample, 1570–3: G.L., MSS 9051/3–4; 9171/15–16; 25626/2; P.R.O., PROB 11/52–55; G.L.R.O., DL/C/358; W.P.L., Will Register Elsam. 1594–7: G.L., MSS 9051/5; 9171/18; 25626/2–3; P.R.O., PROB 11/83–90; G.L.R.O., DL/C/359; W.P.L., Will Register Elsam.
For early sixteenth century, see Brigden, 'Early Reformation', pp. 358–9 and 'Social Obligation', pp. 104–5.

of the desire to have the poor present at the funeral was not incompatible with the exercise of discriminating attitudes.

Moreover, there were ways of securing the attendance of the poor without running the risk of an indiscriminate stampede. Particularly popular were bequests to Christ's Hospital, usually of 20s. to 40s. in return for the presence of the children to sing a psalm over the corpse. In April 1578, for example, Elizabeth Rice of St Botolph Aldersgate left 5s. to the hospital on condition that the children 'maye accompany my body to the buryall from my howse as theie are accustomed to doe to their benefactors'. The accounts of Christ's Hospital record receipts in burial money at an average of eighty funerals a year in the three-year period 1596–9.[85] For wealthy testators the clothing of the poor in funeral gowns provided a way of securing their attendance, and of advertising their own status. Donors usually specified that recipients were to come from particular parishes or from the ranks of the poor of their own companies, leaving the choice to the executors, but occasionally indicating named individuals they thought worthy candidates.[86] Executors clearly had an opportunity to exercise the kind of discrimination envisaged by Richard Elkin, skinner, who instructed that the recipients at his funeral 'shalbe suche as can saie the lordes prayer the articles of their belefe and the tenne commaundementes in englishe without the booke'. It is likely that in most cases executors acted on the recommendation of friends of the deceased. Henry Colthurst requested that the gowns should be bestowed 'uppon suche poore as my especiall friendes shall speake for to be given at the discretion of my executours'.[87] In this way charity was confined to the deserving and the bonds of patronage and deference reinforced in the idealised view of society that the funeral rite articulated. The arrangements Elizabethan Londoners made for their funerals show a nice blend of the continuing quest for the presence of the poor with an insistence on a stricter definition of the boundaries of acceptable behaviour, which reflected the widening social distances of the sixteenth century.

It should also be emphasised that funeral doles only accounted for a small proportion of the money disbursed in poor relief from private sources. For many wealthier testators, in particular, the funeral dole was a token gesture amid many larger benefactions directed at the more disciplined forms of giving. The popularity of institutionalised relief is reflected in the large sums directed to the hospitals. It is also clear that a high proportion of the money disbursed in parochial relief passed through the hands of the parish leaders. Precisely what proportion cannot be determined with any confidence because the absence of instructions to executors to pass on the money to the

[85] G.L., MSS 9051/4, fo. 151; 9171/16, fo. 350ᵛ; 12819/2.
[86] P.R.O., PROB 11/55, fo. 220; G.L., MS 9051/4, fo. 217.
[87] P.R.O., PROB 11/55, fo. 207; PROB 11/85, fo. 127.

Table 5.6. *Value of bequests for charitable purposes, 1570–3 and 1594–7 compared (excluding contingent bequests)*

| | 1570–3 | | 1594–7 | |
	Cash	Endowments	Cash	Endowments
Parochial poor (City)	991	606	2,091	701
Parochial poor (Suburbs)	76	120	404	60
Parochial poor (non London)	444	13	1,016	1,230
Gowns for poor	827	0	2,505	0
Hospitals				
Christ's	594	33	1,561	1,093
St Bart's	254	0	190	0
St Thomas'	397	0	326	0
Bridewell	53	0	162	60
Bethlem	12	0	141	0
Poor in companies	63	167	187	370
Almshouses	66	0	85	97
Prisons	523	20	1,968	195
Marriage portions	270	0	155	0
Ransoming captives	0	0	8	0
Maimed soldiers	0	0	74	0
Stranger poor	67	0	235	155
Companies: general purposes	256	0	456	240
Loan stocks	0	810	0	3,389
Education	440	775	428	2,713
Highways	125	0	59	?
Sermon cycles	186	405	226	650
Church repair	88	?	101	80
Forgotten tithes	2	0	0	0

Figures given are to the nearest £.

Sources:
Will sample, 1570–3: G.L., MSS 9051/3–4; 9171/15–16; 25626/2; P.R.O., PROB 11/52–55; G.L.R.O., DL/C/358; W.P.L., Will Register Elsam.
    1594–7: G.L., MSS 9051/5; 9171/18; 25626/2–3; P.R.O., PROB 11/83–90; G.L.R.O., DL/C/359; W.P.L., Will Register Elsam.
Endowments: *Parliamentary Papers*, 1884. XXXIX, parts IV–V; *Parliamentary Papers*, 1904, LXXI.
    Figures incorporate corrections resulting from search of all company and churchwardens' accounts listed in the bibliography.

Figure 5.7. *Value of endowments for poor relief, 1570–3 and 1594–7 compared*

	1570–3 £ p.a.	1594–7 £ p.a.
Relief of poor in companies	152	251
Relief of poor in parishes	329	658
Relief of poor in prisons	31	107
Relief of poor in almshouses	400	676

For hospital endowments, see Table 5.1.

Sources:
Will sample, 1570–3: G.L., MSS 9051/3–4; 9171/15–16; 25626/2; P.R.O., PROB 11/52–55; G.L.R.O., DL/C/358; W.P.L., Will Register Elsam.
1594–7: G.L., MSS 9051/5; 9171/18; 25626/2–3; P.R.O., PROB 11/83–90; G.L.R.O., DL/C/359; W.P.L., Will Register Elsam.
Endowments: *Parliamentary Papers*, 1884. XXXIX, parts IV–V; *Parliamentary Papers*, 1904, LXXI.
Figures incorporate corrections resulting from search of all company and churchwardens' accounts listed in the bibliography.

churchwardens is by no means a sign that the executors did not act this way in practice. The accounts of the executors of Robert Nowell, attorney of the court of wards, show that they handed over money to preachers like Robert Crowley and James Young, to churchwardens, and to aldermen's deputies, for distribution.[88] The large sums recorded in some parochial records indicate the increasing role played by the churchwardens in the distribution of private charity, and the lists of the recipients of tiny sums kept by the churchwardens demonstrate the care that went into their distribution.[89]

Tables 5.6–5.7 show the results of the valuation of the contribution of private charity. The charity generated by the testators in the will sample is analysed in Table 5.6, while Table 5.7 shows the yield of endowments for poor relief in 1573 and 1597 calculated from the charity commissioners' reports and incorporating the corrections derived from the contemporary documentation. Between 61 per cent and 63 per cent of the philanthropic efforts of Londoners was directed at poor relief. The majority of this was spent in the City and its immediate environs, although donors were increasingly willing to invest their resources in the provinces: whereas in the 1570s

[88] *The Spending of the Money of Robert Nowell*, ed. A. B. Grosart (1877), pp. 90, 92, 96, 98.
[89] W. P. L., E147; G.L., MSS 4824; 4071/1 fo. 94; 9051/3, fo. 259ᵛ.

8.2 per cent of the money intended for poor relief was earmarked for areas outside the City, by the 1590s the proportion was 15.95 per cent. This may reflect a growing confidence in the relief effort in the City and a perception of the difficulties faced by provincial England at the turn of the century. However, it is interesting that the crisis conditions of the later 1590s should have modified the pattern of giving. If we split the 1590s sample into two, separating the testators of 1594/5 from those of 1596/7, by which time the crisis had begun to bite, we find, first that the proportion of total resources directed to poor relief had increased from 57 per cent to 70 per cent, and secondly that the proportion of resources in relief intended for non-metropolitan areas had fallen from 17.4 per cent to 13.2 per cent. Thus the experience of the later 1590s appears to have resulted in some redirection of efforts towards the poor as people became ever more sensitized to their plight, and conditions in the City were such as to cause donors to narrow the horizons of their philanthropy.

The resources available for poor relief from private charity expanded considerably in Elizabeth's reign. The yield of endowments (excluding the endowment of the hospitals, the bulk of which came by grant from the Crown) increased by 86 per cent in cash terms between 1573 and 1597, and by 35 per cent in real terms, after deflation by Rappaport's price index (Table 5.7).[90] Immediate donations to the London poor grew by 133 per cent in cash terms and 70 per cent in real terms (Table 5.6). Taking endowments and cash bequests together, private charity grew by 111 per cent in cash terms and 54 per cent in real terms. In order to appreciate the significance of these changes to potential recipients it is necessary to take into account the increase in the City's population in the intervening period. The overall increase in per capita real terms was 13 per cent, and the net gain to recipients was probably further eroded by the fact that the proportion of the poor in the City population was increasing. Thus the gain to individuals was very limited. However the scale of the achievement is sufficient to put to flight Jordan's more pessimistic critics. It is particularly impressive besides the static poor rate which, because a substantial portion went to Christ's Hospital, in the 1590s only yielded £1,422 p.a. for outdoor relief compared to the £909 p.a. in endowments and £1,312 p.a. in immediate legacies available through companies and parishes in outdoor relief.

What is more difficult to determine is how the philanthropy London merchants dispensed at death compared with the exercise of charity during their lifetimes. The study of private charity from the testamentary evidence is subject to the major limitation that it assumes that charity was a deathbed once-for-all act, whereas various sources indicate that benevolence to the poor was a continuous practice. Thus individual aldermen, like Sir William

[90] Rappaport, *Worlds Within Worlds*, pp. 406–7.

Allen, gained reputations for charitable virtue: 'he would buy wood from the carte and distribute it with his owne hands. Besides he would walke often through the said parish, and such poore as stood in need he gave relief unto'.[91] Such private charity took various forms. It is clear that begging continued. Official policy, in the words of a reform document of 1595, attacked 'the preposterous charity of divers well disposed', but did not outlaw begging. Rather the authorities tried to license beggars and confine their activities to the bounds of a single parish. This continued to be the case after 1598 in apparent recognition of the fact that official relief was still insufficient to provide full support. Moralists were not as united on the question of indiscriminate giving as is often supposed. Silver-tongued Henry Smith, puritan lecturer at St Clement Dane's, answered those who 'make a question of their almes and saie they know not what the partie is that demaundeth reliefe' with the assertion that all should be relieved and, as for the idle poor, 'let theyr bad deedes fall on their own necks, for if they perish for want, we are in danger of God's wrath for them'.[92] But private charity was not necessarily indiscriminate. Much relief was directed at neighbours. Howes hints at the continuing practice of the wealthier households giving out 'the revercion of meat and porrege to the poor'. The daughter of Lawrence Withers claimed that her father wished her to remain in his home in Bread Street for a year after his death 'to thend that she shuld kepe howse in her fathers said howse for the refrrechementt of poor neighbors'. Several wills indicate that Londoners kept children 'of alms', probably local orphans or foundlings.[93] Wealthy householders engaging in regular charity might adopt sophisticated systems in the distribution of relief, such as the tokens issued by Sir John Brugge to the deserving poor of his ward who regularly collected bread from his cart.[94] Support for the institutionalised poor was another means by which resources could be channeled to worthy cases. Robert Offley ordered his son to continue the distribution of 18d. per week in meat pottage and 8d. per week in bread to the inmates of Bedlam, 'they fetchinge the same at my house as they have been accustomed'. Other benevolences could be directed to the churchwardens for distribution. As Burghley's biographer put it, 'he was ever most charitable to the Poore whom he wold better relieve in the Parishes then in Highwaies or Streets'.[95] In the well-documented Westminster parishes large sums were regularly received by the parochial authorities from Lord Treasurer Burghley, Dean Goodman,

[91] W. Jaggard, *A View of All the Right Honourable the Lord Mayors of London* (1601).
[92] C.L.R.O., Remembrancia II, no. 85; Jour. 24, fos. 89ᵛ, 289ʳ⁻ᵛ; B.L. Lansdowne MS 114/4; 39 Eliz. I c. 3 § 10; H. Smith, *The Poore Mens Teares Opened in a Sermon* (1592), p. 13.
[93] *T.E.D.*, III. 426; P.R.O., C24/125, Withers vs. Withers; G.L., MSS 9051/4, fo. 101; 25626/2, fo. 157ᵛ
[94] P.R.O., PROB 11/23, fo. 166ʳ⁻ᵛ.
[95] P.R.O., PROB 11/87, fo. 230; F. Peck, *Desiderata Curiosa* (1732), pp. 29–31, 45, 159–60.

and Lady Dacre. There are parallels in City parishes like the 10s. p.a. paid by Sir John Fortescue to the parish of St Andrew Wardrobe in the 1590s.[96] If such benevolences seem rarer in City parishes than in Westminster, it is perhaps because they were placed in poor boxes and do not therefore appear on regular accounts. Certainly the Church tapped the benevolence of worshippers on numerous occasions. Collections for the poor were always taken at communions, and often at sermons.[97] Where the preachers enjoyed a wide popularity the sums realised could be quite large: at Holy Trinity Minories over the eight-year period 1568–76 receipts at communions and sermons averaged £28 p.a., most of it spent on poor relief out of the parish, often on cases recommended by the preachers.[98]

But it is impossible to get any satisfactory quantitative measure of the overall value of such charity. Few could match the extraordinary largesse of Duke John of Finland wooing Elizabeth on his brother's behalf in 1559 and distributing to all poor households in Southwark 'some 6, some 8, some 12, some 20 dollars'.[99] In Westminster the benevolence was largely borne by a handful of individuals prominent in local society, and was severely haemorrhaged by the death of one benefactor in 1595.[100] The token payments to the poor that one encounters in household accounts do not suggest that Londoners disbursed huge amounts in addition to their poor rate assessments. Richard Stonley, the Exchequer teller, in the year ending Michaelmas 1593, spent a total of 39s. 7d. on the poor, of which 20s. was accounted for by his rate assessment in St Botolph Aldersgate.[101] However the cumulative impact of quite small sums could be considerable. One of godly Master Dering's circle claimed that 'if Mr Hudson kept account of all that he gave to the poor at his door and abroad, he were better to keep two poor all the year long'.[102]

[96] W.P.L., E147; G.L., MS 2088/1. In 1594–5 one-third of receipts for poor relief in St Margaret Westminster came from the benevolence of Lady Dacre: she made two payments of £20 each at Christmas and Midsummer, provided £33 for poor widows, and £6 for coals for the poor. The Dean and Chapter provided forty dishes of meat, forty loaves and forty pence every Sunday (valued at £33. 13s. 4d.), Dean Goodman a further £9. 9s. 8d. from his personal income in bread at Easter and Christmas, and Burghley an annuity of £3. 14s., with supplementary payments in dearth years.
[97] For sermons, see G.L.R.O., P92/SAV/1397; G.L., MS 1432/3, fos. 39^{r-v}, 44, 47^v; for communions, see G.L., MSS 4959, fos. 55–6; 1432/3, fos. 39^{r-v}, 47^v, 58^v; 590/1, 1598–9 acct.; 4524/1, fos. 66, 88; G.L.R.O., P92/SAV/1566; P92/SAV/1397; W.P.L., F 316–25; S.B.H., Little St Bartholomew's C.W.A.: suggesting annual average receipts of 44s. in inner-city parishes and £4 in the extramural parishes. This indicates total receipts for the poor at communions in parishes north of the river of the order of £248 p.a.
[98] E. M. Tomlinson, *A History of the Minories, London* (1907), pp. 325–6, 372–7. Receipts fell with the crackdown on the radical preachers. Only £3. 9s. 1½d. was received in 1593.
[99] B.L., Additional MS 48023, fo. 354.   [100] Lady Dacre (see n. 96) died in 1595.
[101] P.R.O., SP 46/43, fos. 142^v, 156^v; H. Hall, *Society in the Elizabethan Age* (1886), p. 207; Folger Library, MSS V.a. 459–61, esp. 460, fo. 31^v.
[102] H.M.C., *Hatfield*, II. 64.

Table 5.8. *Sources of poor relief in London, 1570–3 and 1594–7 compared*

	1570–3 £ p.a.	1594–7 £ p.a.
Hospitals:		
Endowment		
Christ's	59	603
St Thomas'	814	1,412
St Barts'	647	1,443
Total	1,520	3,458
Legacies & Benevolences		
Christ's	223	586
St Thomas'	83	140
St Bart's	66	132
Total	372	858
City Tolls		
Christ's	231	474
St Bart's	333	265
Total	564	739
Poor Rate		
Christ's	937	828
Other	136	101
Hospitals: total	3,529	5,984
Poor rate disbursed in parishes	1,313	1,422
Company pensions	500	800
Almshouses	417	697
Endowments for relief of poor in companies	152	251
Endowments for relief of poor in parishes	329	658
Private charity at death (companies and parishes)	554	1,312
Endowments for relief of poor in prisons	31	107
Private charity at death for poor in prisons	131	492
Grand total	6,956	11,723
Price index for decade	233	320
Estimated population, city north of river	75,000	115,000
Per capita real terms relief	0.0818	0.0742

Table 5.8 incorporates data from Table 5.1. Population figures on basis of Finlay and Shearer, 'Population Growth and Suburban Expansion', p. 45. Price indices from Rappaport, *Worlds Within Worlds*, pp. 406–7.

Jordan's argument that the poor rate contributed only 7 per cent of the money spent on poor relief was one of his sillier contributions to the discussion about the role of philanthropy in social welfare. But the foregoing discussion will have made it clear that private charity remained a major component in the relief of the poor. In the mid 1590s the private charity quantified in Table 5.8 was contributing £7,833 p.a. (£4,675 excluding the hospital endowment largely granted by the Crown) compared to £2,250 p.a. from the poor rate. It is a still more impressive achievement when we appreciate the scale of informal giving impossible though it is to quantify. And private charity, which registered large increases over the Elizabethan decades and was mobilised by the aldermen in crisis years, was more flexible than the rate, which remained static for much of the reign. The scrutiny of private charity drives home forcefully the message that in discussing the effectiveness of welfare schemes it is essential to take a global view rather than belittling the contribution of individual sources of relief by taking them in isolation.[103] But whether the totals realised were adequate to the challenges confronting the City remains undetermined, and an answer to this question is an objective pursued in the section which follows.

NEEDS AND RESOURCES

That private charity continued to be so important in poor relief is a reminder of the limitations of quantification in estimating the success of the poor relief system in early modern England. However, it has proved possible to obtain estimates of the income for relief available from a wide range of sources: the hospitals, endowed charity, the poor rate, private charity at death, and the pensions paid by livery companies from house stock. This represents the most comprehensive survey of resources available for relief yet attempted. Table 5.8 compares the money available from these sources in 1570–3 and 1594–7. It is one of the problems of the size of London that any absolute figures look impressive: resources apparently increased substantially between the two periods. But once the price inflation and population growth of the intervening period is taken into account it appears that resources actually declined by 9 per cent in per capita real terms. The squeeze on the budgets of individual pauper households was probably the more acutely felt because the location of population growth in the extramural and riverside parishes suggests that the proportion of poor in the population was increasing. The section which follows attempts to take further the argument about the balance between needs and resources, first, by looking at the availability of relief with reference to the numbers of poor in different quarters of the city, and secondly, by reconstructing a budget for a 'typical' pauper household.

There is a considerable amount of evidence which suggests that there were very many more individuals in need of regular support by pensions than the

---

[103] For recent discussions of the balance between public and private relief, see Slack, *Poverty and Policy*, pp. 166–9, and of the importance of informal charity, see Walter, 'Social Economy of Dearth', pp. 113–16. See also below, p. 197.

relief system was able to provide for. The slender resources available for poor relief meant that the bulk of what was available went to the aged, impotent, and very young. This was in accordance with the contemporary dichotomy between the impotent poor, those 'unable to doe anye worke towardes their lyving as old decrepit persons creeples and infantes', and the able-bodied and work-shy, 'the negligent poore being otherwise sturdie & able to earne their whole lyving if they were well sett on worke'.[104] But more sophisticated analyses were available which recognised the possibility of the able-bodied falling into poverty through no fault of their own: thus Christopher Hooke in a sermon of 1603, after noting the normal categories of the widows and orphans, pointed out the difficulties of 'the poore man of occupation, who in this time wanteth woorke, and therefore wanteth foode for him and his familie ... for the sicknesse thus still continuing, & the Winter is hard approaching, and none or little worke, as they say stirrring, the number of the poore and their necessity, do encrease daily'.[105] Thus in 1598 when ordering comprehensive surveys of the poor, the aldermen distinguished carefully between those able to work but 'wanting work', those 'having anie greter chardg then their labors can mainteine', and those who were 'idle & use no labour being hable and have some menes to live by their labor'.[106] But in practice the bulk of relief went to the narrower group of the impotent. None of the pensioners in St Bartholomew Exchange in 1599 was aged under sixty-six.[107] In the same year the aldermen complained that parishes had been too generous in their definitions of eligibility, and in 1602 they ordered that regular relief be confined to lame, impotent, and aged persons.[108] The prejudices that determined access to relief are seen clearly in operation in an episode in 1584 when Deputy Alderman Hilliard and Robert Crowley, that impassioned mid-century advocate of the poor's causes and now minister of St Giles Cripplegate, appeared before the governors of Christ's claiming that thirty parishioners lacked pensions, although 'they hadd sought all meanes that they coulde for the relef of their saide poore'. But the governors were not sympathetic. Only nine received pensions, because 'some of them hadd reasonable pencions and alowaunces oute of halles of the companies of this Citie ... other some semed in all outward aparaunce to be able enoughe to worke for theyr lyvinge'.[109] The prejudice that there was enough work to go round if only the poor could overcome their innate idleness was deep-rooted.

Symptoms of strain on the relief system abound. In 1580, some time before the pressures became really serious, the churchwardens of St Michael Crooked Lane, by no means a very poor parish, explained that they

[104] C.L.R.O., Remembrancia II, no. 87. Cf. Slack, *Poverty and Policy*, pp. 22–8.
[105] Hooke, *Sermon Preached in Paules Church*, sig. C iii[v].
[106] C.L.R.O., Jour. 24, fo. 289[r–v].   [107] *Accounts of Saint Bartholomew Exchange*, p. 8.
[108] C.L.R.O., Rep. 26, fo. 27[r–v].   [109] G.L., MS 12806/2, fos. 345[v], 346[r–v].

supported twelve pensioners, 'and that ther be at the least a dosen more householders within the said parishe that at this present have nede of contynuall relief fallen in great decaye and povertye and contynually increaseth'.[110] City parishes were crowded with poor people awaiting the death of existing pensioners, as the hospital granted numerous reversions to their pensions.[111] Vestries, hospital authorities, and companies all found themselves making lump sum grants 'on condition he is no more suitor'.[112] Although pensions were by no means adequate to provide full support, vestries took advantage of the death of their pensioners to spread the available resources still more thinly by splitting pensions.[113] Some paupers were forced to go to extraordinary lengths to obtain relief, like the poor widow who had to petition a group of aldermen's wives before the lord mayor directed her parish to grant her a pension.[114]

The clearest indication of pressure on the system is the evidence of an increasing determination to restrict responsibilities in the closing decades of the sixteenth century. This manifested itself in an insistence on the need to confine relief to long-term residents and in the harrying of inmates. In 1584, for example, the vestry of St Botolph Aldgate ordered that no one was to receive relief who had not been resident in the parish for three years.[115] Parish accounts throughout the city are littered with payments to remove the poor for whom the masters of the parish would not accept responsibility.[116] From the later 1580s, parishes began to swing in vigorous support of the corporation's campaign against the taking of inmates. In 1589 the vestry of St Dunstan in the East threatened those taking inmates with the loss of their pensions and those placing poor in alleys with fines of £3. 6s. 8d. payable to the poor box, and expulsion from the vestry.[117] Surveyors of inmates were appointed in St Olave Southwark in 1585 'to vewe that none kepe no Inmates nor suffer none with childe nor no other poore to come out of other parishes to the burden of this parishe but that they shall give notice to the deputie and churchwardens yf any suche shall come'.[118] The neighbouring parish of St Saviour followed suit in 1593, ordering the churchwardens to search for inmates fortnightly, and in the next year salarying two parishioners to perform the tours of inspection. The returns of the surveyors of St

---

110 P.R.O., C24/135, Barker vs. Powtney.
111 G.L., MSS 12806/2, fos. 119, 146, 257, 263; 4887, fo. 176.
112 G.L., MSS 594/1, p. 21; 12806/2, fos. 288, 308ᵛ.
113 G.L., MS 4887, fos. 150, 151ᵛ; *Vestry Minutes of Saint Margaret Lothbury*, pp. 22, 25.
114 G.L., MS 2596/1, fo. 212.   115 G.L., MS 9236, fo. 71.
116 For example, in St Andrew Wardrobe payments for getting Lancelot Phillips' daughter out of the parish, sending a poor woman into the country at the lord mayor's command, carrying a woman to Cow Lane, for a warrant to my lord mayor to carry a boy to St Dunstan's: G.L., MS 2088/1, accts. for 1584–5, 1590–1, 1591–2, 1592–3, 1593–4.
117 G.L., MS 4887, fo. 137ʳ⁻ᵛ.
118 Southwark Archives, St Olave's V.M., fos. 69, 73, 82ᵛ, 84ᵛ.

Saviour's show that they executed their offices with zeal, hustling inmates out of the parish or getting them to provide sureties to discharge the parish of responsibility for their support, snooping into the morals of the poor, noting those who kept victualling, and keeping a particularly vigilant eye on single women.[119] These Southwark vestries also put their full weight behind the Crown's attempts to restrict new building and the subdivision of properties in the London suburbs. They petitioned the privy council for action, took distraints on offenders, and arranged for the indictment of some of the recalcitrant.[120] By the later 1590s these concerns had spread even to relatively prosperous inner-city parishes like St Michael Cornhill whose vestry took stern action against offenders. The poor were forced to remove their married children; sureties were taken from those lacking three years' residence; and local landlords threatened with prosecution under the 1593 new building statute.[121] Apart from threatening an extra source of income, the harsh treatment of inmates seems to have prevented many poor families from supporting their kin: thus the vestries of St Gabriel Fenchurch and St Michael Cornhill required the poor to remove their own offspring because of the threat of an extra burden on the rates.[122]

The pressures were most acutely felt in the extramural parishes. In spite of the existence of the mechanism for the redistribution of the income from the rate, resources remained unevenly distributed. In the first place, the bulk of the redistributed rate went to one parish, St Sepulchre, which in 1573 took £203 of the £300 redirected by Christ's. St Botolph Aldgate received only £7 in aid, and St Giles Cripplegate only £31 4s.[123] The hospital authorities were reluctant to subsidise new parishes like St Andrew Wardrobe in difficulties from the mid 1580s, but not receiving any support from outside until 1598.[124] Any new commitments by Christ's would, of course, only diminish the money available for its own operations. Increases in the level of support for the poor in the extramural areas were made still more difficult by the reluctance of inner-city parishes to increase their rates to subsidise what could easily be presented as maladministration in the suburbs. In their dealings with the extramural parishes the aldermen sometimes showed an extraordinary naivety. In 1573, for example, they attached a particularly impractical condition to the continuation of relief payments from the inner-city parishes to St Sepulchre, namely that henceforth there should be

[119] G.L.R.O., P92/SAV/450, pp. 275, 290; P92/SAV/1314–17; H. Raine, 'Christopher Fawcett Against the Inmates', *Surrey Archaeological Collections*, 66 (1966), 79–85.
[120] Southwark Archives, St Olave's V.M., fos. 86ᵛ, 95ᵛ, 96ᵛ, 99; G.L.R.O., P92/SAV/450, pp. 329, 346, 353, 361, 363, 369; A.P.C., XXVIII. 435–6.
[121] G.L., MS 4072/1, fos. 74, 75ᵛ, 76, 84, 87.
[122] Sk. Co., C.M. II, fo. 322ᵛ; G.L., MS 4072/1, fo. 84.
[123] C.L.R.O., Rep. 17, fos. 425ᵛ–6; G.L., MSS 9234/1–7; 12806/2, fo. 346ʳ⁻ᵛ; 12819/2.
[124] G.L., MS 12806/2, fo. 368ᵛ.

no more poor received into the parish, and they optimistically added that as existing pensioners died, cuts might be made in the level of subsidy.[125] It was not until the reorganisation of 1598 that anything like the necessary funds were made available. In place of the £250–£300 which the hospital had been paying to the outer parishes, the City treasurers were appointed to disburse nearly £1,000. For St Botolph Aldgate this meant £91, for St Giles Criplegate £193, while other parishes like St Andrew Wardrobe and St Dunstan in the West were appointed to receive for the first time.[126] The inequitable distribution of resources was exacerbated by the propensity of the wealthy to leave their money in those parishes with which they had long associations. Private charity, therefore, tended to be directed at those parishes with more manageable problems. The extramural parishes which accounted for 44 per cent of the poor recorded in the survey of 1598 received just 23.8 per cent of the cash bequests to the poor in the period 1594–7. The pattern for endowments was exactly the same: in 1597 only 23.2 per cent of the endowments for the relief of the parochial poor were earmarked for these extramural parishes.

Table 5.9 compares the resources available in several London parishes in order to illustrate the range of experiences. St Andrew Wardrobe and St Botolph Aldgate, poor riverside and extramural parishes respectively, were both growing rapidly in the Elizabethan period. Their poverty is evident in the lower proportions of their populations paying subsidy and in the higher crisis mortality ratios of 1593, reflecting their poor and overcrowded housing conditions. St Michael Cornhill and St Stephen Walbrook, on the other hand, were much smaller in size, and had relatively stable populations, a higher proportion of tax payers, and lower crisis mortality ratios.

At one extreme of parochial provision lay the parish of St Stephen Walbrook (per capita expenditure 2.08s.). Although the vast majority of its rate was dispatched to Christ's, this parish of only 350 souls was extremely well endowed with a rental of £60 p.a. in the mid 1590s. The church stock was therefore able to sustain an unusually high level of expenditure on the poor of about £25 p.a., and a further £10 p.a. in four university exhibitions for the children of parishioners. Some of the individual pensions were large: Widows Ludford and Middleton received £5. 4s. and Francis Kindersley 52s. This is even more striking when we realise that these three each received further pensions of £5. 4s. from the Grocers' Company.[127] The experience of these individuals was definitely not typical of the London poor in general. The husband of Widow Ludford had been churchwarden in 1565–6, served as steward of St Bartholomew's Hospital, master of the saunderbeaters at

[125] C.L.R.O., Rep. 17. fos. 425ᵛ–6.   [126] C.L.R.O., Jour. 24, fo. 323.
[127] G.L., MSS 11571/7–8.

Grocers' Hall, and a common broker of the City.[128] In receipt of regular relief since 1577 the family clearly represented tradesmen from families formerly of some standing who had fallen on hard times, the poor at their most respectable.

St Michael Cornhill (per capita expenditure 0.87s.), a larger parish than St Stephen's and one which felt threatened by the number of poor in its alleys in the 1590s, retained over half its rate for the support of its own poor. This probably supported fourteen pensioners which was the number relieved in 1598.[129] In common with a handful of inner-city parishes, St Michael's had been sufficiently well organised and well connected to petition the Crown for a restoration of the monies paid by its fraternities to the poor which had passed to the Crown at the dissolution of the chantries. The result was that in 1554 the Crown had granted an annuity of £12. 4s. 0d. which was used to support a further three pensioners and to provide resources for extraordinary relief in the parish.[130] The Edwardian vestry had also used the money gained from selling off its rich church plate and vestments to build houses in the churchyard which were used to provide accommodation, occasionally rent-free, for poor widows. In this they followed the example of several other city parishes by seizing the opportunities presented by the attenuation of religious ceremonial to convert resources, hitherto supporting their worship, into poor relief.[131] A bequest of £10 to the parish by Thomas Hunt, skinner, in 1557 established one of the earliest fuel stocks in the city.[132] By the 1580s the vestry was also managing loan stocks of £38. 6s. 8d. providing £2 p.a. in interest payments to support the poor.[133] St Michael's therefore illustrates what could be achieved by well-organised parochial enterprise in combination with the private charity of its leading inhabitants.

Poverty in St Andrew Wardrobe (per capita expenditure 0.44s.) was such that the parish was experiencing difficulties in collecting its rate in the mid 1580s, but it continued to make a small contribution to the hospital until 1598. The difficulties it encountered in getting the governors of Christ's to recognise the extent of its problems are suggested by their order in 1585 that, if unable to collect the £12. 8s. 8d. required for the maintenance of its twelve

---

[128] G.L., MS 593/2, fo. 52ᵛ; G.L.R.O., DL/C/358, fo. 224; G.L., MS 11588/1, fos. 201, 258ᵛ, 314, 380ᵛ; C.L.R.O., Rep. 18, fo. 353.

[129] G.L., MS 4071/1, fo. 166ᵛ. [130] Ibid. fos. 35ᵛ, 38, 42ᵛ, 48.

[131] *The Accounts of the Churchwardens of the Parish of Saint Michael Cornhill in the City of London from 1456 to 1608*, ed. W. H. Overall (1883), pp. 69–70, 77–81, 91, 97. Sales of church plate and vestments financed loan stocks for parishioners in St John Zachary and St Thomas Apostle, the purchase of property to support the poor in St Mary Bothaw, and grants in poor relief in St Bride's and St Margaret New Fish Street: P.R.O., E117/4/22, 68, 80, 90, 91.

[132] G.L., MSS 4072/1, fos. 2, 3, 8, 13, 24, 27; 4071/1, fo. 79ᵛ.

[133] G.L., MS 4072/1, fos. 28ᵛ, 56.

Table 5.9. *Resources for poor relief in selected London parishes, c. 1595*

	Saint Stephen Walbrook	Saint Michael Cornhill	Saint Andrew Wardrobe	Saint Botolph Aldgate
Estimated population, *c.* 1595	285	898	1380	5640
Estimated proportion of householders paying subsidy, 1582[a]	45%	50%	19%	18%
Crisis mortality ratio, 1593	3.06	4.15	5.68	6.19
Yield of poor rate (£)	33.13.4	35.13.6	14. 3.6	40. 0.0[b]
Aid from other parishes (£)	Nil	Nil	Nil	7. 0.0
Amount of rate spent locally (£)	2. 3.4	18.11.8	11.18.4	47. 0.0
Endowments for poor relief (£)	0. 3.0	14.16.0	7.14.8	29.16.0
Interest on parish loan stocks (£)	Nil	2. 0.0	Nil	5.10.0
Legacies and benevolences (£)	2.10.0	2. 0.0	5.10.0	12. 0.0
Expenditure on poor from church stock (£)	24.15.0	1.14.8	5. 0.0	Nil
Total expenditure (£)	29.11.4	39. 2.4	30. 3.0	94. 6.0

[a] 1599 for Saint Botolph Aldgate and St Michael Cornhill.
[b] It has been assumed that the rate in East Smithfield yielded the same as that in Portsoken. The two parts of the parish seem to have been of equal size and similar social composition.
Sources: G.L., MSS 4502/1; 9220/1; 4069/1, fos. 77–80ᵛ; 4071/1; 4072/1; 2088/1; 593/2; 9235/1–2; 9234/4–7; P.R.O., E179/251/16; 146/382; 146/392; Bodleian Library, Rawlinson MS D 796B, fo. 86; Will Sample; *The Registers of Saint Stephen's Walbrook, and of Saint Benet Sherehog, London,* ed. W. B. Bannerman (Harleian Society Registers, XLIX, 1919); *Parish Registers of Saint Michael Cornhill, London.*

pensioners, the parishioners should make provision out of the church box rather than coming to the hospital for help.[134] This is particularly striking because after 1598, in addition to its own revised collection of about £24, the parish was appointed to receive no less than £60 in aid from other parishes. With a rental of just £10 p.a. St Andrew's had little property, but it enjoyed access to a number of endowed charities and ate heavily into its church stock in an effort to meet the problems of the 1590s. The vestry did the best it could with the slender resources available, for example by lending out the church stock free of interest to parishioners. But the total resources were clearly inadequate to the challenges confronting the parish.

The poorest of the parishes under consideration was unquestionably St Botolph Aldgate (per capita expenditure 0.33s.). Forty-four per cent of the householders in Portsoken, that part of the parish which was under the

134 G.L., MS 12806/2, fo. 368ᵛ.

government of the City, were recorded as wanting relief in 1595.[135] Its vestry described in 1618 how the parish consisted of many poor, 'most having nether trades nor meanes to live on but by their handy labour, as porters, carmen, waterbearers, chimney sweepers, servants in silk mylls, brewers servants … the rest carpenters, bricklaiers, plaisterers, coopers, smiths, butchers, chandlers, keepers of sylk mills, priests, schoolmasters, vitulers, and brokers'. Analysis of the occupations recorded in the parish register shows that 22.7 per cent of the population were employed in the unskilled and transport sector (labourers, carmen, sailors, waterbearers, porters, and draymen), and 47 per cent in various forms of industrial production, the metal trades being particularly prominent because of the presence of the royal munitions factories.[136] The income from the poor rate in a parish of this size was unimpressive, and the support received from other parishes nugatory until 1598. The situation was improved somewhat by the parish's enjoyment of a number of endowments, the bulk of the income from which came from the bequest of lands to the parish specifically for the purpose of poor relief in 1557. In this respect St Botolph Aldgate may have enjoyed unusual good fortune for an extramural parish because some of the others had little landed endowment for the support of the poor before legacies began to accumulate in the early seventeenth century. The neighbouring parish of St Botolph Bishopsgate, for example, had no landed endowment at all until the bequest of the Half Moon brewhouse in 1600.[137]

Moreover, the problems that the vestry encountered in the management of these properties shed further light on the pressures and constraints under which parish administrators operated. The poor gained very little benefit from the Martyn bequest until 1575, eighteen years after the original gift, because the parish's title was challenged by Martyn's heir-at-law, who had to be bought out. The vestry raised the money by seeking loans from parishioners, the repayment of which consumed the rents in ensuing years. Further litigation surrounded the properties in 1571 when they were granted as concealed lands, and the parish had to pay Lord Wentworth £50 in settlement, again raised by loans from parishioners.[138] The jungle of the

[135] C.L.R.O., Rep. 23, fo. 479ᵛ; Bodl., Rawlinson MS D796B, fo. 86.
[136] Ibid.; G.L., MSS 9234/1–2. On occupational structures, see Beier, 'Engine of Manufacture'; Boulton, *Neighbourhood and Society*, pp. 65–73.
[137] G.L., MS 4524/1.
[138] G.L., MSS 9235/1; 3485/25; 2630; C.P.R., 1569–72, pp. 273–6. The true story is therefore very different from that told by Pearl, 'Social Policy', pp. 121–2. For other problems with the recovery of charities in the same parish see P.R.O., C2, Eliz. I, T5/46; G.L., MS 9234/5A, fos. 79ᵛ, 108ᵛ, 136ᵛ (will of William Newton disputed by his nephew); P.R.O., C93/2/15 (proceedings before the commissioners for charitable uses to recover annuity of John Franke, twenty-three years in arrears in 1605); MT. Co., C.M. VIII, fos. 536ᵛ–7ᵛ (failure of Christ's Hospital to receive poor from Woolsack Alley under terms of bequest of 1552).

Tudor land law left parishes very vulnerable to predatory interests. Secondly, the parish's position as a landlord brought it awkward dilemmas. By the later 1590s the properties comprising the Martyn estate seem to have been in a state of disrepair, and the vestry sought to get its tenants to become leaseholders and take on responsibility for repairs. The tenants resisted with the support of Richard Casy, former alderman's deputy, but now ill at ease with his fellow vestrymen, whom he criticised as 'younge men ... [who] go abowt to undoe and crosse certen thinges and orders before by theire Elders there set downe'. The problem was that the vestry's entrepreneurial management of its property clashed with the tenants' expectations of paternalistic landlordship. One petitioner claimed that in spite of his worthy efforts to earn a living as a schoolmaster he had fallen into debt because of his twenty-two children.[139] The case encapsulates the problems of using property both as a means of supporting the poor through the rents generated and as a means of providing them with accommodation.

A second strategy for assessing the balance between needs and resources is the construction of a typical budget for a poor household, to which the contribution of poor relief can be assessed. In spite of a lot of work on price and wage series this is still a subject on which we are largely in the dark. Wrightson and Levine include a budget for a poor labourer's family in the later seventeenth century in their study of Terling based on payments in overseers' accounts and assuming that these payments reflect full requirements.[140] This assumption cannot be made for the later sixteenth century and the following reconstruction is based on a variety of sources (Tables 5.10–5.11). For the 'typical' pauper household I have chosen the most usual recipient of relief, the widow, using the surveys of the poor to determine the nature of her household.[141]

For dietary requirements the analysis draws on hospital diet sheets of which the most useful is that from Bridewell in 1600. It might be objected that hospital diets reflect the financial well-being of the institution concerned, but Bridewell was the most seriously under-financed of the hospitals, and the diet was actually less generous than that for the projected house of correction at Westminster in 1561 of which we are told that 'although it be slender yet yt wilbe sufficient'. The orders for the London hospitals of 1579 explained that the poor in the house of correction should be kept 'with

139 G.L., MSS 9234/2C, fos. 9ᵛ–10, 74ᵛ–5ᵛ, 82–3ᵛ, 110ʳ⁻ᵛ, 111, 113; 9234/4, fos. 97ᵛ, 138ʳ⁻ᵛ, 173ʳ⁻ᵛ; P.R.O., REQ 2/165/185.
140 K. Wrightson and D. Levine, *Poverty and Piety in an English Village: Terling 1525–1700* (1979), p. 40; Slack, *Poverty and Policy*, pp. 80–2.
141 Boulton, *Neighbourhood and Society*, pp. 122–8.

Table 5.10. *A budget for the London poor, I: diet sheets (daily requirements)*

	Bread	Beer	Beef non-fast days	Dairy produce fast days
Diet A: Non-worker	12 oz.	1 quart	6½ oz.[a]	4 oz. cheese or 2 oz. butter[b]
Diet B: Spinner	16 oz.	1 quart	6½ oz.[a]	4 oz. cheese or 2 oz. butter[b]
Diet C: Working in hemphouse	24 oz.	1 pottel	6½ oz.[a]	4 oz. cheese or 2 oz. butter[b]

[a] As daily average over the year = 4 oz.
[b] As daily average over the year = 0.83 oz. cheese, 0.42 oz. butter.
Diet A costed at 1¼d. per day in early 1580s, 2d. per day in mid-1590s.
Diet B costed at 1½d. per day in early 1580s, 2¼d. per day in mid-1590s.
Compare: allowance of 2d. per day, St. Thomas' Hospital, London, 1576.
        allowance of 2d. per day, Maidstone house of correction, 1583.
        allowance of 4d. per day, Middlesex house of correction, 1616.
Sources: B.C.B. IV, fos. 212[r-v]; G.L.R.O., H1/ST/A24/1; *E.H.R.*, XLII (1927), 260;
Middlesex Sessions Records, new series, III. 139.

thynne diett onely suffizing to susteyne them in health'.[142] The 1600 diet is particularly valuable because it differentiates between several classes of inmate: non-workers, spinners, and those at the mill. The diet suggests minimum daily requirements of 1¼d. in the early 1580s, rising to 2d. in the 1590s (Table 5.10).[143] These estimates are consistent with the statement of the York authorities in 1587 that the poor needed 1½d. per day 'under whiche some a pore creator cannot lyve'.[144] According to the Boroughside survey of the poor of 1618, a poor widow would on average have 0.8 children. The cost of supporting them has been estimated using the lowest payments made by parochial authorities for keeping children they had boarded out, 8d. per week in the 1580s and 12d. per week in the 1590s, although wealthy parishes

[142] S. A. Peyton, 'The Houses of Correction at Maidstone and Westminster', *E.H.R.*, 42 (1927), 260; *Orders Appointed to bee Executed in the Citie of London for Setting Roges and Idle Persons to Work* (1582).
[143] Prices from *Carpenters' Records*, and details of the assize of bread in M. Benbow, 'The Court of Aldermen and the Assizes: the Policy of Price Control in Elizabethan London', *Guildhall Studies in London History*, 4 (1980), 93–118. Beer prices based on the assize of small beer.
[144] *York Civic Records VIII*, ed. A. Raine (Yorkshire Archaeological Society Record Series, CXIX, 1953), pp. 157–8. For diet, see A. Appleby, 'Diet in Sixteenth-Century England: Sources, Problems and Possibilities', in *Health, Medicine and Mortality in the Sixteenth Century*, ed. C. Webster (Cambridge, 1979), pp. 97–116; J. C. Drummond and A. Wilbraham, *The Englishman's Food: a History of Five Centuries of English Diet* (1952).

were paying nurses at rates comparable to those paid by reasonably prosperous inhabitants of the city, up to 20d. per week in St Stephen Walbrook.[145]

Estimating the rent paid by poor families is difficult because of the great range of rents one can show that those in receipt of relief paid. The lowest rents were 4s.–8s. paid on single rooms, such as the chambers in St Dunstan in the East each rented at between 6s. 8d. and 8s. 'for the ease of the poor dwellers there'. More typical were the chambers in the churchyard of St Michael Cornhill let to poor widows on rents of 10s. p.a.[146] However, these low rents may reflect parish paternalism because there is evidence, where pensioners can be linked to rentals of the properties they inhabited, of higher rents being paid in the private sector. Thus the average rent paid by pensioners in St Margaret Westminster in 1578 was 14s. p.a., while some pensioners in St Martin in the Fields in 1603 were paying rents of between 20s. and 40s.[147] Indeed payments of around 20s. are typical of the alley rentals that survive.[148] And where weekly rents were paid, they were likely to be extortionate: a survey of the alien population in 1568 revealed that strangers were paying rents of up to 2s. per week for 'chamber room' in the ward of Bridge Within.[149] What is less clear is the degree to which high rents might be offset by sub-letting. However pensioners who took this option endangered their continued receipt of relief by running foul of local vestries.[150]

Estimates of the cost of heating can be derived from the payments to almsmen in company accounts where it is clear that the company provided all the fuel. The Merchant Tailors spent 12s. p.a. on each of the widows in their new almshouses in the mid 1590s. This estimate is consistent with one derived from the will of John Costyn who specified that each single person receiving the benefit of his legacy should receive one heaped bushel of coal per week, and each couple two or three bushels. The single person allowance cost 9s. p.a. in the 1580s and 12s. p.a. in the 1590s.[151]

[145] For the 1580s, see G.L., MSS 2088/1, 1589–90 acct.; 959/1, fos. 54ᵛ, 57ᵛ; 593/2, fo. 72; for the 1590s, G.L., MSS 3907/1, 1598–9 acct.; 2593/1, fos. 71, 74ᵛ, 84, 88; 5090/2, fo. 141ᵛ; 942A, fo. 2; 4071/1, fo. 156ᵛ; Society of Antiquaries MS 236, fos. 41–2; for middling householders, see *The Private Diary of Dr. John Dee*, ed. J. O. Halliwell (Camden Society, old series, XIX, 1842), pp. 14–17.
[146] P.R.O., C24/142, Bayly vs. Young; G.L., MS 4071/1.
[147] W.A.M. 25029; W.P.L., F 6039; F 329.
[148] Most paid 19s. 8d. in Gregory Alley, St Giles Cripplegate in 1580; about 20s. in Ship Alley, St Botolph Aldgate *c.* 1570; pensioners in St Bartholomew Exchange linked to rental of Bramley's Alley in 1602 paying rents of 20s., 13s. 4d., 40s. and one rent-free; Widow Grace in Clerkenwell occupying two rooms and paying 26s. 8d. rent: G.L., MSS 7086/3, fo. 70; 15874, p. 4; 9171/18, fo. 331; P.R.O., C24/130, Long vs. Barbour; *Accounts of Saint Bartholomew Exchange*, p. 4.
[149] A.P.C., XXVIII. 427–8; *Returns of Aliens*, III. 379.   [150] Above, pp. 184–5.
[151] Stow, *Survey of London*, I. 125; MT. Co., W.A., 1596–7; *Parliamentary Papers*, 1904. LXXI, p. 596.

Clothing has proved the most awkward element in the budget as it is not clear how frequently it needed replacing. Robert Donkyn's bequest for clothing provided a frieze gown, shirt and shoes for twelve men each year and cost 13s. per person in the 1570s and 14s. in the 1590s, but we do not know whether they were changed each year.[152] That they might have been is suggested by the clothing allowance of 20s. p.a. to Alice Todd, pensioner in St Margaret Moses in addition to her pension of 52s. p.a., but she may have been particularly well favoured.[153] Where disbursements to children for clothing can be traced over several years' accounts, they show payments ranging from 8s. to 20s. p.a.[154]

It is arguable that some of the costs on the budget could be reduced. Some might object that the allowance of meat and dairy produce on the diet is too generous: if these products were excluded the cost of the diet could be cut by 25 per cent. The cost of clothing might be reduced by recourse to the second-hand clothing market, and the cost of fuel by the use of the corporation stock of fuel purchased in the summer months and sold to the poor in the winter at prices 10–15 per cent below those in the market.[155] It is for these reasons that the 'saver' budget has been produced, incorporating these lower estimates. However, in other respects the assumptions behind the budget remain optimistic ones. Clothing allowances larger than the one I have assumed can be found, while the estimates for fuel consumption are based on the single person allowance. Moreover the budget excludes some expenditures. For example, it is clear that the poor were expected to contribute to local rates, because pensioners appear on assessments to clerks' wages, fifteenths, the scavengers' rate and tithe. If the pensioners in St Bartholomew Exchange paid the rates to which they were assessed in the 1590s they would have been confronting rates bills of between 3s. and 5s. p.a., that is between 10 per cent and 28 per cent of their pensions.[156] Budgets might also be seriously strained by the cost of sickness. If payments in parish

[152] *Parliamentary Papers*, 1826–7.X, p. 432; MT. Co., W.A., 1570–3, 1594–6.
[153] G.L., MS 3476/1, fo. 144.
[154] Over the four-year period 1591–5 Christopher Laxton received an average of 20s. p.a. in clothing in addition to pension of 52s. p.a. and 6s. p.a. for schooling; Abda Aldermary, a foundling in St Mary Aldermary received 12s. p.a. in clothing 1598–1600; the child kept by Williamson in St Bartholomew Exchange 16s. p.a. in 1599–1603: G.L., MSS 959/1, fos. 61, 63, 67, 68, 71; 6574, 1598–1600 accts.; *Accounts of Saint Bartholomew Exchange*, pp. 6–7, 12, 16.
[155] D. Woodward, '"Swords into Ploughshares": Recycling in Pre-Industrial England', *Ec.H.R.*, second series, 38 (1985), 178–9; C.L.R.O., Rep. 15, fos. 323ᵛ–4; Rep. 22, fos. 37ᵛ–8ᵛ.
[156] Penioners linked to their assessments for fifteenth in 1595, scavenger's rate in 1598, clerk's wages in 1598, and 18d. assumed for tithe (paid on rents at 2s. 9d. in the pound) in all cases: Widow Busby (3s. 6d.), Philip Williamson (3s. 4d.), Widow Pickering (4s. 10d.). See *Vestry Minutes of Saint Bartholomew Exchange*, pp. 32–3, 39–40, 41; *Accounts of Saint Bartholomew Exchange*, p. 4. Four fifteenths a year were levied during the 1590s.

Table 5.11   A budget for the London poor, II: specimen budgets

	Budget 'A'				Budget 'B'			
	Early 1580s		Mid-1590s		Early 1580s		Mid-1590s	
	Standard	Saver	Standard	Saver	Standard	Saver	Standard	Saver
Adult								
Diet	38s.	28s. 6d.	61s.	45s. 9d.	45s. 8d.	34s. 3d.	68s. 6d.	51s. 4d.
Rent	10s	10s.	10s.	10s.	20s.	20s.	20s.	20s.
Clothing	14s.	10s. 6d.	14s.	10s. 6d.	14s.	10s. 6d.	14s.	10s. 6d.
Fuel	10s.	7s. 6d.	12s.	9s.	10s.	7s. 6d.	12s.	9s.
Total	72s.	56s. 6d.	97s.	75s. 3d.	89s. 8d.	72s. 3d.	114s. 6d.	90s. 10d.
Dependants								
Diet	Nil	Nil	Nil	Nil	34s. 8d.	34s. 8d.	52s.	52s.
Clothing	Nil	Nil	Nil	Nil	14s.	10s. 6d.	14s.	10s. 6d.
Total	Nil	Nil	Nil	Nil	48s. 8d.	45s. 1d.	66s.	62s. 6d.
Total requirements	72s.	56s. 6d.	97s.	75s. 3d.	138s. 4d.	117s. 4d.	180s. 6d.	153s. 4d.
Income								
Pension	26s.	26s.	26s.	26s.	26s.	26s.	26s.	26s.
Female earnings	Nil	Nil	Nil	Nil	52s.	52s.	52s.	52s.
Child earnings	Nil	Nil	Nil	Nil	34s. 8d.	34s. 8d.	34s. 8d.	34s. 8d.
Total	26s.	26s.	26s.	26s.	112s. 8d.	112s. 8d.	112s. 8d.	112s. 8d.

Budget 'A': Non-working widow; no dependants.
Budget 'B': Working widow; with one dependant also at work.

accounts can be trusted, then illness might triple weekly requirements. Thus a foundling kept by the parish of St Helen Bishopsgate was paid 3s. per week during a month's sickness instead of the usual 1s. per week.[157] Women in the terminal stages of pregnancy needed much care. The maintenance contracts entered into by the fathers of bastards frequently required support for the woman at the rate of 5s. per week during her lying in.[158] These extraordinary expenditures are not included in the budget.

Table 5.12 indicates the range of pensions paid in London parishes. They appear to have averaged 5d.–6d. in most parishes before the reorganisation of 1598, although slightly larger sums were paid in some extramural parishes, perhaps reflecting the fact that their inhabitants lacked access to other forms of charity such as company pensions (because the extramural parishes had higher proportions of non-freemen) or private charity (because of the bias in the pattern of investment). The effect of the 1598 reorgani-

[157] G.L., MS 6836, fo. 44ᵛ. Cf. G.L., MSS 3907/1, 1586–7 acct.; 593/2, fo. 73ᵛ.
[158] G.L., MSS 12806/2, fos. 209ᵛ, 268ᵛ; 3556/1, fo. 155ᵛ.

Table 5.12. *Size of pensions paid in Elizabethan London parishes*

	Saint Saviour Southwark 1572	Saint Margaret Lothbury 1576–7	Saint Bartholomew Exchange 1598	Saint Bartholomew Exchange 1600	Saint Martin in the Fields 1588–9	Saint Martin in the Fields 1601–2
2s.	0	0	0	2	0	1
20d.	0	0	0	0	0	1
18d.	0	0	0	0	0	5
16d.	0	0	0	0	0	8
12d.	2	0	0	3	8	7
10d.	0	0	0	0	2	2
8d.	2	1	2	4	6	4
7d.	0	1	0	0	0	0
6d.	8	4	4	1	9	9
5½d.	0	1	0	0	0	0
4½d.	0	0	0	0	1	0
4d.	23	3	2	0	0	0
3d.	5	0	2	0	0	0
2d.	0	1	0	0	0	0
Average Pension	4.87d.	5.32d.	5.4d.	12d.	8.5d.	12.2d.

Saint Sepulchre's, 1573, 183 pensioners paid £278: average pension 7d. p.w.
Saint Giles Cripplegate, 1584, 69 pensioners paid £115: average pension 7.7d. p.w.
Sources: Vestry Minutes of Saint Margaret Lothbury, p. 9; Accounts of Saint Bartholomew Exchange, pp. 4, 8; G.L.R.O., P92/SAV/1394; W.P.L., F 315; F 328; C.L.R.O., Rep. 17, fos. 425ᵛ–426; G.L., MS 12806/2, fo. 346ʳ⁻ᵛ.

sation in doubling the level of support can be seen by comparing the figures from St Bartholomew Exchange for 1598 and 1600.

Table 5.11 shows the results of the reconstruction for two types of pensioner, both in receipt of the average London pension of 6d. per week; first, for the non-working widow on Bridewell diet A with no dependants, and paying a low rent, and secondly, for the working widow on diet B with a working dependant living in medium rented accommodation. The Borough-side survey would suggest that this latter was most typical of the pensioner poor. Even in the 1580s, a pension of 6d. per week apparently covered no more than 46 per cent of requirements for the single widow, and in the mid 1590s as needs increased by 35 per cent the proportion covered by the pension fell to 35 per cent. With children to support the situation might become still worse.

It is therefore obvious that the pension was no more than an income supplement. How was the gap bridged? Surveys of the poor from Ipswich, Norwich, and Salisbury show that poor women and children earned a few extra pennies from spinning, laundering, and trades like button making. However, the surveys also suggest that only about half the women listed (forty-six out of ninety-three in St Edmund and St Thomas Salisbury in 1635) were working, and that the earnings of those who were employed averaged only 9d. per week in late Elizabethan Ipswich and 9¾d. per week in Caroline Salisbury. Children rarely made a contribution to the family economy before reaching the age of ten. In St Edmund Salisbury only 8 per cent of the under-tens were at work, compared to 84 per cent of the over-tens. The weekly earnings of the working children aged under fourteen averaged only 5½d. in Ipswich in 1597, and 6½d. in Salisbury in 1635, that is probably barely enough to bear the cost of supporting them.[159] The problem with these figures for earnings is that coming from provincial England, they are not necessarily typical of metropolitan London, where wages for males were 50 per cent above the national norm.[160] Nor do we know the relative balance of the opportunities for female employment in London as compared to the provinces. There are grounds for a pessimistic view of the potential for female earnings in London. The overloaded labour marked which Rappaport has identified in the later sixteenth century made companies determined to maintain and intensify regulations discriminating against the employment of women.[161] These initiatives were accompanied in the later sixteenth century by efforts to keep women out of the more casual labour sectors such as waterbearing and huckstering.[162] Fishwives were the object of a stream of increasingly vituperative regulation by the corporation.[163] Even laundering by the poor might be frowned upon by vestries preoccupied with the threat of the plague, which was thought to spread through infected clothing.[164] The assumption made in Budget B that London women and children earned 33 per cent more than their provincial counterparts might be optimistic. If it is correct, then, even in the 1580s, the pension and earnings of the widow and her child would barely cover their needs, while in the 1590s the proportion of requirements covered by regular income fell to 73 per cent. And it should be

---

[159] *The Norwich Census of the Poor 1570*, ed. J. F. Pound (Norfolk Record Society, XL, 1971); *Poverty in Early Stuart Salisbury*, ed. P. Slack (Wiltshire Record Society, XXXI, Devizes, 1975), pp. 75–80; *Poor Relief in Elizabethan Ipswich*, ed. J. Webb (Suffolk Records Society, IX, 1966), pp. 122–40.

[160] Chartres, 'Food Consumption', pp. 170–2.

[161] Rappaport, *Worlds Within Worlds*, pp. 38–42; V. B. Brodsky, 'Widows in Late Elizabethan London: Remarriage, Economic Opportunity and Family Orientations', in *The World We Have Gained*, ed. Bonfield et al., pp. 140–2; Consitt, *Weavers*, pp. 292, 313–14; G.L., MSS 14789, fo. 18; 15842/1, fo. 17ᵛ; Cw. Co., C.M. I, fo. 204. Cf. S. Wright, 'Charmaids, Huswyfes and Hucksters: the Employment of Women in Tudor and Stuart Salisbury', in *Women and Work in Pre-Industrial England*, ed. L. Charles and L. Duffin (1985), pp. 100–21.

[162] G.L., MS 1311/1, fo. 72.

[163] C.L.R.O., Jour. 17, fos. 299ᵛ–300; Jour. 22, fos. 378ᵛ–80; Jour. 24, fos. 68, 98ᵛ.

[164] G.L., MS 4415/1, fo. 10.

emphasised that the majority of the young in London were not of earning age.

As it stands this analysis remains open to the objection that pensions from the livery companies discussed in the previous chapter might supplement parish relief. The income from the rate (£1,420) combined with disbursements by livery companies out of house stock (£800) amounted to £2,220, capable of providing 1,708 pensions of 6d. per week. There were another 240 almshouses backed by pensions averaging 13d. per week, that is 1,948 individuals on regular relief. How is this likely to have related to the number of candidates for regular relief? As we have seen, this is one of the great imponderables because of the dearth of surveys and listings of the pensioner poor. But the shards of evidence that are available suggest that between 5 per cent and 7 per cent of households fell into the category of those dependent on regular relief. In a population of 115,000, that meant that there were between 1,277 and 1,788 households in the ranks of the structural poor, so that between 160 and 671 extra pensions of 6d. per week would have been available to help bridge the gap between income and needs for some recipients. Even on the most optimistic assumptions about the size of the dependent group, there would still have been 366 households on single pensions alone. On more pessimistic assumptions there would have been over 1,388 households in this position. And even on a double pension the budgets of many of the poor would have remained in deficit, even in the 1580s. In practice the limits of the formal relief system meant that the poor kept their heads above water by selling off what few comforts they had left, and by mobilising the support of their kin and exploiting the informal charity of their neighbours.[165]

It is true that these estimates have not taken into account the role of private charity, whether in the form of endowments (£900 p.a. in the 1590s) or doles and clothing of the poor at funerals (£1,312 p.a.). Piecemeal grants from these funds could close the gap between pensions and expenditure. But it is also the case that the analysis has not begun to tackle the occasional relief of those not thought eligible for regular pensions, but in need of income supplements, a group which in the Boroughside accounted for a further 18.6 per cent of households, households which often included more dependants than those we have been looking at. Even had all the private charity been directed at this group rather than any of it going to the pensioners, then average receipts per household were unlikely to have been higher than 10s. p.a., enough perhaps to clothe a family member, pay the rent in a hard year, or pay a medical practitioner's bill, but little more. This confirms the sense that these underemployed households on the margins of subsistence received only extraordinary relief.

[165] Slack, *Poverty and Policy*, pp. 83–5.

RESPONSES TO CRISIS

The budgets have revealed something of the scale of the problem of the 1590s, raising questions about the responsiveness of the system to crisis conditions. This issue is crucial to the problem of the maintenance of stability in the capital because of the way in which conditions deteriorated for many households normally able to keep their heads above water. As we have seen, the harvest failures of the mid 1590s meant that the poor had to increase their incomes by 33 per cent if they were to maintain their standards of the early 1580s. Moreover the ranks of the poor were swollen as rising prices and unemployment drove many of those on the margins of subsistence into destitution. There were 4,015 householders, 16 per cent of the city's total, declared to be in want of relief in December 1595.[166] Outbreaks of plague produced a similar mushrooming in social problems as quarantine measures prevented households from continuing the economic activity necessary to support their members. Paul Slack suggests that in Salisbury in 1604 the morbidity rate was potentially double the mortality rate, so that the disease's ramifications were more widespread than the data from burials suggest.[167]

The aldermen did not respond to crises by increasing the burden on the rates. On the contrary they argued against the plague rates advocated by the privy council in 1578 on the grounds that rating would cause the income from voluntary contributions to dry up.[168] A handful of parishes experimented with their own plague rates, but they lacked statutory sanction until 1604, and the problems encountered by vestrymen in levying these extra taxes are suggested by the list of twenty-three defaulters in St Margaret Lothbury in 1593.[169] Rather, the corporation's response to plague conditions was exhortation to benevolence by wealthy citizens. In 1563, 1569, and 1592 the aldermen called for weekly collections of the benevolence of inhabitants for plague victims.[170] Their response to harvest failure was similar. In 1596 householders were moved to contribute to special collections 'for that it is a woorke of Charitie for those whom almightie god has blessed in more plentifull measure to releeve their poor and neadie breatheren'.[171] At the height of the crisis in March 1598, the lord mayor required the aldermen to prescribe some fit time of day for the parish poor to receive relief from the houses of the richer sort.[172] The corporation, privy council, and ecclesiastical authorities joined forces in pressing the duty of fasting. Companies were enjoined to forbear their election feasts and use the money

[166] C.L.R.O., Rep. 23, fo. 479ᵛ.   [167] Slack, *Impact of Plague*, pp. 175–6, 188–92.
[168] P.R.O., SP12/98/38, art 1.
[169] Slack, *Impact of Plague*, pp. 281–2; *Vestry Minutes of Saint Margaret Lothbury*, p. 30.
[170] C.L.R.O., Jour. 18, fo. 142; Jour. 19, fo. 192; Jour. 23, fo. 128ᵛ.
[171] C.L.R.O., Jour. 24, fos. 141, 143ᵛ, 148ᵛ.
[172] Ibid. fo. 289.

saved for the relief of the poor. The corporation's Wednesday and Friday fast, introduced in August 1596, received backing from the privy council and archbishop of Canterbury in December, and the ecclesiastical authorities mobilised their machinery to enforce it. Householders were instructed to hand over the monies saved by forbearing Wednesday suppers to parish collectors, and the parish authorities required to make monthly presentments to the archdeacon of those infringing the fast. Parish records show that the orders were widely implemented in the city.[173]

It is extremely difficult to assess the effectiveness of these measures. Churchwardens' accounts, and even the accounts of the collectors for the poor, are not necessarily accurate guides because special funds often received separate accounts: the receipts for collections for plague victims which we know from the vestry minutes to have taken place in St Martin in the Fields in 1593 do not appear among the accounts of the collectors for the poor of that year.[174] The mayor's arguments against rating in 1578 should not be dismissed lightly. In St Margaret Westminster, admittedly perhaps untypical because outside the City and enjoying the patronage of a large number of aristocratic donors and national figures, private charity in the plague years 1592–4 amounted to about £288 compared to £92 in rates.[175] It is true that parish accounts in the City do not give any indication of generosity on this scale, but this may be explained by the fact that by this date benevolences in the City were centrally administered by treasurers appointed by the corporation and often distributed through the aldermen's deputies rather than the parish officers. Therefore churchwardens' accounts may not reflect the true scale of the effort. The machinery for the collection and distribution of benevolences was undoubtedly becoming more sophisticated. Whereas in the earliest collections for plague victims it was left to the discretion of individual parishes to aid other more needy parishes, by 1593 the appointment of City treasurers introduced a more sophisticated redistributive mechanism. The money raised by benevolence in 1596 was again handed over to City treasurers and distributed among the wards after assessment of their needs. The painstakingly compiled lists of recipients of this benevolence are testimony to the great care taken in its distribution.[176] The presentment machinery of the conciliar-backed fast of 1596–7 was probably more successful in directing funds to the poor than Grindal's rather pious hope

[173] C.L.R.O., Jour. 24, fos. 143ᵛ, 149ᵛ, 174ʳ⁻ᵛ, 204; Rep. 24, fos. 60ᵛ–61; A.P.C., XXVI. 96–8, 380–2; G.L., MSS 1431/1, fo. 11; 943/1, fo. 8ᵛ; 2590/1, p. 111; 3570/1, fo. 47; 4072/1, fo. 72; 9234/6, fo. 96ᵛ; *Vestry Minutes of Saint Bartholomew Exchange*, pp. 37–8; Greaves, *Society and Religion*, pp. 480–2, 490–9.
[174] W.P.L., F2001, fo. 32; F320.   [175] W.P.L., E147, accts. for 1592–4.
[176] C.L.R.O., Jour. 18, fo. 142; Jour. 23, fo. 128ᵛ; Jour. 24, fo. 148ᵛ; Rep. 22, fos. 430, 431ᵛ, 438, 443; Rep. 23, fos. 563, 563ᵛ; Rep. 24, fo. 18; G.L., MS 1431/1, fo. 10B.

expressed in 1563 that the monies saved as a result of the fast he had devised for the poor would be directed to the poor in back lanes and alleys.[177] However, even the more sophisticated machinery of the 1590s may have made only a marginal impact on the problem. In September 1596 the lord mayor reported that 4,000 2d. loaves had been distributed to the poor each week since the collections had begun at the end of July. At about £33 per week that looks quite impressive, but it may have been little more than a drop in the ocean, just enough to provide one day's ration in bread each week for one person in each of the households recorded as wanting relief at the beginning of the year.[178]

The aldermen's other response to crisis conditions was an effort to ensure that the markets were properly supplied, profiteering checked, and the assizes enforced. It is true that the periods of intense magisterial activity on the assizes did not necessarily coincide with dearth conditions. The duty of enforcing the assizes was stressed in the mayor's oath as a normal function of the magistrate, and few years passed without a flurry of activity on at least one of the assizes.[179] The decision to press for a rigorous enforcement of the assizes of beer in 1592–3 probably owed more to the reformist enthusiasm of an individual lord mayor than to a perception of the need for immediate action.[180] But crisis conditions prompted a wide range of initiatives rather than concentration on individual offences. Thus in the mid 1590s forestalling and regrating received renewed attention. In November 1594 common council passed an act providing for the disenfranchisement of all freemen found guilty of forestalling victuals and fuel, and in May 1595 appointed committees to look into measures that might be taken to curb regrating. Meanwhile the aldermen disciplined a group of forestallers and regraters of fish.[181] The problem of defective weights and measures was tackled in precepts to the wardmote inquests to search out unsealed weights, the preparation of indictments of those found with unlawful weights and measures, and the public burning of the offending measures in Cheapside.[182] Throughout the 1590s the aldermen grappled with the problem of colliers whose sacks were not properly filled, appointing a succession of individuals to search their sacks, and pillorying offenders or sending them to Bridewell.[183] Dearth conditions in 1595 resulted in a renewed assault on the

[177] B.L., Lansdowne MS 6, fo. 156ᵛ.
[178] C.L.R.O., Jour. 24, fos. 152, 179. The livery companies contributed only reluctantly: MT. Co., C.M. III, fos. 329ᵛ, 352ᵛ; G.L., MSS 12071/2, p. 600; 5570/1, p. 120.
[179] B.L., Additional MS 2177. Market regulation is discussed by Benbow, 'Assizes', and in *Hugh Alley's "Caveat"*.
[180] C.L.R.O., Jour. 23, fo. 111ᵛ; Rep. 22, fo. 438ʳ⁻ᵛ; A.P.C., XXIII, 277.
[181] C.L.R.O., Jour. 23, fo. 334; Jour. 24, fo. 3; Rep. 23, fos. 391, 405ᵛ–6.
[182] C.L.R.O., Rep. 23, fos. 382, 415, 465ᵛ, 519ᵛ, 547.
[183] C.L.R.O., Rep. 23, fo. 444ᵛ, 538ᵛ.

brewers, this time with the strong backing of the privy council, which adopted a high profile in disciplining them.[184]

The corporation was also energetic in its efforts to ensure that the capital was adequately supplied with grain. In times of dearth councillors were bombarded with requests from the City for restraints on the export of grain and beer, for help in releasing grain from counties reluctant to give it up to supply London, and for curbs on the activity of purveyors in the City markets.[185] Through the difficult years of the 1590s the aldermen regularly negotiated contracts with merchants trading to the Baltic for the supply of grain, and channeled some of that provided into their own grain stock financed through loans from the members of the livery companies. Thus from 1594 the corporation financed the purchase of 10,000 quarters of grain each year, ground into meal by the livery companies and sold at slightly below market rates in small quantities to the poor.[186] In November 1597 the companies were instructed to sell their meal to the 'poorer sort' at 4d. per bushel below the prices prevailing in the markets (a saving of about 6.66 per cent) in measures ranging from the half peck to the half bushel, probably just within the range of the poor.[187]

These efforts were crucial to the maintenance of harmony because prices were such a sensitive issue in London. If the magistrates neglected their duties then the populace might take action on their own account, as the *taxation populaire* and assaults on fishwives in the riots of 1595 demonstrated.[188] Years of dearth always strained the fabric of authority in the capital. In October 1573 at the end of Sir Lionel Ducket's mayoralty, which had coincided with high prices, his fellow aldermen promised to punish severely those who had recently slandered him. Typical was Elizabeth Bradley, sentenced to be whipped in Bridewell for wishing that Ducket go to hell, 'because he never did good nor never will and that he was the cause that bread and coles were so deare that she could get none'.[189] Not surprisingly the correspondence between the City and the council on the subject of the food supply reveals a nervousness about the potential for disturbance that might result from bad management. Writing in May 1595 against the practices of purveyors, the aldermen pointed out that their activity 'being

---

[184] C.L.R.O., Jour. 24, fos. 191ᵛ, 207; A.P.C., XXVI. 327, 499, 506–7, 535, 536, 539, 540.
[185] C.L.R.O., Remembrancia II, nos. 104, 106, 108, 109; Rep. 23, fo. 150ᵛ; B.L., Harleian MS 6850, fo. 265.
[186] C.L.R.O., Rep. 23, fos. 571ᵛ, 573ᵛ–4ᵛ; Jour. 24, fos. 161, 249ᵛ; Jour. 25, fos. 123ᵛ, 201–2, 306ᵛ; N. S. B. Gras, *The Evolution of the English Corn Market from the Twelfth to the Eighteenth Century* (Cambridge, Mass., 1915), pp. 78, 82–5; Power, 'Control of Crisis', pp. 372–5; Walter, 'Social Economy of Dearth', pp. 118–19.
[187] C.L.R.O., Jour. 24, fo. 254. However, policy on the sale of the corn was possibly not consistent. In July 1596 the companies were instructed to sell it at 'such rates as the markets will afford': ibid., fo. 139.
[188] Above, p. 6.   [189] C.L.R.O., Rep. 18, fos. 90ᵛ, 97.

noised abroad among the vulgar sorte has been cause of some murmure against the lorde maior and his bretheren as if wee were negligent in preserving of that which was provided for the relief of the poore'. In November 1596, in explaining his policy on the corn supply, the lord mayor again expressed the fear that the 'poorer sort who ar soon mooved both to conceave and report amisse of the magistrate specially in matter of this sort' might be 'moved to exclaime against us as if wee enhaunced the price of corne for our own gaine'.[190]

This heightened sensitivity to the threat of disorder reflects the reality of the recent disturbances. The disturbances themselves may be a sign that the hand of magisterial regulation was faltering. The evidence does not allow us to determine how readily the wards responded to orders for action from the aldermen, nor can we tell how typical are the instances of the disciplining of individual offenders in the absence of full judicial records. The juxtaposition of draconian legislation against forestallers from common council in the autumn of 1594 with the popular indictment of the failures of the magistrates in the riots of the following summer suggests the need to differentiate between magisterial rhetoric and practice. It is true that the aldermen did enough to maintain the fragile fabric of order in subsequent years. The publicity given to the punishment of heinous offenders was one way in which a little effort by the rulers could be made to go a long way.[191] But there are some indications that the initiatives of the 1590s had serious limitations. First, because of their multiplying responsibilities in other fields, the officers of the mayor's household upon whom much of the responsibility for enforcement devolved, were less regularly involved in the presentment of market offences: the Book of Fines shows activity at a much lower level than in the 1560s.[192] Secondly, the 1590s witnessed a number of scandals involving officers with responsibilities for enforcement in the markets, such as the protection racket operated by John Pate, foreign taker.[193] Thirdly, the assize was now enforced on a much narrower range of commodities than in the past: bread and beer remained at the heart of the aldermen's concerns, but wood, tallow, and wine had been abandoned. Moreover the aldermen were increasingly reluctant to use some of the standard devices of the 1560s and 1570s in enforcing the assizes, such as recognisances by victuallers to observe specified prices, and the use of regular searches by the wardmote

---

190 B.L., Harleian MS 6850, fo. 265; C.L.R.O., Remembrancia II, nos. 60, 104; *H.M.C., Hatfield*, VII. 148.
191 C.L.R.O., Rep. 21, fo. 591^v; Rep. 23, fo. 366^v; Rep. 24, fos. 179, 442^v–3.
192 C.L.R.O., Book of Fines, analysed by M. Benbow in Misc MS 363.3: in 1559–63, 75 fines were received for forestalling, regrating and engrossing, 84 for hawking, and 58 for the sale of goods outside the market. The comparable figures for 1594–98 are 29, 8 and 0 respectively.
193 *Hugh Alley's "Caveat"*, pp. 24–5.

inquests to detect offenders.[194] Fourthly, and even more intriguingly, it is possible that whereas earlier the aldermen had been willing to discipline wholesalers for profiteering, by the 1590s the main thrust of their activity was against petty traders, fishwives, and hucksters. Once again the absence of court records for the City makes it difficult to substantiate this argument conclusively, but there are more instances of wholesalers being proceeded against by the aldermen in the mid-Tudor decades than in the 1590s, and they were much more frequently the object of legislation by common council in the earlier period. Against the rather unimpressive legislative achievement of the 1590s should be set enactments of 1571 and 1575 against citizens riding into the country to buy up butter, cheese, and wood, and the action taken by the aldermen in 1576 against brewers profiteering from the resale of grain they had purportedly purchased for use in brewing, and regular action against engrossers of tallow and wood.[195] The increasing preoccupation with the petty dealers reflects mounting hostility to the misdemeanours of the 'poorer sort' in the more socially polarised conditions of the 1590s.

The social fabric held in the 1590s in spite of the tensions. It seems that the action taken by the aldermen to keep the markets supplied, whatever its shortcomings, was just sufficient to retain the confidence of the poor. Poor relief, although limited in scope, might work to promote stability because of the way the exercise of philanthropy served to invest elite figures with reputations for charitable virtue, and because of the way relief could be manipulated by the vestries to promote conformist behaviour. However, to argue that social policy played a role in the maintenance of stability is not the same as claiming that it was successful in relieving poverty and in fulfilling its declared objective of eliminating begging. The pressure placed on resources by the pensioner poor meant that there were only limited funds available for the relief of the 18 per cent or so of householders who fell outside the group, but were nevertheless considered poor. In years of crisis, as the needs of this second group mushroomed, the extra demand placed on resources by the increased cost of living for the pensioner poor meant that the large sums raised in private benevolence made only a marginal impact. Large apparent increases in the scale of charitable provision might mask back-sliding in the level of support for the poor. It is quite clear that there was much unrelieved poverty in London, both because resources were maldistributed, and because the scale of the challenge, particularly in crisis years like the mid 1590s, ultimately proved too much for the authorities.

[194] Benbow, 'Assizes'.
[195] C.L.R.O., Jour. 19, fos. 325ᵛ, 326, 330–1ᵛ; Jour. 20, fos. 131ᵛ–2ᵛ; Rep. 19, fos. 129ᵛ, 130ᵛ, 170ᵛ–1, 366; Rep. 20, fos. 34, 109.

6

Crime and society

A CRIMINAL UNDERWORLD?

Earlier chapters have stressed the integrating functions of the livery companies and of the overlapping institutions of local government, as well as the responsiveness of the elite to the impoverishment of the sixteenth century. But it needs to be recognised that by no means all the city's inhabitants were so well integrated or cared for. The capital was notorious for its criminality and contemporaries firmly believed there to be a counter-culture of deviants. Foreign visitors frequently drew attention to the prevalence of crime about the metropolis and the regular flow of criminals to the gallows.[1] Their verdict is supported by those, like Recorder Fleetwood, who were actively involved in fighting London crime. 'Here are fortie brables and pickeries done abowt this towne more in any one daye than when I first came to serve was done in a moneth', he wrote in 1582.[2] The aldermen concurred, complaining in 1601 of 'the great numbers of idle, lewd, and wicked persons flocking and resorting hither from all parts of this realm which do live here and maintain themselves chiefly by robbing and stealing'.[3] Clerics fulminated against vagrants as 'the very filth and vermin of the common wealth ... the very Sodomites of the land, children of Belial, without God, without minister; dissolute, disobedient, and reprobate to every good work'.[4] The Elizabethan reading public was saturated in the image of a deviant counter-culture. Thomas Harman, a Kentish justice of the peace, in his *Caveat for Common Cursitors* (1566), claimed that an elaborate hierarchy existed within the vagrant population, and described the tricks with which its members gulled the public. It was a theme often repeated during the vogue for rogue

---

[1] *A Relation ... of the Island of England*, ed. C. A. Sneyd (Camden Society, XXXVII, 1847), p. 34; 'London Journal of Alessandro Magno', 148–9; W. B. Rye, *England as Seen by Foreigners in the Days of Elizabeth and James the First* (1865), p. 108.
[2] Wright, II. 171; E. Lodge, *Illustrations of British History* (3 vols., 1838), II. 352.
[3] Rappaport, *Worlds Within Worlds*, p. 65.
[4] Slack, *Poverty and Policy*, p. 25.

literature in the 1590s.[5] Legislators were also convinced of the existence of an organised underworld. According to the preamble of an act against pickpocketing of 1567, there existed 'a certain Kind of evil-disposed Persons, commonly called Cutpurses or Pick-purses who do confeder together, making among themselves as it were a Brotherhood or Fraternity of an Art or Mystery, to live idly by the secret Spoil of the good and true Subjects of the Realm'.[6] London historians are therefore confronted by the problem of the degree to which these perceptions accurately reflected reality. Was Elizabethan London overwhelmed by a 'crime wave'? Were criminals turning the world upside down by rejecting the values of established society? Were the authorities impotent before the challenges of organised crime? It is with these questions that this chapter is concerned.

The sources pose particularly intractable problems for those who seek to penetrate the underworld. Indictments are not a reliable indicator of the level of crime because of the 'dark figure' of unprosecuted crime. As the Somerset justice, Edward Hext, remarked to Burghley in 1596, 'the fyveth person that comytteth a felonye ys not browght to tryall'.[7] Nor are indictments helpful on criminal organisation because they tend to reduce the scope of criminal activity to the one occasion on which the criminal was caught. Those who have been convinced by the reality of the underworld have tended therefore to rely on the literary sources.[8] But these are also highly problematic. One cannot be sure about the representativeness of possibly sensationalised accounts of individual criminals; the frequency with which historians cite the same examples, such as Lawrence Pickering's organisation of weekly meetings of thieves at his house in Kent Street, undermines confidence in the typicality of the phenomena. Moreover, the rogue literature drew heavily on a European literary tradition, the *Liber Vagatorum*, printed in 1510, providing a model for Harman in the 1560s. The relationship between artistic genre and social reality is further complicated by the authors' efforts to secure a market for their works by providing an entertaining narrative rather than an in-depth analysis of the problem of crime. Moreover, the readiness with which contemporaries subscribed to the notion of a criminal counter-culture is another symptom of those mental frameworks inclined to think in terms of binary polarities that historians of ideas see as characteristic of the age. It was by ascribing to the vagrant and the criminal all the characteristics of which respectable opinion disapproved that society's

[5] *The Elizabethan Underworld*, ed. A. V. Judges (1930).   [6] 8 Eliz. I c. 4.
[7] *T.E.D.*, II. 340.
[8] J. McMullan, *The Canting Crew. London's Criminal Underworld, 1550–1700* (New Jersey, 1984). Cf. J. A. S. McPeek, *The Black Book of Knaves and Unthrifts in Shakespeare and Other Renaissance Authors* (Connecticut, 1969); N. Berlin, *The Base String: the Underworld in Elizabethan Drama* (Cranbury, New Jersey, 1968); G. Salgādo, *The Elizabethan Underworld* (1977).

norms could be upheld. Slack concludes that the pamphlets 'do not demonstrate the existence of a rogue society or counter-culture, but people's
determination to believe in one'.[9]

It is because of the difficulties of the literary sources that most historians of
crime have been cautious about accepting the stereotypical criminal at
face-value. Their studies, which have focused on rural areas, have emphasised that the majority of crime was casual and opportunistic, resulting from
the impulse of economic necessity. They have shown that anxieties about
gangs of thieves roaming the countryside and terrorising the inhabitants bore
little relationship to the reality of small groups of poor migrants engaged in
casual theft for subsistence purposes. Even the more serious crimes, like
highway robbery and burglary, were relatively disorganised, characterised
by short-term liaisons and a lack of specialisation.[10] But they have also
emphasised that London provided a particularly favourable and exceptional
environment for organised crime. This was because it offered a high
concentration of valuable targets, and because its anonymity rendered
detection more difficult and the disposal of stolen goods easier.[11] Some of
these suggestions, which generally rest on the literary evidence alone, have
been substantiated by J. M. Beattie's work on late-seventeenth- and early-
eighteenth-century Surrey (incorporating Southwark) and Sussex, comparing the experiences of the urban and rural areas. He has shown that in the
urban areas the value of goods stolen was higher because money and
valuables were more prominent among the goods stolen. He has documented
the infestation of the roads about the capital with gangs of highway robbers,
and unravelled the operation of some of the criminal gangs engaged in
burglaries. But he remains sceptical about their cohesion and longevity. The
gangs were professional in the sense that they depended on crime for their
income, but they did not involve a high level of skill, relying for their
effectiveness on sheer weight of numbers and brute force. People therefore
tended to drift in and out of the gangs rather than having a permanent
allegiance to them.[12]

Talk of the professional criminal underworld is apt to obscure the fact that
crime was an aspect of the problem of youth, and therefore in origins usually
casual. A classic route into vagrancy and petty crime was the breakdown of

---

[9] G. M. Spraggs, 'Rogues and Vagabonds in English Literature, 1552–1642' (Cambridge
Ph.D., 1980); R. Hughes, '"The Canting Crew": Criminal Stereotypes in Popular Literature
and Drama, 1536–1660' (York M.A., 1983); S. Clark, 'Inversion, Misrule and the Meaning
of Witchcraft', *Past and Present*, 87 (1980), 98–127; J. A. Sharpe, *Crime in Early Modern
England, 1550–1750* (1984), pp. 114–16; Slack, *Poverty and Policy*, pp. 24–5, 102–5.

[10] Sharpe, *Crime in Seventeenth-Century England: a County Study* (Cambridge, 1983); Beier,
Masterless Men, ch. VIII.

[11] Sharpe, *Crime in Early Modern England*, pp. 111–17; J. M. Beattie, *Crime and the Courts in
England, 1660–1800* (Oxford, 1986), pp. 252–63.

[12] Ibid. pp. 149–50, 155–6, 158–60, 163–6, 183–90, 252–63.

the master–servant relationship. The records of Bridewell are packed with cases like that of John Devyke, 'a picking naughty boy that will tarry in service with no man'.[13] Apprentices might become disillusioned with their economic prospects, either because of the poor quality of the instruction or care they were receiving, or because of the frustrations resulting from a lengthy period of under-rewarded labour in a city of such fabulous wealth and dizzying distractions as London. The tight restrictions on their leisure time were not surprisingly resented, and apprentices sought outlets beyond the household. One of the standard arguments used to justify action against unlawful games, unlicensed alehouses, and brothels was the temptations they offered to gullible apprentices. Thus in 1559 Thomas Grey was whipped and set to work at the mill in Bridewell as 'a comon player at dyse and inveglyng of other mens servauntes to use that unlawful game to the consumpcion of their masters goodes'. Fulk Mounslow, a client of the prostitute, Jane Harding, testified to his internalisation of this value system when he alleged that Harding 'allureth and entyceth many yonge men to their utter ruyne and decay, not only in expendinge & consumynge their goodes & good name but also in entisinge them to such inconveniences that are & be abhomynable & detestable before the face of god'.[14] As Jim Sharpe has remarked, a 'domino theory' of human character prevailed, as small sins inevitably led to greater ones.[15] It was a theory which fitted the facts in so far as apprentices often stole from their masters to support their illicit pastimes and ran away when threatened with discovery. Many swelled the floating population of master-less men about the city supporting themselves by a succession of odd jobs and petty crime. Lee Beier has demonstrated that an increasing proportion of vagrants arrested in the capital in the sixteenth century came from the city itself and that servants and apprentices were among the groups most prone to vagrancy in London.[16] It is of course impossible to determine what propor-tion of crime was accounted for by men from this sort of background, not least because the indictments of suspects of property crime do not furnish us with evidence relating to their ages. But in the later eighteenth century the

[13] B.C.B. I, fo. 182ᵛ. The problem of youth in early modern England is currently being researched by Paul Griffiths of Jesus College, Cambridge and I am grateful to him for discussions on the subject. In the meantime, see: S. R. Smith, 'The London Apprentices as Seventeenth-Century Adolescents', *Past and Present*, 61 (1973), 149–61 and 'The Ideal and the Reality: Apprentice–Master Relationships in Seventeenth-Century London', *History of Education Quarterly*, 21 (1981), 449–60; Thomas, 'Age and Authority'; S. Brigden, 'Youth and the English Reformation', *Past and Present*, 95 (1982), 37–67; I. K. Ben-Amos, 'Apprenticeship, the Family and Urban Society in Early Modern England' (Stanford Ph.D., 1985); Collinson, *Religion of Protestants*, pp. 223–30.
[14] Below, pp. 216–18; B.C.B. I, fos. 36ᵛ, 72, 125, 175; II, fo. 198ᵛ; G.L., MS 3018/1, fos. 11ᵛ, 35ᵛ.
[15] Sharpe, *Crime in Early Modern England*, pp. 162–4.
[16] Beier, *Masterless Men*, pp. 42, 44, 55, 89.

highest rates of prosecution have been observed in the age group comprising twenty– to twenty-four-year-olds.[17]

So, should we concur with Lee Beier's judgement that London was confronting 'large-scale juvenile delinquency'? There is no straightforward answer because we have no way of assessing the numerical scale of the problem. Steve Rappaport has suggested that the 555 vagrants appearing before the governors of Bridewell in 1600–1 represented a tiny minority of the City's population, and therefore that Beier's conclusions are invalid. But Rappaport fails to appreciate both that more vagrants passed through Bridewell than appear in the court books, and that vagrants might be punished elsewhere, either in special sessions or, crucially after the act of 1598, summarily by local constables. The numbers game is therefore decidedly unhelpful.[18]

We can, however, qualify the impression that might be given of a society about to be overwhelmed by gangs of masterless men by considering whether vagrants were organised in large-scale bands in the capital. Judged by this standard, the problem does not appear really serious. Vagrants, in London as elsewhere, appear to have come to the attention of the authorities in small groups. It is true that 'harbouring houses' of masterless men can be found about the capital. Mrs Philips of Petticoat Lane, for example, was named to the governors of Bridewell in 1599 as a bawd and lodger of cutpurses and breakers of houses. Unlicensed alehouses receiving suspect persons were the staple fare of presentments by the wardmotes and grand jurors.[19] Sometimes we obtain hints of organised crime operating from these establishments. In May 1576 Richard Smethwick named six cutpurses 'with a great nomber more that lye comonly every satturday at night in a barne at the further ende of Tuttle strete' in Westminster; another two lodged at an alehouse in Warwick Lane; and a great number of cutpurses gathered at a barn between Lambeth Marsh and the bishop of Carlisle's house, 'with dyverse whores thear with them'.[20]

But whether the associations formed in these safe houses were anything more than casual is dubious. The literary evidence points to a highly organised fraternity of pickpockets. Thus Robert Greene claimed that they 'have a kind of corporation, as having wardens of their company, and a hall ... where they confer of weighty matters touching their workmanship, for they are provident in that every one hath some trusty friend whom he calleth his treasurer, and with him he lays up some rateable portion of every purse he

[17] Beattie, *Crime and the Courts*, pp. 243–7.

[18] Below, pp. 238–41; A. L. Beier, 'Social Problems in Elizabethan London', *Journal of Interdisciplinary History*, 9 (1978), 203–5; Rappaport, *Worlds Within Worlds*, p. 5.

[19] B.C.B., I, fos. 8ᵛ–9, 46ᵛ; II, fo. 97ᵛ; IV, fo. 102; G.L., MS 3018/1, passim; G.L.R.O., MJ/SR; P.R.O., KB9.

[20] B.C.B. III, fo. 3. Cf. ibid. fos. 167, 273.

draws'.[21] Recorder Fleetwood lends some substance to these claims in his vivid description of a school for pickpockets. One Wotton, a gentleman and former merchant fallen on hard times, had set up an alehouse at Smart's Quay near Billingsgate, and 'procured all the Cuttpurses abowt this Cittie to repaire to his said howse. There was a schole howse sett upp to learn younge boyes to cutt purses'. Among Wotton's teaching aids was a purse containing counters hung with bells. The boys were considered to have graduated when they could take the counters out of the purse without sounding any of the bells.[22] Some of the Bridewell depositions also hint at this kind of organisation. In April 1575, we are told that Goodman Fawkener, an alehouse keeper in Pepper Alley in Southwark, took the money gained by William Tucke and other cutpurses, giving them meat and drink in return. Six months later we learn that Tucke had a similar arrangement with William Clifton who every evening would come to him and his fellows and take all the money they had gained the previous night.[23] Cutpurses were among the more specialised of criminals and in a few cases we are able to trace a career in crime spanning several years. Simon Fawkener, the alehouse keeper named by Tucke in 1575, was eventually sentenced to be hanged for pickpocketing in Westminster at a Middlesex gaol delivery in early 1578.[24] However, there is little to suggest the coherence and centralised control of Greene's account. Individual cutpurses may have had arrangements with the victuallers who lodged them, but they were not necessarily permanent. Tucke had two hosts in 1575; in 1560 Peter Hardwicke confessed that he was taught to cut purses by Thomas Gregory to whom he delivered his gains, but he also says that there was only one other cutpurse associated with Gregory.[25]

The impression of impermanent and shifting alliances is confirmed when we turn to other forms of criminal activity. Professional criminals can be identified with some certainty. There can be little doubt that John Dytche, indicted on nineteen counts of horse theft between May 1582 and November 1583, was a professional horse thief.[26] Some London criminals used the capital as a base for forays into the Home Counties. Benjamin Boorne first turns up at the Surrey assizes in March 1578 when he received benefit of clergy for the theft of fifty-six sheep in Southwark. A year later he was indicted for a petty larceny, again committed in Southwark. But more serious

[21] *Elizabethan Underworld*, ed. Judges, p. 165.   [22] *T.E.D.*, II. 337–9.

[23] B.C.B. II, fos. 95, 183.

[24] B.C.B. II, fo. 95; III, fo. 140ᵛ; G.L.R.O., MJ/SR 213/22. Cf. B.C.B. II, fos. 51, 52, 95; III, fo. 3, and 2 July 1576; G.L.R.O., MJ/SR 198/22 (William Loggens); B.C.B. II, 23 Oct. 1574; G.L.R.O., MJ/SR 206/14; 210/15 (Robert Gibbes). For a network of cozeners, see Spraggs, 'Rogues and Vagabonds', pp. 302–7.

[25] B.C.B. I, fo. 41; III, fo. 95.

[26] G.L.R.O., MJ/SR 247/104–19; Stow, *Annales*, p. 698. Cf. G.L.R.O., MJ/SR 308/36–8, 43–4, 48–53; 347/57; 353/31; 361/41 (William Cappelyn); MJ/SR 205/11, 19; Acc. 565/10 (John Cottingham); MJ/SR 168/19; 187/29 (Ambrose Legg).

crimes lay ahead. In the summer of 1579 he is recorded as having committed highway robberies at Gillingham, Chevening, and Shooter's Hill in Kent. He was sentenced to be hanged at the Kent assizes in March 1580. What is striking, however, is that on each occasion his associates were different people: at Chevening, George Whitehead, William Dawes, Henry Goodman, and John Smith; at Gillingham, James Nailer; and at Shooter's Hill, James Currey, John Miles, William Mannam, Thomas Scarborough, and Richard Turner. On two of these individuals we have a little more information. In the month prior to his escapades on Shooter's Hill Henry Goodman had been engaged in a series of thefts in Whitechapel with one Thomas Robinson. Another associate, James Currey, had recently been reprieved for a highway robbery at Kensington, committed with Simon Candishe and William Farmer.[27] The definite impression one gets is of shifting and kaleidoscopic alignments within the criminal fraternity, possibly casual liaisons formed for specific offences.[28] There was a criminal underworld in the sense of people for whom criminal activity was regular, but it is arguable that its rapidly shifting allegiances made it somewhat easier for the authorities to penetrate it. Likewise, the fact that thieves like John Dytche were prepared to trade information concerning their accomplices for pardons suggests that the ties which bound the thieves were fragile.[29]

Nevertheless, people's fears in later Elizabethan England did have some grounding in reality, and the evidence that crime was committed by organised gangs was growing in the later 1580s and 1590s, because of the problem of disbanded soldiers. Their identification with crime was a commonplace well before the continuous war of the closing years of the century. In August 1560 the privy council, worried by the demobilisation of troops from the recent Scottish expedition, warned that it was necessary for local authorities to devise means to avoid 'the notable burglaries and felonies' which had characterised the previous winter by taking action against 'idle persons'.[30] The habits of violence soldiers had acquired in the wars were compounded by the difficulties of reintegrating with civilian society, particularly in circumstances of rising unemployment and dearth.[31] It was therefore often only by crime that the discharged soldier was able to support himself, and the fulminations of the privy council against the gangs of highway robbers and burglars terrorising the city and its environs become a

---

[27] *Surrey Indictments. Elizabeth I*, pp. 161, 179; *Calendar of Assize Records. Lent Indictments. Elizabeth I*, ed. J. S. Cockburn (1979), pp. 166, 168, 172–3; G.L.R.O., MJ/SR 217/16; 221/10; 222/25–7.

[28] Cf. B. Geremek, *The Margins of Society in Late Medieval Paris* (Cambridge, 1987), pp. 121–5.

[29] Stow, *Annales*, p. 697. Cf. B.L., Lansdowne MS 75/94.		[30] H.M.C., *Bath*, V. 159–60.

[31] H.M.C., *Hatfield House*, IV. 4–5. Cf. D. Hay, 'War, Dearth and Theft in the Eighteenth Century: the Record of the English Courts', *Past and Present*, 95 (1982), 117–60.

depressing theme of its correspondence in the 1590s, as waves of discharged soldiers repeatedly hit the south coast ports and headed for London.[32]

Among the most highly organised sectors of criminal activity in London was prostitution, on which we are remarkably well informed because in the later 1570s the Bridewell authorities embarked on a determined crack-down on commercial sex in the capital, which remarkably included the prosecution of clients, some of them prosperous citizens. Leading pimps were induced to reveal the locations of bawdy houses about London and the names of their keepers, possibly in return for some immunity from prosecution them-selves.[33] The information in the Bridewell records can be supplemented with details concerning other establishments taken from the records of the Middlesex sessions and King's Bench.

The distribution of the bawdy houses traced is shown in Figure 2. The unsavoury reputation enjoyed by areas like Clerkenwell, St John's Street, Whitechapel, and Shoreditch is confirmed, but it is also striking just how many establishments operated within the supposedly much better governed areas under the City's jurisdiction. It was a commonplace of the literary sources that 'Bawdes ... now sit no longer upon the skirtes of the Cittie, but iett up and downe, even in the cloake of the Cittie, and give more rent for a house, then the proudest London occupier of them all'.[34] Such writers were guilty of exaggeration to the extent that most brothels in the areas under the aldermen's control were nevertheless located in the extramural wards, but there were sufficient establishments in the City's commercial heart to give us pause. It was particularly alarming to the authorities that Richard Watwood should have operated a bawdy house in Lime Street for eight years and that John Shaw should have operated so close to the Guildhall that on one particularly boisterous night 'my lord mayor hard the noyse'![35]

Because of the imprecision of contemporary language, we cannot always be sure how intensive was the illicit sexual activity carried on in these establishments. It is clear that many of those brought before the church courts for bawdry were guilty of nothing more than the taking in of pregnant single women to be delivered. The Bridewell governors do not appear to have used the term with this degree of imprecision.[36] Nevertheless, they frequently failed to differentiate between those who kept established houses of prosti-tution where women were employed by a keeper to give sex, and those who

[32] *T.R.P.*, III. 46–8, 96–7, 105–6, 134–6, 196–7.

[33] For an indication of the immunity of one of the pimps on whose testimony the campaign rested, cf. the remark of William Mekins that 'theare was never a whore in England but if she kicked against him he woulde cause her to be brought to Bridewell ... he could go to mr Winche and fetche 3 or 4 crownes of Mr Winche when he had nede': B.C.B. III, fo. 187ᵛ.

[34] T. Dekker, *Newes from Hell* (1606); sig. B ii; *The Dramatic Works of Thomas Dekker*, ed. F. Bowers (4 vols., Cambridge, 1953–61), II. 391 ('Westward Ho' V.iv. 251–2).

[35] B.C.B. III, fos. 115, 120ᵛ.   [36] G.L., MS 9064/13, fos. 24, 49ᵛ, 55ᵛ, 99ᵛ.

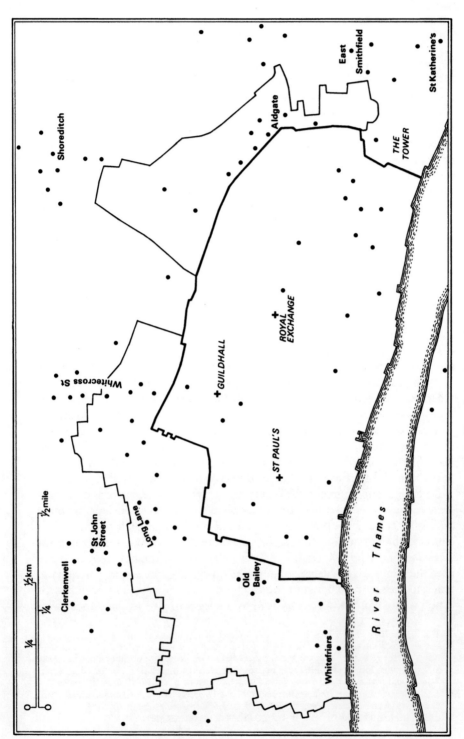

Figure 2 Location of bawdy houses in London, 1575–8.

rented out rooms for independently operating women whose involvement may have been very temporary. The most sophisticated establishments appear to have housed up to nine prostitutes who would pay their keeper a high rent (usually between 4s. and 6s. per week) for lodging and food as well as often also delivering over a portion of their gains (as much as three-quarters) from the clients. These brothels usually had connections with several pimps, men like Melcher Pelse, 'a broker whoe is every day upon thexchange ... a notable bawde and doeth bringe strangers iiij at ones to lewde wemen'.[37] At the other extreme of organisation were the chambers in alleys rented by lodging and alehouse keepers where the more mobile prostitutes did their business. Among the prostitutes themselves there were distinctions between those who rented themselves out as private mistresses forming long-term liaisons, although often residing within a brothel, those whose earnings were tied to the volume of clients they handled, and the more casual prostitutes at the lower end of the market.[38] The first group clearly enjoyed a much greater independence of the control of the brothel keepers, while women in the middle group were likely to be tied much more closely to a particular keeper. The more casual and mobile prostitutes, though nominally independent, were vulnerable to those from whom they rented accommodation, and lacked access to the wealthier clients who patronised the more highly developed establishments with their networks of pimps. The main problem with the Bridewell material is that it furnishes much more evidence on the upper reaches of the market. We know very much more about professional prostitution than we do about the more casual practitioners, and this bias should be borne in mind in the discussion which follows.

The depositions enable the historian to trace connections between the prostitutes, the owners of the bawdy houses and their pimps, and demonstrate the level of cooperation among the brothel keepers who frequently pooled their prostitutes and maintained links with several pimps. Elizabeth Kirkham told the court how she had lodged in Clerkenwell for three months with Gilbert East and his wife, 'abhomynable and lewde persons none worse in the worlde'. Here she served up to four clients a day. But occasionally when another bawd, the infamous Black Luce of Clerkenwell (Mrs Baynam) had 'great guests', she was required to go to her house. Black Luce and East 'agree together and devide the moneye that is given to the harlottes and helpe to tryme them up with swete water and calles (sic) and

---

[37] B.C.B. III, fos. 100 ff., 128ᵛ, 147, 158, 170–1 (Jane Fuller housing nine). For pimps, see ibid. fo. 22ᵛ. For fees, see B.C.B. III, fos. 7ᵛ, 66, 67ᵛ, 113ᵛ, 114, 161, 169, 170ᵛ, 188, 298; IV, fos. 100ᵛ–1.

[38] McMullan, *Canting Crew*, pp. 117–42. For examples of each type, see the careers of Thomasine Breame (B.C.B. III, fos. 13–14ᵛ, 22ᵛ–5), Elizabeth Kirkham (ibid. fos. 279–81), and Ursula Day (B.C.B. II, fos. 82ᵛ, 92, 192; III, fos. 19ᵛ, 254, 422).

The pursuit of stability

cotes and thinges for the purpose fitt for the degree of them that use them'. They divided the profits between themselves.[39] Katherine Jones, 'a little wench' much in demand, was mainly resident at Jane Fuller's on London Wall, but was regularly sent out. Richard Watwood, free of the Grocers and a long-established brothel keeper, often fetched her to his house in Lime Street where her clients included Steelyard men and the son of Alderman Pype, one of the hospital's governors! Thomas Wise who ran a brothel in the Whitefriars carried her to Mr Peter, a Spaniard. Peter also met her at Stephen French's in Basinghall. William Allen, steward to Lady Catlin, met her every Monday at the Bull's Head in Cheap, and one Adamson, an attorney in King's Bench kept her for seven days at Mrs Blewmantel's, yet another bawdy house outside Aldgate.[40] But there were limits to the degree of organisation among the brothel keepers. Although some cooperated with each other at the local level, there are also signs of competition which worked against an integrated network. Leslie Hotson found two brothel keepers taking the peace against each other in 1595.[41] In spite of the fear expressed by the pimp, George Smerken, 'that if it shoulde be knowen that he hath bewrayed this evill rule he shoulde be ill used as thrust with a dagger or crossed on the face with a dagger or such lyke as he goeth in the strete',[42] the authorites gathered evidence with relative ease, another indication of a loose organisation, the contours of which were well known to the agencies of law enforcement. Nor is there any evidence that the relationships between keepers were integrated. Arrangements involving the pooling of prostitutes and the sharing of profits were essentially *ad hoc*. Each keeper was independent and did not owe allegiance to any vertically integrated city-wide network.

It is clear that for some of the brothel keepers prostitution was their main source of income. Of John Shaw, one deponent said that 'he knoweth no trade that Shawe hath to lyve by but bawdrye', of Hamerton and his wife in Southwark, another alleged that 'they harbor many wycked persons and have little other lyveinge'.[43] The precise level of earnings is difficult to establish. Witnesses sometimes recorded their impressions. Mrs Farmer in St John Street 'cannot be soe mayntened as she is with honest lyffe for she hath noe lande or lyveing'. Suspicions had been aroused because she had bought two outfits of silk and two geldings in the space of two months. May's wife without Aldgate, we are told 'hath gotten 3^c li by bawdrye within these 3 yeres'.[44] This is quite plausible, as James Maye was assessed to the 1577 subsidy at £5, placing him among the more substantial inhabitants of

[39] B.C.B. III, fos. 279–80, 281.   [40] Ibid. fos. 100–2, 104, 107, 127, 147^v, 160.
[41] L. Hotson, *Mr W.H.* (1964), p. 253. For further information on the organisation of prostitution, see Archer, 'Governors and Governed', pp. 305–12.
[42] B.C.B. III, fo. 188^v.   [43] Ibid. fos. 10^v, 95^v.   [44] Ibid. fos. 33^v, 328^v.

Portsoken ward. Unfortunately only a few brothel keepers can be traced on the subsidy rolls: whether this reflects their relative lack of wealth or their relatively low profile as a highly mobile group is not clear. Those who can be traced were usually assessed at the £3–£5 level: Richard Watwood, Nicholas Britten, Zachary Marshall, and Robert Whalley at £3, Humphrey Winnington and Robert Barlowe at £5, and Henry Ellis at £7. This placed them in the upper third of London society, among the relatively prosperous craftsmen and petty retailers.[45]

The Bridewell material thus lends some credibility to the literary descriptions of organised prostitution in London. With evidence for at least 100 bawdy houses operating in the later 1570s, it is clear that the closure of the Bankside stews had a minimal effect on the availability of commercial sex in the capital. As one of the keepers put it 'men come to those houses and have harlottes as redely and comenly as men have vittelles honestlye in vittelinge houses for ther monye'.[46] Although metropolitan prostitution lacked centralised control, the leading brothel keepers were well known to each other and prepared to cooperate in pooling their prostitutes.

The records of prosecutions show that there was some truth behind the literary stereotypes; organised pickpocketing and prostitution undoubtedly existed. But the typicality of such crime remains questionable; much crime, in London as elsewhere, was casual and opportunistic, and liaisons, even among the professional criminals, short-term. Furthermore, it would be unwise to assume that the authorities collapsed impotently before the challenges of crime, for the apparatus of criminal prosecution was more highly developed in London than elsewhere, and registered some striking successes, and it is to these issues that the discussion now turns.

THE AGENCIES OF ENFORCEMENT

The household stood in the front line in the maintenance of order throughout early modern English society. Sixteenth-century Englishmen regarded all social and political structures as having their origins in the family, and widely interpreted the fifth commandment to cover obedience to all superiors. As Professor Collinson observes, the writers of the conduct manuals assumed 'a perfect congruence of domestic government with the government of the commonwealth'. Heads of households were vested with kingly authority within the domestic sphere, while the emphasis on the responsibilities of family patriarchs for the household catechising of their children and servants underlined the household's role as a seminary of the church. Such catechising

---

[45] P.R.O., E179/145/252 mm. 14, 16, 59, 79, 81, 146. Unfortunately there are no subsidy assessments for the relevant areas of Middlesex at this date.
[46] B.C.B. III, fo. 318.

also inculcated respect for the earthly hierarchy through its stress on the contribution made by obedience to the achievement of salvation.[47]

The successful fulfilment of these roles was still more crucial to order in the capital because of the high proportion of young people in its population. Rappaport has estimated that apprentices constituted 10 per cent of the City's population in the mid sixteenth century.[48] Through the institution of apprenticeship the young might not only learn a trade but also acquire those habits of piety and respect for authority on which the social order was predicated. The City authorities relied heavily on the commitment of house-holders to social discipline in stressing the responsibilities of masters for their servants' behaviour. Masters were commonly required to pay the costs of maintaining the illegitimate offspring of their servants on the grounds that such a breach of the patriarchal order was the result of their neglect.[49] Likewise a common explanation for outbreaks of disorder in London was the 'want of government' in masters over their servants.[50] In the wake of riots, curfews were routinely imposed on apprentices and masters warned that they would answer for the behaviour of their charges. In the summer of 1596, for example, the aldermen, traumatised by the breakdown in order in the previous year, instructed the beadles to visit every householder to transmit the order that apprentices were to be kept indoors from the beginning of August until Michaelmas.[51]

How effective was the household as a bastion of order? This is a crucial question, requiring much more research than has been possible in the current work. Recent accounts by Ben-Amos, working on Bristol, and Rappaport, working on London, have tended towards an optimistic assessment of apprenticeship as an agency of socialisation. They stress that patriarchal theory was qualified in practice by respect for the personal autonomy of subordinates, that the apprentice's duty to obey was balanced by the reciprocal obligations of the master, and that when relations approached breakdown, there were agencies, in the form of the craft guilds or City courts, available to arbitrate the disputes in ways not always to the master's

---

[47] Hill, *Society and Puritanism in Pre-Revolutionary England*, ch. XIII; S. Amussen, *An Ordered Society: Gender and Class in Early Modern England* (Oxford, 1988), ch. II; J. Morgan, *Godly Learning: Puritan Attitudes Towards Reason, Learning and Education, 1560–1640* (Cambridge, 1986), ch. VIII; Collinson, *The Birthpangs of Protestant England: Religious and Cultural Change in the Sixteenth and Seventeenth Centuries* (1988), ch. III (quotation from p. 60); Todd, *Christian Humanism and the Puritan Social Order*, ch. IV; A. J. Fletcher and J. Stevenson, 'Introduction', in *Order and Disorder in Early Modern England*, ed. A. J. Fletcher and J. Stevenson (Cambridge, 1985), pp. 31–4.

[48] Rappaport, *Worlds Within Worlds*, pp. 232–4; Finlay, *Population and Metropolis*, pp. 66–7.

[49] G.L., MS 12806/2, fos. 39ᵛ, 41, 43ᵛ, 83ᵛ, 163ᵛ, 241.

[50] T.R.P., III. 82–3; C.L.R.O., Jour. 22, fo. 54.

[51] C.L.R.O., Jour. 21, fos. 127ᵛ, 347ᵛ, 356; Jour. 22, fos. 97, 314ᵛ, 476ᵛ; Jour. 23, fo. 114ᵛ; Jour. 24, fos. 11, 18, 19ᵛ, 22ᵛ, 28ᵛ, 37, 141ᵛ; Jour. 25, fos. 238.

favour. It would seem that the reciprocity of the master–servant relationship served to contain tensions, and that the household functioned rather well in identifying its members with the prevailing value system.[52] The contribution of this process to the maintenance of order is suggested by the readiness with which the 'better sort of apprentices' revealed conspiracies to riot to their masters, calling into question the notion of a homogeneous apprentice culture.[53]

But the evidence for the effectiveness of the order of the household is highly ambiguous. Company records provide numerous cases of apprentices complaining that they had not been provided with food and clothing, that they had not been instructed in the craft, and that they had been subjected to unlawful correction of often horrifying severity. The fact that such grievances were treated sometimes sympathetically by the authorities can be interpreted as showing the system's capacity to absorb some of the frustrations of apprenticeship.[54] But these cases should not be discussed without appreciating the power plays that lay behind them. Powerful prejudices worked against apprentices seeking redress from their masters because signs of independence among the young were widely interpreted as mere wilfulness. Thus the assistants of the Mercers' Company complained in 1556 that apprentices 'obstinatlye and wilfullye goe from their masters of there onne free will and follye of stobernes and arrogancie and wolle at their pleasure be sett unto such masters to serve as they will appointe'.[55] It was therefore often difficult for apprentices to achieve redress without the support of their 'friends', that is relatives or other connections prepared to support their claims. Once this is appreciated, the possibility that the cases reaching the assistants represented only a small proportion of the abuses becomes a strong one. In other words the existence of the tensions might be more impressive than the evidence for their successful resolution in what may have been a minority of cases. There can be no doubt that apprenticeship was potentially a highly fraught relationship. The most obvious problem with the reliance on householders to maintain order and socialize the young was the unsuitability of many masters to the demands placed upon them as the complaints by apprentices of ill-treatment clearly demonstrate. For many apprentices, lacking the contacts to achieve an arbitrated settlement with their master or a transfer to another more amenable one, the only recourse was flight. The scale of the breakdown is reflected in the extraordinarily high drop-out rate among London apprentices. Nearly three-fifths of those bound failed to

---

[52] Ben-Amos, 'Apprenticeship'; Rappaport, *Worlds Within Worlds*, pp. 234–7.
[53] *Student's Lamentation; London's Looking-Glasse or the Copy of a Letter Written by an English Travayler to the Apprentices of London* (1621), pp. 39–40.
[54] This is an area in need of further investigation. The Clothworkers' Company records are particularly rich in cases of the type I am rather baldly summarising: Cw. Co., C.M. II–III.
[55] Mc. Co., C.M. II, fo. 286.

complete their terms. Many, perhaps a majority, returned to their homes in the country, but others, hanging about the City, contributed to the problem of vagrancy and petty crime in the capital.[56] We might conclude that although the relationship between masters and servants weakened the solidarity of the young because of the way some apprentices came to identify with their masters, and because of the effects of household catechising, the control of householders and, indeed, the examples they set were never adequate to ensure the full internalisation of the values of order among the young.

Beyond the household, London enjoyed a dense network of highly developed regulatory institutions. The commission of the peace in London was constituted by the recorder and the aldermen who had passed the chair. Sessions of the peace were held to enforce regulative statutes and prosecute misdemeanours such as assault.[57] They were supplemented by special sessions for bawds and scolds and, increasingly in the later sixteenth century, for alehouse regulation.[58] More serious crimes were reserved for the gaol deliveries of Newgate held before judges from the central courts sitting with the mayor, recorder, and senior aldermen. There were between ten and twelve deliveries of Newgate each year compared to the twice yearly assize circuits, so that the capital was much more regularly confronted with the majesty of the law.[59] Elizabethan London also enjoyed a wider range of penal options than many counties at this date because it had been the pioneer of the house of correction. When Bridewell received its charter from Edward VI in 1552, the governors were vested with sweeping powers to search in London and Middlesex and with discretionary powers of punishment. In practice these powers were used against vagrants, disorderly servants, sexual offenders, and an assortment of other offenders against community norms, such as scolds, barrators, and drunks. These offenders were subject to the short, sharp shock treatment of incarceration for average periods of a month and work discipline (beating hemp, scouring City ditches, dredging the Thames, and the like), punctuated by regular whippings.[60] Bridewell's responsibilities overlapped with those of other courts. Hardened vagrants could be indicted at sessions where, between 1572 and 1593, they faced the penalties of felony on a second conviction.[61] Moral offenders could be

---

[56] Rappaport, *Worlds Within Worlds*, pp. 311–15; above, pp. 206–8.
[57] *London Sessions Records*, pp. vii, ix.
[58] Sessions for bawds and scolds are recorded in the journals, e.g. C.L.R.O., Jour. 20, fos. 31ʳ⁻ᵛ, 60, 81, 180, 193, 200. For sessions for the licensing of alehouses, see C.L.R.O., Rep. 22, fo. 164ᵛ.
[59] *London Sessions Records*, p. ix; P.R.O., C 181/1, fos. 11ᵛ–12, 22ʳ⁻ᵛ; G.L.R.O., MJ/SR, gaol delivery wrappers.
[60] *Memoranda on the Royal Hospitals*, p. 84; *Parliamentary Papers*, 1840 XIX. 399; *John Howes' MS 1582*, ed. W. Lempriere (1906), pp. 56–7.
[61] 14 Eliz. I c. 5; 35 Eliz. I c. 7.

presented to the church courts. Although their sanctions of excommunication, penance, and pecuniary fines were less severe than those of Bridewell, they were effective against those with some standing in the community with credit at stake.[62] Masters could bring their disorderly servants before the courts of assistants of their livery companies, which enjoyed the power to whip or stock offenders, or to arrange for their imprisonment on the mayor's commandment.[63] The range of institutions involved in the punishment of crime, and the variety of sanctions they employed, offered prosecutors considerable opportunities to exercise discretion according to their assessment of the severity of the offence.

The effectiveness of these institutions depended on the commitment of the officers of local government to tackling crime. At this level too, regulation in the City was dense. All householders were drafted into the maintenance of order by their obligatory participation in the watch organised on a ward basis, and supervised by the beadle and constable.[64] Each of the twenty-six wards was served by a beadle and subdivided into precincts, of which there were 242 in London, served by constables who were responsible for the maintenance of the queen's peace.[65] The wardmote inquest, a panel of householders elected at the annual wardmotes on 21 December, made presentments of infringements of community norms to the aldermen, and sometimes took discretionary action of its own, for example by requiring offenders to leave the ward. It is true that the regulatory functions of the wardmote inquest were already in decline in the sixteenth century as the enforcement of obligations like the repair of pavements and the cleansing of privies came to outweigh the moral offences, which had been more prominent in the fifteenth century. But, as we have already seen, the withering of the inquest is partly to be explained by the increasing role assumed in local government by the alderman's deputy, the linchpin of order in the capital.[66] At the level of the parish, churchwardens and their sidesmen were required to make regular presentments of offenders to the church courts.[67] Some parishes supplemented this machinery with new officers like the surveyors of inmates, appointed in the Southwark parishes in the closing years of the century to keep a watchful eye over newcomers.[68] The discretionary power wielded by local officers and institutions was reflected in the littering of the city's streets with the apparatus of social discipline. In 1542 the corporation ordered that every alderman provide a set of stocks in his ward, and in 1598,

[62] R. Wunderli, *London Church Courts and Society on the Eve of the Reformation* (Cambridge, Mass., 1981); Ingram, *Church Courts*, ch. XI.
[63] Rappaport, *Worlds Within Worlds*, pp. 209, 234.   [64] G.L., MS 3505, fos. 22ᵛ–3.
[65] Foster, *Politics of Stability*, pp. 29–31.
[66] Pearl, 'Change and Stability', pp. 16–26; above, pp. 68–9.
[67] G.L., MS 9236, second foliated section, fos. 8, 10ᵛ, 12ᵛ, 13, 13ᵛ.
[68] Above, pp. 184–5.

with the passage of new vagrancy legislation which allowed the punishment of vagrants at the discretion of constables, whipping posts were set up in every parish.[69]

Although it is true that in most cases the initiative for the detection and prosecution of property crime lay with the victim, and that such a system had graver weaknesses in the more anonymous city than in rural England, it should already be clear that London's anonymity can be easily exaggerated.[70] Because the primary units of local government were small, the close regulation of the lives of inhabitants was a practical proposition. One of the duties of the beadles attached to each ward was to ensure that newcomers were registered, and that they had testimonials of their good behaviour on their departure. A testimonial system was also in operation in Westminster in the early seventeenth century.[71] It is striking that parishes which paid beadles to find the mothers of foundlings laid in their streets were sometimes rewarded with success.[72]

Moreover, victims of property crime were not entirely unaided. The Goldsmiths' Company records make it clear that individuals who had suffered the theft of plate or jewellery would have the details circulated among the practising goldsmiths to whom the thief might have recourse, and the wardens were diligent in searching out for suspect sales.[73] Legislation by common council in 1595 sought to tighten controls over the second-hand dealers who were thought to provide an outlet for the sale of stolen goods. Registrars were to record all goods pawned or sold, together with personal details concerning those from whom the brokers had received them, 'to the intent ... that every person from whome any such things have been unlawfully taken or convaighed, may make search in the saide Register bookes for the same'.[74] Likewise, a statute of 1589 aimed to make the disposal of stolen horses more difficult by requiring vouchers of vendors.[75] Finally, there are signs that the justices of the peace took a more active role in the detection of certain thefts, particularly where the victims were prominent men. The occasional records of the setting up of privy watches to apprehend suspects, of the use of torture on the orders of the privy council in the investigation of certain large-scale property crimes, and of payments by the

---

[69] C.L.R.O., Rep. 11, fo. 41ᵛ; 39 Eliz. I c. 4; Churchwardens' accounts listed in bibliography.
[70] C. Herrup, 'New Shoes and Mutton Pies: Investigative Responses to Theft in Seventeenth-Century East Sussex', *Historical Journal*, 27 (1984), 811–30.
[71] C.L.R.O., Samuel Barton's Book, fo. 69ᵛ; W.P.L., Minutes of the Court of Burgesses, I.
[72] G.L., MSS 4524/1, fo. 52; 1046/1, fos. 10, 38.
[73] Gs. Co., Reg. K, pp. 100, 118, 132, 184, 185, 255; Reg. L, p. 219.
[74] *Retailing Brokers. Commune Concilium* (1595). For efforts to extend the system to the suburbs, see *L.J.*, II. 208, 209, 214, 217, 219; D'Ewes, *Journals*, p. 545; *H.M.C., House of Lords*, XI. 57–60 (1597); C.L.R.O., Rep. 25, fo. 296; Remembrancia II, nos. 213, 214; *H.M.C., Third Report*, p. 10; *L.J.*, II. 232, 233 (1601).
[75] P. Edwards, *The Horse Trade of Tudor and Stuart England* (Cambridge, 1988), pp. 108–11.

City chamberlain for the pursuit of cozeners, probably all conceal a much wider range of magisterial activity.[76]

For the more mundane offences the victim of a crime could call on the aid of the local constable. Constables played a crucial part in the maintenance of order. They were responsible for the apprehension of vagrants, the supervision of the watch, the enforcement of curfews, and the carrying of offenders to gaol on receiving warrants from the justices of the peace. As the men at the blunt end of local government they have been much maligned.[77] It is hard not to be struck by the complaints of the ever exasperated lord mayors, annoyed that their precepts had been slenderly executed, convinced that the failure to clear the streets of vagrants was due to the poor quality of the men chosen as constables.[78] This is another of those areas where the evidence is highly ambiguous. For every negligent constable prosecuted at the sessions for failure to participate in searches for vagrants, another was launching an indictment for an assault suffered in the conscientious discharge of his duties.[79] But there are also problems with revisionist assessments of constabulary performance. Constables' accounts, which have been used by Joan Kent to show the vigour with which constables approached their duties, cannot entirely demolish the force of contemporary critiques because there is no real comparative standard: we do not know what proportion of vagrants constables ever arrested.[80] Certainly some features of the stereotype of the ignorant and negligent constable of lowly social standing are not applicable in the metropolitan context. They were by no means inexperienced men, usually having served as scavenger, inquestman, and collector of the poor before holding the constableship. Nor were they poor. The majority of constables were assessed to the subsidy, albeit usually on the lower ratings, but this still put them in the wealthiest one-third of London householders.[81] A search of indictments at the Middlesex sessions and in King's Bench for mention of those who served as constables in the precinct of St Katherine's suggests that they were respectable men in the sense that they had not been guilty of serious disorderly conduct.[82] Constables were numbered among those guilty of breaking the assize and of nuisance

[76] Wright, II. 72–3; Lodge, *Illustrations of British History*, II. 15, 205; B.C.B. I, fos. 113–14; J. H. Langbein, *Prosecuting Crime in the Renaissance. England, Germany, France* (Cambridge, Mass., 1975), pp. 45–54; J. S. Cockburn, *Calendar of Assize Records. Home Circuit Indictments. Elizabeth I and James I. Introduction* (1985), pp. 93–101; J. H. Langbein, *Torture and the Law of Proof* (1977), pp. 96–118; C.L.R.O., Chamber Accounts I, fos. 34, 214.

[77] Salgado, *Elizabethan Underworld*, pp. 164–6; McMullan, *Canting Crew*, pp. 180–3.

[78] For a few examples, among many, see C.L.R.O., Rep. 20, fo. 169ᵛ; Rep. 21, fos. 126ᵛ, 247ᵛ; Jour. 25, fos. 257, 290ᵛ.

[79] Contrast P.R.O., KB9/699/36, 61–7 with KB9/699/44, 52.

[80] J. Kent, *The English Village Constable, 1580–1640* (Oxford, 1986), G.L., MS 9680.

[81] Archer, 'Governors and Governed', pp. 283–5.

[82] G.L., MS 9680; search of P.R.O., KB9/662–709; 1030–42; G.L.R.O., MJ/SR 254–400.

offences such as blocking sewers or failing to maintain pavements, but such infractions were probably near universal. For the more serious regulative offences (keeping unlicensed alehouses, lodging suspect persons, running bawdy houses, allowing unlawful games, and receiving inmates) only one man who served the constableship in St Katherine's was prosecuted.[83] It is true that the practice of appointing deputies to perform the office means that it is not always clear who actually discharged the constables' functions. However, because the mayor had to approve deputies, and because deputies were expected to have served the office in their own right, the consquences of deputisation were probably not as serious as we might at first assume and, on the contrary, the practice may have ensured a certain amount of continuity in the office.[84]

Given that the constables were respectable men counted among the more substantial members of their communities, why was there so much complaint of their negligence? The view that one gets from a reading of the fulminations of the aldermen and privy council is highly skewed. First, it draws attention away from embarrassing failures at the upper levels of government. For example, London tradesmen were rather more consistent in their opposition to the theatres than the privy council, which wavered inconsistently between the demands of public order and the pressures of the aristocratic patrons of the stage.[85] As we shall see, much of the blame for the failure of the civic campaign against prostitution should be laid at the door of court interests. Secondly, the complaints against officials ignore the practical problems in the enforcement of the law: the statutory requirement that vagrants be passed from constable to constable once discharged from the city had obvious weaknesses, while the small size of the precincts for which the constables were responsible encouraged them to content themselves with merely passing the vagrant out of their area.[86] Thirdly, there are signs that if adequately coordinated from above the system could achieve at least temporary success. Fleetwood recorded after a privy search in January 1582 that there was 'not one rooge stirring'.[87] It was not a situation which was likely to have lasted for long because London was constantly threatened by new waves of immigrants. Constables were therefore often the scapegoats for failures the real causes of which lay elsewhere. Finally, it should be emphasised that the majority of the complaints relate to only one aspect of constabulary activity, namely the campaign against vagrancy. There are no

---

[83] P.R.O., KB9/670/45; 674/31; E180/105 (John Soper, cook).
[84] C.L.R.O., Remembrancia II, no. 76; Jour. 25, fos. 223ᵛ–4; Jour. 17, fo. 132; G.L.R.O., DL/C/211, fos. 181ᵛ–2.
[85] E. K. Chambers, *The Elizabethan Stage* (4 vols., Oxford, 1923), I. 269–307.
[86] *Middlesex Sessions Records*, new series, ed. W. le Hardy (4 vols., 1936), II. 213.
[87] Wright, II. 166.

complaints that constables failed to cooperate in apprehending suspects of theft and conveying them to gaol on the warrant of the justices.

Nevertheless, the need for a firmer line against vagrancy was an increasingly pressing concern for the City authorities in the later sixteenth century. Two solutions were tried. The first was the multiplication of officials to deal with the problem; the second was the effort to secure better coordination among the constables. Among initiatives of the first kind should be counted the appointment of the beadles attached to the hospitals, each patrolling a group of wards, and serving sensitive points like London Bridge and the Exchange by rotation.[88] The aldermen also tried to extend the responsibility for tackling vagrancy by stressing the obligations of householders. In 1573 vestries were ordered to appoint weekly surveyors for the arrest of vagrants. This office was supposed to rotate among householders, but many vestries appointed one man to fulfil the duties of all, paid by a special rate.[89] Among initiatives of the second kind were the appointment of one of the officers of the mayor's household to oversee constables in 1580, and the appointment of provost marshals by the City in 1596. The large number of fines taken from constables for their failure to obey the marshals shows how heavily their regime bore on the lower levels of City government.[90]

None of these schemes eventually satisfied their promoters. Constantly admonished to 'travayle to clense the stretes of the greate nombres of beggers that noye the citie dayly', and frequently disciplined for their negligence, it is clear that the beadles and surveyors had only a marginal impact on the problem.[91] The problem was that as salaried persons the incumbents were generally lowly members of the community, sometimes lacking in rather essential qualities. Vestries and hospitals had to discipline surveyors and beadles for their disordered lives, even for consorting with vagrants in alehouses.[92] Ratepayers were reluctant to provide the money for the surveyors and the rates were sometimes in arrears. Some vestries doubted whether the money should be paid at all; that of St Bartholomew Exchange, responding to renewed pressure to appoint a surveyor in 1602 and, finding the money collected inadequate to provide the full salary, decided that 'it was

---

[88] G.L., MS 12806/2, fos. 15ᵛ–16, 27, 297ᵛ; B.L., Lansdowne MS 11/19; S.B.H., Ha1/2, fos. 194ᵛ–5.

[89] C.L.R.O., Rep. 18, fos. 126ᵛ–7ᵛ; Jour. 20, fo. 325ʳ⁻ᵛ; *Vestry Minutes of St Margaret Lothbury*, pp. 4, 12; *Vestry Minutes of St Bartholomew Exchange*, pp. 6, 10, 14, 15, 20, 26, 35; G.L., MSS 593/2, fos. 74ᵛ, 76ᵛ, 78; 819/1, fos. 6ᵛ, 7ᵛ; 4165/1, pp. 10, 41.

[90] C.L.R.O., Rep. 20, fos. 169ᵛ, 220ᵛ, 295ᵛ; Rep. 23, fos. 483ᵛ, 502, 517ᵛ; Jour. 24, fo. 250ᵛ; J. Stow, *Abridgement or Summarie of the English Chronicles* (1607), p. 502; B.L., Lansdowne MS 114/4.

[91] G.L., MSS 12806/1, fos. 41ᵛ, 42; 12806/2, fos. 27, 29ᵛ, 32; C.L.R.O., Rep. 15, fo. 461.

[92] G.L., MSS 12806/2, fos. 38ᵛ, 41ᵛ, 64, 93, 207; 594/1, p. 14; S.B.H., Ha1/2, fo. 195; Ha1/3, fo. 218; G.L.R.O., H1/ST/A1/1, fo. 3; *Vestry Minutes of St Margaret Lothbury*, p. 12.

the Constables Charge to looke unto & noe Reason whye the paryshioners should be at any Charge to ease him'.[93]

Nor were the marshals successful in the long term. In 1602 Samuel Rowlands claimed that 'there be more notorious strumpets and their mates about the city than ever there were before the marshal was appointed'.[94] Nor was anyone convinced of the success of the campaign against vagrancy. The privy council was threatening martial law again in 1598, and in 1602 the governors of Bridewell were complaining that the discipline of the constables had broken down with the result that the statute for the restraint of the poor 'is almost utterlie frustrated'.[95] Their failure was a product of financial problems and of the way their responsibilities multiplied. It was essential to pay a decent salary to attract men who would apply themselves diligently to the task in hand, but this raised problems about how the money was to be obtained. After a series of stop-gap measures (including a gift from the aldermen and a loan from the City Chamber), the aldermen settled on supporting the marshals through two-and-a-half City fifteenths, a move which cannot have added to their popularity. Doubts were expressed about whether the City could afford such a high level of funding and Marshal Simpson was not replaced on his death.[96] Moreover, the marshals aroused a great deal of ill-will because constables resented the extra pressures placed upon them. Within a few months of their appointment the aldermen were complaining that 'the Marshalles have been deverslye abused, by certen unruly and disordered persons aswell with threatnings as with reprochfull speeches as by resistance & open violence to their greate discouragement'.[97] These resentments, of course, may be a sign that the marshals were making a real impact. But in the typical response of a hard pressed administration with very limited resources, the initial successes of the marshals simply encouraged the aldermen to multiply their responsibilities into matters as varied as market regulation, the pressment of troops, the suppression of alehouses, and the enforcement of plague regulations.[98] The inevitable result was that their subsequent performance was impaired.

This study of the measures taken to make the campaign against vagrancy more effective sends out conflicting signals. On the one hand, to the extent that they failed to clear the streets of vagrants, they must be counted a failure. But on the other hand, the seriousness of that failure is open to question

[93] *Vestry Minutes of St Bartholomew Exchange*, pp. 14, 20, 47–8; G.L., MS 4165/1, p. 41.
[94] Cited in *Philip Stubbes' Anatomy of Abuses in England in Shakspere's Youth*, ed. F. J. Furnivall, New Shakspere Society, series VI, nos. 4, 6, and 12 (1879–82), p. 281.
[95] T.R.P., III. 196–7; B.C.B. IV, 2 Nov. 1602; C.L.R.O., Jour. 26, fos. 36ᵛ, 49ʳ⁻ᵛ.
[96] C.L.R.O., Rep. 23, fos. 503, 511; Rep. 24, fo. 169; Jour. 24, fos. 111, 226, 310ᵛ.
[97] C.L.R.O., Jour. 24, fo. 150ᵛ; Rep. 23, fos. 508ᵛ, 521ᵛ, 532ᵛ, 538ᵛ, 548ᵛ; Rep. 24, fos. 23, 41, 57, 83ᵛ.
[98] C.L.R.O., Book of Fines, fos. 226, 228; Rep. 26, fo. 179.

because the fears of the elite about the threat that vagrants posed were exaggerated, and because it would be wrong to reach conclusions about the effectiveness of the entire system by judging its success against a problem that was probably insoluble, especially in the context of the subsistence migration of the 1590s. Moreover, the range of initiatives taken by the aldermen is an indication of their responsiveness to the problems confronting them: they did not collapse impotently before the challenge.

Another way of explaining the City's failings is to point to the problems of the suburban districts outside its control. Offenders could easily slip between jurisdictions, and the success of action against vagrancy depended on the diligence of the suburban authorities as much as upon the energy of the City's officers. Unfortunately we are handicapped by a chronic lack of evidence for the suburbs with the important execption of Westminster. It would be wrong to draw the contrast between the strict and punctual government of the City and the disorderly suburbs too starkly because, as we have seen, some forms of petty crime, such as prostitution, flourished in areas under the City's control. But although the extramural City and suburban parishes shared the social problems that came from rapid growth, immigration, and poverty, it is also true that the local governors of Middlesex were less well placed to meet the challenges. In Cornhill there were four constables for 260 households (1:65); in the extramural ward of Portsoken there were four for probably 500 households (1:125). Although the western suburbs showed ratios as favourable as those within the City, 1:140 in St Martin in the Fields and 1:63 in St Margaret Westminster, the situation in the eastern suburbs was more worrying. In the suburban precinct of St Katherine's there were two for probably 490 households (1:245); and in Stepney five or six for 1575 households (1:262 or 315).[99]

The second source of weakness in the suburbs lay at the intermediate level between the justices of the peace and the petty constables, for there was no officer equivalent to the alderman's deputy who played such a crucial role in the City. The four high constables who served the whole of Ossulston hundred (an area covering the suburban districts from Acton and Willesden in the west to Bromley and Hackney in the east, and extending as far north as Finchley and Hornsey) received county rates and supervised the levy of

---

[99] These ratios depend in most cases on estimates of population drawn from baptisms recorded in the parish registers and assuming a mean household size of 4.5: *Register of St Martin in the Fields; Memorials of St Margaret's Church Westminster: the Parish Registers 1539–1660*, ed. A. M. Burke (1914); *The Registers of St Katharine's by the Tower, London*, ed. A. W. Hughes Clarke (Harleian Society Registers, LXXV, 1945); M. J. Power, 'The Urban Development of East London, 1550–1700' (London Ph.D. 1971), pp. 304–6. Figures for the number of households in Cornhill and Portsoken are based on a rate assessment and a contemporary estimate respectively: G.L., MS 4069/1, rakers' wages assessment, 1598; Bodl., Rawlinson MS D796B, fo. 86. Lists of constables occur regularly in the Middlesex sessions records: G.L.R.O., MJ/SR.

troops, but were not involved in day-to-day routine in the way the deputies were.[100] There is an exception to this picture of the weakness of the intermediate levels of government, and it is an exception which nevertheless proves the rule. In 1585 parliament passed a statute establishing the government of Westminster, modelling it very consciously upon that of London. The city was divided into twelve wards, each represented by a burgess chosen by the dean or high steward, and an assistant chosen by the dean or high steward acting with the burgesses. The burgesses were given authority 'to heare examyne determine and punyshe, accordinge to the laws of this Realme or the lawdable Custome of London, all Matters of Incon-tynences, common scoldes, and of Inmates, and common Annoyaunces'. Every burgess with his assistant was to 'doe and deale in everie thinge and thinges as Aldermens deputies in the Cittie of London'.[101] The minutes of their weekly meetings, which commence in 1610, show that strict and punctual government was their watchword as the burgesses implemented a vigorous regime against inmating, fornication, and drunkenness, often proceeding by summary conviction.[102]

No other suburb could have enjoyed a government as sophisticated as this. It is true that the manorial authorities which provided the main institutions of local government in the suburbs were more flexible than has previously been thought,[103] but there is no sign that the leets met regularly enough to provide the kind of tough regulation which characterised Westminster. Indeed a proposal for the statutory government of Westminster, possibly dating from 1585 but much less sophisticated than the measure which eventually passed, points up the weakness of a system of government by leets: 'there is no lawfull warraunte to poonische sooch malefactours but by the Leete or Lawday which by lawe is to be houlden but twise in the yeare only Against which time beeing well knowen sooch malefactors doo avoide and flee from the City and Liberty untill the said Courte and sitteng be past. And then in moquerye retoorne and contynue without any punischmente.'[104] Moreover, where court leet presentments do survive, as in Southwark, they are overwhelmingly concerned with local nuisances and marketing offences. There are a few presentments for moral offences and unlicensed victualling, but hardly in proportion to the prevalence of such offences, nor is there much

---

[100] G.L., MS 9680; W. Lambarde, *The Dueties of Constables, Borsholders, Tithingmen, and Such Other Lowe Ministers of the Peace* (1583), pp. 28–32.

[101] 27 Eliz. I c. 31; B.L., Lansdowne MS 43, fo. 179.

[102] W.P.L., Minutes of the Court of Burgesses I; B.L., Harleian MS 1831; W. Manchée, *The Westminster City Fathers, 1585–1901* (1924).

[103] M. Carlin, 'The Urban Development of Southwark, c. 1200–1550' (Toronto Ph.D., 1983), pp. 571ff., G. Rosser, 'Medieval Westminster: the Vill and the Urban Community, 1200–1540' (London Ph.D., 1984), ch. V.

[104] P.R.O., SP12/177/29.

sign that inmates were regulated through leets.[105] It is true that in some circumstances parish vestries, like that of St Saviour Southwark, could appropriate a considerable amount of regulative power through officers like the surveyors of inmates. But St Saviour's was in some respects untypical (even City parishes like St Botolph Aldgate were slower off the mark with measures to regulate inmates), and vestries always lacked the summary powers enjoyed by the Westminster burgesses.[106] It is unlikely that the powers enjoyed by constables to inflict summary punishments on offenders like drunkards without the involvement of the higher authorities were exercised against any but the most marginal members of the society. Most offenders, for example those rounded up in the periodic tours of inspection by the churchwardens and sidesmen for drinking or victualling during service time, were presented to courts with formal jurisdiction over the offences.[107] The more formal the jurisdiction, the greater was the time spent in securing a conviction, and the more intermittent the prosecution of the offence.

A third problem in the suburbs was the small number of active justices, with the result that the Middlesex magistracy was overworked. The evidence of the justices signing recognisances suggests that in the early 1560s over 70 per cent of the routine work was borne on the shoulders of three men, the noted London lawyer, Robert Chidley, the retired lord chief justice, Sir Roger Cholmeley, and the obscure William Amondesham. Again in the mid 1580s the routine work of the commission was dominated by three men, the undersheriff of the City, Humphrey Smith, the lawyer and former client of the duke of Norfolk, Robert Harris, and the grocer and customs official, Richard Young.[108] Although such records of attendance as survive indicate that more were involved at the sessions themselves,[109] the recognisances understate the burdens on the individual justice because there was so much activity out of sessions which did not necessarily give rise to formal

105 C.L.R.O., Southwark Manor Court Book, 1539–1564; King's Manor Presentments, 1620 and 1624; Guildable Manor Presentments 1620 and 1624.
106 Above, pp. 184–5; *Memorials of Stepney Parish*, ed. G. W. Hill and W. H. Frere (1890–1); G.L., MSS 9234/1–7. Cf. G.L.R.O., P92/SAV/793 for the claims of the St Saviour's vestrymen that theirs was a model administration.
107 G.L., MSS 9064/13, fos. 113ᵛ, 172ʳ⁻ᵛ, 216; 9064/15, fos. 45ᵛ, 74ᵛ, 159, 173ʳ⁻ᵛ, 161ᵛ.
108 Analysis of recognisances taken 1561–3, 1585–7, 1595–7: G.L.R.O., MJ/SR 109–24; 193–203; 258–69; 326–52. For the justices named, see *House of Commons, 1509–1558*, I. 644–6 (Cholmeley); *A Calendar of the Inner Temple Records*, ed. F. A. Inderwick (5 vols., 1896–1901), I, passim; C.L.R.O., Rep. 9, fos. 128ᵛ, 163; Rep. 10, fo. 241ᵛ (Chidley); *House of Commons, 1558–1603*, II. 260 (Harris); III. 396–7 (Smith); Benbow, 'Index'; C.L.R.O., Jour. 22, fo. 347; P.R.O., C66/1312, mm. 40–1 (Young).
109 P.R.O., E362/1/5–8; 1/14; 1/16A; E137/23/3. For example, Dean Goodman was regular in attendance at sessions of the peace, and signed the poor relief accounts of the Westminster parishes, though not taking many recognisances: W.P.L., F304–24.

documentation. Two justices of the peace had the power to suppress and license alehouses, to imprison those refusing to pay poor rates, to determine responsibility for the maintenance of bastard children, to imprison servants refusing the prescribed wages, and to grant security for good abearing. Among the powers of the single justice, Lambarde lists the imprisonment of those keeping unlawful games, the dispatch of vagrants to gaol, and the arbitration of disputes between masters and servants.[110]

The burdens of attendance at sessions were that much greater in the metropolitan area than elsewhere. Gaol deliveries in London and Middlesex took place up to twelve times a year in the later sixteenth century in contrast to the twice yearly deliveries of the gaols of the counties on the assize circuits.[111] Each gaol delivery was accompanied by a sessions of inquiry at which indictments were examined by the grand jury to be found true or not. These were usually held on the day before the commission of gaol delivery sat. Thus in 1586 Fleetwood notes the holding of a sessions of inquiry for London on Thursday 1 July in the morning, and at Finsbury for Middlesex in the afternoon at which 'all such as were to be arraigned for felonie at the gaole delyvery were indycted'. On the following day the gaol was delivered at the Justice Hall in the Old Bailey, the justices sitting from 7 a.m. to 7 p.m.[112] The supervision of privy searches for vagrants, on which Fleetwood claimed to spend 100 nights a year, were also exacting. 'I have not leasure to eat my meat, I am so called upon', he lamented.[113] The recorder may not have been quite so remarkable as his self-advertisement suggests; the evidence of committals to Bridewell confirms the suggestions of the recognisances that Jasper Fisher was a more diligent justice.[114] Finally the magistracy was only a part-time occupation because most of the active core of Middlesex justices held other burdensome offices.[115] The strains on the commission are reflected in Fleetwood's complaint against a bill of 1585 requiring that bail be not granted except before two justices: 'the Recorder of London must be made a dogbolt to run to Justice Young at Estcheap & Justice harrys in St Johns, Mr lyvetenant at the tower'.[116] In the same parliament it was pointed out in the debates on the bill for the government of Westminster that there were few resident justices of the peace in Westminster, and that if non-

[110] W. Lambarde, *Eirenarcha, or of the Office of the Iustices of the Peace* (1581), pp. 190–272, esp. 191–4, 243–4, 266–72. Cf. C. Read, *William Lambarde and Local Government: his 'Ephemeris' and Twenty-nine Charges to Juries and Commissions* (Ithaca, New York, 1962), pp. 15–52; G. Leveson-Gower, 'Notebook of a Surrey Justice', *Surrey Archaeological Collections*, 9 (1888), 161–232; A. J. Fletcher, *Reform in the Provinces: the Government of Stuart England* (1986), pp. 80–3, 148–58.
[111] National Library of Wales, Chirk Castle MS A 17; P.R.O., E137/23/3; G.L.R.O., MJ/SR, gaol delivery wrappers.
[112] Ibid. II. 186.   [113] Ibid. II. 171.   [114] B.C.B. II and III, passim.
[115] Archer, 'Governors and Governed', pp. 293–4, 296.
[116] B.L. Lansdowne MS 43, fo. 172.

residents dealt with Westminster causes it would be to the detriment of the government of their own areas.[117]

One suspects that the pressure of routine work was such that the magistrates were unlikely to have felt enthusiastic about extraordinary policing activity such as the coordination of privy searches for vagrants. It is striking that the bouts of reforming zeal against alehouses and vagrants recorded in Fleetwood's letters always came in response to a directive from the centre, privy councillors or the queen herself.[118] When the court was away from the capital, groups of councillors would be left in London to keep an eye on affairs in the city, regularly reporting to the councillors in attendance. Periodically representatives of the metropolitan authorities would be summoned to the Star Chamber to be given instructions on those areas of policy currently exercising the council.[119] Sir William Cordell and Sir Gilbert Gerrard as successive masters of the rolls seem to have been used by the council as coordinators of the metropolitan magistrates. They frequently headed the list of addressees of letters from the council concerning such matters as searches for vagrants and the enforcement of regulations relating to building and Lent.[120] Towards the end of the reign Lord Chief Justice Popham also adopted a high profile in the policing of the capital. It was probably Popham who was responsible for the requirement that Middlesex constables make fortnightly reports on aspects of social regulation in March 1602; he was definitely responsible for the investigations of the following year into the operation of the poor laws in the metropolitan area; he badgered the Middlesex and Surrey authorities into providing houses of correction; he advised local authorities on the statutes against subdivision of tenements; and his hostility to prostitution earned him a reputation for the prosecution of 'poor pretty wenches out of all pity and mercy'.[121]

Although difficult to quantify because of the informal means by which pressure was often exercised and because letters from the council did not always reflect an initiative which originated there,[122] conciliar involvement in the policing of the capital was becoming more intense in the later 1580s and 1590s when social problems escalated and poverty assumed more threatening forms. From the earliest years of the war the council was regularly prodding the metropolitan magistrates into action against vagrancy, instructing the Middlesex and Surrey authorities to confer with the

[117] Ibid. fo. 179.   [118] Wright, II. 18–19, 88, 164–6.   [119] Ibid. II. 18–19.
[120] Ibid. II. 18–19, 62, 66, 67, 164; A.P.C., IX. 388; X. 40, 146–7, 218; XII. 37; XIV. 356; XV. 418; XVI. 336–7; XVII. 214; XIX. 278–80.
[121] P.R.O., SP46/163, fo. 216; W.P.L., F6039; G.L., MS 9680, fo. 12; G.L.R.O., P92/SAV/450, pp. 346, 353; *Chamberlain Letters*, I. 48; B.L., Harleian MS 6686, fo. 308. Cf. Fletcher, *Reform in the Provinces*, pp. 137–8, 231, 356.
[122] C.L.R.O., Rep. 21, fos. 475ᵛ–6; A.P.C., XV. 256.

230 The pursuit of stability

lord mayor to coordinate their searches.[123] Deteriorating standards of public order contributed to the council's greater involvement in this period. The agitation of disbanded soldiers, newly returned from the Portuguese expedition in August 1589, resulted in the drawing up of orders for standing watches by Walsingham and Wolley, and prompted the council to take greater precautions against the return of the next wave of soldiers in November. The justices of the peace within six miles of London were ordered to confer with the master of the rolls and the lord mayor to set up nightly watches, and provost marshals were appointed within the Home Counties.[124] A further tightening of the screws occurred after the riots of 1595. Martial law was imposed on the City and a special commission consisting of London and Middlesex magistrates established to sit twice a week for the examination of vagrants. Although the mayor made the initial request for martial law, it is clear that the council was losing confidence in his government. Burghley himself drafted the order for Wilford's appointment as marshal, and the memorandum for his appointment is in his hand.[125] Searches of vagrants in the 1590s were regularly conducted at the council's behest: round-ups in March, April, and June 1591, August 1592, April 1593, and early 1594 were definitely prompted by the council. In March 1595 Burghley himself drafted orders for a privy search through London and Westminster.[126]

The council's increasing intervention in the policing of the capital in these years in part reflected the severity of the pressures to which the city was subjected, but it was probably also related to a weakening of the bonds between the City magistrates and their suburban colleagues. Whereas the bench of the 1570s and 1580s had been dominated by figures with strong City connections, that of the mid 1590s apparently had fewer such ties with the aldermen. Only John Croke, the recorder, and Nicholas Collins, a member of the City's legal counsel, can be linked with the City establishment. On two occasions in this decade the council complained that as soon as alehouses were suppressed by one set of justices they were set up again by others.[127] Although the commission of the 1590s was more broadly based than its predecessors, with more justices taking an active role, it may have lost something in coordination.

---

[123] A.P.C., XVI. 136, 336–7; C.L.R.O., Jour. 22, fos. 128ᵛ, 188ᵛ, 239ᵛ, 245, 250.
[124] Stow, *Annales*, p. 756; A.P.C., XVII. 453–4; XVIII. 54–5, 222–5, 229; T.R.P., III. 39–40, 44–8; C.L.R.O., Jour. 22, fos. 309ᵛ, 312, 313ᵛ, 314, 317ᵛ, 341, 347ᵛ.
[125] T.R.P., III. 82–3, misdated by the editors; B.L., Lansdowne MSS 66/93–95; 78/53; 78/64; *Orders Prescribed...* (1595; S.T.C., 8243).
[126] C.L.R.O., Jour. 23, fos. 6ᵛ, 8ᵛ, 15ᵛ, 18ᵛ (March/April 1591), 34 (June 1591), 123, 126ʳ⁻ᵛ, 127ʳ⁻ᵛ; B.L., Harleian MSS 6995/81; 7018/6 (August 1592); A.P.C., XXIV. 193–4; *An Order to be Published...* (1593; S.T.C. 16713.5); C.L.R.O., Jour. 23, fos. 260, 264, 268ᵛ, 296ᵛ (early 1594); B.L. Lansdowne MS 75/89 (March 1594).
[127] A.P.C., XXV. 437; XXX. 176–7.

To emphasise the privy council's role in coordinating action against crime in the metropolitan area is to run the risk of too readily adopting its own rather skewed perception of the world where failures were always the result of shortcomings at the lower levels of government. But when we look at the informal dimension to the involvement of the court and council in the campaign against crime a more complex picture emerges. Court connections, for example, have a major role to play in explaining the failure of the civic campaign against prostitution. Many brothels apparently remained immune from prosecution for long periods after the governors of Bridewell received information on them. They failed, for example, to take action against John Honman of Southwark until June 1578, although they had known about his activities as early as December 1576.[128] Some establishments were apparently not proceeded against at all, either in Bridewell or at the sessions. Most extraordinary is the immunity of such notorious offenders as Black Luce of Clerkenwell. In other cases the sanctions applied by Bridewell appear to have been relatively slight. Elizabeth Hamerton who kept a bawdy house in Lord Montague's liberty in Southwark was required in June 1576 to enter sureties for her honest behaviour, and to depart within twelve days.[129] Later in the same year, Joanne Higgens, the keeper of Worcester House, was discharged on one Mr Somerset's word that he would be bound for her.[130] Anne Bartifield, 'who some do calle Ladie Bartifeld ... an naughtie lewde and evell woman', was discharged at the suit of George Dudley and Thomas Morris, who were bound for her good behaviour and departure from the city. Such sanctions often lacked effect. Bartifield turned up nine months later in Lambeth.[131] Indeed the only impact the campaign seems to have had besides contributing to the occupational hazards of brothel keeping lay in the way in which it contributed to their mobility. Driven out of one quarter of the city they would set up elsewhere.[132]

The immunity from prosecution enjoyed by some keepers was the result of protection from figures at court. London's bawdy houses were another of the capital's service industries directed towards gentry visitors. Several witnesses recorded their impressions: 'dyvers gentlemen with cheynes of golde' patronised Mrs Farmer's establishment in St John's Street; Honman's in Southwark was the resort of 'very Auncyent folkes and welthye'; Mary Dornelly was abused by 'gentlemen and welthye men with velvett gaskens and such

[128] B.C.B. III, fos. 125, 188, 319.   [129] Ibid. fo. 19.   [130] Ibid. fo. 62ᵛ.
[131] B.C.B. I, fos. 142ᵛ, 209ᵛ.
[132] For other examples, see C.L.R.O., MC1/5B/184; B.C.B. III, fos. 193ᵛ–6, 197ʳ⁻ᵛ, 266; P.R.O., KB9/1022/65 (Gilbert East); B.C.B. III, fos. 115, 118–24, 359ᵛ, 417; G.L.R.O., MJ/SR 215/5 (John Shaw); B.C.B. III, fos. 115, 316ᵛ; C.L.R.O., Jour. 20, fo. 411ᵛ (Richard Watwood); B.C.B. II, fo. 214; III, fos. 128, 147; P.R.O., KB9/648/57; 1021/280 (Jane Fuller); C.L.R.O., Jour. 19, fo. 395; B.C.B. II, fo. 105ᵛ; III, fos. 317ᵛ, 379; G.L.R.O., MJ/SR 215/9; 220/9; 228/11 (Thomas Bowmer).

apparell and not for the comen sorte'; Shaw's wife catered for merchants of the Steelyard 'for she will have none but merchantes to her house to the wemen'.[133] The firmer profiles of the clientele of these brothels, which can be obtained from the extraordinarily detailed depositions of some of the pimps and keepers, confirm that most clients were recruited from the foreign merchant community, the staffs of the embassies, the gentlemen of the Inns of Court, servants to prominent court or government figures, and sometimes from the ranks of prominent citizens.[134] These patterns of clientage meant that Bridewell's investigations often stirred muddy waters near the centre of power. In January 1579 the governors found themselves listening to the revelations of one Gilbert Periam who pimped for his master, Sir Horatio Palavacino, luminary of Elizabeth's court, diplomat, and financier. Palavacino had required his servant to find 'some mayden to abuse who had not been dealte with all before'. Periam reported that he was unable to find such a girl in London, so his master dispatched him with a horse and 10s. to Guildford![135] It is hardly surprising that well-connected establishments were assured the protection of powerful interests. Jane Fuller's boast that 'the Quenes pardon will save her' was not unfounded.[136] In 1559 Lord Robert Dudley intervened on behalf of Helen Andrewes indicted by the wardmote inquest of Cheap; in 1564 the earl of Pembroke and other privy councillors wrote on behalf of John Thrush similarly indicted; John Hollingbrig, gentleman, who was running a brothel in Holborn in the mid 1570s wore the livery of Lord Ambrose Dudley.[137] When the City constables attempted to close down Mrs Higgens' brothel operating out of Worcester House, the earl of Worcester counter-attacked with suits in King's Bench against the officers involved.[138] Elizabeth Barlowe, sentenced in May 1578 by a sessions for bawds and scolds to the pillory and incarceration in Bridewell, was spared punishment at the suit of 'Mr Browne which kepeth my Lord of Lecesters house'.[139]

When the authorities attempted to take action against wealthy or well-connected offenders, the controversies surrounding Bridewell were openly aired with highly embarrassing consequences to the City. In 1577 a wealthy London goldsmith, Anthony Bate, filed a bill in the court of Star Chamber accusing Robert Winch, the treasurer of Bridewell, of having framed him on a charge of sexual incontinency. Winch was accused of the most dubious methods in his quest for evidence. Henry Boyer, a pimp, claimed that he was

[133] B.C.B. III, fos. 27^v, 134^v, 279, 359^v.   [134] Ibid. fos. 118–24.
[135] Ibid. fo. 377. Cf. B.C.B. II, fo. 235.
[136] Ibid. fo. 50^v.
[137] C.L.R.O., Rep. 14, fo. 149^v; Rep. 15, fos. 306^v, 338; B.C.B. II, fo. 117^v; *Middlesex County Records*, I. 94–5.
[138] C.L.R.O., Rep. 19, fo. 198.
[139] B.C.B. III, fos. 311, 380; C.L.R.O., Jour. 20, fo. 411^v.

kept prisoner for five days having nothing to lie on 'other than the bare earth and the meate he then had was onely suche thynne porredge and black breade as a dogge would skarse eate', that he was made to witness the whipping of a prostitute with forty lashes, and advised that he would receive such a whipping every Saturday until he confessed.[140] In fact Bate was unquestionably guilty, finally admitting as much before the aldermen in 1581.[141] That Bate was a charlatan is not of course the point. The truth is that he was able to convince many influential people that the Bridewell establishment was corrupt, and the controversies convinced others that the campaign against prostitution was a misdirected effort. Bate's campaign was accompanied by the strenuous lobbying of courtiers and councillors: the pimp, Richard Rolles, had poured forth his grievances before Sir James Croft and boasted that 'he had given the masters of Bridewell such a pusshe that Bridewell shoulde be putt downe by the wordes he had spoken before Sir James Acrofte'.[142] By 1579 the aldermen were complaining that the case was causing 'great troubles threateninges and daunger of assaultes to the governors'.[143] That this pleading was not exaggerated is shown by John Richardson's assault on Winch 'quyetly syttinge at his doore in Chepesyde', and by Sir George Carey's dismissal of Winch as a man whom 'I know and shortelie the world will iudge to be one of the worst members that can live in our common wealth'.[144] Even someone as sympathetic to the hospitals as John Howes, looking back over the controversies of the past few years in 1582, felt that the governors were wasting their time in the 'carefull and dilligent searching oute of mens wyves and other gallant gyrles' while the poor still swarmed in the streets.[145]

This telling evidence of the way in which court connections compromised the City's campaign against prostitution raises the question whether similar pressures affected more serious types of crime. Influence at court was regularly mobilised by convicted felons to secure reprieves and pardons. As Douglas Hay puts it, 'mercy was part of the currency of patronage'.[146] There is no more insistent complaint in Fleetwood's letter than that of the traffic in reprieves at court: 'these secretories, chamberkepers, and solicitors in the court, procure many letters from theire lords and ladies upon untrue suggestions, the which letters do greatly hurte ... twentie poundes for a reprieve is nothing although it be but for ten daies'. Well might he agree with the marquess of Winchester that 'when the court is furthest from London,

[140] P.R.O., STAC5/B11/18; B21/3; B53/40; B108/33.
[141] C.L.R.O., Rep. 20, fos. 115v–16.
[142] P.R.O., STAC5/B11/18; B.C.B. III, fos. 165v, 186v, 190v–1, 242, 296, 329.
[143] B.L., Additional MS 48019, fo. 151.
[144] C.L.R.O., Rep. 19, fo. 211v; Remembrancia I, no. 80.   [145] *T.E.D.*, III. 441.
[146] D. Hay, 'Property, Authority and the Criminal Law', in *Albion's Fatal Tree*, ed. D. Hay, P. Linebaugh *et al.* (Harmondsworth, 1975), pp. 40–9.

then is there the best justice done in all England'.[147] But there is no way we can determine how far reprieves undermined the efforts of the authorities against crime because we do not know in what circumstances they were issued. Were they another means by which discrimination entered the operation of the criminal law, mitigating its severity in order to filter out the hardened offender from those whose criminality reflected personal misfortunes? Or were they an indication that people on the fringes of the court themselves had connections among the criminal fraternity?[148] The very peculiarity of the patterns of clientage of prostitution suggests that the connections of brothel keepers with the court were not typical of other types of criminal activity, and it would therefore be unwise to read sinister motives into the involvement of courtiers in the granting of reprieves.

There remains the problem of the extent to which the liberties about London posed a threat to the maintenance of law and order. The liberties were the private franchises ringing the City which had passed at the Reformation from ecclesiastical corporations to the Crown and thence to private interests to whom they were sold. John McMullan has alleged that the liberties were 'free zones immune from city policing and authority ... independent and unregulated deviant territories', and that their 'communities gave widespread support to and participated in criminal projects'.[149] But although the liberties were undoubtedly a thorn in the flesh of the corporation, as shown by its largely fruitless efforts to purchase them and the litigation it frequently launched against their owners, it is far from clear that their existence had the dire consequences McMullan has asserted.

It is true that in an emotional moment in the parliament of 1601, when the City's pretensions to suppress the liberties were attacked, Sir Stephen Soame claimed that the liberties were 'the very sink of sin, the nurcery of naughty and lewd people, the harbour of rogues, theeves, and beggars, and maintainers of idle persons; for when our shops and houses be robbed, thither they fly for relief and sanctuary'.[150] But the liberties were not utterly lawless. On the contrary, local government was sometimes well developed. In the 1590s the precinct of St Katherine's boasted two resident justices, the master of the precinct, Sir Julius Caesar, and the more active Henry Thoresby. The accounts of the two constables chosen each year by the master show the enforcement of local sanctions such as the carting and ducking of offenders, as well as illustrating the at least intermittent responsiveness to directives from above: constables answered articles at the sessions and carried vagrants off to the Sessions House or Bridewell in periodic round-ups.[151] Likewise, in

[147] Wright, II. 21, 170, 243, 245, 247.
[148] C. B. Herrup, *The Common Peace: Participation and the Criminal Law in Seventeenth-Century England* (Cambridge, 1987), chs. V–VII; McMullan, *Canting Crew*, pp. 144–6.
[149] Ibid. pp. 52–63; Tomlinson, *Minories*, p. 165; Archer, 'Governors and Governed', p. 301.
[150] Townshend, *Historical Collections*, p. 325.   [151] G.L., MS 9680; P.R.O., E180/105.

a petition to Burghley and Bacon against the bowling allies set up by Henry Naillor, the inhabitants of the Blackfriars claimed that hitherto 'by the care and industry of such of better sort and calling' the precinct had been kept 'in good order'. Constables were appointed by the justice of the verge who was also responsible for the licensing of victuallers. Incontinent persons were carted, sent to Bridewell, and presented to the church courts.[152] Soame's outburst in 1601 was the only occasion on which it was alleged by the City authorities that the liberties harboured felons and fugitives from justice. The complaints usually turned on much more mundane matters such as the enforcement of trade regulations and the liability of the residents to pay City taxes and serve offices in the City.[153] Indeed, it seems to have been accepted that the aldermen enjoyed jurisdiction over felons sheltered in the liberties. In 1581 the judges ruled that robberies and murders occuring in the friars should be enquired of within the City as in the past. When deferring the implementation of their report the privy council's injunction to the City authorities against meddling in the liberties was qualified by a proviso for the punishment of felons 'as heretofore'.[154]

Clearly there were problems in the policing of the capital, but they should be kept in perspective. The City proper had a relatively well-coordinated system of policing, and machinery was available for the close regulation of the life of the inhabitants. In the suburbs the problems were more serious because constables were thinner on the ground, the links between constables and the justices were weak, the justices themselves were overworked, and manorial institutions did not offer the same opportunities for close social regulation as the summary powers of the deputies. Some of the alleged weaknesses are much less compelling. Although the Middlesex justices were not always well coordinated among themselves, at least there is little evidence of jurisdictional conflict with the City authorities. The multiplication and duplication of jurisdictions that is so frequently alleged as a source of serious weakness in tackling crime and delinquency did not necessarily have deleterious effects. Bridewell, for example, duplicated some of the functions of the church courts in the investigation of sexual misdemeanours but, apart from some friction in Mary's reign, there is little indication of tension between them. On the contrary, High Commission sometimes sent offenders into Bridewell for punishment, and in other cases the only consequence of duplication was that delinquents were punished twice for the same offence.[155] The time spent by the privy council in dealing with the

[152] P.R.O., SP46/15, fo. 41; A.P.C., XIII. 76–7; B.L., Lansdowne MS 155, fos. 80ᵛ–1; B.C.B. II, fos. 23, 24; III, fo. 62. Bridewell's warrants were effective in the liberties: B.C.B. II, fos. 57 (Blackfriars), 98ᵛ, 104ᵛ (Norton Folgate).
[153] C.L.R.O., Rep. 16, fos. 316ᵛ, 318ᵛ; Rep. 17, fos. 179ᵛ, 261ᵛ; Rep. 18, fo. 178; Rep. 25, fo. 349; B.L., Lansdowne MS 74/32.
[154] C.L.R.O., Rep. 20, fo. 19ᵛ; A.P.C., XII. 19.   [155] B.C.B. III, fos. 302ᵛ, 327, 339.

problems of metropolitan policing should not be read simply as an indictment of the performance of the local officers, but is testimony to their own fears of disturbance in the capital, and these fears were certainly exaggerated in the 1590s.[156] The higher profile they adopted does not necessarily mean that the local administration was collapsing. Nor are there any signs that some areas become entirely 'no-go areas' for the forces of law and order. The authorities did not collapse impotently before the challenges. Rather they responded to them with initiatives like the closer regulation of second-hand dealers in the 1590s to tackle the problem of receiving. Action against prostitution was less successful than against other types of crime, but this was because of a lack of consensus within the elite about the wisdom of moral reformation when it ascended the social gradient.

Moreover, there are some indications that the authorities achieved a high level of knowledge about the contours of the underworld. This is of course a judgement which it would never be possible to prove conclusively: one could always argue that the knowledge of the authorities covered only a small fraction of criminal activity. But there are one or two striking pieces of evidence. Those criminals who were apprehended frequently disgorged details concerning others. Sixteen cutpurses were named by Thomas Getley in 1560, eight by Richard Smethwick in May 1576; a bill found on one William Deane in the same year gave the names of sixteen cozeners about the city.[157] One advantage of the terrifying penal sanctions of the period was that they could be manipulated to encourage the flow of information. Stow explains that John Dytche, the professional horse thief, was reprieved because he revealed the names of accomplices about the capital.[158] Fleetwood's letters hint at an intimate knowledge of the criminal population of the metropolis. In July 1585 he was able to name forty-four 'Maisterless men and Cut-purses whose practice is to robbe Gentlemen's chambers and Artificers' shoppes in and about London', and eighteen notorious 'Harboring-houses for Maisterless-men' about the capital.[159]

Equipped with this level of knowledge, the agencies of law enforcement had more impact on the problem than we might at first think possible. Greene suggests that general warrants against cutpurses were issued by the magistrates using the information on the underworld they had gathered. Whenever a purse of 'great value' was stolen, the victim obtained warrants from the justices to the keepers of Newgate 'to take up all the nips and foists about the City, and let them lie there while the money be re-aunswered unto the party'. One can see little reason why he should have fabricated such a

---

[156] Above, pp. 8–9.
[157] B.C.B. I, fo. 90; III, fos. 3, 287. Getley was discharged after promising to help the authorities in apprehending them.
[158] Stow, *Annales*, p. 697. Cf. B.L., Lansdowne MS 75/94.   [159] Wright, II. 248–50.

story.[160] Fleetwood himself hints at such practices when promising to compile a list of cutpurses 'that I may know what new be sprung up this last year and where to find them if need be'.[161]

Occasionally a note of optimism entered Fleetwood's letters. At Whitsun 1586 he was able to report that there were few dealings in criminal causes because most of the leading criminals were in prison. The apprehension of key individuals could make a substantial impact on the problem: in the same letter he reports that the 'Genner or Ingen' (sic) was in custody 'the want wherof is a great stay of many burglaries'.[162] There is, of course, an element of self-congratulation and wishful thinking in this remark, and it would be ludicrous to suggest that there was any hope of eliminating crime. But ultimately the system's claims to effectiveness rest on its deterrent impact, impossible to quantify, in the theatre of execution. Londoners were regularly treated to spectacles which drove home the lesson that crime did not pay. Writing of the near-monthly sessions of gaol delivery, William Smith remarked in 1588:

> there is condemned at one sessions, 30, 40, 50, yea sometymes 60 parsons, besydes those that are burned in ye hand & quitt by proclamacion of which parsons so condemned there is executed in one day 20 or 30 & I have knowne 36 at a tyme to suffer And within a moneth after peradventure as many more.[163]

This was, we should not forget, probably the bloodiest period in the history of the English criminal law, and the lessons of order were regularly articulated.

PUNISHMENTS AND POLICIES

The difficulties involved in exploring trends in the prosecution of crime in London are even more forbidding than elsewhere. This is, in the first place, a reflection of the very partial coverage of the sources. There is no extant sessions material for the City proper until the early Jacobean period, and the Elizabethan Middlesex gaol delivery files are by no means complete.[164] The scale of the loss is impossible to estimate without the gaol delivery calendars which do not commence until the early seventeenth century. This means that one crucial variable, namely the volume of indicted crime, cannot be established. We cannot be certain whether the pattern of indicted crime in the metropolitan area followed that of the Home Counties, where large increases

---

[160] *Elizabethan Underworld*, ed. Judges, p. 165. Cf. Bodl., Ashmole MS 195, fo. 196ᵛ.
[161] Wright, II. 74.
[162] Ibid. II. 292–3.
[163] B.L., Harleian MS 6363, fo. 10ʳ⁻ᵛ; J. A. Sharpe, '"Last Dying Speeches": Religion, Ideology and Public Execution in Seventeenth-Century England', *Past and Present*, 107 (1985), 144–67.
[164] *Middlesex County Records*, I. xx–xxiv, xxix–xxx; *London Sessions Records*, pp. xii–xiii.

have been observed in the later sixteenth century.[165] There is a strong presumption in favour of such a trend as the volume of surviving indictments is certainly much greater in the 1580s and 1590s, and the case load at individual sessions greater to judge from the occasional calendars of prisoners. But it is difficult to be more precise than this in an area where precision is important because of the particularly acute problem of the relationship of an increasing volume of indictments to an increasing population. We cannot be certain whether the per capita prosecution rate was higher in the 1580s and 1590s without firm statistics on the volume of indictments, and preferably statistics which included crime prosecuted in the City, which will never be obtainable for the Elizabethan period. Given the nature of the record survival all that we can meaningfully establish is the changing treatment of the various classes of property crime by the juries and judges.[166]

The Bridewell material is rich in depositions, but the court books only survive patchily, and where they are extant do not appear to record all the offenders incarcerated in the house of correction. This is clear from a comparison of the 954 offenders recorded in the year 1600–1 with the 2,730 that the governors said passed through in that year in their annual report.[167] A discrepancy of this size is difficult to account for. It is probable that the court books did not consistently record the offenders sent in from other jurisdictions, like the Spaniards sent there by the privy council or those dispatched to Bridewell from the sessions of gaol delivery, where examination by the governors was not necessary.[168] Alternatively, it is likely that many offenders were dealt with by small numbers of governors acting informally out of court. The orders of 1557 gave the treasurer acting with one almoner considerable discretionary power to examine 'all such beggers, vagabondes, strumpets, or single women gotten with childe, and other personnes that shall happen to be taken and brought before you . . . and them to . . . comit to prison, reprove, banishe, put to labour, punishe, or being deseased, to admit into the hospitals at your discretion'.[169] Therefore arguments about shifts in patterns of prosecution have to rest on the assumption, which must remain unproven, that those recorded in the court books are representative of the full range of offenders.

The interpretation of the trends in the types of offender appearing before

---

[165] J. S. Cockburn, 'The Nature and Incidence of Crime in England, 1559–1625: a Preliminary Survey', in *Crime in England, 1550–1800*, ed. J. S. Cockburn (1977), pp. 66–7.

[166] Below, pp. 245–8.

[167] B.C.B. IV, 28 Mar. 1601. The numbers of inmates passing through were 2,043 in 1598–9, 1,952 in 1599–1600: ibid. 4 Apr. 1599, 4 Apr. 1600.

[168] A.P.C., XVI. 205, 210; XXII. 41–2, 220; XXIII. 373; XXIV. 190–1; T.E.D., III. 417; G.L.R.O., MJ/SR 180/16; 209/23; B.C.B. III, fos. 266, 266ᵛ, 286.

[169] *Memoranda on the Royal Hospitals*, p. 87.

Table 6.1. *Cases heard before the governors of Bridewell, 1559–60, 1576–7, and 1600–1 compared*

	1559–60	1576–7	1600–1
Prostitutes	97	69	41
Bawds/Pimps	58	42	13
Clients of prostitutes	16	73	9
Other fornication/adultery: males	20	111	104
females	30	128	139
Bigamy	3	6	4
Rape	6	6	2
Child abuse	2	0	0
Sexual offenders: total	232	435	312
Vagrants	84	176	503
Vagrants with false licences	0	9	0
Forging licences	0	3	1
Vagrancy: total	84	188	504
Runaway, disobedient servants	33	23	16
Thieving and pilfering by servants	50	14	0
Encouraging servants in lewdness	9	0	0
Servants playing unlawful games	2	0	0
Theft	25	19	4
Cozenage	0	9	9
Cutpursing	5	5	3
Receiving stolen goods	6	3	0
Drunkenness	0	7	3
Scolding	7	3	0
Defamation	6	0	0
Abusing officers	4	0	3
Miscellaneous	4	7	25
Offence unclear or unstated	0	9	75
Total offenders	467	722	954

Sources: B.C.B. I; III; IV; years beginning 26 April 1559, 7 May 1576 and 1 Sept. 1600.

the governors and their treatment (Tables 6.1–6.3) is rendered difficult by the variety of jurisdictions in the city. All of the offences punished in Bridewell could be punished in other courts. The investigation and punishment of fornication was duplicated not only by the church courts, but also by Christ's Hospital, and there is evidence that summary action was taken by the deputies in the wards. Disorderly servants could be disciplined through the courts of the livery companies and by justices of the peace acting on their

Table 6.2. *Treatment of fornication/adultery cases by Bridewell, 1576–7 and 1600–1*

	1576–1	1600–1
Cases in which both parties appear	82 (82F+82M)	69 (69F+71M)
Cases in which female only appears	46 (46 F)	70 (70F)
Cases in which male only appears	28 (29M)	32 (33M)
Total number of cases	156	171
Cases in which pregnancy is at issue	64 (41%)	107 (63%)
Number of females:		
appearing	128	139
punished	82 (64%)	72 (52%)
discharged without punishment	9	9
whose fate is unknown	37	58
Number of males:		
appearing	111	104
punished	56 (50%)	57 (55%)
fined	7	12
discharged without punishment	10	1
whose fate is unknown	38	34

M = Males
F = Females

own. Thus alterations in the numbers accused of a particular class of offence may reflect shifts in jurisdiction rather than changes in attitudes towards that offence, still less changes in the incidence of the offence. We have already seen the problems that result from the disagreements between Lee Beier and Steve Rappaport over how the statistics on vagrancy are to be interpreted.[170] Nevertheless, I would argue that some of the trends in Table 6.1 are significant. The failure of the determined moralism of the 1570s is clear from the drop in the number of clients of prostitutes prosecuted between 1576–7 and 1600–1, and from the way in which vagrants came to predominate over other types of offender. There appears to have been a distinct narrowing in the range of social groups affected by the drive for social discipline.

Another set of problems is illustrated by a consideration of the changes in the treatment of vagrants (Table 6.3). The most impressive change lies in the decline in the proportion of vagrants who were sentenced to labour in Bridewell, and a corresponding increase in the proportion who were punished and immediately discharged, usually with passports, or who were discharged apparently without punishment. One might interpret these

[170] Above, p. 208.

Table 6.3 *Treatment of vagrants by Bridewell, 1576–7 and 1600–1*

	1576–7	1600–1
To work, punished and to work	72 (41%)	77 (15%)
Punished	33 (18%)	86 (17%)
Punished and discharged	55 (31%)	241 (48%)
Discharged without punishment	11 (6.3%)	99 (20%)
Other	2	0
Unknown	3	0
Total	176	503

Sources: B.C.B., III; IV.

changes in terms of increasing leniency towards vagrants, the growing humanitarianism of Elizabethan Englishmen. But the changes were at least partly the result of practical constraints because the limited capacity of Bridewell to house the vagrants meant that the ideal of setting the poor to work and inuring them with labour discipline had to be sacrificed for the more limited objective of getting them out of London. Moreover, because vagrants formed a composite category, including both subsistence migrants and petty criminals, the increase in the proportion of those discharged without punishment may reflect a shift in the balance between the two types of vagrancy, as the volume of subsistence migration, and hence of poor genuinely in search of work, increased in the straitened circumstances of the 1590s. Perhaps in discharging without punishment the governors were filtering out the more deserving cases from the hardened offenders. Because the court books fail to give details of the circumstances which gave rise to a vagrancy charge, this must remain a speculation rather than demonstrable fact.

Most commentators on penal trends in the early modern period have emphasised the shifts occurring in the period 1580–1620 when social polarisation, often reinforced by the puritan ideology of the village elites, resulted in the increased prosecution of regulative offences such as alehouse keeping and the building of cottages without the statutory four acres attached and in a surge in the prosecution of property crime.[171] The applicability of such a model to the metropolitan context is rendered dubious by the complexity of urban institutions and traditions of social regulation, by the peculiar pressure exerted by the privy council on policing in the capital, by the different chronology of impoverishment and the higher profile the

[171] Cockburn, 'Nature and Incidence of Crime', pp. 66–7; Wrightson, *English Society*, pp. 142–8; Sharpe, *Crime in Early Modern England*, ch. VIII.

poor always had in London, and by the earlier impact of protestantism in the metropolitan context. What is needed for London is a multi-layered model of changes distinguishing between slowly developing shifts (for example, those promoted by economic change) and short-term variations (resulting from the role of individual personalities, or from the crises, whether perceived or real, caused by war, riot, or rebellion), and allowing for the role of movements like the Reformation, which might produce abrupt transitions as well as having effects over the longer term. It is also important that allowances are made for changes in the institutional framework, that is changes in the way the law was administered, as well as for the forces of social and economic change.

Social polarisation in the sense of society filling out at the bottom was, as we saw in the previous chapter, a feature of London's development in the sixteenth century. The growth in the city's population, fuelled by an immigration which at least partly reflected 'push' factors, was accompanied by an increase in the proportion of poor in the population.[172] The profile of poverty was heightened by the tendency for the poor to cluster in alleys, increasingly a target for official disapproval. Alleys, noted an act of common council in 1551, contributed to the growth in poverty and vagrancy, and were responsible for much 'evell rule'. The 'multitude of buildings being stuffed with poore, needie, and of the worst sort of people', explained Recorder Fleetwood, was to blame for the rising metropolitan crime rate.[173] The other major demographic development of the period was probably an increase in the proportion of young people in the city's population. Rappaport has demonstrated a massive expansion in apprentice recruitment outstripping the rate of population growth in the 1530s and 1540s on the crest of the cloth export boom. Adolescents came to form a significantly higher proportion of the population of the capital than elsewhere: probably at least 10 per cent of the city's population were apprentices in 1550. It is also clear that more than half the apprentices recruited failed to complete their terms. London's rulers were therefore confronted not only with more young people than they were accustomed to, but also evidence to confirm all their assumptions about the headstrong nature of youth.[174] Social polarisation, and the heightened perception of the threat the poor and the young represented, explain the growing preoccupation with regulative offences and the petty delinquencies of the poor: the keeping of inmates which was thought to encourage poverty, the proliferation of alehouses which encouraged evil rule and fed on the spendthrift habits of the poor, and the keeping of unlawful games and dancing schools which drew the young away from their masters and tempted them into vice. The concern of the authorities with

---

[172] 'Above, pp. 12–13; V. B. Elliott, 'Mobility and Marriage', pp. 178–91 (push factors).
[173] C.L.R.O., Jour. 16, fos. 120ᵛ–1; Wright, II. 171.   [174] Above, pp. 206–8, 217–18.

these offences was acute in the later 1540s and early 1550s, resurfaced in the 1570s, and acquired the familiar intensity in the 1590s.

In the mid-Tudor period we find a whole range of initiatives which suggest a tightening in social regulation. In 1552 the aldermen took action against the proliferation of alleys requiring, somewhat implausibly, that their inhabitants should pay an annual sum equivalent to their rent to the hospitals.[175] They anticipated and then vigorously enforced the parliamentary measure of 1552 against alehouses, and cracked down on tippling in service time.[176] Bowling alleys and dancing schools were outlawed within the City, and the aldermen lobbied parliament for legislation against licences for unlawful games.[177] The establishment of Bridewell represented an effort to toughen the policing of petty delinquency and a widening in the range of penal options.[178] As we shall see, these developments reflected more than merely responses to economic and demographic pressures: ideological factors may help to explain the hints that there was an effort to reform the whole society rather than merely the vices of the poor. Rappaport's conclusion that real wage levels held up reasonably well between 1540 and 1560 should not, however, blind us to the fact their trend was firmly downwards until 1552. Although the scale of the impoverishment of this period may have been exaggerated in the past, there undoubtedly was a heightened perception of the problem of poverty, fed by a succession of short-term crises and by the appropriation of the cause of the poor by the protestant reformers as another polemical weapon against the old religion.[179] Moreover, the preoccupation with the problems of youth may have been particularly acute in this period because the demographic development was a comparatively recent one. The closure of the Southwark stews was justified on the grounds that 'youth is provoked, enticed, and allowed to execute the fleshly lusts'.[180] The authorities intervened in the ways in which apprentices spent their leisure time as traditional festivals like May Day became the object of magisterial hostility, and buckler playing (a form of fencing) was outlawed.[181] In August 1553 masters were instructed to improve the

---

[175] C.L.R.O., Jour. 16, fos. 120ᵛ–1; Rep. 13, fo. 532ʳ⁻ᵛ.

[176] C.L.R.O., Rep. 11, fos. 384ᵛ, 389ᵛ, 391, 395ᵛ–6; Rep. 12, fos. 173ᵛ, 403, 412, 518ᵛ; Rep. 13, fos. 272, 408ᵛ, 415ᵛ, 431ᵛ; Jour. 16, fos. 60ᵛ, 101ᵛ; Letter Book 'Q', fo. 232; Letter Book 'R', fos. 128ᵛ, 146, 157ᵛ, 158; *C.J.*, I. 5; 5 & 6 Ed. VI c. 25; *The Select Works of Robert Crowley*, ed. J. M. Cowper (E.E.T.S., extra series, XV, 1872), pp. 8–9.

[177] C.L.R.O., Jour. 16, fos. 328, 330ᵛ; *Wriothesley's Chronicle*, II. 43, 105; *C.J.*, I. 34, 36; 2 & 3 Ph & M c. 9.

[178] Above, pp. 218, 238–41.

[179] Rappaport, *Worlds Within Worlds*, pp. 132–5, 148–9; Brigden, 'Popular Disturbance', pp. 270–2.

[180] *T.R.P.*, I. 365–6.

[181] Stow, *Survey of London*, I. 143–4; *Machyn's Diary*, p. 20; C.L.R.O., Jour. 16, fo. 277ᵛ; Rep. 12, fos. 91ᵛ, 498ᵛ; Rep. 13, fos. 113, 113ᵛ, 146ᵛ.

discipline of their servants 'and suffer them not to ron & wandere abroad in such sort as this of late have used & been accustomed to the no little increase of vyce syn & stubborness of the same apprentices servants and journeymen'.[182] The willingness of masters to discipline their disobedient servants through Bridewell rather than the courts of their livery companies shows that some took the warnings to heart.[183]

The 1570s witnessed a recrudescence of the corporation's concern with inmates which had been rather muted in the previous decade. This manifested itself in a new act of common council in 1570 and in the royal proclamation against new buildings, secured at the City's behest in 1580.[184] Committees of the court of aldermen laboured to improve the execution of the poor laws. Orders issued in 1576 required vestries to appoint surveyors of the poor to remove vagrants and instructed constables to make fortnightly searches of alleys for inmates. The comprehensive orders for the poor of 1579 show an even greater concern with the regulation of the poor, who were to be visited daily by a member of the vestry to determine whether they were working, and whose delinquencies were to be presented monthly to the wardmotes.[185] The explanation for such concerns lies in the increasing scale of immigration which is suggested by the rapidly accelerating baptismal curves of the extramural parishes in this decade.

The difference that the 1590s made was that the local authorities, hitherto rather hesitant in their support of these initiatives, now swung strongly behind them. We have already seen how salaried surveyors of inmates appeared in the Southwark parishes and how concern about population growth is evident even in some inner-city areas.[186] The vagrancy legislation of 1593 and 1598, although replacing ear-boring and death with the milder penalties of whipping, also ensured that they would be better enforced by placing the power to apply them in the hands of the constables and minister of the parish. Quarter sessions were now only involved in the punishment of dangerous and incorrigible rogues who could be banished. Whipping posts appeared all over London, and payments in accounts show that they were regularly used in ensuing years.[187] Secondly, the increased intensity of regulation is clear from the number of precepts relating to specific offences: thus there were no less than nine orders for a general review of alehouse

---

[182] C.L.R.O., Jour. 16, fos. 251ᵛ–2.

[183] Table 6.1; P.R.O., REQ 2 213/36, 254/57, 283/38 for the use made by masters of the threat of punishment in Bridewell as a sanction against disobedient servants.

[184] C.L.R.O., Jour. 19, fo. 255ʳ⁻ᵛ; Rep. 20, fos. 136ᵛ–8; T.R.P., II. 466–8.

[185] C.L.R.O., Jour. 20, fos. 325ʳ⁻ᵛ, 499ᵛ–503ᵛ.

[186] Above, pp. 184–5.

[187] 35 Eliz. I c. 7; 39 Eliz. I c. 4. For the disagreements over the penalties applicable to vagrants, see Slack, *Poverty and Policy*, pp. 124–6.

licences in the 1590s compared to just six in the previous thirty years.[188] Thirdly, the range of marginal groups which came under official scrutiny in this decade is striking. The 1590s witnessed a series of initiatives which resulted in a tightening in the regulation of fishwives, hucksters, colliers, second-hand dealers, and rag-and-bone men. The disciplining of fishwives and hucksters was a major objective of a scheme for market regulation in 1599 which established new officers (the overseers of the markets) to inform on offences.[189] Colliers were regulated through a succession of special officers, and they provided many victims for the pillory in the 1590s.[190] Second-hand dealers were placed under registrars in 1595, and rag-and-bone men under the jurisdiction of Bridewell in 1600.[191] These initiatives contributed to the marginalisation of key ways in which the poor might make a living.

The impact of social polarisation on the prosecution of property crime is impossible to determine because of the absence of full series of indictments, although there is little reason to suppose that the trends observed on the Home Circuit would not have been replicated in the metropolitan area. We are on firmer ground in looking at changes in the treatment of different types of offences (Table 6.4). It is at first surprising that the period should have been characterised by increasing leniency in the treatment of suspects of property crime. The most significant changes were registered in the treatment of simple grand larceny, for which the bulk of suspects in property crime were indicted. Juries were increasingly inclined to bring partial verdicts, undervaluing the goods stolen and convicting the offender of petty larceny for which the penalty was a whipping, although such verdicts were not brought against more than about 5 per cent of those appearing before the trial jury until the early seventeenth century. But the proportion of those convicted who were eventually hanged fell quite sharply from 52 per cent to around 27 per cent. Offenders were much more likely to receive benefit of clergy, with the milder sanction of branding, at the end of the period than at the beginning. The proportion of convicted offenders receiving benefit rose from about 44 per cent in the 1560s and 1570s to about 70 per cent in the 1590s. The rejection of requests for benefit was also less frequent: in the 1560s and 1570s 12.7 per cent of applicants failed to pass the literacy test, often on the grounds that they had enjoyed benefit before, whereas in the 1590s the proportion failing was only 3.8 per cent, and it is likely that the judges were allowing it to men who were technically ineligible. The increased

[188] C.L.R.O., Rep. 15, fo. 401ᵛ; Rep. 17, fo. 213ᵛ; Rep. 18, fo. 412; Rep. 21, fos. 162, 327; Rep. 22, fo. 164ᵛ; Jour. 18, fo. 285; Jour. 20, fo. 230ᵛ; Jour. 22, fo. 356ᵛ; Jour. 23, fos. 126ʳ⁻ᵛ, 341ᵛ; Jour. 24, fos. 52ᵛ, 95ᵛ, 153ᵛ, 204; Jour. 25, fos. 41, 155ᵛ.
[189] *Hugh Alley's "Caveat"*, pp. 15–16, 22–7.
[190] C.L.R.O., Jour. 22, fos. 261ᵛ, 316; Rep. 23, fos. 291ᵛ, 444ᵛ.
[191] Above, p. 220; C.L.R.O., Jour. 25, fos. 201–2, 216ᵛ–17.

Table 6.4. *Treatment of property crime at Middlesex gaol deliveries,*
1560–99

	1560–9	1570–9	1580–4	1585–9	1590–4	1595–9
Simple grand larceny: males						
Size of sample[a]	143	211	137	185	184	277
Percentage of suspects pleading guilty	0	6.2	18.3	30.8	26.1	32.5
Percentage of suspects found guilty	85.7	85.2	76.6	70.1	76.6	79.7
Percentage of suspects acquitted	14.3	12.4	17.5	25.0	20.1	15.6
Percentage of suspects found guilty on partial verdicts	0	2.4	5.8	4.9	3.3	4.7
Percentage of those convicted receiving benefit of clergy	44.1	46.9	60.0	76.4	73.0	70.2
Percentage of those convicted sentenced to hang	51.7	50.8	38.5	22.0	24.8	27.1
Simple grand larceny: females[b]	1560–9	1570–9	1580–4	1585–9	1590–4	1595–9
Size of sample[a]	28	40	27	34	36	38
Percentage of suspects pleading guilty	0	2.5	0	2.9	5.6	10.5
Percentage of suspects found guilty	82.1	50.0	55.6	32.4	52.8	50.0
Percentage of suspects acquitted	17.9	47.5	22.2	58.8	41.7	31.6
Percentage of suspects found guilty on partial verdicts	0	2.5	22.2	8.8	5.6	18.4
Percentage of those convicted receiving discharge for pregnancy	18.2	15.0	13.3	36.4	31.6	15.8
Percentage of those convicted sentenced to hang	68.2	65.0	33.3	0	36.8	31.6
Horse theft	1560–9	1570–9	1580–4	1585–9	1590–4	1595–9
Size of sample[a]	61	61	45	45	48	81
Percentage of suspects pleading guilty	13.1	13.1	17.8	13.3	10.4	24.7
Percentage of suspects found guilty	90.2	90.2	88.9	82.2	64.6	80.2
Percentage of suspects acquitted	9.8	9.8	11.1	17.8	35.4	19.8
Percentage of those convicted sentenced to hang	89.8	96.3	95.0	73.0	93.5	90.6
Highway robbery	1560–9	1570–9	1580–4	1585–9	1590–4	1595–9
Size of sample[a]	22	40	26	29	55	67
Percentage of suspects pleading guilty	4.5	15.0	0	3.4	5.5	6.0
Percentage of suspects found guilty	95.5	95.0	80.8	69.0	67.3	67.2

Percentage of suspects acquitted	4.5	5.0	19.2	31.0	32.7	32.8
Percentage of those convicted sentenced to hang	95.2	97.4	95.2	85.0	94.6	95.6

Burglary	1560–9	1570–9	1580–4	1585–9	1590–4	1595–9
Size of sample[a]	24	23	11	36	45	89
Percentage of suspects pleading guilty	4.2	8.7	9.1	19.4	11.1	14.6
Percentage of suspects found guilty	95.8	73.9	72.7	50.0	68.9	56.2
Percentage of suspects acquitted	4.2	13.0	9.1	30.6	15.6	18.0
Percentage of suspects found guilty on partial verdicts	0	13.0	18.2	19.4	15.6	25.8
Percentage of those convicted sentenced to hang	82.6	82.4	75.0	94.4	80.6	92.0

[a] The samples are comprised of all the cases going to trial for which the indictments survive and the proceedings are legible, in the periods indicated.
[b] The large number of cases where the outcome of a plea of pregnancy is unknown makes discussion of changes in the treatment of female felons particularly difficult.
Sources: G.L.R.O., MJ/SR/94–373; stray indictments in Accessions (Code Acc.).

availability of benefit of clergy was directly related to the increased proportion of suspects who put in guilty pleas: this figure rose from zero to between a quarter and a third of suspects at the end. Those who put themselves on the mercy of the court were much more likely to receive benefit than those who pleaded not guilty: whereas 55.4 per cent of those convicted of simple grand larceny who had pleaded not guilty between 1580 and 1599 received benefit of clergy, the proportion among those pleading guilty was 86.5 per cent. Recent historians have emphasised the degree of judicial discretion in access to clergy: suspects whom the judges thought unworthy would be denied an opportunity to apply for benefit or would be set more difficult passages. It was a way of sifting out the petty criminals from those thought to be a greater threat to society.[192] In so far as the availability of clergy was extended, the exercise of judicial discretion was also extending. It is also striking that the majority (76 per cent) of those appearing before the trial jury on indictments for petty larceny, both those originally thus indicted and those whose indictments were altered in the course of trial, put in guilty pleas, and became subject to the relatively mild sanction of a whipping.

[192] C. B. Herrup, 'Law and Morality in Seventeenth-Century England', *Past and Present*, 106 (1985), 102–23; P. Lawson, 'Crime and the Administration of Criminal Justice in Hertfordshire, 1580–1625' (Oxford D.Phil., 1982), pp. 199–202; Cockburn, *Calendar of Assize Records. Introduction*, pp. 118–21.

The more selective application of the death penalty is evident in other aspects of the law. Whereas successful pleas of pregnancy by women in the 1560s had often provided only a temporary reprieve because they had been followed by the summoning of another jury after the woman's delivery, by the 1590s it seems that a successful plea of pregnancy was tantamount to a pardon.[193] Discretion in the treatment of suspects of highway robbery and horse stealing, which were non-clergyable offences, seems to have operated through an increasing acquittal rate. Partial verdicts were increasingly used to spare burglary suspects from the gallows: they might be found guilty only of grand larceny opening the way to a plea for benefit of clergy or, particularly where thefts of food were involved, they might be found guilty only of petty larceny. Whereas they had been absent in the 1560s, such mitigations accounted for about one quarter of verdicts in the later 1590s.

Some of these changes are explicable in terms of the overloaded calendars confronting the judges. This is Cockburn's explanation for the introduction to the Home Circuit of plea bargaining, which obviated the need for jury trial.[194] But it is worth emphasising that as it increased the element of judicial discretion in the criminal process, it may also have contributed to the increase in the volume of prosecutions. Hext identified as one of the most serious obstacles to the efficient prosecution of crime the fact that 'the simple Cuntryman and woman, lokynge no farther then ynto the losse of ther owne goods, are of opynyon that they wold not procure a mans death for all the goods yn the world'.[195] The increasing discrimination in the operation of the law, achieved through plea bargaining, partial verdicts, and possibly manipulated acquittals, may therefore have removed some of the obstacles to prosecution. The law was becoming a more subtle and flexible instrument discriminating between degrees of seriousness in crime. As this occurred victims of crime probably became more willing to use the law rather than ignore a crime or settle it out of court. This illustrates the way in which changes in the administration of the law could themselves have an impact upon the level of prosecutions.

Historians are generally agreed on the role of the social changes of the sixteenth century in the more intense prosecution of crime. They are less agreed, however, on the importance of the ideological variable, in other words whether there was a relationship between protestantism and the efforts to reform popular manners. In their study of the Essex village of Terling, Keith Wrightson and David Levine have suggested that there was a correlation between the arrival of puritan ministers in the village and the tightening of social regulation.[196] But they have been criticised for confusing with puritanism 'the officious respectability of the dozen or so farmers of

---

[193] Ibid. pp. 121–3.   [194] Ibid. pp. 65–9.   [195] *T.E.D.*, II. 341.
[196] Wrightson and Levine, *Poverty and Piety*.

substance who ran the parish'. Martin Ingram, studying the Wiltshire clothing village of Keevil, has found a pattern of concerns similar to those of the Terling elite, but he is much less convinced that a knot of committed puritan reformers lay behind them. Margaret Spufford has noted the similarities between the regulative drives of the early fourteenth century and those of the later sixteenth and early seventeenth centuries, in the former case without the presence of village elites motivated by puritanism. These historians have therefore asserted the primacy of the socio-economic over the ideological variable.[197] The problem with their arguments is that no one ever argued that the religious factor alone was responsible for the reformation of manners. Rather it was the interaction between social and religious changes which produced campaigns of peculiar intensity. The difference that religion makes therefore lies in the intensity of the campaign, rather than its presence or absence. Such variations in intensity will be extraordinarily difficult to measure because of the range of variables involved in any comparison between communities. But one symptom of the intensity of godly commitment to the reformation of manners lies in that willingness to prosecute people higher up the social scale that we can see in the efforts of the governors of Bridewell Hospital to discipline the clients of prostitutes in the later 1570s. Moreover, most of the debate has concentrated on the early seventeenth century rather than on the early years of the Reformation. There are good reasons for that, because it was only at the turn of the century that the message of protestantism got through to much of rural England, but historians of urban communities should consider the role of protestantism at an earlier date because the impact of the Reformation occurred much earlier in the towns. In London we can see the way in which the Reformation effected an abrupt transition in the treatment of certain types of offence. In particular, it was the polemics of early protestants which explain the harsher treatment of illicit sexuality evident in the mid-Tudor period.

The argument that illicit sexuality was more harshly treated at this time is one which an early modernist advances at his peril because of the lack of research on social regulation in later medieval England. It is particularly a problem because London's magistrates in the sixteenth century always stressed the customary basis of the powers they were exercising. The secular authorities in the City had long been involved in the punishment of illicit sexuality. Bawds had long been presented by the wardmote inquests for punishment by special sessions for bawds and scolds. Some mayors were particularly vigilant against prostitution and earned approving comment

---

[197] M. Spufford, 'Puritanism and Social Control?', in *Order and Disorder*, ed. Fletcher and Stevenson, pp. 41–57; M. Ingram, 'The Reform of Popular Culture? Sex and Marriage in Early Modern England', in *Popular Culture in Seventeenth-Century England*, ed. B. Reay (1985), pp. 129–65; Collinson, *Birthpangs*, p. 153.

from the chroniclers. In 1474 'the mayer dyd dyligent & sharp Ćorrecion on
Venus servauntys, and cawsid theym to be Garnysshid & attyrid wyth Raye
hodys, and to be shewid abowth the Cyte wyth theyr mynstralsy beffore
theym ... and sparid noon ffor mede nor ffor ffavour'.[198] But the distinct
impression is that such vigorous action was exceptional and rarely sustained.
Moreover, prostitution was licensed on the manors of the bishop of
Winchester in Southwark, so that it was the unregulated prostitution in the
northern and eastern suburbs against which the magistrates most often
acted.[199] From the later 1530s onwards, however, the evidence for a much
higher profile taken by the secular authorities mounts. The greater sensitivity
of neighbourhood opinion is reflected in a petition from the wardmotes in
December 1537 concerning the 'hawnting of commen hoores from the
stewes & such other places yn excessyve and gorgious apparill to the evyll
example of mennys wyffes maydens & chyldern'. Heightened hostility to
prostitutes also emerges in the order of the court leet of the Guildable manor
of Southwark in 1543 that no prostitute should enter the manor, echoing an
order from the aldermen in December 1542 that tavern keepers should not
allow prostitutes to enter their houses to eat and drink.[200] A decisive break
with the past was made in 1546 with the closure of the Southwark stews.
Now an outright ban on prostitution replaced efforts at regulation.[201]
Meanwhile, old penalties were revived. In February 1543 the aldermen
agreed that 'all the good & laudable auncyent lawes actes and ordenaunces
heretofore made & devysed for the ponyshement of harlottes & bawdes of
the stewys & other incontynent women of theyr lyvyng shall from henceforth
by my lord mayer [be] duelye observyd & put in spedye & strength
execucion from tyme to tyme as the case shall requyre'. John Cotes, the lord
mayor in this year, arranged for the ducking of prostitutes in the Thames.[202]
Other mid-century mayors also enjoyed reputations as stern moralists,
notably Rowland Hill in 1550, and George Barne in 1553. Hill caused the
wardmote inquests to make new presentments in April 1550, 'upon which
indictments the lord mayor sat many times', punishing the offenders,
including significantly some of high position, by carting. 'Some citizens', we
are told, 'went to the lord mayor and told him that it was not right to be so
severe, and said that it would cost him dear when he finished his office, but he

---

[198] G. May, *Social Control of the Sex Expression* (1930), pp. 131–4; E. J. Burford, *The Orrible
      Synne* (1973), chs. VI and VII; *Calendar of Plea and Memoranda Rolls, 1413–1427*, ed.
      A. H. Thomas (1943), pp. 122, 124, 131, 132, 134, 138, 151, 152, 154, 157; *Great
      Chronicle of London*, p. 222; C.L.R.O., Rep. 13, fo. 481ᵛ.
[199] R. M. Karras, 'The Regulation of Brothels in Later Medieval England', *Signs*, 14 (1989),
      399–433; J. B. Post, 'A Fifteenth-Century Customary of the Southwark Stews', *Journal of
      the Society of Archivists* (1977), 418–28.
[200] C.L.R.O., Rep. 10, fos. 13ᵛ, 27, 300; Carlin, 'Urban Development of Southwark',
      pp. 501–6.
[201] *T.R.P.*, I. 365–6.   [202] C.L.R.O., Rep. 10, fos. 309ᵛ, 318ᵛ, 338ᵛ, 343, 344ʳ⁻ᵛ, 348.

did not cease on that account, although many men would have paid large sums of money to be saved from disgrace'.[203]

Hill was also a leading light behind the foundation of Bridewell which clearly marked the widening involvement of the secular arm in the punishment of illicit sexuality. The campaign against prostitution was now capable of more central direction. During the 1570s, for example, the governors used warrants to haul in the brothel keepers and clients named by the pimps. Secondly, the range of sanctions widened. The traditional penalties of carting and banishment continued to be used, particularly by the Middlesex sessions and the local authorities of Westminster, but they were now supplemented by the incarceration, work discipline, and regular whippings which characterised Bridewell.[204] Thirdly, the scope of secular action widened to include the routine investigation and punishment of fornication. Whereas the fifteenth-century wardmote presentments were predominantly concerned with the professionals, now non-commercial sexual relations were disciplined. A major preoccupation here was the responsibility for maintenance payments, but there was a strong moral dimension as well, demonstrated by the large number of cases in which pregnancy was not at issue (Table 6.2). Fourthly, the willingness to prosecute the clients of prostitutes and the statistics relating to the treatment of male fornicators shown in Table 6.2 suggest that male sexuality was now more harshly treated and the double standard eroded. It is true that more women than men appeared in fornication cases and that men sometimes escaped punishment on the payment of a fine, but the preponderance of females was by no means overwhelming (128:111 in 1576–7), and the numbers of men escaping by fines relatively small (less than 7 per cent in the same year).[205]

This tougher attitude towards illicit sexuality was partly a symptom of the generally heightened concern with order that resulted from social change and the anxiety of elites unnerved by the popular rebellions of 1549, but religious change was also important. The Reformation served to heighten the sense of sin. For protestants attacks on sin were both a means of indicting the old order and validating the new, for God was clearly on the side of those who

---

203 *Chronicle of King Henry VIII of England*, ed. M. A. S. Hume (1889), pp. 167–9; *Wriothesley's Chronicle*, II. 36–7, 43; 80–1; C.L.R.O., Rep. 12, fos. 247ᵛ, 273ᵛ.
204 *Middlesex County Records*, I. 95, 114, 189, 234, 235, 286; W.P.L., Minutes of Court of Burgesses, I. For comments on the discipline of Bridewell, see G. von Bulow, 'A Journey through England and Scotland made by Lupold von Wedel in the years 1584 and 158', *T.R.H.S.*, new series, 9 (1895), 233; 'The London Journal of Alesandro Magno', p. 144; G. von Bulow, 'Diary of the Journey of Philip Julius, Duke of Stettin-Pomerania through England in the year 1602', *T.R.H.S.*, new series, 6 (1892), 11. For a different perspective, see the ballad 'Whipping Cheer' in *A Pepysian Garland: Black Letter Broadside Ballads of the Years 1595–1639*, ed. H. F. Rollins (Cambridge, 1922), pp. 39–43.
205 K. V. Thomas, 'The Double Standard', *Journal of the History of Ideas*, 20 (1959), 195–216. Cf. Fletcher, *Reform in the Provinces*, p. 257.

were most vehement against sin, and opposed to those who appeared to condone it. Protestant attacks on the 'great and myghtie abhomination of vyce, that now rayneth within this your Highnesse realme' were legion.[206] The Catholic Church was highly vulnerable on the question of sexuality, clerical incontinence becoming a major polemical weapon in the hands of early protestants. Thus Simon Fish claimed that no man's wife or daughter was safe from the sexual machinations of the clergy, that the clergy had made 100,000 idle whores, and that they were responsible for the spread of venereal disease. These were arguments with strong resonances for London audiences where pre-Reformation wardmote presentments had identified priests as among the most prominent patrons of prostitutes. The presence of the Southwark stews on the manors of the bishop of Winchester, none other than Stephen Gardiner, hammer of the protestants, was a conservative 'own goal'. In the rhetoric of the reformers the association between unbridled sex and superstition was forged; the Catholic Church's vulnerability on sex encouraged its identification as the whore of Babylon.[207] Moreover, protestants altered some of the emphases in the conventional attacks on fornication. First, one of their major preoccupations was with ensuring that the offences of the wealthier sort did not pass unpunished. Thus Henry Brinklow highlighted the hypocrisy of conventional attitudes: 'If a poor man keep a whore besides his wife, and a poor wife play the harlot, they are punished as well worthy. But let an alderman, a gentleman, or a rich man keep whore or whores, what punishment is there?'[208] Secondly, several reformers pressed for harsher penalties. Latimer and Brinklow both demanded the death penalty for adultery; an anonymous tract addressed to Edward VI on the distresses of the commonwealth (*c.* 1550) called for the penalties for fornication to be increased to six months' imprisonment and fine at the king's pleasure for the first offence, and death on the second, while any adultery by man or woman was to be judged a felony. Less bloody, but none the less severe, were the penalties proposed in the abortive reform of canon law, the *Reformatio Ecclesiasticarum Legum* of 1552: perpetual imprisonment and loss of the property rights gained by marriage for adultery, and the application of unspecified punishments of

[206] *The Lamentacyon of a Christen Agaynst the Cytye of London*, ed. J. M. Cowper (E.E.T.S., extra series, XXII, 1874), p. 75; *A Supplication of the Poore Commons*, ed. J. M. Cowper (E.E.T.S., extra series, XIII, 1871), p. 82; *A Supplycaion to our moste Soveraigne Lorde Kynge Henry the Eyght*, ed. J. M. Cowper (E.E.T.S., extra series, XIII, 1871), pp. 52–3; *Lever's Sermons*, ed. E. Arber (1870), pp. 42, 76, 86.

[207] *A Supplicacyon for the Beggers*, ed. F. J. Furnivall (E.E.T.S., extra series, XIII, 1871), pp. 6–7; *Lamentacyon*, pp. 63–4, 110; J. Bale, *Dramatic Writings*, ed. J. S. Farmer (Early English Drama Society, 1907), pp. 23–31, 55–6; Guy, *Tudor England*, pp. 219–20. Cf. L. Roper, 'Discipline and Respectability: Prostitution and the Reformation in Augsburg', *History Workshop*, 19 (1985), 3–28.

[208] *Lamentacyon*, p. 91.

'great bitterness' to harlots.[209] Thirdly, the reformers were much more willing than their enemies to support the secular magistrate in the correction of sin. Latimer urged a firmer line before the young Edward VI; and it was at the instigation of Bishop Ridley that the king made the gift of Bridewell Palace to the City. Exhortations to magisterial action thundered forth from the protestant pulpits. The chronicles record that it was at the urging of the protestant clergy that Hill moved vigorously against illicit sexuality in 1550, although somewhat cattily suggesting that they were seeking revenge on the laity for their mocking of clerical marriage.[210]

Conservative credentials were besmirched by the hostages to polemical fortune in Aquinas' justification of licensed prostitution and by Bridewell's unpopularity with some sections of the Marian establishment. The relationship between Bridewell and the church courts was fraught during the catholic reaction. The City was forced to defend its customs on the punishment of bawds before the commissioners for ecclesiastical causes in November 1556; and the aldermen took very seriously indeed the slander of a preacher at Paul's Cross who had claimed that an apprentice had been punished in Bridewell 'in such sort that he should die thereof'. Some Marians were willing to deploy Aquinas' arguments in favour of licensed prostitution. William Harrison later claimed that the clergy sought to have the stews set up once more 'for the stewes, saith one of them in a sermon made at Paules crosse are so necessary in a comon welthe as a iaxe in a mannes house'.[211]

The establishment of Bridewell therefore set up a framework within which initiatives like that undertaken in the later 1570s were possible. Although it is impossible to obtain explicit evidence concerning the motivation of the campaign associated with Winch's treasureship, the investigation of the character of the governors most closely involved in it suggests that religious ideology provided the impetus. Of the ten governors attending over 30 per cent of the meetings in the key year, 1576–7, six were puritans, and the lack of proof on another three may be explained in terms of the lack of surviving wills for them because wills provide one of a very few clues as to religious orientation. Thomas Aldersey, William Ormeshawe, and James Hewishe signed the godly petition in support of Thomas Barber, the suspended lecturer at St Mary Bow. Aldersey appointed a known nonconformist to the lectureship he established at Bunbury in Cheshire. Hewishe left £20 to 'such

209 Ibid. p. 18; *Sermons of Bishop Hugh Latimer*, ed. G. E. Corrie (Parker Society, XXII, 1844), pp. 196, 244; B.L., Kings MS 17B, XXXV, fo. 20ᵛ; *The Reformation of the Ecclesiastical Laws*, ed. E. Cardwell (1850).
210 *Sermons of Latimer*, pp. 196, 244; *Lever's Sermons*, p. 42; *T.E.D.*, III. 416; *Chronicle of Henry VIII*, pp. 167–9.
211 C.L.R.O., Rep. 13, fos. 455, 457ᵛ, 458, 479ᵛ; Rep. 14, fos. 24ᵛ, 29ᵛ, 49; *John Howes' MS 1582*, pp. 71–2; *Harrison's Description of England in Shakspere's Youth*, ed. F. J. Furnivall (New Shakspere Society, 1877–8), Part I, pp. li–lii.

godly and zealous preachers as are or shalbe restrained from the publique
exercise of theire ministerie'. Clement Kelke's will included a detailed
testimony of his faith and asserted his confidence of election among the
saints. Others showed signs of that stern moralism characteristic of the
godly. John Mabb emphasised that the recipients of his charity should be 'of
honest behavyour and good conversacion and no drunkarde nor swearer'.
John Clerk arranged for the distribution of clothing and money to the poor
attending sermons in his parish church. Given the notorious difficulties of
unravelling individual religious commitment, these are certainly suggestive
indications.[212] The quest for an internal assurance of their election through
their zeal for God's glory gave the Bridewell governors the impetus they
needed to take the campaign for moral reform up the social gradient.

Short-term variations in the pattern of prosecution and punishment might
be produced by the sense of vulnerability felt by new regimes, by the rise in
the crime rate usually associated with the demobilisation of soldiers, by
plague, and by riot and rebellion. These all fed the sense that order was under
threat, and that a tougher stance against crime, and stricter social regulation
were necessary. The hard line taken by the City at the privy council's behest
in June 1559 against vagrants and bowling alleys in the wake of affrays in
Smithfield reflects the vulnerability of Elizabeth's new councillors.[213] One of
the most interesting initiatives of the early Elizabethan period, namely the
controversial extraordinary commission of May 1561 and its successors of
1563 and 1565, with their powers to search out felons, issue warrants for
arrest, and make claims from the Exchequer for expenses incurred in the
investigation of crime, perhaps reflected similar concerns, although there is
no documentation which might illuminate their genesis.[214] As we have seen
the demobilisation of soldiers was routinely followed by instructions for a
firmer line against vagrancy, and this accounts for much of the council's
greater pressure on the metropolitan authorities in the later 1580s and
1590s.[215] Because disease was linked with sin, and because plague was
thought to spread by means of vagrants, epidemics might fuel the drive for
regulation. Dr Caius attributed the sweating sickness of 1551 to alehouse
gadding by the poor, while preachers exhorted the magistrates to action
against vice in years of plague. Thus Thomas White, preaching at Paul's
Cross in 1577 in time of plague, goaded the mayor to action: 'you must play

212 B.C.B. III, analysis of attendances; *Seconde Parte of a Register*, II. 219–21; P.R.O.,
PROB 11/71, fo. 70 (John Mabb); PROB 11/76, fo. 182ᵛ (James Hewishe); PROB 11/77,
fo. 135ᵛ (William Ormeshawe); PROB 11/82, fo. 210ᵛ (Clement Kelke); PROB 11/90,
fo. 71ᵛ (John Clerke); PROB 11/93, fo. 68 (Thomas Aldersey). The other active governors
were Robert Winch, Edmund Bragge, Francis Dodd and Robert Brett.
213 C.L.R.O., Rep. 14, fos. 173ᵛ, 175, 176ᵛ; Jour. 17, fos. 132, 166.
214 *C.P.R., 1560–1563*, pp. 237, 523; *C.P.R., 1563–6*, p. 257; C.L.R.O., Rep. 15, fo. 116ᵛ; F.
Bacon, *Works*, ed. J. Spedding *et al.* (14 vols., 1857–74), VII. 514.
215 Above, pp. 210–11; H.M.C., *Bath*, V. 159–60; C.L.R.O., Letter Book R, fo. 85ᵛ.

both the Phisition and Surgeon, you muste awake out of Endimions sleepe, and thrust dilligently your sword of iustice in, to launce out all corruption and bagage which is gathered in the bowels'.[216] In the plague year of 1593 the aldermen moved to suppress bear-baitings, bowling alleys, and 'such like profane exercises'. Temporary breakdowns in public order might also lead to regulative drives. The riots of the mid 1590s emphasised the fragility of order in the capital, and drove the magistrates into tougher policing measures with the appointment of provost marshals as City officials in 1596. In the years which followed they coordinated action against vagrants within the City, shut down alehouses, and disciplined marginal groups like fishwives and colliers.[217] The perceived crisis was also evident in the way in which the long-term trends in the direction of increasing 'leniency' in the treatment of suspects of property crime were arrested. A significantly higher proportion were found guilty in the later 1590s than in the late 1580s, and the proportion of those convicted who were sentenced to be hanged also increased slightly (Table 6.4).

It should now be clear that the forces for change just described might interact and reinforce each other to give particular periods a strong 'law and order' flavour. Thus in the late 1540s and early 1550s the determination to build a godly commonwealth reinforced the anxieties of magistrates already sensitised by the evidence for impoverishment and the problems of youth and by the provincial rebellions of 1549. In the 1590s continuing immigration and widespread impoverishment as real wages fell dramatically, contributed to accelerating social polarisation. Tensions were exacerbated by the riots of 1595 and by the waves of disbanded soldiers who thronged the capital. The paucity of records of prosecutions for the sixteenth century in general, and for the middle decades of the century in particular, make comparisons between the two periods difficult. But we might hazard two speculations. First, in the middle decades of the century there are some signs of a determination to reform the failings of the whole society: early protestants made much of the necessity to tackle the vices of the rich, and some of the preoccupations of the mid-century disciplinarians reflect vices to which the wealthy may actually have been more prone than the poor. Bowling alleys, dancing, and fencing schools were rather more prominent than alehouses, the stock concern of later decades. By the 1590s the frustrations experienced by the moral reformers of the 1570s encapsulated in the Bate case, and the

---

[216] Slack, 'Social Policy and the Constraints of Government', p. 97; T. White, *A Sermon Preached at Pawles Crosse on Sunday the Thirde of November 1577 in Time of Plague* (1578), p. 93; J. Stockwood, *A Sermon Preached at Paules Cross on Barthelmew Day Being the 24 of August 1578* (1578), pp. 85–6; H. Holland, *Spirituall Preservatives Against the Pestilence* (1603 edn), sig. A i; C.L.R.O., Rep. 23, fo. 50ᵛ.

[217] Above, pp. 223–4; C.L.R.O., Rep. 23, fos. 517ᵛ, 521ᵛ, 573; Rep. 24, fos. 6, 41, 48, 71, 73ᵛ, 129, 173; Rep. 26, fo. 179; B.C.B. IV, passim.

much greater prominence of the problem of poverty, meant that the drive for
social regulation fell more heavily on the backs of the poor. Godly energies
came to be directed at those vices and those social groups where there was a
consensus within the elite on the need for action.[218] The second difference
between the two periods is that the instruments of regulation were becoming
more sophisticated as an increasingly bureaucratised poor relief gave the
authorities greater opportunities to mould the behaviour of the poor, as the
corporation and parishes elaborated mechanisms and officials to deal with
the poor, and as the greater discretion in the operation of the criminal law
made it more effective in the disciplining of the petty offender.

---

[218] Cf. J. Kent, 'Attitudes of Members of the House of Commons to the Regulation of "Personal
Conduct" in Late Elizabethan and Early Stuart England', *B.I.H.R.*, 46 (1973), 51–5;
Collinson, *Birthpangs*, pp. 18–19; *Hugh Alley's "Caveat"*, p. 23.

—————————————————— ≪ *7* ≫ ——————————————————

Conclusion

We saw in the introduction how the absence of a conflagration in London in the 1590s belies the very real tensions to which the social and economic pressures of that decade contributed. Londoners turned against the traditional scapegoats for economic misfortune, the aliens resident in their midst, and in 1592–3 the aldermen confronted the very real possibility of a repetition of the rioting that had characterised Evil May Day in 1517. But more serious developments lay ahead. It was especially worrying to the elite that during the escalation of economic difficulties in the years which immediately followed the attacks broadened and members of the elite were directly criticised.

The social fabric was highly flammable, but it failed to ignite. A key variable in ensuring that stability was maintained was the cohesion of the elite, a lesson which is obvious from a comparison of London in the 1590s with earlier less stable periods in its history and with other European cities at the same time. That London escaped the fate of Paris was due to England's successful containment of the religious passions unleashed by the Reformation. The catholic threat in the capital had long since receded. There is little sign that the London elite's forward protestant façade cracked during the 1590s, and although some, like Alderman Richard Martin, had probably favoured still more radical forms of protestantism, there was little desire to rock the boat in the 1590s in view of the queen's commitment to war against the Antichrist, while Whitgift's policy of isolating the presbyterian contagion proved remarkably effective in reminding most puritans, in London and elsewhere, of what they had in common with the Established Church. It is true that the earl of Essex enjoyed widespread support within the City, but it was only within the framework of loyalty to the Crown and the Church, and outside that framework, he was unable to mobilise his support. London emerged from the court battles of the twilight years of Elizabeth's reign relatively unscathed. The elite presented a united front before the forces of popular disorder.

We are sometimes in danger of underestimating the informal coercive powers at the elite's disposal. Aldermen were responsible for the licensing of alehouse keepers, hucksters, and fishwives; they were usually prominent landlords; and as major consumers their choice of suppliers was a powerful sanction. The immense discretionary jurisdiction exercised by the aldermen and their deputies is another reminder of the power they wielded in local society. Because of the frequency with which they were employed as arbitrators, citizens had every reason to remain on good behaviour to retain their favour. The wider availability of poor relief administered by the local authorities encouraged the internalisation of deferential attitudes through repeated exchanges, which underlined the dependence of the poor on the wealthier. The operation of the criminal law offered a finely calibrated mechanism for the disciplining of those who fell foul of social norms. It is true that the power of the aldermen was diluted by the necessity that they work through the livery companies, parishes, and wards, in the running of which middling householders were often heavily (although not to the extent suggested by some recent historians) involved. But we have noted at several points a process analogous to that observed by Keith Wrightson in rural England whereby the rulers of local society came to align themselves with the value system of the national elite. The growth of the capital and the ever-expanding problem of poverty caused vestrymen and assistants to see the necessity for stricter social control. By the 1590s vestrymen were willing accomplices in the campaign to discipline the poor, as their adoption of surveyors of inmates, their recourse to Bridewell, and their liberal use of the whipping posts set up after 1598 testify. Assistants showed themselves more hostile to traditional recreational practices among the journeymen of their companies. In both companies and parishes, it has been argued, social relations came to be articulated in more strictly hierarchical terms. Older practices of commensality were eroded and the social bond was most commonly expressed in charity, increasingly distributed through these institutions.

If the elite were united and possessed of a veritable armoury of informal sanctions, the populace they ruled was weak and divided. A model of social relations based on the straightforward dichotomy between elite and populace has serious limitations because of the divisions among the poorer inhabitants of the City. The craft-bounded horizons of many Londoners acted as a barrier to common action, and craftsmen in different companies with common grievances, for example against aliens and foreigners, were competitors on other issues. Within individual companies the coherence of the artisans' position *vis-à-vis* the rulers was undermined by divisions over the use of non-free labour and the size of enterprises. Within the parishes the differential impact of the campaign for godliness opened up another line of division, as a striving for respectability among the godly poor brought many of the poorer inhabitants into line with elite concerns in the drive for discipline. Vestries fostered another line of division by using the poor as warders or searchers of inmates to discipline immigrants, and by showing greater favour to long-term residents in the distribution of relief.

Nevertheless, in their quest for stability the aldermen could not rely on crude social control, however far they elaborated its mechanisms in the 1590s with provost marshals and surveyors of inmates, nor on the divisions among the populace, however far these were widening under the impact of the pressures of the 1590s. Their formal coercive powers were weak because of the system's ultimate reliance on an unpaid constabulary: they were astonishingly vulnerable to a concerted challenge from below, and an awareness of that vulnerability shaped the panic-stricken rhetoric of the 1590s. What they could not achieve through the formal machinery of government, the aldermen sought through the tyranny of vocabulary. By emphasising the threats to the social order, they might hope to mobilise the support of the middling sort. For the identification of this group with their regime was still partial and conditional. Many of the men of middling status who wielded power in local government and the companies sympathised with the grievances of the craftsmen relating to alien competition, and their attitudes towards the poor were shaped by the awareness of the transitory nature of their own business fortunes. Thus wardmote petitions agitated for improved poor relief and for measures against aliens. Moreover, the existence of disorder, however limited in scope, was testimony to powerful potential threats to the established order. Stability depended on ameliorating popular grievances to the extent that the poor could feel some prospect of improvement within the system.

That London escaped serious disorder in the 1590s is tribute to the elite's responsiveness to popular grievances. We have seen how the aldermen energetically organised the provisioning of the capital, the prosecution of offenders against market regulations, and the mobilisation of the benevolence of the wealthy. That they were relatively speaking so successful was a reflection of a highly developed infrastructure: London was one of the pioneers of the hospitalisation of the poor and parochially administered relief, and the aldermen had a long tradition of involvement in provisioning the City and controlling the markets. These traditions were themselves a reflection of the strength of the corporate ideal, the sense that the magistrate should rule for the benefit of all citizens, which was pushed repeatedly in the sermons of the period. We have seen how a similar rhetoric was articulated by the rulers of the companies in their promotion of craft grievances. Significantly the later 1580s and 1590s witnessed a revival of parliamentary lobbying against aliens and the intense harassment of aliens and foreigners by the companies in the law courts. The assistants in several key companies became more responsive to craft grievances over apprentice recruitment, as in the Clothworkers, wholesaling in raw materials, as in the Skinners, and guaranteed employment, as in the Merchant Tailors.

This responsiveness to pressure from below was one guarantee of the loyalty of the poorer sections of society to the institutions of companies, parishes, and wards. It has been one of this book's major arguments that the generation of these institutional loyalties was crucial to stability in so far as they ensured that the pursuit of the redress of grievances remained institutionally focused. The majority of Londoners were locked into a matrix of overlapping communites each of which created a hold on their loyalties and contributed to their sense of identity. The less advantaged could manipulate the obligations of the wealthier that membership of a community entailed to mobilise elite support for the redress of their grievances.

But just as there are dangers in exaggerating the 'control' element in explaining the stability of Elizabethan London, so also do we run risks if we push the 'community' arguments too far. The functioning of institutions depended very much on the distribution of power within them, and it has been shown that however much participation the middling sort enjoyed, initiative still lay with those in the upper echelons of society. This meant that there were limits to the responsiveness of those in authority, and that in some circumstances frustrations could build up. Certain kinds of petitioner were more likely to be listened to than others; certain kinds of grievance were more likely to be taken up than others. Widows and orphans were the favoured candidates for relief; official suspicions of the able-bodied made their quest for relief an arduous one. The rulers of the companies were selective on those petitions on which they acted: it was relatively easy to secure action on quality control, but much more difficult to persuade rulers to discipline wholesalers or those who expanded the size of their enterprises beyond reasonable limits. Very few measures of the latter nature reached parliament, and when they did, the artisans appear to have felt that the support of their rulers was lacking. The distribution of power also meant that there were limits to what could be achieved. Ratepayers who ran vestries, for example, were resistant to increases in the poor rate, and the aldermen reluctant to take any measures to coerce them, until they had experienced the harrowing conditions of the 1590s. The tensions were contained because the elites were sufficiently responsive to ensure that popular attitudes towards them remained ambiguous. It was recognised that elite action was wanting on some issues, but it was also appreciated that little could be achieved without their support. In some cases, as with an unpopular mayor like Spencer, or with a rather isolated elite like that in the Skinners' Company, the tensions were threatening, but such cases remained the exception rather than the rule.

BIBLIOGRAPHY

MANUSCRIPT SOURCES

CORPORATION OF LONDON RECORD OFFICE

Rep. 1–28	Repertories of the Court of Aldermen, 1495–1609
Jour. 11–26	Journals of the Court of Common Council, 1506–1605
Rem. I–II	Remembrancia
M.C.1	Mayor's Court, Original Bills
	Letter Books, P, Q, R, and S
	Chamber Accounts, vol. I, fragmentary accounts mainly from the 1560s; vol. II for 1584–6
	Common Serjeant's Book, vol. I, 1586–1614
	Book of Fines, 1517–1628
	Book of Oaths
	'A Book Containing the Manner and Order of a Watch to be Used in the Cittie of London Uppon the Even at Night of Sainct John Baptist and Sainct Peeter as in Tyme Past hath bin Accustomed'
	'Samuel Barton's Book; Articles of the Charter and Liberties of London'

Southwark Manorial Records

Misc. MS 169.1	Bailiffs' Accounts of the Manor of Southwark
Misc. MS 169.6	Survey of Southwark, *c.* 1562
Southwark Box 2	Guildable Manor Court Leet Presentments, 1620–4
Southwark Box 2	King's Manor Court Leet Presentments, 1620–4
	Southwark Manors Court Book, 1539–64

GUILDHALL LIBRARY, LONDON

Parochial Records

819/1	Allhallows the Great, Vestry Minutes, 1574–1684
5090/1	Allhallows London Wall, Churchwardens' Accounts, 1455–1536
5090/2	Allhallows London Wall, Churchwardens' Accounts, 1566–1681
4957/1	Allhallows Staining, Vestry Minutes, 1574–1655
4956/2	Allhallows Staining, Churchwardens' Accounts, 1534–1628
4959	Allhallows Staining, Sacramental Acounts, 1585–1664
4958/1	Allhallows Staining, Assessments for Clerk's Wages, 1539–75

261

4958/2	Allhallows Staining, Assessments for Clerk's Wages, 1574–1605
9163	Christ Church, Churchwardens' Accounts, 1593–5
4835/1	Holy Trinity the Less, Churchwardens' Accounts, 1582–1662
1264/1	St Alban Wood Street, Vestry Minutes, 1583–1676
7673/1	St Alban Wood Street, Churchwardens' Accounts, 1584–1639
1431/1	St Alphage Cripplegate, Vestry Minutes, 1593–1608
1432/2	St Alphage Cripplegate, Churchwardens' Accounts, 1553–80
1432/3	St Alphage Cripplegate, Churchwardens' Accounts, 1580–1631
1278/1	St Andrew Hubbard, Vestry Minutes, 1600–78
1279/2	St Andrew Hubbard, Churchwardens' Accounts, 1525–1621
2088/1	St Andrew Wardrobe, Churchwardens' Accounts, 1570–1668
2089/1	St Andrew Wardrobe, Poor Accounts, 1613–68
4502/1	St Andrew Wardrobe, Register of Baptisms, 1558–1812
4507/1	St Andrew Wardrobe, Register of Burials, 1558–1812
1046/1	St Antholin, Churchwardens' Accounts, 1574–1708
1568	St Benet Gracechurch, Churchwardens' Accounts, 1549–1723
877/1	St Benet Paul's Wharf, Vestry Minutes, 1578–1674
943/1	St Botolph Billingsgate, Vestry Minutes, 1592–1673
942A	St Botolph Billingsgate, Poor Accounts, 1598–1663
4887	St Dunstan in the East, Vestry Minutes, 1515–1651
4241/1	St Ethelburga Bishopsgate, Churchwardens' Accounts, 1569–1681
4791	St George Botolph Lane, Parish Register, 1546–1617, including Vestry Minutes, 1593
951/1	St George Botolph Lane, Churchwardens' Accounts, 1590–1676
6419/1	St Giles Cripplegate, Parish Register, 1561–1606
6836	St Helen Bishopsgate, Vestry Minutes and Churchwardens' Accounts, 1565–1654
4810/1	St James Garlickhithe, Churchwardens' Accounts, 1555–1627
4824	St James Garlickhithe, Gifts to the Poor Distribution Book, 1598–1630
577/1	St John Walbrook, Churchwardens' Accounts, 1595–1679
590/1	St John Zachary, Churchwardens' Accounts, 1591–1682
1124/1	St Katherine Coleman Street, Churchwardens' Accounts, 1609–71
2590/1	St Lawrence Jewry, Vestry Minutes, 1556–1669
2593/1	St Lawrence Jewry, Churchwardens' Accounts, 1579–1640
3907/1	St Lawrence Pountney, Churchwardens' Accounts, 1530–1681
3476/1	St Margaret Moses, Churchwardens' Accounts, 1547–97
1175/1	St Margaret New Fish Street, Vestry Minutes, 1578–1789
1176/1	St Margaret New Fish Street, Churchwardens' Accounts, 1576–1678
4570/2	St Margaret Pattens, Churchwardens' Accounts, 1558–1653
1311/1	St Martin Ludgate, Vestry Minutes, 1576–1715
959/1	St Martin Orgar, Vestry Minutes, 1555–1643, and Churchwardens' Accounts, 1574–1707
3570/1	St Mary Aldermanbury, Vestry Minutes, 1569–1609
3556/1	St Mary Aldermanbury, Churchwardens' Accounts, 1569–92
2500A/1–6	St Mary Aldermanbury, Assessments for Clerk's Wages and Tithe, 1577, 1591, 1593, 1594, 1595, 1596
6574	St Mary Aldermary, Churchwardens' Accounts, 1597–1665

2596/1   St Mary Magdalen Milk Street, Vestry Minutes and Church-
         wardens' Accounts, 1518–1606
1542/1   St Mary Staining, Churchwardens' Accounts, 1586–8
1013/1   St Mary Woolchurch, Churchwardens' Accounts, 1560–1672
1002/1   St Mary Woolnoth, Churchwardens' Accounts, 1539–1641
3579   St Matthew Friday Street, Vestry Minutes, 1576–1743
1016/1   St Matthew Friday Street, Churchwardens' Accounts, 1547–1678
4072/1   St Michael Cornhill, Vestry Minutes, 1463–1697
4071/1   St Michael Cornhill, Churchwardens' Accounts, 1455–1608
1188/1   St Michael Crooked Lane, Churchwardens' Accounts, 1617–93
2895/1   St Michael le Querne, Churchwardens' Accounts, 1514–1604
4415/1   St Olave Old Jewry, Vestry Minutes, 1574–1680
4409/1   St Olave Old Jewry, Churchwardens' Accounts, 1586–1643
645/1   St Peter Westcheap, Churchwardens' Accounts, 1435–1601
645/2   St Peter Westcheap, Churchwardens' Accounts, 1601–1702
4165/1   St Peter Cornhill, Vestry Minutes, 1574–1717
4457/2   St Stephen Coleman Street, Churchwardens' Accounts, 1586–1640
4449/1   St Stephen Coleman Street, Parish Register, 1617–93
594/1   St Stephen Walbrook, Vestry Minutes, 1587–1614
593/2   St Stephen Walbrook, Churchwardens' Accounts, 1549–1637
4249   St Andrew Holborn, Bentley Register
6667/1   St Andrew Holborn, Register of Baptisms, 1558–1623
6673/1   St Andrew Holborn, Register of Burials, 1556–1623
1453/1   St Botolph Aldersgate, Vestry Minutes, 1601–52
1454   St Botolph Aldersgate, Churchwardens' Accounts, 1466–1636
9234/1   St Botolph Aldgate, Memorandum Book, 1583–4, 1586–8
9234/2   St Botolph Aldgate, Memorandum Book, 1588–90, 1591–2
9234/3   St Botolph Aldgate, Memorandum Book, 1590–1
9234/4   St Botolph Aldgate, Memorandum Book, 1593–4
9234/5   St Botolph Aldgate, Memorandum Book, 1594–6, 1598–1600
9234/6   St Botolph Aldgate, Memorandum Book, 1596–7
9234/7   St Botolph Aldgate, Memorandum Book, 1597–8
9235/1   St Botolph Aldgate, Churchwardens' Accounts, 1547–85 (also
         contains the Accounts of the Renters for the Poor's Lands,
         1559–99)
9235/2   St Botolph Aldgate, Churchwardens' Accounts, 1586–1691
9236   St Botolph Aldgate, Vestry Minutes and Memoranda, 1583–1640
2630   St Botolph Aldgate, Book of Deeds (19th cent. copy)
9220   St Botolph Aldgate, Register of Baptisms and Marriages, 1558–
         1625
9222/1   St Botolph Aldgate, Register of Burials, 1558–1625
4524/1   St Botolph Bishopsgate, Churchwardens' Accounts, 1567–1632
3016/1   St Dunstan in the West, Vestry Minutes, 1588–1663
2968/1   St Dunstan in the West, Churchwardens' Accounts, 1516–1608
10342   St Dunstan in the West, Parish Register, 1558–1632
9680   St Katharine's Precinct, Constables' Accounts, 1598–1706

Ward Records

4069/1	Cornhill Ward, Wardmote Inquest Book, 1571–1651
3018/1	St Dunstan in the West, Wardmote Inquest Book, 1558–1823
2505/1	Bassishaw Ward, Wardmote Inquest Minutes, 1655–1752
3505	Bassishaw Ward, Record and Assessment Book, 1610–63
3461/1	Bridge Ward, Wardmote Inquest Book, 1627–62

Hospital Records
Christ's Hospital

12806/1	Court Minutes, 1556–63
12806/2	Court Minutes, 1562–92
12806/3	Court Minutes, 1592–1632
12819/1	Treasurers' Accounts, 1552–8
12819/2	Treasurers' Accounts, 1561–1608
12818/1	Admission Register, 1554–99
12815/1	Book of Wills, 1552–1702

Bridewell Hospital
These records, the originals of which are at King Edward's School, Witley, have been consulted in microfilm copies available at the Guildhall Library and Bethlem Royal Hospital, Beckenham, Kent.

C.B. I	Court Book, Apr. 1559–June 1562
C.B. II	Court Book, Mar. 1574–May 1576
C.B. III	Court Book, May 1576–Nov. 1579
C.B. IV	Court Book, Feb. 1598–Nov. 1604

Probate Records
Archdeaconry of London

9051/2	Will Register, 1549–60
9051/3	Will Register, 1561–70
9051/4	Will Register, 1570–82
9051/5	Will Register, 1594–1604
9065A/1A	Depositions in Testamentary Causes, 1562–7
9065A/2	Depositions in Testamentary Causes, 1594–7
9065A/3	Depositions in Testamentary Causes, 1597–1603

Commissary Court of London

9171/15	Will Register, 1559–70
9171/16	Will Register, 1570–8
9171/17	Will Register, 1585–92
9171/18	Will Register, 1592–7
9171/19	Will Register, 1597–1603

St Paul's Peculiars

25626/1	Will Register, 1535–60
25626/2	Will Register, 1560–93
25626/3	Will Register, 1593–1608

Other Ecclesiastical Court Records
9064/12   Acta quoad Correctionem Delinquentium, 1582–7
9064/13   Acta quoad Correctionem Delinquentium, 1588–93
9064/14   Acta quoad Correctionem Delinquentium, 1593–9
9064/15   Acta quoad Correctionem Delinquentium, 1599–1603
9056   Archdeaconry Court, Depositions, 1566–7

Livery Companies
Armourers' Company
12071/1   Court Minutes, 1413–1559
12071/2   Court Minutes, 1559–1621
12073   Yeomanry Court Minutes, 1552–1604
12065/1   Wardens' Accounts, 1497–1563
12065/2   Wardens' Accounts, 1563–1616
12110   Charter and Ordinance Book
12079/1   Apprentice Bindings and Freedom Admissions, 1535–1602
12079/2   Apprentice Bindings and Freedom Admissions, 1603–61
12085   Livery Quarterage Book, 1604–65

Bakers' Company
5177/1   Court Minutes, 1537–61
5177/2   Court Minutes, 1561–92
5177/3   Court Minutes, 1592–1617
5174/2   Wardens' Accounts, 1548–86
5174/3   Wardens' Accounts, 1586–1625
5179/1   Quarterage Book, 1518–56
5179/2   Quarterage Book, 1556–1630
5195   John Storer's Remembrancia
5182/2   Wheat Book, 1582–1631

Blacksmiths' Company
2881/1   Court Minutes, 1605–11
2883/1   Court Minutes, 1495–9, 1547–55, 1557–65
2883/3   Wardens' Accounts, 1597–1625
2943   Charter and Ordinance Book

Brewers' Company
5445/2   Court Minutes, 1557–63
5445/3   Court Minutes, 1563–8
5445/4   Court Minutes, 1568–73
5445/5   Court Minutes, 1573–8
5445/6   Court Minutes, 1578–82
5445/7   Court Minutes, 1582–6
5445/8   Court Minutes, 1586–9
5445/9   Court Minutes, 1590–7
5445/10   Court Minutes, 1597–1600
5445/11   Court Minutes, 1601–3
5445/12   Court Minutes, 1604–12
5442/3   Wardens' Accounts, 1547–62
5442/4   Wardens' Accounts, 1563–81

5442/5	Wardens' Accounts, 1582–1616
7885/1	Yeomanry Wardens' Accounts, 1556–86
7885/2	Yeomanry Wardens' Accounts, 1586–1618
5496	Ordinance Book

Broderers' Company
| 14789 | Ordinance Book |

Butchers' Company
6440/1	Wardens' Accounts, 1544–88
6440/2	Wardens' Accounts, 1593–1646
9808	Ordinance Book

Carpenters' Company
4329/1	Court Minutes, 1533–73
4329/2	Court Minutes, 1573–94
4329/3	Court Minutes, 1600–18
4326/2	Wardens' Accounts, 1546–73
4326/3	Wardens' Accounts, 1555–92
4326/4	Wardens' Accounts, 1574–91
4326/5	Wardens' Accounts, 1593–1613

Coopers' Company
5602/1	Court Minutes, 1567–96
5602/2	Court Minutes, 1597–1627
5603/1	Rough Court Minutes, 1552–67
5606/1	Wardens' Accounts, 1529–71
5606/2	Wardens' Accounts, 1571–1611
5633	Memorandum Book

Cordwainers' Company
| 7351/1 | Wardens' Accounts, 1595–1636 |
| 8033 | Memorandum Book |

Curriers' Company
14346/1	Wardens' Accounts, 1557–94
6117	Memorandum Book
6195	Licence to buy Leather, 1567

Cutlers' Company
| 7151/1 | Court Minutes, 1602–70 |
| 7147/1 | Wardens' Accounts, 1586–1621 |

Fishmongers' Company
| 5570/1 | Court Minutes, 1592–1610 |
| 5578A/1 | Quarterage Book, 1610–42 |

Fletchers' Company
| 5977/2 | Quarterage Rolls, 1559–1602 |

Grocers' Company
11588/1   Court Minutes, 1556–91
11588/2   Court Minutes, 1591–1616
11571/6   Wardens' Accounts, 1555–78
11571/7   Wardens' Accounts, 1579–92
11571/8   Wardens' Accounts, 1592–1601
11571/9   Wardens' Accounts, 1601–11
11616   Evidence Book

Haberdashers' Company
15842/1   Court Minutes, 1583–1652
15868   Yeomanry Wardens' Accounts, 1601–61
15869   Yeomanry Wardens' Triumph Accounts, 1604–99
15857/1   Register of Freedom Admissions, 1526–1642
15873   Book of Benefactions
15874   'The State of the Charities, 1597'

Ironmongers' Company
16967/1   Court Minutes, 1555–1602
16967/2   Court Minutes, 1603–11
16988/2   Wardens' Accounts, 1539–92
16988/3   Wardens' Accounts, 1593–1616
16987/2   Yeomanry Wardens' Accounts, 1593–1628
16977/1   Register of Freedom Admissions, 1555–1740
17003   Will and Charter Book
16960   Charter, Ordinance and Memoranda Book

Joiners' Company
8059   Charter and Ordinance Book

Merchant Tailors' Company
The microfilms of these records in the Guildhall Library have been consulted.
C.M. I   Court Minutes, 1562–74
C.M. II   Court Minutes, 1575–95
C.M. III   Court Minutes, 1575–1601
C.M. IV   Court Minutes, 1595–1607
C.M. V   Court Minutes, 1601–11
W.A. IV   Wardens' Accounts, 1545–57
W.A. V   Wardens' Accounts, 1569–81
W.A. VI   Wardens' Accounts, 1581–92
W.A. VII   Wardens' Accounts, 1592–1601
W.A. VIII   Wardens' Accounts, 1601–4
Anc. MS. II   Ordinances, 1579
Anc. MS. V   Benefactors' Gift Book
Anc. MS. VI   Ordinance Book
Anc. MS. VII   Pageant Book, 1556, 1561, 1568
Anc. MS. VIII Evidence Book
Anc. MS. IX   Wills Book
Anc. MS. X   Statutes, 1606

Paviors' Company
182/1   Quarterage Lists, 1565–1611

Pewterers' Company
7090/1   Court Minutes, 1551–61
7090/2   Court Minutes, 1561–89
7090/3   Court Minutes, 1589–1611
7086/2   Wardens' Accounts, 1530–72
7086/3   Wardens' Accounts, 1572–1663
7094   Yeomanry Wardens' Accounts, 1494–1635
7109   Register of Wills
7110   Inventory and Record Book
7114   Charter and Ordinance Book

Pinmakers' Company
184/1–3   Ordinances and Charter, 1605–6

Plasterers' Company
6122/1   Court Minutes and Wardens' Accounts, 1571–1634
6127/1   Quarterage Book, 1604–34
6132   Ordinance Book

Plumbers' Company
2210/1   Wardens' Accounts, 1593–1661
2207   Ordinance Book

Saddlers' Company
5385   Court Minutes, 1605–65
5385A   Ordinance Book

Tallow Chandlers' Company
6152/1   Court Minutes, 1549–85
6152/2   Court Minutes, 1585–1653
6156   Yeomanry Court Book, 1607–36, 1646–95
6155/1   Yeomanry Wardens' Accounts, 1519–49
6155/2   Yeomanry Wardens' Accounts, 1550–1627
6174/1   Ordinance Book

Turners' Company
3295/1   Court Minutes, 1605–33
3297/1   Wardens' Accounts, 1593–4, 1604–70
3308   Ordinance Book

Tylers and Bricklayers' Company
3043/1   Court Minutes, 1580–1667
3054/1   Wardens' Accounts, 1605–31
3047/1   Search Book, 1605–50
4318   Memorandum Book

Vintners' Company
15201/1   Court Minutes, 1608–10
15333/1   Wardens' Accounts, 1522–82
15333/2   Wardens' Accounts, 1582–1617
15211/1   Register of Freedom Admissions, 1428–1602
15211/2   Register of Freedom Admissions, 1602–61
15364   Will Book
15197   Ordinance Book

Waxchandlers' Company
9485/1   Court Minutes, 1584–1689
9493   Search Book, 1574–1652

Woolmen's Company
6901   Wardens' Accounts
6907   Ordinance and Memorandum Book

GREATER LONDON RECORD OFFICE

Parochial Records
Records listed below relate to St Saviour Southwark unless otherwise stated.
P92/SAV/449   Vestry Minutes, 1556–81
P92/SAV/450   Vestry Minutes, 1582–1628
P92/SAV/787–798   Documents Relating to Controversies over Constitution of
                   Vestry, 1606
P92/SAV/1566–72   Accounts of College of Poor, 1589–90, 1597–1602, 1603–4,
                   1606–7
P92/SAV/1383   Account of Collectors for the Poor, 1552–3
P92/SAV/1384   Account of Gifts to the Poor Besides their Weekly Stipends,
                   c. 1562
P92/SAV/1385   Account of Collectors for the Poor, ? date
P92/SAV/1386   Account of Money Received by Legacy, 1563
P92/SAV/1387   Account of Collectors for the Poor, 26 June–3 Oct. 1563
P92/SAV/1394   Account of Collectors for the Poor, 1572
P92/SAV/1395   Account of Collectors for the Poor, 1573
P92/SAV/1397   Account of Collectors for the Poor, ? date
P92/SAV/1314–17   Views of Inmates, 1593–5
P92/SAV/1463   Warrant from J.P.s to Distrain Non-Contributors to Poor,
                   1599
P92/SAV/1465   Survey of Poor, 1618
P92/SAV/1477   Will Book
P92/SAV/356   Parish Register, 1538–63
P92/SAV/357   Parish Register, 1563–71
P92/SAV/3001   Parish Register, 1571–1610

P71/OLA/9   St Olave Southwark, Parish Register, 1583–1627

St Thomas' Hospital

H1/ST/A1/1	Court Minutes, 1557–64
H1/ST/A1/2	Court Minutes, 1564–8
H1/ST/A1/3	Court Minutes, 1568–80
H1/ST/A1/4	Court Minutes, 1580–1608
H1/ST/A24/1	Book of Court, including 1576 Ordinances and Treasurers' Accounts, 1561–82
H1/ST/E29/2	Hospital Rental, including Treasurers' Accounts, 1583–1619

Sessions Records

MJ/SR/	Middlesex Gaol Delivery Files
	Stray indictments and recognisances are to be found among the Accessions (Code Acc.) of the Record Office.

Ecclesiastical Records

DL/C/358/1	Consistory Court, Will Register, 1560–91
DL/C/359	Consistory Court, Will Register, 1592–1609
DL/C/301	Consistory Court, Act Book, Mar. 1584–July 1586
DL/C/210	Consistory Court, Deposition Book, Nov. 1566–Feb. 1569
DL/C/211/1	Consistory Court, Deposition Book, Apr. 1572–Jun. 1574
DL/C/212	Consistory Court, Deposition Book, Jun. 1574–Mar. 1576
DL/C/629	Consistory Court, Deposition Book, Apr. 1578–Nov. 1580
DL/C/213	Consistory Court, Deposition Book, Dec. 1586–Jun. 1591
DL/C/214	Consistory Court, Deposition Book, Jun. 1591–Nov. 1594

Other Records

SKCS 18	Proceedings of the Surrey and Kent Commissioners of the Sewers, 1569–1606

E144	St Margaret Westminster, Accounts of Collectors for the Poor, 1561–2, 1565–71
E145	St Margaret Westminster, Accounts of Collectors for the Poor, 1572–80
E146	St Margaret Westminster, Accounts of Collectors for the Poor, 1580–9
E147	St Margaret Westminster, Accounts of Collectors for the Poor, 1589–97
E148	St Margaret Westminster, Accounts of Collectors for the Poor, 1598–9
E149	St Margaret Westminster, Accounts of Collectors for the Poor, 1599–1608
F304–F329	St Martin in the Fields, Accounts of Collectors for the Poor, 1577–1603
F2001	St Martin in the Fields, Register of Parochial Memoranda
F6039	St Martin in the Fields, Answer to Warrant Concerning Poor Relief, 1603
	Will Registers, Bracy and Elsam
	Minutes of the Westminster Court of Burgesses, vol. I, 1610–13

WESTMINSTER ABBEY MUNIMENTS

25029   View of Poor, St Margaret Westminster, 1578
9340   Orders for Poor in Vandon's Almshouses
9353   Survey of Poor in Pickering's Ward, 1595
13550   Summary Accounts of Collectors for the Poor, St Botolph Aldersgate, 1620s

SOUTHWARK ARCHIVES

St Olave Southwark, Churchwardens' Accounts, 1546–92
St Olave Southwark, Vestry Minutes, 1552–1604
St Mary Magdalen Bermondsey Street, Accounts of Collectors for the Poor, 1599–1625
St George the Martyr, Book of Distributions to the Poor, 1609–67

SOCIETY OF ANTIQUARIES, LONDON

MS 236   St Olave Southwark, Churchwardens' Accounts, 1592–1608

ST OLAVE'S GRAMMAR SCHOOL, ORPINGTON

SOI/1/1   St Olave's Grammar School, Governors' Minutes, 1571–1690
SOII/1/1   St Saviour's Grammar School, Governors' Minutes, 1571–1650
SOII/1/8   Orders made for the Grammar School late erected in Southwark in the Parish of St Saviour's

SAINT BARTHOLOMEW'S HOSPITAL

Ha1/1   Court Minutes, 1549–61
Ha1/2   Court Minutes, 1567–86
Ha1/3   Court Minutes, 1586–1607
Hb1/1   Treasurers' Accounts, 1547–61
Hb1/2   Treasurers' Accounts, 1562–88
Hb1/3   Treasurers' Accounts, 1589–1614

St Bartholomew the Less, Churchwardens' Accounts, 1575–1666

BARBER SURGEONS' HALL

5257/1   Court Minutes, 1550–86
5257/2   Court Minutes, 1566–1604
5257/3   Court Minutes, 1598–1607
5255/1   Wardens' Accounts, 1603–59

CLOTHWORKERS' HALL

C.M. I	Court Minutes, 1539–58
C.M. II	Court Minutes, 1558–81
C.M. III	Court Minutes, 1581–1605
R.W.A.	Renter Wardens' Accounts, 1558–1603 (bundles for each year separately foliated)
Q.W.A.	Quarter Wardens' Accounts, 1558–1603 (bundles for each year separately foliated)
	'Wills Book'
	'Benefactors' Book'
	Directory of Freedom Admissions, 1535–1661

DRAPERS' HALL

Rep. A	Court Minutes, 1547–52
Rep. B	Court Minutes, 1552–7
Rep. C	Court Minutes, 1557–61
Rep. D	Court Minutes, 1567–74
Rep. E	Court Minutes, 1574–84
Rep. F	Court Minutes, 1584–94
Rep. G	Court Minutes, 1594–1603
W.A.	Wardens' Accounts (bundles for each year separately foliated)
R.W.A.	Renter Wardens' Accounts (bundles for each year separately foliated)
	'Dinner Book', 1563–1602
	'Poor Roll', 1595–1616
	Bachelors' Ordinances, 1560
	Yeomanry Wardens' Accounts, 1616–90

GOLDSMITHS' HALL

Reg. K	Court Minutes, 1557–69
Reg. L	Court Minutes, 1569–79
Reg. N	Court Minutes, 1592–9
Reg. O	Court Minutes, 1599–1604
	'Register of Deeds'

LEATHERSELLERS' HALL

Liber Curtes I	Wardens' Accounts and Inventories, 1471–1584
Liber Curtes II	Wardens' Accounts and Inventories, 1584–1647

MERCERS' HALL

C.M. II	Court Minutes, 1527–60
C.M. III	Court Minutes, 1560–95

C.M. IV Court Minutes, 1595–1629
Renter Wardens' Accounts, 1538–77
Renter Wardens' Accounts, 1577–1603
Register of Writings, vol. II
Register of Benefactors' Wills
'Black Book'

SALTERS' HALL

J1/2 Wardens' Accounts, 1599–1600 only
C5/1/1 Will Book, commenced 1611

SKINNERS' HALL

C.M. I Court Minutes, 1551–1617
C.M. II Court Minutes, 1577–1617
W.A. III Wardens' Accounts, 1564–96
W.A. IV Wardens' Accounts, 1596–1617
Register of Freedom Admissions and Apprentice Bindings, 1496–1602

BRITISH LIBRARY

Lansdowne Manuscripts
Harleian Manuscripts
Cottonian Manuscripts
Additional Manuscripts
Hatfield Manuscripts (microfilm copies)
Royal Manuscripts

PUBLIC RECORD OFFICE

C2 Chancery, Proceedings
C3 Chancery, Proceedings
C24 Chancery, Town Depositions
C66 Chancery, Patent Rolls
C93 Chancery, Proceedings of Commissioners for Charitable Uses
C181 Chancery, Entry Books of Commissions (Crown Office)
C203 Chancery, Certificates of Lenten Searches
C265 Chancery, Certificates of Lenten Searches
E117 Certificates of Church Goods
E137 Exchequer, King's Remembrancer, Estreats
E159 Exchequer, King's Remembrancer, Memoranda Rolls
E179 Exchequer, King's Remembrancer, Lay Subsidies (assessments, certificates etc.)
E180 Victuallers' Recognisances
E190 Port Books
E351 Exchequer, Various Accounts
E362 Estreats
KB9 King's Bench, Ancient Indictments

PROB 11	Prerogative Court of Canterbury, Will Registers
REQ2	Court of Requests, Proceedings
SP11	State Papers Domestic, Mary I
SP12	State Papers Domestic, Elizabeth I
SP14	State Papers Domestic, James I
SP15	State Papers Domestic, Addenda
SP46	State Papers Domestic, Supplementary
STAC5	Star Chamber Proceedings, Elizabeth I
STAC8	Star Chamber Proceedings, James I

HOUSE OF LORDS RECORD OFFICE
Main Papers, 1582–1607

LAMBETH PALACE LIBRARY
Cartae Miscellanae VII–VIII: Papers Relating to the Great Tithe Cause
Holy Trinity Minories, Churchwardens' Accounts, 1566–1686

BODLEIAN LIBRARY, OXFORD
MS Eng. Hist. *c.* 429 Papers of William Herrick, goldsmith, including Renter Wardens' Account for 1600–1
Rawlinson Manuscripts
Ashmole Manuscripts

CAMBRIDGE UNIVERSITY LIBRARY
Mm. 1.29　Notebook of Thomas Earle

BUCKINGHAMSHIRE RECORD OFFICE
D138/22/1　Speeches of Sir John Croke, Recorder of London

NORTHAMPTONSHIRE RECORD OFFICE
Fitzwilliam of Milton Manuscripts

NATIONAL LIBRARY OF WALES
Chirk Castle MS A17 Newgate Gaol Delivery Calendar, 1541–3

FOLGER SHAKESPEARE LIBRARY, WASHINGTON
MSS V.a. 459–461　Diaries of Richard Stonley

HENRY E. HUNTINGTON LIBRARY, SAN MARINO, CALIFORNIA
Ellesmere Manuscripts

PRINTED SOURCES

Place of publication is London, unless otherwise stated.

Accomptes of the Churchwardens of the Paryshe of St Christofer's in London, 1575–1662, ed. E. Freshfield (1885)

The Account Books of St Bartholomew Exchange, ed. E. Freshfield (1895)

The Accounts of the Churchwardens of the Parish of St Michael Cornhill in the City of London, from 1456 to 1608, ed. W. H. Overall (1883)

Acts of Court of the Mercers' Company, 1453–1527, ed. L. Lyell and F. D. Watney (Cambridge, 1936)

Acts of the Privy Council of England, ed. J. R. Dasent (32 vols., 1890–1907)

Hugh Alley's "Caveat": the London Markets in 1598, ed. I. W. Archer, C. M. Barron and V. Harding (London Topographical Society, 1988)

Analytical Index to the Series of Records Known as the Remembrancia Preserved Among the Archives of the City of London, 1579–1664, ed. W. H. and H. C. Overall (1878)

Bacon, F., *Works*, ed. J. Spedding *et al.* (14 vols., 1857–74)

Bale, J., *Dramatic Writings*, ed. J. S. Farmer (Early English Drama Society, 1907)

Ballads and Broadsides Chiefly of the Elizabethan Period, ed. H. L. Collman (Oxford, 1912)

Balmford, J., *A Short Dialogue Concerning the Plagues Infection* (1603; *S.T.C.* 1338)

Barron, C. M., Coleman, C., and Gobbi, C. (eds.), 'The London Journal of Alesandro Magno, 1562', *London Journal*, 9 (1983), 136–52

Birch, T., *Memoirs of the Reign of Elizabeth from the Year 1581 till her Death* (2 vols., 1754)

Birch, W. de G., *Historical Charters and Constitutional Documents of the City of London* (second edition, 1887)

A Breefe Discourse, Declaring and Approving the Necessarie Maintenance of the Laudable Customes of London (1584; *S.T.C.* 16747)

Bush, E., *A Sermon Preached at Pauls Crosse* (1576; *S.T.C.* 4183)

Calendar of Assize Records: Home Circuit Indictments. Elizabeth I and James I, ed. J. S. Cockburn (11 vols., 1975–85)

A Calendar of the Inner Temple Records, ed. F. A. Inderwick (5 vols., 1896–1901)

Calendar of the Patent Rolls, Edward VI, Philip and Mary, Elizabeth (1924–)

Calendar of Plea and Memoranda Rolls of the City of London, ed. A. H. Thomas *et al.* (7 vols., Cambridge, 1924–61)

Calendar of State Papers, Domestic, vols. I–VIII, ed. R. Lemon and M. A. E. Green (1856–75)

Calendar of State Papers, Venetian, vol. XV, ed. A. B. Hinds (1909)

Camden, W., *The History of the Most Renowned and Victorious Princess Elizabeth* (1675)

Chamber Accounts of the Sixteenth Century, ed. R. B. Masters (London Record Society, XX, 1984)

The Letters of John Chamberlain, ed. N. E. McClure (2 vols., Philadelphia, 1939)

The Charters of the Merchant Taylors' Company, ed. F. M. Fry and R. T. D. Sayle (1937)

The Charters, Ordinances and Bye Laws of the Mercers' Company (1881)

Christ's Hospital Admissions, 1554–1599, ed. G. A. T. Allan (1937)

Chronicle of King Henry VIII of England, ed. M. A. S. Hume (1889)

Contemporaneous Account of the Foundation and Early History of Christ's Hospital, and of Bridewell and St Thomas' Hospitals by John Howes (1889)

Crowley, R., *A Sermon Made in the Chappel at the Gylde Halle in London* (1575; S.T.C. 6092)

Select Works, ed. J. M. Cowper (Early English Text Society, extra series, XV, 1872)

Cupper, W., *Certaine Sermons Concerning Gods Late Visitation in London and Other Parts of the Land* (1592; S.T.C. 6125)

Darell, W., *A Short Discourse of the Life of Servingmen* (1578; S.T.C. 6274)

The Private Diary of Dr John Dee, ed. J. O. Halliwell (Camden Society, old series, XIX, 1842)

Dekker, T., *Dramatic Works*, ed. F. Bowers (4 vols., Cambridge, 1953–61)

Newes from Hell (1606)

'A Description of England and Scotland by a French Ecclesiastic in the Sixteenth Century', *The Antiquarian Repertory*, 4 (1809), 501–20

D'Ewes, S., *The Journals of All the Parliaments During the Reign of Queen Elizabeth* (1682)

Drant., T., *Two Sermons Preached, the one at S. Maries Spittle 1570 and the other at the Court at Windsor the viij of January, 1569* (?1570; S.T.C. 7171)

Queen Elizabeth and her Times, ed. T. Wright (2 vols., 1838)

The Elizabethan Underworld, ed. A. V. Judges (1930)

Fisher, W., *A Sermon Preached at Paules Crosse* (1580; S.T.C. 10920)

Four Supplications, 1529–1553, ed. F. J. Furnivall (Early English Text Society, extra series, XIII, 1871)

Grafton, R., *Chronicles* (2 vols., 1809)

The Great Chronicle of London, ed. A. H. Thomas and I. D. Thornley (1938)

Harrison, W., *Harrison's Description of England in Shakspere's Youth*, ed. F. J. Furnivall (New Shakespeare Society, 1877–8)

Haynes, S., *A Collection of State Papers ... Left by William Cecil, Lord Burghley* (1740)

Hessels, J. H. (ed.), *Ecclesiae Londino-Batavae Archivum, Epistulae et Tractatus* (3 vols., Cambridge, 1889–97)

Historical Manuscripts Commission:

　Third Report (1872)

　Hatfield House (24 vols., 1883–1976)

　Frankland-Russell-Astley (1900)

　Bath (3 vols., 1904–8)

　Pepys (1911)

　De L'Isle and Dudley (4 vols., 1925–42)

　Various (8 vols., 1901–14)

　House of Lords, new series, vol. XI (1962)

History of Queen Elizabeth, Amy Robsart, and the Earl of Leicester, being a Reprint of Leycester's Commonwealth, 1641, ed. F. J. Burgoyne (1904)

The History of Sir Richard Whittington. By T. H(eywood), ed. H. B. Wheatley (Chap-Books and Folk Lore Tracts, first series, V, Villon Society, 1885)

Holinshed's Chronicles of England, Scotland and Ireland (6 vols., 1807–9)

Holland, H., *Spirituall Preservatives Against the Pestilence* (1603 edn.; S.T.C. 13588)

Hooke, C., *A Sermon Preached in Paules Church in Time of Plague* (1603; S.T.C. 13703)

John Howes' MS 1582, ed. W. Lemprière (1906)

John Isham, Mercer and Merchant Adventurer: Two Account Books of a London Merchant in the Reign of Elizabeth I, ed. G. D. Ramsay (Northamptonshire Record Society, XXI, 1962)

Jaggard, W., *A View of All the Right Honourable the Lord Mayors of London* (1601; S.T.C. 14343)

Journals of the House of Commons, vol. I (1852)

Journals of the House of Lords, vols. I–II (1846)

Lambarde, W., *The Duties of Constables, Borsholders, Tithingmen, and Such Other Lowe Ministers of the Peace* (1583; S.T.C. 15145)

  Eirenarcha, or of the Office of the Iustices of the Peace (1581; S.T.C. 15163)

William Lambarde and Local Government: His "Ephemeris" and Twenty-Nine Charges to Juries and Commissions, ed. C. Read (Ithaca, 1962)

The Lamentacyon of a Christen Agaynst the Cytye of London, ed. J. M. Cowper (Early English Text Society, extra series, XXII, 1874)

Latimer, H., *Sermons*, ed. G. E. Corrie (Parker Society, XXII, 1844)

Letters and Papers, Foreign and Domestic of the Reign of Henry VIII, 1509–47, ed. J. S. Brewer, J. Gairdner and R. H. Brodie (21 vols., 1862–1910)

Lever, T., *Sermons*, ed. E. Arber (1870)

Levenson-Gower, G. (ed.,), 'Notebook of a Surrey Justice', *Surrey Archaeological Collections*, 9 (1888), 161–232

Lodge, E., *Illustrations of British History* (3 vols., 1838)

London and Middlesex Chantry Certificate, 1548, ed. C. J. Kitching (London Record Society, XVI, 1980)

London's Looking-Glasse or the Copy of a Letter Written by an English Travayler to the Apprentices of London (1621)

London Sessions Records, 1605–1685, ed. H. Bowler (Catholic Record Society, XXXIV, 1934)

The London Surveys of Ralph Treswell, ed. J. Schofield (London Topographical Society, 1987)

London Viewers and their Certificates, 1509–1558, ed. J. S. Loengard (London Record Society, XXVI, 1989)

Lord Mayors' Pageants of the Merchant Taylors' Company, ed. R. T. D. Sayle (1931)

The Diary of Henry Machyn, Citizen and Merchant-Taylor of London, 1550–1563, ed. J. G. Nichols (Camden Society, old series, XLII, 1848)

Memoranda, References and Documents Relating to the Royal Hospitals of the City of London (1836)

Memorials of St Margaret's Church Westminster: the Parish Registers, 1539–1600, ed. A. M. Burke (1914)

Memorials of Stepney Parish, ed. G. W. Hill and W. H. Frere (1890–1)

Middlesex County Records, ed. J. C. Jeaffreson (4 vols., 1886–92)

Middlesex Sessions Records, ed. W. le Hardy (4 vols., 1936–41)

Narratives of the Days of the Reformation, ed. J. G. Nichols (Camden Society, old series, LXXVII, 1859)

Norton, T., 'Instructions to the Lord Mayor of London, 1574–5', in *Illustrations of Old English Literature*, ed. J. P. Collier (3 vols., 1866), III, item 8

The Norwich Census of the Poor, 1570, ed. J. F. Pound (Norfolk Record Society, XL, 1971)

Orders Appointed to bee Executed in the Citie of London, for Setting Roges and Idle Persons to Work (1582; S.T.C. 16709)

Orders Prescribed for the Observation of Her Maiesties Present Proclamation (1595; S.T.C. 8243)

An Order to be Published by the Lord Mayor for Avoyding of Beggars (1593; S.T.C. 16713.5)

The Ordinances of the Clothworkers' Company (1881)

The Book of Ordinances Belonging to the Company of the Tylers and Bricklayers Incorporated in the City of London (?date; 17th. cent.)

Parish Fraternity Register: Fraternity of the Holy Trinity and SS Fabian and Sebastian in the Parish of St Botolph Without Aldersgate, ed. P. Basing (London Record Society, XVIII, 1982)

The Parish Registers of St Michael Cornhill, London, ed. J. L. Chester (Harleian Society Registers, VII, 1882)

Parliamentary Papers, 1840, XIX, part I, Thirty-Second Report of the Commissioners for Inquiring Concerning Charities

Parliamentary Papers, 1884, XXXIX, parts I–V, Report of Her Majesty's Commissioners Appointed to Inquire into the Livery Companies of the City of London

Parliamentary Papers, 1904, LXXI, Accounts and Papers, vol. XXIII: Endowed Charities (County of London)

Peck, F., *Desiderata Curiosa* (1732)

A Pepysian Garland: Black Letter Broadside Ballads of the Years 1595–1639, ed. H. F. Rollins (Cambridge, 1922)

Thomas Platter's Travels in England, ed. C. Williams (1937)

Poor Relief in Elizabethan Ipswich, ed. J. Webb (Suffolk Records Society, IX, 1966)

The Port and Trade of Early Elizabethan London: Documents, ed. B. Dietz (London Record Society, VIII, 1972)

Poverty in Early Stuart Salisbury, ed. P. Slack (Wiltshire Record Society, XXXI, Devizes, 1975)

Proceedings in the Parliaments of Elizabeth I, 1558–1581, ed. T. E. Hartley (Leicester, 1981)

Records of the Court of the Stationers' Company, 1576–1602, ed. W. W. Greg and E. Boswell (Bibliographical Society, 1930)

The Records of Two City Parishes. A Collection of Documents Illustrative of the History of St Anne and Agnes, Aldersgate, and St John Zachary, London, ed. J. McMurray (1925)

Records of the Worshipful Company of Carpenters, ed. B. Marsh, J. Ainsworth and A. M. Millard (7 vols., 1914–68)

The Reformation of the Ecclesiastical Laws, ed. E. Cardwell (1850)

The Registers of St Katherine's by the Tower, London. Part I: 1584–1625, ed. A. W. Hughes Clarke (Harleian Society Registers, LXXV, 1945)

The Register of St Lawrence Jewry, London, ed. A. W. Hughes Clarke (Harleian Society Registers, LXX, 1940)

A Register of Baptisms, Marriages, and Burials in the Parish of St. Martin in the Fields ... from 1550 to 1619, ed. T. Mason (Harleian Society Registers, XXV, 1898)

The Registers of St Stephen's, Walbrook, and of St Benet Sherehog, London, ed. W. B. Bannerman (Harleian Society Registers, XLIX, 1919)

A Transcript of the Registers of the Stationers' Company, 1554–1640, ed. E. A. Arber (5 vols., London and Birmingham, 1875–1894)

A Relation, or Rather a True Account, of the Island of England; with Sundry Particulars of the Customs of these People, and of the Royal Revenues under

King Henry the Seventh, about the Year 1500, ed. C. A. Sneyd (Camden Society, old series, XXXVII, 1847)

Retailing Brokers. Commune Concilium (1595; *S.T.C.* 16715)

Returns of Aliens Dwelling in the City and Suburbs of London, ed. R. E. G. and E. F. Kirk (Huguenot Society Publications, X, 4 vols., 1900–8)

Returns of Strangers in the Metropolis, 1593, 1627, 1635, 1639, ed. I. Scouloudi (Huguenot Society Publications, LVII, 1985)

Rymer, T., *Foedera, Conventiones, Litterae etc.* (1704–35)

St Martin in the Fields. The Accounts of the Churchwardens, 1525–1603, ed. J. V. Kitto (1901)

The Seconde Parte of a Register, ed. A. Peel (2 vols., Cambridge, 1915)

Smith, H., *The Poore Mens Teares Opened in a Sermon* (1592; *S.T.C.* 22683)

The Spending of the Money of Robert Nowell, ed. A. B. Grosart (1877)

The Statutes of the Realm, ed. A. Luders etc. (1810–28)

Stockwood, J., *A Sermon Preached at Paules Crosse on Barthelmew Day, being the 24 of August 1578* (1578; *S.T.C.* 23284)

Stow, J., *A Survey of London*, ed. C. L. Kingsford (2 vols., Oxford, 1908)

   The Annales or Generall Chronicle of England (1615; *S.T.C.* 23338)

   The Abridgement or Summarie of the English Chronicle Continued unto 1607. By E. Howes (1607; *S.T.C.* 23330)

Philip Stubbes' Anatomy of Abuses in England in Shakspere's Youth, ed. F. J. Furnivall (New Shakspere Society, series VI, nos. 4, 6, and 12, 1879–82)

A Students Lamentation that hath Sometime been in London an Apprentice, for the Rebellious Tumults lately in the Citie Hapning (1595; *S.T.C.* 23401.5)

A Supplicacyon for the Beggers, ed. F. J. Furnivall (Early English Text Society, extra series, XIII, 1871)

A Supplycacion to our Moste Soveraigne Lorde Kynge Henry the Eyght, ed. J. M. Cowper (Early English Text Society, extra series, XIII, 1871)

A Supplication of the Poore Commons, ed. J. M. Cowper (Early English Text Society, extra series, XIII, 1871)

Three Fifteenth-Century Chronicles, with Historical Memoranda by John Stowe, ed. J. Gairdner (Camden Society, new series, XXVIII, 1880)

Townshend, H., *Historical Collections, an Exact Account of the Last Four Parliaments of Elizabeth* (1680)

Tudor Economic Documents, ed. R. H. Tawney and E. Power (3 vols., 1924)

Tudor Royal Proclamations, ed. P. L. Hughes and J. F. Larkin (3 vols., 1964–9)

Turnbull, R., *An Exposition Upon the Canonicall Epistle of Saint James* (1606 edn; *S.T.C.* 24341)

The Vestry Minute Books of the Parish of St Bartholomew Exchange in the City of London, 1567–1676, ed. E. Freshfield (1890)

Minutes of the Vestry Meetings and other Records of St Christopher-le-Stocks in the City of London, ed. E. Freshfield (1886)

The Vestry Minute Book of the Parish of St Margaret Lothbury in the City of London, 1571–1677, ed. E. Freshfield (1887)

Vicary, T., *The Anatomie of the Bodie of Man*, ed. F. J. and P. Furnivall (Early English Text Society, extra series, LIII, 1888)

Von Bulow, G. (ed.), 'Diary of the Journey of Philip Julius, Duke of Stettin-Pomerania through England in the Year 1602', *Transactions of the Royal Historical Society*, new series, 6 (1892), 1–67

   (ed.), 'A Journey through England and Scotland made by Lupold von Wedel in the

Years 1584 and 1585', *Transactions of the Royal Historical Society*, new series, 9 (1895), 223–70

Wardens' Accounts of the Worshipful Company of Founders of the City of London, 1497–1681, ed. G. Parsloe (1964)

White, T., *A Sermon Preached at Pawles Crosse on Sunday the Thirde of November 1577 in the Time of the Plague* (1578; S.T.C. 25406)

A Sermon Preached at Pawles Crosse on Sunday the Ninth of December 1576 (1578; S.T.C. 25405)

'The Journal of Sir Roger Wilbraham', ed. H. S. Scott, *Camden Miscellany X* (Camden Society, third series, IV, 1902)

Willet, A., *Synopsis Papismi* (1613 edn; S.T.C. 25699)

Wills, Leases and Memoranda in the Book of Records of the Parish of St Christopher-le-Stocks in the City of London, ed. E. Freshfield (1895)

Wilson, T., 'The State of England Anno Dom. 1600', *Camden Miscellany XVI* (Camden Society, third series, LII, 1936)

Wriothesley, C., *A Chronicle of England During the Reigns of the Tudors*, ed. W. D. Hamilton (2 vols., Camden Society, new series, XI and XX, 1875–1877)

York Civic Records VIII, ed. A. Raine (Yorkshire Archaeological Society Record Series, CXIX, 1953)

SECONDARY SOURCES

Adams, S. L., 'Eliza Enthroned? The Court and its Politics', in *The Reign of Elizabeth I*, ed. C. A. Haigh (Basingstoke, 1984), pp. 55–77

'The Lurch into War', *History Today*, 38 (May 1988), 18–25

Alford, B. W. E., and Barker, T., *A History of the Carpenters' Company* (1968)

Alldridge, N., 'Loyalty and Identity in Chester Parishes, 1540–1640', in *Parish, Church and People: Local Studies in Lay Religion*, ed. S. Wright (1988), pp. 85–124

Amussen, S. D., *An Ordered Society: Gender and Class in Early Modern England* (Oxford, 1988)

Appleby, A. B., *Famine in Tudor and Stuart England* (Liverpool, 1978)

'Diet in Sixteenth-Century England: Sources, Problems, Possibilities', in *Health, Medicine and Mortality in the Sixteenth Century*, ed. C. Webster (Cambridge, 1979), pp. 97–116

Archer, I. W., 'The London Lobbies in the Later Sixteenth Century', *Historical Journal*, 31 (1988), 17–44

Arkell, T., 'The Incidence of Poverty in England in the Late Seventeenth Century', *Social History*, 12 (1987), 1–22

Ashton, R., *The City and the Court, 1603–1643* (Cambridge, 1979)

Reformation and Revolution, 1558–1660 (1984)

Barron, C. M., 'Ralph Holland and the London Radicals, 1438–1444', in *A History of the North London Branch of the Historical Association, Together with Essays in Honour of its Golden Jubilee*, ed. A. L. Rowse and C. M. Barron (1971), pp. 60–80

The Parish of Saint Andrew Holborn, London (1979)

Revolt in London: 11th to 15th June 1381 (1981)

'The Parish Fraternities of Medieval London', in *The Church in Pre-Reformation Society: Essays in Honour of F. R. H. du Boulay*, ed. C. Harper-Bill and C. M. Barron (1985), pp. 13–37

Beattie, J. M., *Crime and the Courts in England, 1660–1800* (Oxford, 1986)

Beaven, A., *The Aldermen of the City of London* (2 vols., 1908–13)

Beier, A. L., 'Vagrants and the Social Order in Elizabethan England', *Past and Present*, 64 (1974), 3–29

'Social Problems in Elizabethan London', *Journal of Interdisciplinary History*, 9 (1978), 203–21

'The Social Problems of an Elizabethan Country Town: Warwick, 1580–90', in *Country Towns in Pre-Industrial England*, ed. P. Clark (Leicester, 1981), pp. 46–85

Masterless Men: the Vagrancy Problem in England, 1560–1640 (1985)

'Engine of Manufacture: the Trades of London', in *London, 1500–1700: the Making of the Metropolis*, ed. A. L. Beier and R. Finlay (1986), pp. 141–67

Bellamy, J., *The Tudor Law of Treason: an Introduction* (1979)

Benbow, M., 'The Court of Aldermen and the Assizes: the Policy of Price Control in Elizabethan London', *Guildhall Studies in London History*, 4 (1980), 93–118

Benedict, P., *Rouen During the Wars of Religion* (Cambridge, 1981)

Berlin, M., 'Civic Ceremony in Early Modern London', *Urban History Yearbook*, 1986, 15–27

Berlin, N., *The Base String: The Underworld In Elizabethan Drama* (Cranbury, New Jersey, 1968)

Bindoff, S. T. (ed.), *The House of Commons, 1509–1558* (3 vols., 1982)

Bird, R., *The Turbulent London of Richard II* (1949)

Bittle, W. G. and Lane, R. T., 'Inflation and Philanthropy in England: a Reassessment of W. K. Jordan's Data', *Economic History Review*, second series, 29 (1976), 203–10

Black, J. B., *The Reign of Elizabeth, 1558–1603* (Oxford, 1936)

Bobart, H. H., *Records of the Basketmakers' Company* (1911)

Boulton, J. P., 'The Limits of Formal Religion: the Administration of Holy Communion in Late Elizabethan and Early Stuart London', *London Journal*, 10 (1984), 135–54

Neighbourhood and Society: a London Suburb in the Seventeenth Century (Cambridge, 1987)

Bowden, P., *The Wool Trade in Tudor and Stuart England* (1962)

Boynton, L. O. J., 'The Tudor Provost Marshal', *English Historical Review*, 77 (1962), 437–55

Bradshaw, B., 'The Tudor Commonwealth: Reform and Revision', *Historical Journal*, 22 (1979), 455–76

Brenner, R., 'The Civil War Politics of London's Merchant Community', *Past and Present*, 58 (1973), 53–107

Brigden, S., 'Popular Disturbance and the Fall of Thomas Cromwell and the Reformers', *Historical Journal*, 24 (1981), 257–78

'Youth and the English Reformation', *Past and Present*, 95 (1982), 37–67

'Religion and Social Obligation in Early Sixteenth-Century London', *Past and Present*, 103 (1984), 67–112

London and the Reformation (Oxford, 1989)

Brodsky, V., 'Widows in Late Elizabethan London: Remarriage, Economic Opportunity and Family Orientations', in *The World We Have Gained: Histories of Population and Social Structure: Essays to Peter Laslett on his Seventieth Birthday*, ed. L. Bonfield, R. M. Smith and K. Wrightson (Oxford, 1986), pp. 122–54

Brooks, C. W., *Pettyfoggers and Vipers of the Commonwealth: the "Lower Branch" of the Legal Profession in Early Modern England* (Cambridge, 1986)

Burford, E. J., *The Orryble Synne: A Look at London Lechery from Roman to Cromwellian Times* (1973)

Burke, P., 'Popular Culture in Seventeenth-Century London', *London Journal*, 3 (1977), 143–62

Cain, P., 'Robert Smith and the Reform of the Archives of the City of London, 1580–1623', *London Journal*, 13 (1987–8), 3–16

Carlton, C., *The Court of Orphans* (Leicester, 1974)

Carrington, R. C., *Two Schools: a History of the St Olave's and St Saviour's Grammar School Foundation* (1971)

Chambers, E. K., *The Elizabethan Stage* (4 vols., Oxford, 1923)

Chaney, E. P. de G., '"Philanthropy in Italy": English Observations on Italian Hospitals', in *Aspects of Poverty in Early Modern Europe*, ed. T. Riis (Florence, 1981), pp. 183–217

Chartres, J., 'Food Consumption and Internal Trade', in *London, 1500–1700: the Making of the Metropolis*, ed. A. L. Beier and R. Finlay (1986), pp. 168–96

Cheyney, E. P., *A History of England from the Defeat of the Armada to the Death of Elizabeth* (2 vols., 1914–26)

Clark, P. and Slack, P., 'Introduction', in *Crisis and Order in English Towns, 1500–1700: Essays in Urban History*, ed. P. Clark and P. Slack (1972), pp. 1–55

Clark, P., 'The Migrant in Kentish Towns, 1580–1640', in *Crisis and Order in English Towns, 1500–1700: Essays in Urban History*, ed. P. Clark and P. Slack (1972), pp. 117–63

Clark, P. and Slack, P., *English Towns in Transition, 1500–1700* (Oxford, 1976)

Clark, P., 'Popular Protest and Disturbance in Kent, 1558–1640', *Economic History Review*, second series, 29 (1976), 365–82

'A Crisis Contained? The Condition of English Towns in the 1590s', in *The European Crisis of the 1590s*, ed. P. Clark (1985), pp. 44–66

'Migrants in the City: the Process of Social Adaptation in English Towns', in *Migration and Society in Early Modern England*, ed. P. Clark and D. Souden (1987), pp. 267–91

Clark, S., 'Inversion, Misrule and the Meaning of Witchcraft', *Past and Present*, 87 (1980), 98–127

Clode, C. M., *The Early History of the Guild of Merchant Taylors* (2 vols., 1888)

Memorials of the Guild of Merchant Taylors (1875)

Cockburn, J. S., 'The Nature and Incidence of Crime in England, 1559–1625: a Preliminary Survey', in *Crime in England, 1550–1800*, ed. J. S. Cockburn (1977), pp. 49–71

Calendar of Assize Records. Home Circuit Indictments. Elizabeth I and James I. Introduction (1985)

Collinson, P., *The Elizabethan Puritan Movement* (1967)

The Religion of Protestants: the Church in English Society, 1559–1625 (Oxford, 1982)

The Birthpangs of Protestant England: Religious and Cultural Change in the Sixteenth and Seventeenth Centuries (1988)

Consitt, F., *The London Weavers' Company* (Oxford, 1933)

Cooper, J. P., 'Henry VII's Last Years Reconsidered', *Historical Journal*, 2 (1959), 103–29

Cressy, D., *Literacy and the Social Order: Reading and Writing in Tudor and Stuart England* (Cambridge, 1980)

Croft, P. (ed.), *The Spanish Company* (London Record Society, IX, 1973)

Cust, R., and Hughes, A., 'Introduction: After Revisionism', in *Conflict in Early Stuart England: Studies in Religion and Politics, 1603–1642*, ed. R. Cust and A. Hughes (1989), pp. 1–46

Davies, C. S. L., 'Popular Disorder', in *The European Crisis of the 1590s*, ed. P. Clark (1985), pp. 244–60

Davis, N. Z., 'The Sacred and the Body Social in Sixteenth-Century Lyon', *Past and Present*, 90 (1981), 40–70

Davis, R., *English Overseas Trade, 1500–1700* (1973)

Dean, D. M., 'Public or Private? London, Leather and Legislation in Elizabethan England', *Historical Journal*, 31 (1988), 525–48

De Krey, G. S., *A Fractured Society: the Politics of London in the First Age of Party, 1688–1715* (Oxford, 1985)

Dictionary of National Biography, ed. L. Stephen and S. Lee (1885–1900)

Dietz, B., 'Overseas Trade and Metropolitan Growth', in *London, 1500–1700: the Making of the Metropolis*, ed. A. L. Beier and R. A. P. Finlay (1986), pp. 115–40

Drummond, J. C. and Wilbraham, A., *The Englishman's Food: a History of Five Centuries of English Diet* (1952)

Duffy, E., 'The Godly and the Multitude in Stuart England', *The Seventeenth Century*, 1 (1986), 31–55

Dyer, A., *The City of Worcester in the Sixteenth Century* (Leicester, 1973)

Edwards, P., *The Horse Trade of Tudor and Stuart England* (Cambridge, 1988)

Elliott, J. H., *Imperial Spain, 1469–1716* (Harmondsworth, 1970)

Elton, G. R., 'Henry VII: Rapacity and Remorse', in G. R. Elton, *Studies in Tudor and Stuart Politics and Government* (3 vols., Cambridge, 1974–82), I. 45–65

'Henry VII: a Restatement', in G. R. Elton, *Studies in Tudor and Stuart Politics and Government* (3 vols., Cambridge, 1974–82), I. 66–99

Reform and Renewal: Thomas Cromwell and the Commonweal (Cambridge, 1973)

'Piscatorial Politics in the Early Parliaments of Elizabeth I', in *Business Life and Public Policy: Essays in Honour of D. C. Coleman*, ed. N. McKendrick and R. B. Outhwaite (Cambridge, 1986), pp. 1–20

The Parliament of England, 1559–1581 (Cambridge, 1986)

Englefield, W. A. D., *A History of the Painter-Stainers' Company of London* (1923)

Finlay, R. A. P., *Population and Metropolis: the Demography of London, 1580–1650* (Cambridge, 1981)

Finlay, R. A. P. and Shearer, B., 'Population Growth and Suburban Expansion', in *London, 1500–1700: the Making of the Metropolis*, ed. A. L. Beier and R. A. P. Finlay (1986), pp. 37–59

Fisher, F. J., 'Commercial Trends and Policy in Sixteenth-Century England', *Economic History Review*, 10 (1940), 95–117

'The Development of London as a Centre of Conspicuous Consumption in the Sixteenth and Seventeenth Centuries', *Transactions of the Royal Historical Society*, fourth series, 30 (1948), 37–50

'London's Export Trade in the Early Seventeenth Century', *Economic History Review*, second series, 3 (1950), 151–61

Fletcher, A. J., *Reform in the Provinces: the Government of Stuart England* (1986)

Fletcher, A. J. and Stevenson, J., 'Introduction', in *Order and Disorder in Early Modern England*, ed. A. J. Fletcher and J. Stevenson (Cambridge, 1985), pp. 1–40

Foster, F. F., *The Politics of Stability: a Portrait of the Rulers of Elizabethan London* (1977)

Friedrichs, C. R., 'German Town Revolts and the Seventeenth-Century Urban Crisis', *Renaissance and Modern Studies*, 26 (1982), 27–51

Garrioch, D., *Neighbourhood and Community in Paris, 1740–1790* (Cambridge, 1986)

Geremek, B., *The Margins of Society in Late Medieval Paris* (Cambridge, 1987)

Gillis, J. R., *For Better, For Worse: British Marriages, 1600 to the Present* (Oxford, 1985)

Gras, N. S. B., *The Evolution of the English Corn Market from the Twelfth to the Eighteenth Century* (Cambridge, Mass., 1915)

Grassby, R., 'The Personal Wealth of the Business Community in Seventeenth-Century England', *Economic History Review*, second series, 23 (1970), 220–34

Graves, M. A. R., 'The Management of the Elizabethan House of Commons: the Council's "Men of Business"', *Parliamentary History*, 2 (1983), 11–38

Greaves, R. L., *Society and Religion in Elizabethan England* (Minneapolis, 1981)

Greengrass, M., 'The Later Wars of Religion in the French Midi', in *The European Crisis of the 1590s*, ed. P. Clark (1985), pp. 106–34

Greg, W. W., *A Companion to Arber* (Oxford, 1967)

Griffith, E., *Cases of Supposed Exemption from the Poor Rates Claimed on Grounds of Extra-Parochiality, with a Preliminary Sketch of the Ancient History of the Parish of Saint Andrew Holborn* (1831)

Guy, J., *Tudor England* (Oxford, 1988)

Hadwin, J. F., 'Deflating Philanthropy', *Economic History Review*, second series, 31 (1978), 105–17

Haigh, C. A., 'The Church of England, the Catholics and the People', in *The Reign of Elizabeth I*, ed. C. A. Haigh (Basingstoke, 1984), pp. 195–219

(ed.), *The English Reformation Revised* (Cambridge, 1987)

Hall, H., *Society in the Elizabethan Age* (1886)

Harper-Bill, C., *The Pre-Reformation Church in England, 1400–1530* (1989)

Harris, T., *London Crowds in the Reign of Charles II: Propaganda and Politics from the Restoration until the Exclusion Crisis* (Cambridge, 1987)

Harrison, C. J., 'The Petition of Edmund Dudley', *English Historical Review*, 87 (1972), 82–99

Hasler, P. W., (ed.), *The House of Commons, 1558–1603* (3 vols., 1981)

Hay, D., 'Property, Authority and the Criminal Law', in *Albion's Fatal Tree: Crime and Society in Eighteenth-Century England*, ed. D. Hay, P. Linebaugh, J. G. Rule, E. P. Thompson and C. Winslow (Harmondsworth, 1975), pp. 17–63

'War, Dearth and Theft in the Eighteenth Century: the Record of the English Courts', *Past and Present*, 95 (1982), 117–60

Heal, F., 'The Idea of Hospitality in Early Modern England', *Past and Present*, 102 (1984), 66–93

Herlan, R. W., 'Social Articulation and the Configuration of Parochial Poverty in London on the Eve of the Restoration', *Guildhall Studies in London History*, 2 (1976), 43–53

'Poor Relief in the London Parish of Dunstan in the West During the English Revolution', *Guildhall Studies in London History*, 3 (1977), 13–36

'Poor Relief in the London Parish of Antholin's Budge Row, 1638–1664', *Guildhall Studies in London History*, 2 (1977), 179–99

Herrup, C. B., 'New Shoes and Mutton Pies: Investigative Responses to Theft in Seventeenth Century East Sussex', *Historical Journal*, 27 (1984), 811–30

'Law and Morality in Seventeenth-Century England', *Past and Present*, 106 (1985), 102–23

The Common Peace: Participation and the Criminal Law in Seventeenth-Century England (Cambridge, 1987)

Hill, C., *Society and Puritanism in Pre-Revolutionary England* (1964)

Hind, A. M., *Engraving in England in the Sixteenth and Seventeenth Centuries; a Descriptive Catalogue with Introductions* (3 vols., Cambridge, 1952–64)

Holmes, G., *The Good Parliament* (Oxford, 1975)

Hotson, L., *Mr W.H.* (1964)

Ingram, M., 'Ridings, Rough Music and the "Reform of Popular Culture" in Early Modern England', *Past and Present*, 105 (1984), 79–113

'The Reform of Popular Culture? Sex and Marriage in Early Modern England', in *Popular Culture in Seventeenth-Century England*, ed. B. Reay (1985), pp. 129–65

Church Courts, Sex and Marriage in England, 1570–1640 (Cambridge, 1987)

James, M. E., 'At a Crossroads of the Political Culture: the Essex Revolt, 1601', in M. E. James, *Society, Politics and Culture: Studies in Early Modern England* (Cambridge, 1986), pp. 416–65

Johnson, A. H., *The History of the Worshipful Company of Drapers of London* (5 vols., Oxford, 1914–22)

Johnson, D. J., *Southwark and the City* (1969)

Jones, D. W., 'The "Hallage" Receipts of the London Cloth Markets, 1562–1720', *Economic History Review*, second series, 25 (1972), 567–87

Jones, E., 'London in the Early Seventeenth Century: an Ecological Approach', *London Journal*, 6 (1980), 126–33

Jordan, W. K., *Philanthropy in England, 1480–1660: a Study of the Changing Pattern of English Social Aspirations* (1959)

The Charities of London, 1480–1660: the Aspirations and Achievements of the Urban Society (1960)

Karras, R. M., 'The Regulation of Brothels in Later Medieval England', *Signs*, 14 (1989), 399–433

Keene, D., 'A New Study of London Before the Great Fire', *Urban History Yearbook*, 1984, 11–21

Keene, D., and V. Harding (eds.), *A Survey of Documentary Sources for Property Holding in London Before the Great Fire* (London Record Society, XXII, 1985)

Kent, J., 'Attitudes of Members of the House of Commons to the Regulation of "Personal Conduct" in Late Elizabethan and Early Stuart England', *Bulletin of the Institute of Historical Research*, 46 (1973), 41–71

The English Village Constable, 1580–1640 (Oxford, 1986)

Kiernan, V. G., *State and Society in Europe, 1550–1650* (Oxford, 1980)

Kishlansky, M., *Parliamentary Selection: Social and Political Choice in Early Modern England* (Cambridge, 1986)

Lang, R. G., 'Social Origins and Social Aspirations of Jacobean London Merchants', *Economic History Review*, second series, 27 (1974), 28–47

Langbein, J. H., *Prosecuting Crime in the Renaissance: England, Germany and France* (Cambridge, Mass., 1975)

Torture and the Law of Proof (1977)

Lindley, K., 'Riot Prevention and Control in Early Stuart London', *Transactions of the Royal Historical Society*, fifth series, 33 (1983), 109–26

MacCaffrey, W. T., *Exeter, 1540–1640: the Growth of an English Country Town* (1975)

McCampbell, A. E., 'The London Parish and the London Precinct, 1640–1660', *Guildhall Studies in London History*, 2 (1976), 107–24

McIntosh, M. K., 'Local Responses to the Poor in Late Medieval and Tudor England', *Continuity and Change*, 3 (1988), 209–45

McMullan, J., *The Canting Crew: London's Criminal Underworld, 1550–1700* (New Jersey, 1984)

McPeek, J. A. S., *The Black Book of Knaves and Unthrifts in Shakespeare and Other Renaissance Authors* (Connecticut, 1969)

Manchée, W. H., *The Westminster City Fathers, 1585–1901* (1924)

Manning, R. B., 'The Prosecution of Sir Michael Blount, Lieutenant of the Tower of London, 1595', *Bulletin of the Institute of Historical Research*, 57 (1984), 216–24

Village Revolts: Social Protest and Popular Disturbances in England, 1509–1640 (Oxford, 1988)

Martz, L., *Poverty and Welfare in Habsburg Spain: the Example of Toledo* (Cambridge, 1983)

Masters, B. R., 'The Mayor's Household before 1600', in *Studies in London History*, ed. A. E. J. Hollaender and W. Kellaway (1969), pp. 95–114

May, G., *Social Control of the Sex Expression* (1930)

Miller, H., 'London and Parliament in the Reign of Henry VIII', *Bulletin of the Institute of Historical Research*, 35 (1962), 128–49

Moore, N., *The History of St Bartholomew's Hospital* (2 vols., 1918)

Morgan, J., *Godly Learning: Puritan Attitudes to Reason, Learning and Education, 1560–1640* (Cambridge, 1986)

Newcourt, R., *Repertorium Ecclesiasticum Parochiale Londinense: an Ecclesiastical Parochial History of the Diocese of London* (2 vols., 1708–10)

Nicholl, J., *Some Account of the Worshipful Company of Ironmongers* (1866)

Nightingale, P., 'Capitalists, Crafts and Constitutional Change in Late Fourteenth-Century London', *Past and Present*, 124 (1989), 3–35

O'Connell, L. Stevenson, 'The Elizabethan Bourgeois Hero-Tale: Aspects of an Adolescent Social Consciousness', in *After the Reformation: Essays in Honour of J. H. Hexter*, ed. B. Malament (Manchester, 1980), pp. 267–90

Oddy, D. J., 'Urban Famine in Nineteenth-Century Britain: the Effect of the Lancashire Cotton Famine on Working-Class Diet and Health', *Economic History Review*, second series, 36 (1983), 68–86

Outhwaite, R. B., 'Dearth and Government Intervention in English Grain Markets, 1590–1700', *Economic History Review*, second series, 34 (1981), 389–406

'Dearth, the English Crown and the Crisis of the 1590s', in *The European Crisis of the 1590s*, ed. P. Clark (1985), pp. 23–43

Owen, H. G., 'Tradition and Reform: Ecclesiastical Controversy in an Elizabethan London Parish', *Guildhall Miscellany*, 2 (1961), 63–70

'Lectures and Lecturers in Tudor London', *Church Quarterly Review*, 167 (1961), 63–76

Oxley, J. E. *The Fletchers and Longbowstringmakers of London* (1968)

Palliser, D. M., *Tudor York* (Oxford, 1979)

The Age of Elizabeth: England Under the Later Tudors, 1547–1603 (1983)

Pearce, A., *The History of the Butchers' Company* (1929)

Pearl, V., *London and the Outbreak of the Puritan Revolution: City Government and National Politics* (Oxford, 1961)

'Change and Stability in Seventeenth-Century London', *London Journal*, 5 (1979), 3–34

'Social Policy in Early Modern London', in *History and Imagination: Essays in Honour of H. R. Trevor-Roper*, ed. H. Lloyd-Jones, B. Worden and V. Pearl (1979), pp. 115–31

Pendrill, C., *Old Parish Life in London* (1937)

Pettegree, A., *Foreign Protestant Communities in Sixteenth-Century London* (Oxford, 1986)

Peyton, S. A., 'The Houses of Correction at Maidstone and Westminster', *English Historical Review*, 42 (1927), 251–61

Phelps-Brown, E. H., and Hopkins, S. V., *A Perspective of Wages and Prices* (1981)

Phythian-Adams, C., *Desolation of a City: Coventry and the Urban Crisis of the Late Middle Ages* (Cambridge, 1979)

Post, J. B., 'A Fifteenth-Century Customary of the Southwark Stews', *Journal of the Society of Archivists* (1977), 418–28

Power, M. J., 'London and the Control of the "Crisis" of the 1590s', *History*, 70 (1985), 371–85

'The Social Topography of Restoration London', in *London, 1500–1700: the Making of the Metropolis*, ed. A. L. Beier and R. Finlay (1986), pp. 199–223

'A "Crisis" Reconsidered: Social and Demographic Dislocation in London in the 1590s', *London Journal*, 12 (1986), 134–45

Pullan, B., 'Catholics and the Poor in Early Modern Europe', *Transactions of the Royal Historical Society*, fifth series, 26 (1976), 15–34

Raine, H., 'Christopher Fawcett Against the Inmates', *Surrey Archaeological Collections*, 66 (1966), 79–85

Ramsay, G. D., 'Industrial Discontent in Early Elizabethan London: Clothworkers and Merchant Adventurers in Conflict', *London Journal*, 1 (1975), 227–39

The City of London in International Politics at the Accession of Elizabeth Tudor (Manchester, 1975)

'Clothworkers, Merchant Adventurers and Richard Hakluyt', *English Historical Review*, 92 (1977), 504–21

'The Recruitment and Fortunes of some London Freemen in the Mid-Sixteenth Century', *Economic History Review*, second series, 31 (1978), 526–40

'Victorian Historiography and the Guilds of London: the Report of the Royal Commission on the Livery Companies of London, 1884', *London Journal*, 10 (1984), 155–66

The Queen's Merchants and the Revolt of the Netherlands (Manchester, 1986)

Ransome, D., 'The Struggle of the Glaziers' Company with the Foreign Glaziers, 1500–1550', *Guildhall Miscellany*, 2 (1960), 12–20

Rappaport, S., 'Social Structure and Mobility in Sixteenth-Century London: Part I', *London Journal*, 9 (1983), 107–35

'Social Structure and Mobility in Sixteenth-Century London: Part II', *London Journal*, 10 (1984), 107–34

Worlds Within Worlds: Structures of Life in Sixteenth-Century London (Cambridge, 1989)

Rawcliffe, C., 'The Hospitals of Later Medieval London', *Medical History*, 28 (1984), 1–21
Reddaway, T. F., *The Early History of the Goldsmiths' Company, 1327–1509* (1975)
Reynolds, S., *An Introduction to the History of English Medieval Towns* (Oxford, 1977)
   'Medieval Urban History and the History of Political Thought', *Urban History Yearbook*, 1982, 14–23
Richet, D., 'Aspects socio-culturels des conflits religieux à Paris dans la seconde moitié du XVIᵉ siècle', *Annales, Economies, Sociétés, Civilizations*, 32 (1977), 764–89
Rigby, S., 'Urban "Oligarchy" in Late Medieval England', in *Towns and Townspeople*, ed. J. A. F. Thomson (1988), pp. 62–86
Roper, L., 'Discipline and Respectability: Prostitution and the Reformation in Augsburg', *History Workshop*, 19 (1985), 3–28
   'The "Common Man", "the Common Good", "Common Women": Gender and Meaning in the German Reformation Commune', *Social History*, 12 (1987), 1–21
Rosser, G., 'The Essence of Medieval Urban Communities: the Vill of Westminster, 1200–1540', *Transactions of the Royal Historical Society*, fifth series, 34 (1984), 91–112
Rubin, M., *Charity and Community in Medieval Cambridge* (Cambridge, 1987)
Rye, W. B., *England as Seen by Foreigners in the Days of Elizabeth and James the First* (1865)
Salgado, G., *The Elizabethan Underworld* (1977)
Scarisbrick, J., *The Reformation and the English People* (Oxford, 1984)
Schofield, J., *The Building of London from the Conquest to the Great Fire* (1984)
Schofield, R., 'Taxation and the Political Limits of the Tudor State', in *Law and Government Under the Tudors: Essays Presented to Sir Geoffrey Elton*, ed. C. Cross, D. Loades and J. J. Scarisbrick (Cambridge, 1988), pp. 227–55
Seaver, P., *The Puritan Lectureships: the Politics of Religious Dissent, 1560–1662* (Stanford, 1970)
   Wallington's World: a Puritan Artisan in Seventeenth-Century London (1985)
Shakespeare, J., and Dowling, M. (eds.), 'Religion and Politics in Mid-Tudor England Through the Eyes of an English Protestant Woman: the Recollections of Rose Hickman', *Bulletin of the Institute of Historical Research*, 55 (1982), 94–102
Sharpe, J. A., *Crime in Seventeenth-Century England: a County Study* (Cambridge, 1983)
   Crime in Early Modern England, 1550–1750 (1984)
   '"Last Dying Speeches": Religion, Ideology and Public Execution in Seventeenth-Century England', *Past and Present*, 107 (1985), 144–67
Sharpe, R. R., *London and the Kingdom* (3 vols., 1894–5)
Shipley, N. R., 'The City Lands Committee, 1592–1642', *Guildhall Studies in London History*, 2 (1977), 161–78
Slack, P., 'Poverty and Politics in Salisbury, 1597–1666', in *Crisis and Order in English Towns, 1500–1700*, ed. P. Clark and P. Slack (1972), pp. 164–203
   'Mortality Crises and Epidemic Disease in England, 1485–1610', in *Health, Medicine and Mortality in Sixteenth-Century England*, ed. C. Webster (Cambridge, 1979), pp. 9–59
   'Social Policy and the Constraints of Government, 1547–58', in *The Mid-Tudor Polity, c. 1540–1560*, ed. J. Loach and R. Tittler (1980), pp. 94–115

'Poverty and Social Regulation in Elizabethan England', in *The Reign of Elizabeth I*, ed. C. Haigh (1984), pp. 221–41

The Impact of Plague in Tudor and Stuart England (1985)

'Metropolitan Government in Crisis: the Response to Plague', in *London, 1500–1700: the Making of the Metropolis*, ed. A. L. Beier and R. Finlay (1986), pp. 60–81

Poverty and Policy in Tudor and Stuart England (1988)

Smith, S. R., 'The London Apprentices as Seventeenth-Century Adolescents', *Past and Present*, 56 (1973), 149–61

'The Ideal and the Reality: Apprentice–Master Relationships in Seventeenth-Century London', *History of Education Quarterly*, 21 (1981), 449–60

Spaeth, D., 'Common Prayer? Popular Observance of the Anglican Liturgy in Restoration Wiltshire', in *Parish, Church and People: Local Studies in Lay Religion*, ed. S. Wright (1988), pp. 125–51

Spufford, M., *Small Books and Pleasant Histories: Popular Fiction and its Readership in Seventeenth-Century England* (Cambridge, 1981)

'Can We Count the 'Godly' and the Conformable in the Seventeenth Century?', *Journal of Ecclesiastical History*, 36 (1985), 428–38

'Puritanism and Social Control?', in *Order and Disorder in Early Modern England*, ed. A. J. Fletcher and J. Stevenson (1985), pp. 41–57

Stacey, M., 'The Myth of Community Studies', *British Journal of Sociology*, 20 (1969), 134–47

Stone, L., 'The Peer and the Alderman's Daughter', *History Today*, 11 (1961), 48–55

Strype, J., *A Survey of the Cities of London and Westminster ... Reprinted and Augmented by the Author ... Now Lastly Corrected* (2 vols., 1720)

Annals of the Reformation and Establishment of Religion ... During Queen Elizabeth's Happy Reign (4 vols., 1824)

Thirsk, J., *Economic Policy and Projects: the Development of a Consumer Society in Early Modern England* (Oxford, 1978)

Thomas, K. V., 'The Double Standard', *Journal of the History of Ideas*, 20 (1955), 195–226

'Age and Authority in Early Modern England', *Proceedings of the British Academy*, 67 (1976), 205–48

Thompson, E. P., 'The Moral Economy of the English Crowd in the Eighteenth Century', *Past and Present*, 50 (1971), 76–136

Thompson, I. A. A., 'The Impact of War', in *The European Crisis of the 1590s*, ed. P. Clark (1985), pp. 261–84

Thomson, J. A. F., 'Piety and Charity in Late Medieval London', *Journal of Ecclesiastical History*, 16 (1965), 178–95

Thrupp, S., 'The Grocers of London: a Study of Distributive Trade', in *Studies in English Trade in the Fifteenth Century*, ed. E. Power and M. M. Postan (1933), pp. 247–92

The Merchant Class of Medieval London, 1300–1500 (Chicago, 1948)

Todd, M., *Christian Humanism and the Puritan Social Order* (Cambridge, 1987)

Tomlinson, E. M., *A History of the Minories, London* (1907)

Underdown, D., *Revel, Riot and Rebellion: Popular Politics and Culture in England, 1603–1660* (Oxford, 1985)

Unwin, G., *Industrial Organization in the Sixteenth and Seventeenth Centuries* (Oxford, 1904)

The Gilds and Companies of London (4th edn, 1963)

Veale, E., *The English Fur Trade in the Later Middle Ages* (Oxford, 1966)
Wales, T. C., 'Poverty, Poor Relief and the Life-Cycle', in *Land, Kinship and Life-Cycle*, ed. R. M. Smith (Cambridge, 1984), pp. 351–404
Wall, A., 'Patterns of Politics in England, 1558–1625', *Historical Journal*, 31 (1988), 947–63
Walter, J., and Wrightson, K., 'Dearth and the Social Order in Early Modern England', *Past and Present*, 71 (1976), 22–42
Walter, J., 'A "Rising of the People"? The Oxfordshire Rising of 1596', *Past and Present*, 107 (1985), 90–143
'The Social Economy of Dearth in Early Modern England', in *Famine, Disease, and the Social Order in Early Modern Society*, ed. R. Schofield and J. Walter (Cambridge, 1989), pp. 75–128
Welch, C., *History of the Worshipful Company of Pewterers of the City of London* (2 vols., 1902)
Willan, T. S., *Studies in Elizabethan Foreign Trade* (Manchester, 1959)
Williams, D. A., 'London Puritanism: the Parish of St Stephen Coleman Street', *Church Quarterly Review*, 115 (1959), 464–82
'London Puritanism: the Parish of St Botolph without Aldgate', *Guildhall Miscellany*, 2 (1960), 24–38
Williams, P. H., *The Tudor Regime* (Oxford, 1979)
'The Crown and the Counties', in *The Reign of Elizabeth I*, ed. C. A. Haigh (1984), pp. 125–46
Wood, A. C., *A History of the Levant Company* (Oxford, 1935)
Woodward, D., 'Wage Rates and Living Standards in Pre-Industrial England', *Past and Present*, 91 (1981), 28–46
'"Swords into Ploughshares": Recycling in Pre-Industrial England', *Economic History Review*, second series, 38 (1985), 175–91
Wright, S., 'Charmaids, Huswyfes and Hucksters: the Employment of Women in Tudor and Stuart Salisbury', in *Women and Work in Pre-Industrial England*, ed. L. Charles and L. Duffin (1985), pp. 100–21
Wrightson, K., and Levine, D., *Poverty and Piety in an English Village: Terling, 1525–1700* (New York, 1979)
Wrightson, K., *English Society, 1580–1680* (1982)
'The Social Order of Early Modern England: Three Approaches', in *The World We Have Gained: Histories of Population and Social Structure. Essays Presented to Peter Laslett on his Seventieth Birthday*, ed. L. Bonfield, R. M. Smith and K. Wrightson (Oxford, 1986), pp. 177–202
Wrigley, E. A., and Schofield, R. S., *The Population History of England, 1541–1871: a Reconstruction* (1981)
Wunderli, R., *London Church Courts and Society on the Eve of the Reformation* (Cambridge, Mass., 1981)
Youings, J., *Sixteenth-Century England* (Harmondsworth, 1984)
Young, S., *The Annals of the Barber Surgeons* (1890)

UNPUBLISHED SECONDARY SOURCES

Adamson, N. L., Urban Families: the Social Context of the London Elite, 1500–1603' (Toronto Ph.D., 1983)
Anderson, K., 'The Treatment of Vagrancy and the Relief of the Poor and the Destitute in the Tudor Period, Based on the Local Records of London to 1552,

and Hull to 1576' (London Ph.D., 1933)

Archer, I. W., 'Governors and Governed in Late Sixteenth-Century London, *c.* 1560–1603: Studies in the Achievement of Stability' (Oxford D.Phil., 1988)

Barron, C. M., 'The Government of London and its Relations with the Crown, 1400–1450' (London Ph.D., 1970)

Barry, J., 'The Cultural Life of Bristol, 1640–1775' (Oxford D.Phil., 1985)

Ben-Amos, I. K., 'Apprenticeship, the Family and Urban Society in Early Modern England' (Stanford Ph.D., 1985)

Benbow, M., 'Index of London Citizens Involved in City Government, 1558–1603', copy on deposit at Centre for Metropolitan History, Institute of Historical Research, London

Brigden, S., 'The Early Reformation in London, 1522–47: the Conflict in the Parishes' (Cambridge Ph.D., 1979)

Carlin, M., 'The Urban Development of Southwark, *c.* 1200–1550' (Toronto Ph.D., 1983)

Dingle, A. M., 'The Role of the Householder in Early Stuart London, *c.* 1603–1630' (London M.Phil., 1975)

Duncan, G. D., 'Monopolies Under Elizabeth I, 1558–1585' (Cambridge Ph.D., 1976)

Elliott, V. B., 'Mobility and Marriage in Pre-Industrial England' (Cambridge Ph.D., 1978)

Foster, F. F., 'The Government of London in the Reign of Elizabeth I' (Columbia Ph.D., 1968)

Gronquist, G., 'The Relationship Between the City of London and the Crown, 1509–1547' (Cambridge Ph.D., 1986)

Hughes, R., '"The Canting Crew": Criminal Stereotypes in Popular Literature and Drama, 1536–1660' (York M.A., 1983)

Kennedy, J., 'The City of London and the Crown, *c.* 1509–*c.* 1529' (Manchester M.A., 1978)

Lang, R. G., 'The Greater Merchants of London in the Seventeenth Century' (Oxford D.Phil., 1963)

Lawson, P. G., 'Crime and the Administration of Criminal Justice in Hertfordshire, 1580–1625' (Oxford D.Phil., 1982)

Leese, F. E., 'A Calendar and Analysis with Introduction of two Elizabethan Port Books' (Oxford, B.Litt, 1963)

Macfarlane, S., 'Studies in Poverty and Poor Relief in London at the end of the Seventeenth Century' (Oxford D.Phil., 1982)

Owen, H. G., 'The London Parish Clergy in the Reign of Elizabeth I' (London Ph.D., 1957)

Power, M. J., 'The Urban Development of East London, 1550–1700' (London Ph.D., 1971)

Rappaport, S., 'Social Structure and Mobility in Sixteenth-Century London' (Columbia Ph.D., 1983)

Rosser, A. G., 'Medieval Westminster: the Vill and the Urban Community, 1200–1540' (London Ph.D., 1984)

Spraggs, G. M., 'Rogues and Vagabonds in English Literature, 1552–1642' (Cambridge Ph.D., 1980)

Yarborough, A., 'Bristol's Apprentices in the Sixteenth Century: the Cultural and Regional Mobility of an Age Group' (Catholic University of America Ph.D., 1977)

INDEX

Acton (Middlesex), 225
Adams, Theophilus, 158
Adamson, Mr, 214
adultery, 252
Aldermary, Abda, 193
aldermen: business interests of, 47–9;
    charity of, 53, 178–9; cost of
    office-holding by, 18; decision-making
    among, 40–2; elections of, 18, 23, 33;
    expectations of, 6, 7–8, 49–57, 59,
    259; homogeneity of, 19, 22, 23–7,
    32, 39–49, 257; patronage of, 60,
    258; pattern of recruitment of, 14, 18,
    50–1; policies towards crime, 204,
    222, 223, 233, 235, 250, 253, 255;
    popular attitudes towards, 1, 5, 8,
    20–1, 25, 26–7, 28–9, 40–1, 49–57,
    140, 201–2, 257; powers of, 18, 258;
    relations with common council, 19,
    22; relations with livery companies,
    18–19, 20, 21–25, 26, 51, 61, 102,
    103, 116, 128, 133, 134, 136, 139,
    142–3, 146, 148; relations with
    vestries, 51, 93; religious attitudes of,
    44–6; residence of, 51–2; social
    policies, 6, 8, 105, 157, 160, 163,
    183, 184, 185–6, 189, 198–203, 244,
    treatment of riots, 1–9, 216; wealth
    of, 18; wives of, 184
aldermen's deputies, 67–8, 78, 80, 96,
    177, 183, 190, 199, 219, 225–6, 239,
    258
Aldersey, Thomas, haberdasher, 46, 47,
    253
Alderson, Anthony, tallow chandler, 105
aleconners, 30
alehouses: campaigns against, 31, 81, 207,
    218, 222, 224, 226, 241, 242, 243,
    244–5, 254, 255; licensing of, 60, 63,
    235, 258; links with criminal activity,
    208–9, 213

aliens: attitudes of government towards,
    137–8, 140; churches of, 131;
    economic rights of, 31, 134–5;
    numbers of, 4, 131–2; organisation
    among, 62, 137–8; policies of livery
    companies towards, 7, 32, 58,
    131–40, 141, 145, 146, 259–60;
    popular hostility towards, 1, 2, 5, 7,
    52, 58, 131–40, 257; skills of, 132,
    137, 146; support for poor of, 170,
    172, 176
Allen, Sir William, leatherseller and
    mercer, 18, 178–9
Allen, William, 214
alleys, 13, 77, 79, 81–2, 184, 192, 200,
    242, 243, 244
almoners, 155, 238
almshouses, 91, 98, 120, 121, 122, 123,
    168, 170, 172, 176, 177, 181, 192
Altham, James, clothworker, 41, 42
Altham, Thomas, clothworker, 105
Alva, duke of, 48
America, 47
Amondesham, William, 227
Andrewes, Helen, 232
Antwerp, 32, 47, 124
apparel, 61
apprentices: bequests for, 164; criminality
    of, 206–8, 217–18, 243–4; drop-out
    rate of, 15, 217; leisure of, 94, 207,
    242, 243–4; numbers per master,
    limits on, 106, 108, 125, 127–9,
    130–1, 135; proportion of in
    population, 216; recruitment patterns
    of, 4, 14, 242, 260; regulations
    relating to aliens and, 137, 138;
    rioting by, 1–9, 216; sexuality of, 3;
    socialisation through experience of,
    215–18; solidarity of, 7; status
    uncertainties of, 4; tensions with
    gentlemen, 3–4; visibility of, 77

292

economy of, 9–11

environment of, 76–7, 81–2

food supply of, 7–8, 11, 20, 38, 52, 53, 60, 136, 201–2, 259

freedom and citizenship of: privileges of, 20, 22, 29, 34, 50–1, 74–5, 100; proportion of inhabitants enjoying, 19, 61, 113–14

immigration to, 10, 13, 15, 51, 61, 150, 225, 241, 255

patronage available to, 34

population of, 12–13, 17, 19, 83, 84, 152, 186, 188, 242

social integration through loyalty towards, 60–1, 74–5

relations with Crown, 10–11, 12, 17, 20, 25–7, 32–9, 41, 44, 50–1, 140

as social centre for gentry, 11

London, companies:

Armourers, 20, 81, 104, 114, 116, 118, 119, 126, 131, 132, 133, 147

Barber Surgeons, 20, 108–9, 111, 141

Blacksmiths, 20, 104, 115, 132, 133, 147

Brewers, 20, 37, 79, 110, 115, 118, 128

Bricklayers, 125, 146–7

Broderers, 126

Brown Bakers, 42

Butchers, 20, 104

Carpenters, 116, 121, 128, 133

Clothworkers, 19, 39, 42, 51, 101, 102, 104, 105–7, 108–9, 114, 123–4, 125, 126, 127, 129, 141, 144, 145, 147, 217, 260

Coopers, 20, 79, 104, 114, 115, 132, 136, 137, 139, 142, 144

Cordwainers, 20, 104, 126, 133, 136, 137, 140, 142, 147, 148

Curriers, 20, 39, 139, 142, 147, 148

Cutlers, 131, 137, 139, 147

Drapers, 19, 23, 24, 110, 113, 114, 116–17, 118, 147

Dyers, 133, 147

Feltmakers, 144

Fishmongers, 19, 24, 104, 114, 115, 119, 126, 130, 231

Founders, 20, 114, 132

Freemasons, 143

Goldsmiths, 103, 121, 122, 123, 129, 220

Grocers, 19, 20, 23, 24, 46, 51, 120, 122, 123, 124, 127, 128–9, 186–7

Haberdashers, 51, 101, 102, 108, 113, 115, 119, 120, 124, 129, 141, 144–5

Holy Trinity, brethren of, 62

Horners, 55

Ironmongers, 19

Joiners, 133

Leathersellers, 37, 38

Mercers, 19, 27, 34, 51, 121, 124, 146, 217

Merchant Tailors, 19, 24, 25, 34, 42, 51, 101, 102, 104, 106, 107, 108, 109, 110, 113, 114, 119–20, 121, 122, 124, 128, 129, 139, 141, 143, 145, 147, 192, 260

Painter-Stainers, 146–7

Pewterers, 20, 106, 113, 119, 130

Pinmakers, 126

Plasterers, 20, 104, 105, 113, 128, 135, 139, 142, 146–7, 148

Plumbers, 20, 101, 114

Saddlers, 104

Skinners, 51, 88, 100, 101, 102, 106, 110, 116, 124, 126, 127, 141, 144, 145, 148, 260

Tallow Chandlers, 20, 104, 105, 112, 113, 114, 115, 121, 146

Vintners, 39, 115

Weavers, 1, 118, 131, 132, 134, 148

White Bakers, 42, 113, 133

London, courts of:

commission of peace, 18, 218

commission of gaol delivery, 3, 18, 218, 228, 238

court of aldermen, 18–19; *see also* aldermen

court of common council, 19, 22, 23, 30, 32, 40, 50; acts of, 29, 30, 133, 138, 200, 202, 220, 244; bill to, 146; *see also* common councillors

court of common hall, 19–20, 28, 30

court of conscience, 18; beadle of, 35

court of hustings, 18

court of orphans, 18

mayor's court, attorney of, 34

sheriff's court, 18

see also wardmote inquests

London, diocese of:

archdeacon of London, 199

archdeaconry court, wills proved in, 172, 174

bishop of London, 70, 137, 199–200

commissary court, wills proved in, 75, 172, 174

consistory court, wills proved in, 172, 174

London, hospitals:

Bethlem, 5, 170, 172, 176

Elsyng Spittle, 154

St Bartholomew's, 79, 154, 156, 158, 159, 170, 172, 176, 181, 186

St Mary without Bishopsgate, 154

Cambridge Studies in Early Modern British History

Titles in the series

The Common Peace: Participation and the Criminal Law in Seventeenth-Century England*
CYNTHIA B. HERRUP

Politics, Society and Civil War in Warwickshire, 1620–1660
ANN HUGHES

London Crowds in the Reign of Charles II: Propaganda and Politics from the Restoration to the Exclusion Crisis*
TIM HARRIS

Criticism and Compliment: The Politics of Literature in the England of Charles I*
KEVIN SHARPE

Central Government and the Localities: Hampshire, 1649–1689
ANDREW COLEBY

John Skelton and the Politics of the 1520s
GREG WALKER

Algernon Sidney and the English Republic, 1623–1677
JONATHAN SCOTT

Thomas Starkey and the Commonwealth: Humanist Politics and Religion in the Reign of Henry VIII
THOMAS F. MAYER

The Blind Devotion of the People: Popular Religion and the English Reformation
ROBERT WHITING

The Cavalier Parliament and the Reconstruction of the Old Regime, 1661–1667
PAUL SEAWARD

The Blessed Revolution: English Politics and the Coming of War, 1621–1624
THOMAS COGSWELL

Charles I and the Road to Personal Rule
L. J. REEVE

George Lawson's 'Politica' and the English Revolution
CONAL CONDREN

Puritans and Roundheads: The Harleys of Brampton Bryan and the Outbreak of the English Civil War
JACQUELINE EALES

An Uncouncelled King: Charles I and the Scottish Troubles, 1637–1641
PETER DONALD

The Pursuit of Stability: Social Relations in Elizabethan London
IAN W. ARCHER

* Also published as a paperback

Printed in the United Kingdom
by Lightning Source UK Ltd.
125323UK00002B/127/A